Magic Trees of the Mind

Magic Trees of the Mind

How to Nurture Your Child's
Intelligence, Creativity, and Healthy
Emotions from Birth Through
Adolescence

Marian Diamond, Ph.D.
Janet Hopson

A DUTTON BOOK

DUTTON
Published by the Penguin Group
Penguin Putnam Inc., 375 Hudson Street,
New York, New York 10014, U.S.A.
Penguin Books Ltd, 27 Wrights Lane,
London W8 5TZ, England
Penguin Books Australia Ltd, Ringwood,
Victoria, Australia
Penguin Books Canada Ltd, 10 Alcorn Avenue,
Toronto, Ontario, Canada M4V 3B2
Penguin Books (N.Z.) Ltd, 182–190 Wairau Road,
Auckland 10, New Zealand

Penguin Books Ltd, Registered Offices:
Harmondsworth, Middlesex, England

First published by Dutton, an imprint of Dutton Signet,
a member of Penguin Putnam Inc.

First Printing, January, 1998
10   9   8   7   6   5   4   3   2   1

Drawings on page 18 adapted from *Neuroscience: Exploring the Brain* by Mark F. Bear, Barry
W. Connors, and Michael A. Paradiso, Williams and Wilkins, 1996.

"The Mind Is an Enchanting Thing" reprinted with the permission of Simon & Schuster
from *Collected Poems of Marianne Moore.* Copyright 1944 by Marianne Moore; copyright
renewed © 1972 by Marianne Moore.

Poem 632 from *The Complete Poems of Emily Dickinson*, edited by Thomas H. Johnson.
Copyright 1929, 1935 by Martha Dickinson Bianchi, copyright © renewed 1957, 1963 by
Mary L. Hampson. By permission of Little, Brown and Company (Inc.).

Drawings on pages 106, 107, and 193 from *The Postnatal Development of the Human Cerebral
Cortex* by J. LeRoy Conel (Cambridge, Mass.: Harvard University Press), Vol. I, Copyright
© 1939 by the President and Fellows of Harvard College, © 1967 by Jesse LeRoy Conel;
Vol. III, Copyright © 1947 by the President and Fellows of Harvard College, © 1975 by
Jesse LeRoy Conel; Vol. VI, Copyright © 1959 by the President and Fellows of Harvard
College; and Vol. VIII, Copyright © 1967 by the President and Fellows of Harvard College.

REGISTERED TRADEMARK—MARCA REGISTRADA

LIBRARY OF CONGRESS CATALOGING-IN-PUBLICATION DATA:
Diamond, Marian Cleeves.
    Magic trees of the mind : how to nurture your child's intelligence, creativity, and
healthy emotions from birth through adolescence / Marian Diamond, Janet Hopson.
        p.   cm.
    Includes bibliographical references and index.
    ISBN 0-525-94308-0 (alk. paper)
    1. Children—Intelligence levels.   2. Teenagers—Intelligence levels.   3. Creative ability
in children.   4. Creative ability in adolescence.   5. Emotions in children.   6. Emotions
in adolescence.   7. Child rearing.   I. Hopson, Janet L.   II. Title.
BF432.C48D53   1998
649'.1—dc21   97-36971
                                                                                      CIP

Printed in the United States of America
Set in New Baskerville
Designed by Leonard Telesca

This book is printed on acid-free paper.

With much love, to Will Colin-Diamond and
his new generation.—M. D.

For Jerry, Barri, Alisa, Allen, and Emily,
with love and hope for a stimulating future.—J. H.

Contents

Prologue and Acknowledgments ix

Introduction: Experience Is the Best Sculptor   1

1: Trees That Grow So Fair: Neural Forests of the Mind   10

2: An Enchanted Thing: The Brain's Network of Connections   36

3: Feed My Brain: Influences in the Womb   65
   An Enrichment Program for the Unborn Child   97

4: Dreaming Eyes of Wonder: Nurturing the Very Young   101
   An Enrichment Program for Babies and Toddlers   140

5: These Become Part of the Child: Stimulating the Mind in the Preschool Years   148
   An Enrichment Program for Preschool Children   180

6: Letting the Future In: The Power of Experience in Middle Childhood   189
   An Enrichment Program for Grade School Children   228

7: Plant Another Tree: Continuing Mental Development in Adolescence   233
    An Enrichment Program for Teenagers   259

8: Learning Not by Chance: Enrichment in the Classroom   264

9: As Morning Shows the Day: How Social Factors Shape Future Minds   285

Resource Guide: Additional Tools for Enrichment
    *Articles   307 / Books   310 / Organizations   317
    On-line Resources   324 / Catalogs and Commercial
    Sources   327 / Parent-Recommended Enrichment
    Tools   330*

Notes   421

Index   451

Prologue and Acknowledgments

We met on a sunny day in June 1984, and started our long collaboration without even knowing it.

On dozens of previous occasions, one of us had ushered reporters into her laboratory cluttered with microscopes, bottles of chemicals, and human brains soaking in formaldehyde. The writers had come like pilgrims up the treadworn stairs and down the dusky halls of the old life sciences building on the University of California campus to learn about Marian Diamond's work on the brain, its blanket of interconnected nerve cells, and about the remarkable, mind-expanding discovery that Diamond and her colleagues had made in 1963: Given the appropriate mental, physical, and/or sensory stimulation, the brain's interconnected neurons sprout and branch.

Over the years, the other of us had carried her notepad and tape recorder to dozens of similar laboratories in blocky campus or corporate buildings to hear researchers describe their achievements for magazine or book audiences. Some sources had been affable, some arrogant, but most were at least interesting. Jan Hopson looked forward to interviewing a woman neuroanatomist—an unusual commodity.

On that June morning in 1984, we stood in the doorway sizing each other up while the acrid smell of chemicals and the whir of a centrifuge drifted across from a nearby room. There we were, two tall, athletic women in summer dresses, shaking hands firmly and smiling broadly. After chatting a few minutes, it became clear we were a perfect, reciprocal, transgenerational match: a willing explainer, an eager questioner; a scientific popularizer, a media counterpart; a pair of tennis enthusiasts from way back; two career women who also loved family and home. As we talked, there was clearly brain chemistry—a mental attraction, an igniting of ideas surrounding the simple but profound notion that the brain grows with deliberate stimulation. Diamond's was a life-transforming idea: enrich your own experiences and enlarge your cerebral cortex; deprive yourself of stimulation and the brain will shrink from disuse. Our meeting lasted long into the afternoon.

Ten years after the interview, we were still in touch and still intrigued by the enrichment concept. By now, researchers around the world had applied it to rats, mice, gerbils, cats, monkeys, human children, and adults in the laboratory and in real life surroundings. Diamond was being asked with increasing frequency to lecture large groups of parents and teachers on the implications of enrichment for children's rapidly developing minds. Audience members inevitably asked for books and articles on childhood brain development and enrichment, yet few materials existed beyond Diamond's rather challenging book *Enriching Heredity*, published in 1988.

Seeing a clear need, we decided to collaborate on a popular-level book about childhood brain development and enrichment. We spent three years researching, writing, conducting original surveys, and working to produce the version you see now. We profiled each stage of childhood development, and described the changes taking place in the brain, then went on to explain the implications for behavior, for learning, and for the child's growing abilities and interests. We wanted to convey the fascinating research spreading far beyond the Diamond lab on how experience sculpts the child's brain and influences his or her future. Beyond this, for both readers familiar with the enrichment concept and for others new to the idea of deliberate stimulation, we wanted to suggest stimulating toys, books, games, lessons, and excursions. Many of the ideas we include come straight from a survey we conducted with three hundred parents. These ideas are highlighted at the ends of chapters 4, 5, 6, and 7, and are presented in detail in the Resource Guide on page 330. We hope our enrichment tips will represent productive new avenues to explore in homes and schools.

Co-authors often face a dilemma: In a book by two individuals, which single voice will tell the story most effectively? We were unwilling to silence either team member. So we chose to use two separate points of view: Diamond's personal reminiscences of the 1963 discovery that launched a modern field; her enrichment work with public school children, including own sons and daughters; plus her latest research on important medical topics. And Hopson's third-person accounts of enrichment research in and beyond the Diamond lab; anecdotes about children and the effects of stimulation on mental growth; discussions of the social and educational implications of brain growth; and specific enrichment programs for each age group during childhood.

There is another inherent issue in a book like ours: Children who have suffered adverse medical conditions or extremes of mental stimulation deserve strict anonymity. Descriptions of their histories could reveal too many identifying details and in so doing, invade their well-deserved privacy. We therefore made an editorial decision to rename all subjects in our anecdotes; to change all locations in these same examples; and in some cases to merge the details of several anecdotes so that no real child, parent, or teacher can be identified. In every case history you read in *Magic Trees of the Mind*, when we provide only first names it is a signal that both names and locations have been changed. In all other discussions throughout the book, we give full first and second names for those we discuss, as well as accurate home states, cities, and institutions, and all the references we consulted. Using these, readers can verify our sources if they wish and judge our conclusions.

There was one final issue to consider in planning the book: Diamond's reputation is built on laboratory work with rats, yet parents and teachers are concerned about *children's* brain development and ways to enhance it. Because of this, we felt it important to hit upon three areas in our text: (1) All the relevant human brain research we could locate, interpreted through Diamond's four decades of experience as a brain anatomy professor and presented in a user-friendly writing style. (2) The very close similarities between animal and human neurons and brain structure. And (3) Diamond's forty-year history of directly enriching children through parenting, through working with thousands of California school children, and through the directorship of a children's discovery center on the University of California campus. Professors seldom venture outside lecture halls and laboratories to interact with local communities—their youngest members even less frequently. Diamond's long-term involvement lends a uniquely valid perspective to the human enrichment issue.

In producing *Magic Trees of the Mind,* any mistakes we may have made are inadvertent and regretted. Any congratulations we may receive belong, as well, to the dozens of people who assisted us.

We are indebted to those at Lawrence Hall of Science who assisted us with our enrichment survey: Barbara Ando, Elouise Dickerson, Lisa Eriksen, Gerri Ginsburg, and Phil Stone. Cecile Kim also provided tireless and invaluable assistance with research and computer work on our surveys. And of course, the survey would have been impossible without the willing spirit of the three hundred parents and five hundred children who participated in the survey questionnaire.

Ingrid Radkey in the University of California Biosciences Library was enormously helpful with literature searches, as was biology student Rashmi Shukla. Three consultants assisted with survey research planning: Percy Tannenbaum, Selina Monsky, and Elliott Medrich.

We thank the Albany, California, school administrators and teachers for their active involvement in the original survey of children's time use we conducted for *Magic Trees of the Mind:* Sandi Adams, Dan Bearson, Craig Boyan, Terry Corpuz, Sarah Danielson, Chris Engemann, Chiyo Masuda, Dena Peterson, Marian Rothchild, and Victoria Sears. Our gratitude also goes to the two hundred parents and children who took time to answer and return the time-use questionnaires for this survey.

Mary Jean Haley, writer, editor, and computer-literate mom, provided important reviews and information for our coverage of children's CD-ROMs, as well as general feedback.

Dozens of busy professors and researchers took time to talk with us on the record and to provide background perspective, and we much appreciate their generosity: Linda Acredolo, Robert Alexander, Jane Holmes Bernstein, John Bruer, Frances Campbell, Philip Cogen, Harry Chugani, Richard Coss, Anthony De-Casper, Adele Diamond, Glenn Doman, Kurt Fischer, Rochel Gelman, Kathleen Gibson, Patricia Goldman-Rakic, Susan Goodwyn, Harriet Green, Norman Krasnegor, Helen Neville, James McGaugh, Bruce Perry, Michael Phelps, Martha Pierson, Claudia Pogreba, Michael Posner, Marcus Raichle, Craig Ramey, Mary Rothbart, Oren Sandel, Arnold Scheibel, Gordon Shaw, Donald Shetler, Elizabeth Spelke, F. Rene Van de Carr, Merlin Wittrock, Norman Wessells, and Karen Wynn.

Finally, this project would have been impossible without the steady guidance and editorial acumen of our agent, Sarah Lazin, our former editor Matthew Carnicelli, and our current editor Deirdre Mullane and the production staff at Dutton.

Introduction

Experience Is the Best Sculptor

Experientia does it.
—Charles Dickens, *David Copperfield*

The child's mind is filled with magic genies, sorcerers, and fairy godmothers; magic wands, shields, ponies, and frogs. And conjuring them all, animating these charmed apparitions, are tangled forests of branching, treelike nerve cells that interconnect at a million billion contact points and converge into a living fabric of consciousness. Electrochemical currents ripple through groves of these neural trees like wind stirring a shady thicket. And from these stirrings our human faculties arise: the generation of images, thoughts, words, feelings, and music, and the belief itself in genies and magic frogs.

In the 1990s, researchers made remarkable gains in understanding how a child's brain develops, grows, and produces uniquely human capacities. At the same time, they discovered new ways to foster greater intelligence by nurturing brain growth during its most active phases. Where society once viewed the child's brain as static and unchangeable, experts today see it as a highly dynamic organ that feeds on stimulation and experience and responds with the flourishing of branching, intertwined neural forests. This discovery presents us with a way of helping our children reach their fullest and healthiest mental development. But it has a dark side, as well, if the child's mind is understimulated and underused.

Like any remarkable tale, the story of modern brain research and enrichment is peopled by fascinating characters: A professor who hears "celestial music" in the harmonious beauty of human nerve cells. A young girl who loses one half of her brain to disease yet goes on to live a normal childhood and to graduate from high school and college. A deaf child who can see with the hearing region of her brain. Parents who teach words, numbers, and musical notes to their unborn child. A one-year-old who learns to communicate with a special form of baby sign language before she can speak. A six-year-old who learns how to read, speak Japanese and Italian, and play the violin years before starting school. A teacher who touches hundreds of lives each year with techniques that stimulate children's brains in particular ways. And many more.

The story of enrichment research is expansive as well as populous—rooted in the nineteenth century but branching into the intricate knowledge and practice of the late twentieth century. More than 150 years ago, insightful scholars of the human brain guessed that exercising our organ of thought could cause it to change and grow. Not until the 1960s, however, would a group of researchers from the University of California at Berkeley, with a colony of laboratory rats, prove this idea and overturn the tenacious dogma that, once developed in a child or adult, a brain can never change!

From this beginning, the science of brain enrichment has blossomed. Curious investigators have explained many mysteries stemming from a single basic phenomenon: The brain's outer layer can grow if a person or animal lives in stimulating surroundings, but the zone can shrink if the environment is dull or unchallenging. The implications of the discoveries are profound, and span a range from molecular minutia—such as how the nerve cells that allow an infant to see and hear become activated and fine-tuned—to far-reaching family and social issues—like how best to raise and educate our children in an age of diminishing resources and advancing technology.

The emerging message is clear: The brain, with its complex architecture and limitless potential, is a highly plastic, constantly changing entity that is powerfully shaped by our experiences in childhood and throughout life. In Charles Dickens's novel *David Copperfield*, Mrs. Micawber conveys her father's sage advice that

"Experentia does it" to young David, twisting the phrase of the Roman historian Tacitus: *"experientia docet"* (experience teaches). Nevertheless, Mrs. Micawber's malapropism was uncannily, unwittingly perfect for our modern-day tale of discovery. For when it comes to the brain, *experience does it.* Our collective actions, sensations, and memories are a powerful shaper of both function and anatomy. What's left for the wise parent or teacher, hoping to promote their children's healthiest mental development, is to pick the *right* experiences at the *right* time. That's why we wrote this book.

Despite numerous public lectures and articles for the general audience, the average person on the street has no inkling that the brain can change and no idea of how to stimulate it for best effect. Dogmas die hard, and the somewhat counterintuitive finding that brains can change has been slow to penetrate. At the same time, a few entrepreneurs have marketed specific formulas for growing a child's brain that are ... let's just say, unproven.

We sought to write a book about enrichment in accurate detail and answer the fundamental questions a parent, an educator, a policy maker, or any other curious reader would ask:

- How can brain tissue, the most complicated matter in the universe, change at any age?
- What is and isn't known about how experience induces nerve cells in the brain to expand or shrivel?
- How does the human brain develop, starting at conception and continuing through adolescence and early adulthood?
- What have researchers discovered about childhood experiences and brain plasticity?
- How large a role does heredity play in intelligence and how much is left to experience?
- How can one determine whether a child is getting an appropriate level of stimulation, too much, or too little?
- What do experts and involved parents recommend for enriching children of different ages?
- What are the case histories and outcomes of children who have lived in deprived environments, average ones, and/or enriched surroundings?

- How will enrichment affect a child, a class, a school, or society?

We wanted to give readers a sense of the enormous and exciting opportunities children have today for stimulation and learning. And we felt it was crucial to tell the story now because the subject has started, in recent months, to receive more attention in the popular press, and some of it is unnecessarily discouraging. A few articles have suggested that doors open and close in the brain for certain subjects and skills at specific ages. These have gone on to imply that if a child doesn't start a foreign language, let's say, or a musical instrument by a certain age, then the mind's door will close and he or she might as well forget trying.

Ours is a different, and we hope, more encouraging message. Childhood is a special, magical time when the brain is metaphorically spongelike and when learning new skills can be both fun and effortless. But with very few exceptions, the normal, healthy brain can still absorb all types of information and a person can acquire all sorts of skills and experiences at any age. It may be more taxing to take up tennis at thirty-seven rather than seven, more time-consuming to learn the flute at forty than at ten, and less successful to start a foreign language after adolescence. But we all know friends and relatives who have taken up new hobbies, languages, sports, even careers in adulthood and triumphed. The brain doesn't snap shut or fill up. And the suggestion that a potential linguist is washed up at eight or a would-be musician is a has-been at twelve is untrue, discouraging, and a waste of human resources. The late-bloomer may not become a United Nations translator or a concert violinist, but then neither do most of us who go on to enjoy knowing second languages, playing in a small instrumental group, or competing on a C-level tennis ladder. Isn't the object an interesting, varied life and the realization of our fullest, broadest potential? We think so, and we want to encourage—not discourage—children, parents, teachers, and others interested in human development.

Thirty years ago, researchers used to say that if a child lost part of the brain's left hemisphere to disease and/or surgical removal by age two, the right hemisphere would take over the language functions and the child would grow up able to listen, speak, and read normally. Twenty years ago, after additional research and surgical experience, the figure grew to five years of age. Today, it stands at ten. And no one knows what future research will reveal and future medical techniques will make possible. Science never stops moving forward and today's closed door may be tomorrow's open portal. We are careful in *Magic Trees of the Mind* to encourage a wide variety of safe experiences once a child is developmentally ready for them. As you will see—to quote the poet Marianne Moore—the mind is an enchanted thing. Its capabilities are astonishing, and we are just at the threshold of understanding this most complex living matter.

We had a second reason for wanting to tell the enrichment story now, even though it, like the rest of medicine, psychology, and life science, is ongoing and open-ended: While millions of children are already getting fine educations and a range of stimulating free-time activities, *the typical American child does not experience an enriched environment.* He or she watches three to four hours of television each day while in preschool and grade school. Is rather sedentary. Doesn't read very well. Doesn't particularly like school. Doesn't do much homework. Doesn't have many hobbies. Eats a less-than-optimal diet. Drops out of sports by ninth or tenth grade. Experiments in high school with alcohol and drugs that can potentially stunt brain development. Listens to rock or rap music from two to six hours per day as a teenager. Spends far more time dating and earning pocket money than studying, volunteering, or engaging in new and challenging activities. And overall, grows up with a disenchanted mind that never reaches its fullest potential—or even comes close.

In modern society, we are all bombarded daily with news and features about our nation's high rates of teen pregnancy and children living in poverty; about school delinquency and dropout rates; drug abuse and crime; failed teaching methods, the burgeoning of prison cells, and the clamoring need all around us. We don't see enrichment as a mystical panacea for society's ills, but we do think it can change lives for the better—and the need has never been greater.

As we trace enrichment's history and potential, some readers may be surprised to find that the story begins with rats and ends with people. Human brain research, however, is a devilishly difficult challenge because people almost always object to giving chunks of their gray matter to curious scientists.

Think of the shocking tabloid stories we'd see beside the checkout counter if a researcher took, say, a kindergarten class, divided the children into experimental and control groups, chained one group to cartoon reruns and set the other loose in a children's museum, then, after days or weeks, removed and examined pieces of their brain tissue for changes based on these experiences! Such a thing could never happen, of course. So only laboratory animals will do for many kinds of questions involving enriched environments and the brain. (Even then, researchers are strictly limited in the procedures they can use so that the animal's housing, feeding, handling, treatment, and eventual sacrifice are as clean, humane, and pain-free as possible.)

Like so many other significant discoveries in medicine and life science, the history of enrichment research starts with the laboratory rat. The rodent's brain is smoother, simpler, and of course, far smaller than a person's. However, the nerve cells, the living units that comprise most of the rat brain, are virtually identical to human brain cells and work in exactly the same major ways. This is true of the cat, dog, guinea pig, and monkey, as well. Because of the close similarities, human neural research can rest comfortably on a furry foundation of mammalian anatomy, physiology, and behavior. In fact, in many ways, animal research is superior because the investigator can intentionally control so many of the variables. Research on the human brain, by contrast, relies on volunteer subjects, on indirect methods of measurement, and on brain tissue that people bequeath to science.

The story of enrichment in the rat's smooth pink brain is fascinating in its own right, and our first chapter not only presents the history of a dogma-shattering find, but also serves to introduce most of the neuroanatomy we'll need to consider. We then tour the marvelous organ inside the human skull, from its beginnings as an "embryonic inchworm" to its plump, furrowed fullness in the child and adult. From there we plunge microscopically into the magic forest of branching, treelike nerve cells that fill the cerebral cortex layers and can grow when excited and stimulated, or shrivel when underused.

We also look at our most intimate connection with a child— the prenatal environment—and how some people accidentally deprive or deliberately enrich a fetus in this quiet, watery world. We present a gentle program for enriching your own child prenatally, as well as information to help you identify and avoid substances that could harm the developing brain. We then trace the budding and flowering of a baby's mind as it learns to grasp, hold, walk, talk, and think. And we tell the stories of parents who do just the right—and wrong—things for their one- and two-year-olds.

In Chapter 5, we describe the blooming brain of the preschooler, and the special opportunities that abound for the three-to-five age group. Parents, teachers, and researchers debate the right type and amount of stimulation for children in their years at home or in day care, including a controversial and widely publicized flash card method. We cover this topic in detail, then present our own ideas and those of our survey parents.

Chapter 6, the longest in the book, looks at children in their enrichment prime time, ages six to twelve. Some are "overprogrammed" with multiple activities; some are thriving in unexpected ways; some are channeled into high performance levels in sports or music; and some sit for hours in front of Nintendo, television, or computers. The children we surveyed for their freetime activities were from seven to twelve years old, and so we summarize the results of that study in this chapter and give many specific ideas gathered from the hundreds of participating parents. The complete survey results appear in the Appendix on page 330.

We focus next on the difficult but exhilarating teenage transition as the brain continues to change and mature. In this preadult period, some children display splendid accomplishments and the fruits of varied experiences and active mental and physical effort. Some teens are on career paths. Some are adrift in pop music and culture. Some are abusing drugs in or out of school. And some are raising their own children. Parents and teachers have less impact on enrichment in teenagers than in younger children; the adolescent must seek his or her own healthy stimulating experiences. It's never too late to start, though—even after a childhood of dullness or deprivation—and we offer a program of tips and ideas for the thirteen- to seventeen-year-old in this chapter.

Although American children spend far more time out of school than in, preschool, grade school, junior high, and high school education still plays an important role in enriching the developing brain. Chapter 8 discusses that role, as well as its inverse: Enrichment ideas and brain research are inspiring an entire education reform movement in the 1990s. Some dismiss it, others embrace it. But the proof is in the children who are learning to read with better comprehension, to work math problems with real understanding, and to like school for the first time, based on new teaching methods influenced by brain research.

Some fear that America is becoming dangerously segmented into a pampered, privileged minority, a struggling middle class, and a growing underclass mired in poverty. Our last chapter explains how brain enrichment and deprivation have contributed to these divisions, and how a society given to an ethic of careful, deliberate stimulation could alter the future. Some families are already operating under that ethic in their local communities, and are bringing about impressive change.

Finally, a Resource Guide starting on page 307 presents book titles, organization names, and other types of support for readers who want to create and pursue enrichment plans for their children.

We like to think this book can change how people view childhood and its cognitive opportunities, how they see human brain development and its ongoing plasticity, and how they perceive their children's—and their own—everyday activities and routines. Youngsters are so highly adaptable that they feel natural in virtually any pattern their parents set. Fully two-thirds of American adults have sedentary lifestyles; and the majority have high-fat, high-calorie diets; seldom read or create things for pleasure; and watch television for hours every day. It would be surprising, then, if the average child had a regimen any different. If our book has the kind of positive effect we envision, it will inspire a new level of mental and physical activity in all age groups.

It doesn't take money to create a climate for enchanted minds to grow. It just takes information, imagination, motivation, and effort. Once the habit of active involvement is entrained, experience will take over and those stimulated minds will do the rest for themselves in surprising and delightful ways.

Chapter 1

Trees That Grow So Fair:
Neural Forests of the Mind

Of all the trees that grow so fair
Old England to adorn . . .
                    —Rudyard Kipling, "A Tree Song"

. . . My love affair with the brain started when I was a child growing up in the country. At night, I would look up at the stars and wonder where the sky ended. When I learned that the universe had no end, I wanted something easier, more circumscribed, to think about. So I started concentrating on brains and the little bit I knew about them. Ironically, most scientists agree today that the brain is the most complex structure in the universe.

One day as a teenager I accompanied my father on his rounds at the hospital. I can still see that visit as if it were yesterday. Walking down the antiseptic-smelling corridors, I would look into each door as I passed by, and I was stunned by what I saw in one room: Four men in white coats stood by a little medical tray no larger than a card table and stared at an object in the center of it, a human brain. I never found out what they were doing with that organ. But I remember saying to myself in amazement and without a trace of the horror one might expect from a young girl, "That mass used to think! How can living cells—well, previously living cells—produce ideas?"

After that day, I would look at people and wonder what was behind their eyes. Most other processes of the body you could hear or feel or see, like the blood pumping, or the muscles contracting, or the veins running down an arm or leg. But the mass inside your skull was forever hidden and that intrigued me. It was, in a way, a kind of narcissism: nerve cells in love with their own obscure image.

About that same time—the year was 1941 and I was fourteen—I wrote out an essay in my squiggly, adolescent hand. It said: "I, Marian Cleeves, will go to the University of California at Berkeley, because those who don't wish they did." Both my parents and four of my sisters and brothers had been students there, and indeed, I did go to the idyllic campus in northern California. My first years there I studied the broader subject of biology, and then in graduate school, my passion, the brain.

Along the way, I became fascinated with a control region called the hypothalamus. I went to a cocktail party once, and when someone asked, "What do you do?" I answered breathlessly, "I study the hypothalamus!" They'd never heard of it. So I explained, "If you put one index finger between your eyebrows and other one above your left ear, where the lines would meet inside your head there is a brain region that weighs just four grams, like a grape. Yet that part controls thirst, hunger, body temperature, sex, emotions. Wow, what a remarkable piece of tissue!" I'm not sure how contagious my enthusiasm was that night. But my zeal propelled me through a doctoral degree on the brain's "master gland," and, as it turns out, led me to the teaching and research that would be my real life's work.

After Berkeley and a short postdoctoral stint at Harvard, I arrived with my first husband, Dick Diamond, a nuclear chemist and physicist, at Cornell University in upstate New York. Most afternoons, I would get a baby-sitter for our infant daughter and hang out at the zoology department on campus. Marcus Singer, a brain expert I had read about and wanted to study with, worked in that department. Singer eventually gave me a little research project to carry out. But then, in the middle of fall semester—I think it was 1955—Singer was indicted for contempt of Congress. The president of the university was not going to let someone teach Cornell students after he had been blacklisted for attending communist meetings. So he immediately terminated Singer, and this left a class of 250 undergraduates in human biology stranded. Generously, Singer turned in my name as a possible substitute. It was a "Can you lecture tomorrow?"

sort of thing, and I agreed. The following semester another professor took a sabbatical and I filled in for his comparative anatomy class. One course led to another, and in all, I spent four years working as the first woman science instructor at Cornell.

Part-time teaching was an ideal situation for a woman with, by now, two small children. I could keep up with the field of anatomy by preparing my lectures at home, going to campus to deliver them, then coming home again. One day, I was sitting in our big green leather living room chair, reading an issue of *Science* magazine while the children slept. I saw an article by three researchers at U.C. Berkeley, who had been studying the brain chemistry of smart and dull rats. David Krech, Mark Rosenzweig, and Edward Bennett used one strain of "maze-bright rats," which could make their way through a standard wooden maze quickly and easily. The team also used another strain of "maze-dull rats," which made their way through a maze slowly and laboriously. The team compared the amount of one particular chemical in the "bright" brains with the same chemical in the "dull" brains. Their finding was significant: They showed, for the first time, a link between the physical makeup of an animal's brain and its behavior—in this case, its ability to learn.

I sat in that green chair even more thrilled than I was at the sight of the disembodied brain of my youth. "That's exactly what I want to do!" I told myself, to work with this team, but to study the structure of those rat brains, not their chemistry. As luck would have it, Dick Diamond got an offer to return to U.C. Berkeley, and my immediate response to packing up the children and all the household possessions was, "Boy, that's perfect!"

By the time I got settled in, taught a few courses, and went down to see Krech, Rosenzweig, and Bennett, they had moved on to an even more exciting project. Their new work was inspired by a man named Donald Hebb at McGill University. It turns out that the Hebbs allowed their children's pet rats to run freely around the house, and this gave Hebb an inspiration. After a few weeks of free roaming, Hebb took the rats to his lab to run mazes and compared the results with maze-running by rats living in laboratory cages. Interestingly, the free-ranging rodents ran a better maze than the locked-up lab rats. Hebb speculated that rats confined to small unstimulating cages would develop brains worse at solving problems than animals growing up in a stimulating environment like a large house with hallways, staircases, and human playmates.

From Hebb's observation the Berkeley team got the idea of deliberately raising baby rats in two kinds of cages: a large "enrichment cage," filled with toys and housing a colony of twelve rats; and a small "impoverishment cage" housing a solitary rat with no toys. Indeed, the rats growing up in a deliberately enriched environment ran better mazes than the "impoverished rats" raised in unstimulating confinement. And like the bright and dull rats that Krech and his colleagues had already tested, the deliberately enriched rats had more of that particular brain chemical than the impoverished rats. This time, however, it was apparently nurture at work, not nature.

When I showed up at the Krech and Rosenzweig lab, full of enthusiasm for their work and anxious to look at the rats' brains, they were surprised but accepting. In those days, money was readily accessible to add new people to scientific projects. So within days, my wish was coming true.

The research process involved removing the brain of a deceased laboratory rat, chemically fixing, or preserving, the brain tissue and making thin slices of it, viewing the slices under a microscope, then very carefully measuring the thickness of the cerebral cortex from the rats raised in both kinds of cages, enriched and impoverished. I did see variations: The enriched rats had a thicker cerebral cortex than the impoverished rats. But the difference was not the sort you could observe casually; you had to compare the brain tissue under the microscope, and the cerebral cortex of the enriched rats was only 6 percent thicker than the cortex of the impoverished rats. Nevertheless, it was highly statistically significant; nine cases out of nine showed a 6 percent difference. This was the first time anyone had ever seen a structural change in an animal's brain based on different kinds of early life experiences. Could it really be true?

I took another year and repeated the experiment with nine more animals. Then I started to get excited. It was about 1963 by then, and my life was really hectic. I now had three babies, I was only at the university half time, and I was doing demanding, pioneering work in the lab. In some ways, that period is hard to recall. But I do remember very clearly the day I took the results over to show David Krech. I ran across campus with the papers in my hand and laid them out on his desk. He stared at them, then at me, and immediately said, "This is unique. This will change scientific thought about the brain." It was a great thrill—truly an emotional high—to sit with him and share that moment.

In 1964, we published the results in a paper by Diamond, Krech, and Rosenzweig called "Effects of Enriched Environments on the Histology of the Cerebral Cortex." And a year after that, I found myself standing in front of a session on the brain at the annual meeting of the American Association of Anatomists.

We were at a hotel conference room in Washington, D.C., and I was scared silly. There were hundreds of people in the room—very few of them women—and this was the first scientific paper I had presented at a big conference. I explained the project as calmly as I could, people applauded politely, and then—I'll always remember this—a man stood up in the back of the room and said in a loud voice, "Young lady, that brain cannot change!"

It was an uphill battle for women scientists then—even more than now—and people at scientific conferences are often terribly critical. But I felt good about the work, and I simply replied, "I'm sorry, sir, but we have the initial experiment and the replication experiment that shows it can." That confidence is the beauty of doing anatomy. Ed Bennett used to say to me, "Marian, your data will be good from here to eternity, because it is based on anatomical structure." Eternity is a long time, of course. But so far—and it's been thirty-four years—Bennett has been right. And the man in the back row? My entire research career, all the scientific findings that stemmed from it, and—as we hope this book will show—the experiences of your own life and your children's show how wrong he was. . . .

Answers Lead to Questions

The discovery that a rat's brain can grow when it is raised in a spacious environment full of toys and companions led to celebrations in the Berkeley lab—but the hurrahs died out quickly. Virtually all fundamental revelations about nature and its laws propagate new questions for every new answer. The dogma-shattering fact that a mammalian cerebral cortex could grow when stimulated by the environment was no exception, and the focus quickly shifted to new questions of mechanism and meaning: Exactly how could a brain region get thicker? Why does it get thicker or, for that matter, thinner? Is an animal with a thicker cerebral cortex smarter, and if so, how much? Do other parts of the brain grow with experience, too? Can age and sex influence the phenomenon? Do other animals show the same effect? And what about people? Answers—and the inevitable crop of still more questions—started coming soon after the infamous anatomy conference in Washington.

The idea of brain enhancement excited biologists, behaviorists, and educators alike. But neurologists, the group of life scientists specializing in brains and nervous systems, were at once both curious and strongly skeptical about the prospects of brain growth. They, after all, had created the theory that the Man in the Back Row was merely espousing: the notion that the brain is equipped at birth with all the nerve cells it will ever have, and that a portion of these inevitably dwindle and die off during life. Schoolchildren in the 1960s learned to recite the dictum, "You lose 100,000 brain cells every day." And nutritionists of that era focused on the body but ignored the head. They reasoned that nothing, including diet, was going to alter the gelatinous mass with the "gray ceiling"—an intelligence level fixed at birth and immutable throughout life save for the inescapable decay of senses and reason.

Neurologists, you see, had *measured* the dwindling of brain cells in rats and humans over the typical life span. They could see shrinkage with a microscope, they could count the disappearance of nerve cells in a given region over time, and they could weigh the ever-lighter whole brain at later and later ages. In what was probably the central study of brain shrinkage with age, a professor in Rochester, New York, procured two brains from deceased twenty-year-olds and two from octogenarians who had passed on. The researcher then removed one tiny region of the cerebral cortex from each of the four brains and counted the nerve cells. He found a 20 percent decrease in the number of cells between the young and old brains. This seemed to coincide with the cell loss another neurologist had seen in the surface area of the human brain between ages twenty and eighty. Finally, a third neurologist took the data from the first two and extrapolated the figure of 100,000 cells lost each day between young adulthood and old age. This loose chain bound together the data and a popular notion at least as old as Shakespeare: "When the age is in, the wit is out." Combinations of apparent fact and anecdotal observation are often the birthplace of dogma, and so it was with assumptions about the brain.

Ironically, the Berkeley group's theory of enriched and impoverished environments could easily explain the apparently dwindling nerve cells by looking to the *source* of those experimental brains. Before the 1964 Diamond paper appeared, researchers paid little attention to where a brain came from or to its owner's life history. In most cases, human researchers got brains from coroners, who, in turn, received the bodies of indigents, alcoholics, or bedridden soldiers who had died in Veteran's Hospitals. Likewise, animal researchers invariably housed mice, rats, and other lab animals in small sterile cages. Whether a cage is built of steel, or of drugs, poverty, and illness, it is the picture of mental impoverishment. In death, the inhabitants' brains usually reflected the long-term effects of too little stimulation, sensation, exploration, and learning. Inadvertently, *the neurologist's standard model was based on starving brains,* and their pessimism for the fate of all brains was founded on too few examples and impoverished lives of the mind. When researchers collect brain tissue from enriched research animals or from people who have lived healthy, mentally active lives, they do not find a thinning of the cortex or a relentless loss of neurons with age. Nevertheless, despite this historic oversight, it was the neurologist's standard unit of study, the neuron, or nerve cell, that ultimately explained how a rat's brain could grow with enrichment.

A Rodent's Brain Revealed

All rats—whether the red-eyed, white-furred laboratory varieties or the dusky types that prowl alleys and attics—have the same type of brain. This organ is the size of a small oyster, the consistency of week-old Jell-O, and the light pink color inside a puppy's ear, and it sits encased in a thin, bony skull as big as a pecan shell. In life, the brain controls all the animal's body functions and behaviors. In death, that organ can be removed very gingerly from its protective case and its four major divisions examined easily. Viewed from the tail end, a smooth brain stem (including the medulla) is contiguous with the spinal cord running down the back. Next comes the cerebellum, a small, highly wrinkled lump sitting on top of the medulla; then two larger very smooth lobes, the right and left cerebral hemispheres, mushroom out; and finally up front, small twin orbs protrude—the right and left olfactory bulbs. The brain stem controls basic body functions like breathing, alertness, blood circulation, and body temperature; the cerebellum governs muscle coordination, balance, and learning; the cerebral hemispheres process vision, hearing, sensations, movement, and thinking (a rat's version, anyway); and the olfactory bulbs interpret incoming smells.

The most notable features of a rat's small oyster brain are the smoothness of the cerebral hemispheres and the relatively huge size of the olfactory lobes. These reveal that the rat depends heavily on its nose to suss out features of the surrounding world. In a larger-brained animal like a cat or a sheep, the cerebral hemispheres are so fissured, folded, and convoluted that the surface looks like a topographic map merged with a jumbled pile of large pasta noodles. The cat and sheep olfactory bulbs are proportionately smaller than a rat's and less distinct, but they still protrude and reveal a nose-centered existence. In a more intelligent organism like a human, a dolphin, or a chimpanzee, the cerebral hemispheres are proportionately huge. They obscure all but a portion of the wrinkled cerebellum, and the cerebral surface is so densely convoluted that it stops resembling anything but the aptly named brain coral.

On every mammal's brain there is a thin "bark" layer covering the gelatinous mass. It's hard to believe that this narrow sheet could contain all of an animal's cunning or a person's intellect. But it does. Life scientists have known for over a century that if

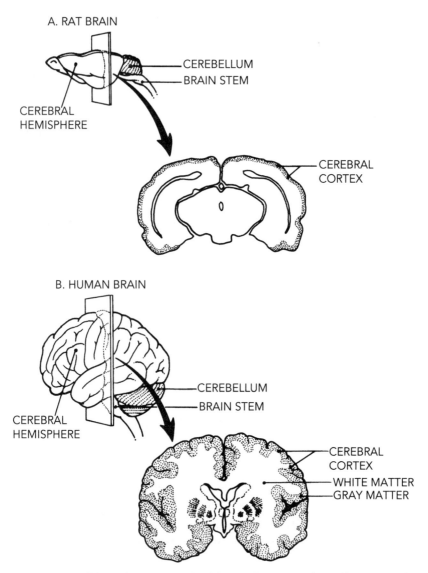

(a) A rat's small brain has two cerebral hemispheres enveloped by a smooth, very thin layer of nerve cells, the cerebral cortex. (b) The human brain is, of course, much larger, and the cerebral cortex is deeply fissured and folded.

you take the brain from a furry animal or person that has died and slice the organ in the ear-to-ear direction, there is a layer of nerve cells $1/32$ to $1/8$ inch thick at the outer edge, just below a diaphanous protective membrane. Because the thin layer of nerve cells has the same position as bark on a tree, it came to be known as the cerebral *cortex* (Latin for "bark").

In a living animal, the cortex is pink, like the rest of the brain, since it is crisscrossed with a hundred miles or more of minute blood vessels. But seventeenth-century scientists began calling the cortex the "gray matter" due to the ashen hue it turns when a brain is pickled in alcohol or another fixative. The rest of the mass enveloped by the cortex layer contains nerve fibers sheathed with a white fatty covering (called *myelin*). In common parlance, it is the "white matter."

Over many centuries of probing the gray and white matter, physicians and scientists located regions responsible for particular bodily and mental functions. In the early 1900s, for example, a German brain anatomist assigned nearly fifty specific capacities to patches of the human cerebral cortex, including vision, hearing, touch, movement, speech, and planning. Others did the same for the smaller, simpler rat brain. It was perfectly logical, therefore, that after Krech, Rosenzweig, and Bennett altered rats' maze-navigating behavior by enriching their environments, the next step was to search for physical changes in the cerebral cortex. Whatever intelligence a rat can claim, that brain power lies in the cortex. When the Diamond team found a thicker cortex in the stimulated rats and a thinner cortex in their unstimulated siblings, the finding made a startling kind of sense, even though no one had ever before looked for a brain change of that kind.

The rat was a fortuitous choice for the Berkeley group as an animal model. The smooth little cortex of that oyster-sized brain is less than $1/8$ inch thick all around. Because of that uniformity, it was a relatively straightforward exercise to measure any change in cortical thickness based on a rat's exciting or boring environment. By comparison, a human brain, with the hills and valleys of its wildly convoluted surface, has a cerebral cortex that varies from $1/32$ inch in some places to $1/4$ inch thick in others. It took nearly thirty years—and the development of sophisticated, computer-driven laboratory methods—before researchers would figure out how to document subtle thickness changes in the human cortex. The smooth-brained rat simply provided a running start for enrichment science.

In addition to its small size and smooth bark layer, the rat cortex had another beneficial feature: its interior architecture. The rat cortex is like a living, six-layered "fabric" made of densely packed nerve cells and fibers. In rats, cats, humans, and all other mammals, the cortex is cut from the same cloth with a similar six-layer construction, and the fibers contain the same kinds of branching cells. Scientists refer to the cells as *neurons* and they call the mammalian cortex the *neocortex* because it is the newest evolutionary addition to the cortical architecture—that is, the latest structure to evolve. From rat to cat to person, the neocortex differs mainly in area, not in basic interior design. The entire surface area of a rat's cortex is about four square centimeters, or the size of a postage stamp. A person's cortex—if stretched out flat—would be about two and one-half feet square, or the size of a very large table napkin. A postage-stamp cortex fits comfortably inside a pecan-shell skull; that's why a rat's cortex remains smooth and why, in turn, it's so useful for brain research. A large square napkin, however, has to bunch and pleat to fit inside a coconut-shell-sized skull like our own, and that explains the myriad convolutions of our brain surface. Because the six-layered neuron-packed fabric of the mammalian cortex remains very similar from one species to the next, however, some of its fundamental secrets are the same, too, and the rat's brain will yield them generously. Ultimately it was the neurons in the rat cortex that answered the first questions arising from the Diamond discovery: How do brains grow thicker when they are enriched?

The Heart of Enrichment: Nerve Cell Branching

The nerve cell or neuron may be the neurologist's standard unit of study but there is nothing standard about it as living cells go. The typical rat or human cell is a compact globular or squarish unit, while the neuron tends to look more like a spindly, uprooted plant with tiny leaves and a bulbous base.

Some neurons in the cerebral cortex have a body shaped like a pyramid and others like a star. Regardless, most have an elaborate network of spiny branches sprouting profusely from the

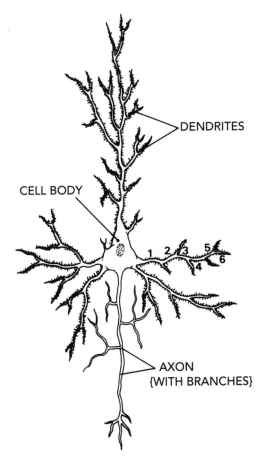

The nerve cell, or neuron, resembles a miniature tree with its cell body, its axon bearing a few long thin extensions, its luxuriantly branching dendrites, and its thornlike spines that grow, change shape, or shrink as a person experiences the world.

"bulb"; these branches are the *dendrites* (named after the "little trees" they so closely resemble) and they are a kind of antenna that either receives input from an organism's environment or from other neurons, distant or nearby. Neurons also have a long thin extension, the *axon*, that emerges from one side of the cell and often bears fewer, simpler branches. Axons act like telephone wires carrying messages away from nerve cells. Many of the axons from nerve cells in your brain, however, transmit messages only between layers of the thin cortical fabric or from one brain region to another. These axons can be less than a millionth of an inch long. But a few spectacular axons can be a yard long or longer: An axon from a single nerve cell in your spinal cord, for example, could easily run all the way to your big toe and transmit the messages that lead you to point your toe or flex it.

One man who has spent most of his long research career admiring neurons is Arnold Scheibel, former director of the Brain Research Institute at the University of California at Los Angeles. Scheibel—a man with the heart of a poet, the humor and looks of Sid Caesar, and the intonation of an Elizabethan actor—thinks of his hours peering through a microscope at neurons as a "perpetual voyeur's paradise. It is so delightful," he says, "and it lends a sense of reverence that you are looking at the stuff that has made biological life sensate."

While there are more elaborate microscopes and more sophisticated, specialized stains available now, the voyeur's keys to neural paradise have long been the light microscope and a type of staining preparation using silver chromate called the Golgi stain that reveals individual neurons. "Golgi has always been exciting and remains so," says Scheibel, "because a fortunate preparation with it shows glimpses of everything—the cells, their dendrites, axons, and their connections." The cells and their dendritic trees usually stain an inky black, while the background remains a golden color. "The effect is a bit like a Japanese print," Scheibel muses. "But the beauty is that it only picks out one element in a thousand or ten thousand." If Golgi stained every neuron, "you'd just see a black mass," because the cortical fabric is so dense with crisscrossing cell bodies, dendrites, and axons. Instead, says Scheibel, "you get, in a sense, fragments of a circuit diagram, and if you put them all together, you get a little celestial music."

If that music had lyrics, it would sing *"Surface area!"* Neurons without branching dendrites would be like trees without leaves to soak up sunshine. "Only when the neuron develops these extensions from itself," Scheibel explains, "does it begin to significantly increase its surface area as a total unit and provide more and more of a 'landing field' " for incoming information transmitted through other dendrites, axons, and cell bodies.

Surface area is a useful solution that nature first invented, then elaborated upon. A plant's leaves are its collectively huge solar surface, and likewise, the 300 million tiny balloonlike bags packaged into your two lungs give you a surface area the size of a badminton court for absorbing oxygen and liberating carbon dioxide. Or take your small intestine, which is longer than a 1965 Cadillac. It has an inner surface thrown into millions of folds, each covered with fingerlike projections themselves carpeted with microscopic brushes. If this byzantine structure could be ironed into a single flat sheet, the surface area would surpass that of a tennis court! No other organ, however, holds a candle to the "landing fields" of our three-pound human brain. Of its 100 billion neurons, more than one third are jammed into the cerebral "bark" and branch luxuriantly into dendritic trees. No one that we know of has ever calculated the surface area of all those branching nerve cells, but it must be truly vast.

Now, at the time the Diamond team published their work on changes in rats' brains with varying environments, neurologists knew about dendritic branching and neural surface area, as well as how these branches fill most of the gray matter. The Diamond group had noticed an additional fact: In the thicker cortex of each enriched rat, the nerve cell bodies were farther apart than in the thinner cortex of each impoverished rat. In their 1964 article, they speculated that branching of dendrites might explain the additional thickness of the enriched cerebral cortex. Later that same year, a U.C. Berkeley student named Ralph Holloway jumped into the brain enrichment fray, and found that, indeed, neurons in the rat's cerebral cortex were sending out more dendritic branches in response to environmental stimulation. Holloway also found that this branching, at least in part, *was causing the cortex to grow thicker.* When Holloway published this finding in 1966, it helped dissolve some of his fellow neurologists' skepticism about brain growth: Here was a plausible mechanism for how the cortex could get thicker. But as the next few years would show, there were still more levels of detail to the story.

The more researchers have learned about the dendrites in our nervous systems and brains, the more appropriate seems the term "little trees." The trunk of a maple tree, for instance, divides into two or three thick major branches, each of these splits into smaller secondary branches, and eventually, the whole system will ramify into thousands of small leaf-bearing twigs. Similarly, a neuron's dendritic branches bifurcate again and again in such a way that in just one portion of a nerve cell, a neurologist can count the first, second, third, fourth, fifth, sixth, and occasionally seventh or eighth branching points. "The successive branching," Arnold Scheibel explains, "is what we call lower order and higher order. By lower order, we mean the first, second, and third branches of the dendritic system, and by higher order we mean the fourth, fifth, sixth, and sometimes more."

Scientists like Scheibel have found that dendrites bear some resemblance to public stocks: The longer a dendritic branch grows, the more likely it is to split. Scheibel and colleagues also found that when a child is born, the neurons in its cerebral cortex tend to have some or all of its lower-order dendrites already in place, whereas the higher-order branches develop well after birth. Could one say that the branching of the lower-order dendrites is determined by a person's genes and the higher-order branching pattern by interaction with their environment? "It's not quite that tidy," replies Scheibel, "but it's in that direction."

One telling exception is the dendrites in a baby rat's olfactory bulb—a brain region responsible for receiving and processing odor cues. "When we studied these," says Scheibel, "we found they were beautifully heavily branched and all set to go, because the little one at birth has to be mature enough to smell out and seek out the nipple. Within hours after birth, a rat pup is nipple-specific—it will go back to its own spigot and nothing else." Clearly, higher-order branches result from experience *unless* survival requires them to be present at birth in certain parts of the brain.

A researcher at the University of Illinois, William Greenough, became interested in enriched environments and the brain after the Berkeley team published their work in the mid 1960s. Six years after Diamond's student Ralph Holloway found that a rat's cortex grows thicker because its neural dendrites are branching and growing, Greenough published an article elaborating on that fact. He found more higher-order branches in an enriched rat's dendrites and more lower-order branches in an impoverished rat's dendrites. Somehow, stimulation from the rat's environment was inducing the dendritic trees in that smooth, thin little rodent cortex to branch like a young tree in the spring sunshine. The image is seductive: miniature trees of the mind growing like poplars in the sun, reaching ever wider and higher to bask in a shower of information—sensations, physical challenges, social contacts—from the outside world.

This image hints at a neuron's raison d'être and it opens one more level of detail in the story of brain enrichment: thorns on the remarkable neural trees.

Nubbins, Umbrellas, and Lollipop Trees

Most of the cells in living things have specialty jobs: Muscle cells are built to contract, goblet cells in the stomach lining to secrete mucus, and hair follicle cells to generate hair shafts. The neuron, too, has an important mission: to communicate. Whether possessed of long or short axon "wires" and of bushy or unforked dendritic "antennae," a neuron is specialized to receive information about the state of the outside environment, like heat or cold, as well as information about internal states like hunger or pain. Further, it is designed to interpret these states and orchestrate responses that could set the animal to fighting, fleeing, hunting, eating, seeking shelter, or understanding a sentence. Biologists have known for half a century that in order for information to flow from one neuron to another, parts of neurons must come into close contact with each other. And the regions of close contact usually involve a branch of one neuron's transmitting fiber (axon) getting very close and intimate with a neighboring cell's receiving antenna (dendrite).

The communicating axon and dendrite are not actually welded together at their point of near-contact. Instead, a little buttonlike ending on the axon (a *bouton*, from the French for "button") nestles very close to a little bulbous ending on the dendritic branch, leaving a minute gap between them like the firing surface of a spark plug. This bulb-and-button unit is a *synapse* (literally a "clasp") and it works something like this: When an electrical signal traveling down one neuron's axonal wire reaches the buttonlike ending at the wire's terminus, a chemical message crosses the gap in the synapse. If the information is compelling enough to spark interest in the receiving cell, the electrical transmission

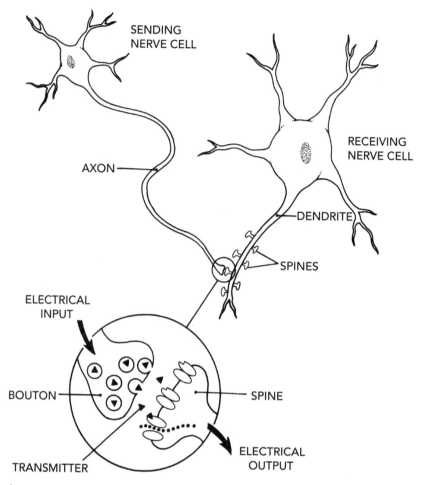

Among neurons, communication is an electrical-chemical affair. Here, it is taking place across a narrow gap between the sending nerve cell's bulbous axon tip and the receiving cell's thornlike spine.

continues on down *that* cell's receptive antenna or dendrite, to *its* cell body, and into *its* axon wire. From there it may pass across a synaptic junction to yet another neighboring cell where yet another transmission can take place. Although you are unaware of it, this same sparking and transmission is going on right now a billion times a second between your own neurons as you read, shift in your chair, blink, swallow, visualize what's going on in your brain, and reach up to turn the page.

The exciting implication for the story of brain enrichment is that almost all of the close-contact points (synapses) on dendrites occur at little thornlike protrusions called *spines*. And as University of California researchers (including the Diamond group) have found, *these dendritic spines themselves grow, change shape, or shrink* as an animal experiences the world.

One student in the Diamond lab, James Connor, became interested in how social isolation could affect a rat's brain, particularly in an elderly rat. He housed some advanced-age rodents together with a set of their aged friends, then housed other elderly rats alone. After the animals died, he looked at the spines on the dendrites in their cortex layers and found two surprising things: First, Connor saw that the spines resembled either three-dimensional lollipops with a ball on a stalk (like Tootsie Pops), or else they were short, squat nubbins with no stalk. Second, he found that older rats housed alone had lots of nubbin spines on their dendrites. Could there be various lollipop shapes, depending on experience? And in a lonely, deprived animal, could the lollipop spines go unused and eventually collapse into gnarled old nubbins, less capable of receiving information from other neurons? Or was there another explanation?

A researcher at the University of California at Davis, Richard Coss, found some answers in the tiny brains of honeybees. Coss and some coworkers looked at the dendritic spines from young honeybees that had never left the hive, then compared them to the spines of bees that had made just *one single flight* out into the meadows near the university and back. They also looked at dendritic spines in forager bees that make repeated forays in search of pollen and nectar, and at spines in nurse bees that remain in the hive permanently and tend the larvae. The Coss team found a number of spine shapes—not just lollipops and nubbins—depending on the bees' level of stimulation from the outside world: Young bees that had never flown had lollipop spines, with small heads on tall stalks. In bees that had made a single flight, many of these lollipops had grown bigger heads! In the forager bees, with their extensive real-world navigating experience, the spines had very large heads and very short stalks. We think of this latter shape as umbrellalike because it can be cupped, like an inside-out umbrella; flattened, like a decorative Japanese umbrella; or rounded, like a standard British bumbershoot.

Experience—even just an hour or two's worth of flying through the meadow—obviously had a dramatic enlarging effect on a bee's dendritic spines. Richard Coss found similar changes in the dendrites of socially enriched and deprived jewel fish. Another team found a change from lollipop to umbrella-like spines in young myna birds who listened to tapes of human speech. A third group found that young mice that ran on exercise wheels had more dendritic branching and many more spines than littermates prevented from moving around. Finally, several researchers have studied the somewhat confusing landscape of dendritic spines in people—specifically, the cerebral cortices of mentally retarded children. By using high-powered microscopes to examine the brain tissue of deceased children, researchers found an abundance of long-stalked lollipop spines but an absence of umbrella and nubbin spines. Another group found that before birth, the dendritic spines in a fetus with Down's syndrome were identical to those of a nonaffected fetus, but by four months after birth, the Down's syndrome child had fewer spines and these were mostly lollipops with thin, elongated stalks.

Human dendritic spines are so tiny and hard to study that today, at the turn of the twenty-first century, they are still largely a mystery to neurologists. Researchers, however, do tend to agree about some things: Lollipop spines on dendrites in the cerebral cortex may represent a virgin condition—that is, the spines may assume this ball-and-stick shape before they have been stimulated much. The narrow stalks below the rounded heads may slow incoming impulses or prevent them from reaching the nerve cells. Only with repeated use will the spines' shape change and the transmission of information become easier—a correlate of learning and memory. Umbrella spines may represent that initiated state of regular use, and the bigger head and broader, shorter stalk may pass along nerve impulses more easily. The nubbin spines may represent an old or collapsed umbrella, perhaps due to disuse of the brain region it occupies.

Regardless of how the neuron's differently shaped spines may act, it is clear that in everything from insects to primates, the cerebral cortex (or its equivalent) is packed with forests of minute thorn trees, each capable of bearing tens of thousands of differently shaped spines. These, spines, in turn, twitch and vibrate in response to inflowing information, and the transmission process itself transmutes their shape. In some way, the shimmering, pulsating neural arbors help modulate learning and memory. And the more stimulating the animal's environment, the more extensive the arbor.

All of this structural detail explains beautifully *how* the cortex grows thicker with use. Why, then, aren't we outfitted at birth with the thickest possible cortex so we are ready for whatever challenges the environment might present? The answer rests with nature and its basic conservatism.

Richard Coss of the University of California at Davis, explains it succinctly: "An animal is only as smart as it needs to be." A nurse bee sequestered inside the hive apparently doesn't need as many umbrella spines, a cortex as thick, or a bee "mind" as smart as a worker buzzing through the meadows and orchards. As a result, a nurse bee has a less-developed cortex. All animals' bodies are tuned to conserve energy (and most of us have the spare tire to prove it). So nature programs parts of the brain to sharpen up when—and only when—experience demands it. A person is infinitely smarter than a honeybee, of course, and every normal human brain is large and convoluted. But there is always growing room and no apparent cap on what we can learn and absorb. We laugh at the cartoon showing a student who raises his hand in class and says, "Professor, can I be excused? My brain is full!" because we know from common experience that our learning capacity is boundless and lifelong.

On the other hand, just as the muscles are programmed to grow smaller and weaker with disuse, the dendritic trees and spines will shrivel and the cortex grow thinner with lack of mental activity. Nature's conservatism is survival-oriented and geared to save energy for the inevitable bad times. In good times, if we do nothing but lounge around, eat snacks, and watch TV, the same conservative mechanism can make us both fatter and dumber!

Rats Revisited

For two decades after their first finding of brain changes in rats, the Diamond lab group studied enrichment and impoverishment with great intensity. They wanted to learn everything they could about the enrichment effect and what might influence it; with its matriculatory parade of graduate students and post-doctoral candidates, the lab produced over 150 scientific papers.

One of the first adjustments the Berkeley team made in their overall strategy was to start splitting experimental animals into three groups instead of two: a standard or intermediate condition in which three rats inhabit a small cage with no toys; an impoverishment condition in which a solitary rat lives in a small cage without toys; and an enrichment condition in which twelve rats inhabit a much larger cage with a rotating array of toys such as exercise wheels, platforms, and ladders.

This three-way split gave the researchers a control group against which to compare the impoverished and enriched experimental groups. This improved the science and it helped allay a perennial criticism: Some observers pointed out that laboratory rats, regardless of cage type, are slower-witted and thinner-cortexed than even the dimmest wild rodent. A rat trying to survive in an alley or a sewer would certainly be bombarded with sensations, challenged with physical barriers, and constantly in search of food—all of which would sharpen its cerebrum far more than a stay of any length in a cushy enrichment cage. Could researchers be doing nothing more with their wheels and ladders than restoring cage-bound dullards to the native state? The critics had a point, but the use of an intermediate condition as a control helped persuade them that indeed, an animal's cortex can expand and contract in response to experiential input. And this finding is potentially valid for students in dormitories, or prisoners in solitary confinement; for senior citizens living together in comfort or alone in poverty; for children treated well or malnourished and abused; and for all other vagaries of the human condition.

With their three cage types, the Diamond team fleshed out the basic principles of brain enrichment:

- The impact of a stimulating or boring environment is widespread throughout the regions involved in learning and remembering. Neurons in other parts of the brain besides the cerebral cortex can also respond by growing new dendritic branches and spines (or by shrinking).
- Enriching the environment of a pregnant female rat can result in newborn pups with a thicker cerebral cortex than in pups born to impoverished females.
- Nursing rat pups show the effects of enrichment on the brain. In just over a week, the enriched youngsters developed a cortex from 7 to 11 percent thicker than in deprived infants. After two weeks in the enrichment cage with toys, one particular brain area involved in sensory integration grew 16 percent thicker in the enriched pups—the biggest increase in any brain region at any age.
- In young weaned rats, an enriched environment had a mild positive effect on cortical thickness. In "teenage" rats, the impact was even greater. A more startling result, however, was the impact of *boredom* in young and adolescent rats: A boring environment had a more powerful *thinning* effect on the cortex than an exciting environment had on cortex *thickening*. Young rats are obviously very susceptible to losing mental ground when not challenged, and that shrinkage shows up after just four days. In rodent "teenagers," at least, the shrinkage can begin to be reversed again after four days of enrichment.
- Brain changes were found in young adult rats, in "middle-aged" rats, and even in rats the equivalent of ninety-year-old humans. "Use it or lose it," is clearly a lifelong prospect for both rats and people.

These brain changes were exciting news, but the question remained: *Does a thicker cortex mean a smarter animal?* The answer was "Yes!" Building on the Berkeley group's data, psychologists have learned that enriched rats of varying ages can figure out the twists and turns of a maze more quickly than a standard-colony or deprived rat, and they can arrive in less time at the food reward waiting in the maze's end zone.

These varied findings lead to the inescapable fact that a mammal's brain—especially the forests of thorn trees with their nubbin, umbrella, and lollipop spines flourishing in the narrow cerebral bark—can grow when environmental stimulation demands a smarter animal. It's also clear that a confining, solitary environment lacking in challenges requires a duller brain and nature responds by shrinking the cortex and reinvesting elsewhere the energy resources it would take to maintain a thicker cortex capable of more computing power. The upshot is obviously a way to generate smarter rats. But what good is a brainy rodent, aside from its illustrative value as an animal model? If that model translates to people and means that we can also deliberately enrich a person's environment and cause his or her brain to grow, then a smart rat is a priceless commodity. So *does* it translate?

Enrichment and the Human Brain

As long ago as 1819, an Italian anatomist speculated that thoughts and actions could in some unspecified way alter the structure of our brains. And in 1911, a Spanish researcher who studied the makeup of nerve cells suggested that exercising the human brain would specifically cause our neurons to grow bigger and form more interconnections. But a modern researcher, Arnold Scheibel of U.C.L.A., has tried to answer the question of human brain enrichment directly. Ironically, he was introduced to the subject by two forward-looking European researchers who had already been contemplating genetics, experience, and the brain for a decade before the Berkeley team studied rat brains, two decades before Scheibel met those Berkeley scientists, and three decades before he married Diamond.

Back in 1954, Scheibel and his first wife, Madge Scheibel, were studying in Europe and visited the laboratory of an elderly couple, Oscar and Cecille Vogt, who had been exploring the human brain for years. The Vogts showed Scheibel some slides of brain tissue from talented Europeans, and it was, Scheibel recalls, "The first time I had ever seen any evidence that a correlation exists between brain structure and what we do in life." One slide was from the cerebral cortex of an artist who, Scheibel reminisces, "had what is called the capacity for eidetic imagery—essentially photographic mind. The exciting thing is, this fellow who had this remarkable visual imagery capability all his life had a layer four in his visual cortex—which is the layer where visual information comes in from the eyes—that was at least twice as wide as those of normal people!"

The man had passed away, and the Vogts had studied a sample of his brain tissue. An ordinary laboratory stain revealed his thicker fourth layer quite clearly. "Then," Scheibel goes on excitedly, "to cap it all, they had also studied a tissue specimen from a Belgian violinist who had apparently been born with the gift of perfect pitch." In the part of his cerebral cortex responsible for hearing, the receptive layer, layer four, was once again about twice as thick as normal. "I found this extremely exciting," says Scheibel, and after returning to the United States, "I kept wondering how we could obtain and study samples from extraordinary people—creative artists, great raconteurs." Unfortunately, it was rare at that time for people to leave their brain to science. "Today," Scheibel adds, "it's a lot more acceptable."

Scheibel kept busy studying other aspects of the brain for nearly twenty years, and then, in the early 1970s, he had a new idea: Instead of studying a unique ability like photographic mind or perfect pitch, he would focus on a faculty that virtually every person possesses—language—so that he could obtain and study specimens more easily. Scheibel and coworkers conducted experiment after experiment on the language areas of the human cerebral cortex as well as on other regions controlling diverse mental and physical activities.

Through this work, Scheibel's group revealed three important generalities about the brain and human experience. First, in the part of the cortex concerned with producing speech (called Broca's area, together with an adjacent motor zone that governs mouth and lip movements) they found distinct differences in the dendritic trees. In this region on the left side of the cerebral cortex, the dendrites had more extensive branching, including fourth-, fifth-, and sixth-order split-offs. On the right side, the dendritic trees showed mostly first-, second-, and third-order branching. Significantly, the left side, not the right side, controls speech production in about 90 percent of all people, and in this well-used left side, the neural trees were growing more luxuriantly.

Second, a graduate student in Scheibel's lab, Bob Jacobs, along with colleague Matthew Schall, looked at the area of the human cortex responsible for understanding speech, so-called Wernicke's area. The team found that the higher a person's educational level, the more fourth-, fifth-, and sixth-order branching they could observe and document in the dendritic trees. Perhaps, their data suggest, by learning and using more words and complex ideas, the more highly educated person stimulates Wernicke's area dendrites to grow and branch.

Third, Scheibel and colleagues looked at two separate regions of the human cortex, one receiving sensations to the body trunk and another to the hands and fingers. They also explored a third brain region involved with planning and a fourth with logic. They speculated that they might find a continuum of "branchiness" in the dendritic trees for these areas, with the least branching in the trunk region dendrites, intermediate branchiness in the hand/finger region dendrites, and extreme branching in the areas devoted to higher-level thinking and planning.

Their continuum did not hold up entirely, but they did find the least dendritic branching connected with skin sensations in the trunk. And they saw fuller dendritic trees in the hand/finger cortex region of people whose jobs demanded dexterity and less branching when the job was less hand-oriented. For example, they saw impressive levels of dendritic branching in the brains of two deceased typists, while in a mechanic and a chef, the dendrites were only slightly fuller in the hand/finger region than in the trunk region. And in two other deceased subjects—a civil servant/salesman and a tailor—the hand/finger dendrites were no bushier than the trunk dendrites. One might have expected a tailor to have bushier neural trees representing finger dexterity. This man had died at age seventy-four, however, and may well have been retired from his vocation for a decade or more. As provocative as Scheibel's findings are, he interprets them cautiously; in the future, he says, studies like these need to be based on brain specimens from people whose jobs, hobbies, educations, intellectual habits, and lifestyles are fully known to the researcher.

All the same, Scheibel remains convinced that the human brain responds to stimulation. "It's always going to be more problematic to study human enrichment," he concedes, "because you can't do experiments" that deliberately control and manipulate a person's environment, as one can with lab animals. And of course a person must donate his or her brain to science before it can be examined. Nevertheless, he finds "a correlation between dendritic complexity and the length and levels of education and of vocation in life. Correlation says nothing about causality," he cautions, "but on the basis of what we know and have seen from animal experiments, it seems a likely inference" that the same phenomenon in rats, mice, cats, and monkeys holds for humans, as well: Increase the level of environmental stimulation and challenge, and you will increase the branching of the dendrites and the thickness of the human cortex.

It seems logical that if adult dendrites respond to their owner's education, jobs, and hobbies, and if young rats grow thicker brains in response to enrichment, then a human child should also show the phenomenal flourishing of dendritic trees when stimulated and enriched. A child's brain is hundreds of times bigger and more complicated than a rat's and its full development spans sixteen to eighteen years, not sixty days. So is there proof that as the child's brain develops, the dendrites—the magic trees of the mind—really *do* change in response to experience? These are the next parts of our story—and the plot literally thickens.

Chapter 2

An Enchanted Thing:
The Brain's Network of Connections

The Mind Is an Enchanting Thing

is an enchanted thing
    like the glaze on a
katydid-wing . . .

—Marianne Moore

• A few years ago, a West Virginia couple, expecting their first child, went to the obstetrician for a routine ultrasound examination. The results, however, were unexpected and frightening: The fetus was showing signs of hydrocephaly, or swelling in one of the brain's fluid-filled spaces. This swelling could cause the baby to have a thinned skull, a greatly enlarged head, and to be mentally retarded. The couple could, however, elect for mother and fetal son to undergo surgery for the installation of a plastic shunt that would drain off the excess fluid into the amniotic sac. Apprehensive but hopeful, they underwent the procedure. The swelling was relieved successfully, and their baby was born with a healthy brain and normal intelligence.

• A five-year-old Florida girl started experiencing ten to twelve seizures a day after the right side of her brain became infected. Doctors were able to cure the infection with drugs, but the best alternative they could offer for the devastating seizures was to completely remove the right hemisphere to eliminate the area where the convulsions were originating. The condition had deprived the girl of movement in her left leg and arm, but the surgery and extensive follow-up physical therapy restored much of that movement. Even though one half of her brain was replaced by a cavity containing only cerebrospinal fluid, the child's speech, emotions, problem solving, and other capacities recovered quickly and fully. Researchers followed her progress for twenty years, and found that her intelligence remained above normal, she could speak fluently, and she eventually graduated from college.

• Many decades ago, a baby boy was born with no cerebellum, the highly folded region inside the base of the skull. He grew up, lived for six decades, and then, after he died, a famous British physician at Cambridge University acquired and studied his brain. The researcher showed this unusual specimen to Arnold Scheibel, visiting Cambridge from U.C.L.A., and asked his guest, "What do you think his life was like?" Scheibel thought for a moment, then speculated, "He must have been wheelchair-bound and he could hardly control his hands." With a twinkle in his eyes, the Cambridge don replied, "Actually, he was a hod carrier—he had everything. Mobility. Balance. Strength. Coordination." Now, says Scheibel, "I have more humility when asked what something does in the brain."

The Brain: A Close-up View

The human brain is often called the most complex matter in the universe, and anyone who has ever taken a neuroanatomy final or even thumbed through an atlas of the brain and nervous system would have to agree. The gelatinous mass we each carry above our necks, behind our eyes, and between our ears contains *100 billion* nerve cells, or *neurons.* It also houses one trillion additional supporting cells, the *glia,* that surround and nourish the neurons. Together, the nerve cells make *1,000 trillion synaptic contact points* with each other—a number far greater than all the stars and planets in all the galaxies. A popular book on brain anatomy published in 1992 was aptly titled *The Three Pound Universe;* but in 1862, long before modern neuroscience, Emily Dickenson described the organ in appropriately cosmic terms in her poem 632:

The Brain—is wider than the sky—
For—put them side by side—
The one the other will contain
With ease—and You—beside.

Even more astonishing than the brain's structural complexity are its origins and its continual dynamics. Less than one week after a human egg is fertilized, a tiny layer of cells has divided and a fraction of those is destined to become the brain and the rest of the nervous system. Before a woman has missed her first period, three sections of her embryo's brain have already been demarcated as if an elongated balloon (albeit extremely small) had been pinched into segments. In less than thirty-three weeks, the fetal brain has been sculpted from a proliferating mass of dancing, migrating neurons. And birth, at thirty-eight weeks, marks just one point along a continuum of development that will encompass the next sixteen to eighteen years. By voting age, the brain will have emerged via a process guided by both nature and nurture, genes and upbringing.

In the last chapter, we asked, Can experience alter a child's brain in the same way the environment shapes a rat's brain? The short answer is "yes." The long answer fills this chapter and the next five.

When a pregnant woman first feels the momentary flutter of life inside her uterus, her experience of impending motherhood changes dramatically: She moves beyond sore breasts and morning sickness, and beyond daydreams of parenting. For the next five to six months, she becomes viscerally aware that her body is inhabited, and that this new being is active and constantly growing. Ironically, the single most crucial phase of embryonic development—the emergence of the future brain—took place before she knew that a new life was pending. In time, confirmation comes, she identifies the first flutter of "quickening," and she observes the obvious enlargements and gymnastics going on inside her midsection. In no way, however, can the woman sense the fantastic processes that produce the fetal brain and, with it, the basis of her future child's personality, emotion, and thought.

For all the brain's eventual complexity, early brain development is stunningly fast. Let's say the fertilization of an egg took place on a Monday. By Thursday, the embryo would consist of thirty cells clustered together like a colorless blackberry no bigger than a pinpoint. By Saturday, the cluster would have burrowed into the woman's uterine wall, and by Tuesday of the second week, a layer would have emerged within the cluster, destined to become the ectoderm, or future skin, sense organs, and the nervous system—the brain included. The ectoderm proper appears by the start of the third week, and by day nineteen, the future brain is already visible as a bulge on a flat disc of cells. In under a month, the embryo resembles a minute fish, and the head end contains a double-flexed tube, smaller than a comma in this sentence. The two flex zones demarcate the forebrain from the midbrain and the midbrain from the hindbrain. And by the fifth week after fertilization, when the mother has suspected or confirmed pregnancy, those three primitive brain regions have subdivided into two forebrain areas, one midbrain, and three hindbrain regions—five embryonic parts that will produce the forty or so major brain structures and the hundreds of smaller tracts, nuclei, fibers, ganglia, nerves, bodies, pathways, canals, and membranes that must form for the brain to function normally.

For some, a list of major brain structures will have all the charm of a warehouse inventory. But naming and defining those parts can give readers a sense of their own complex anatomy. And it also suggests the explosion of development that was touched off in each of us as our father's sperm entered our mother's egg.

The embryo's forebrain regions will give rise to:

- Retinas and optic nerves of our eyes
- Relay stations of the thalamus, a region that also coordinates our movements and sensations
- Hypothalamus, the master integrator, which regulates our body temperature, water and salt balance, and our appetites for food and sex, among other functions
- Olfactory bulbs, allowing us to detect odors
- Most of the white matter inside our brain's two hemispheres
- Corpus callosum, a fibrous bundle of axons (300 million of them!) forming a bridge between the brain's two hemispheres
- Corpus striatum, a complex set of cells and connecting fibers that enable us to move smoothly

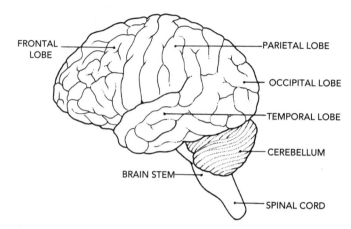

From the exterior, a human brain—seat of knowledge, passion, speech, and action—looks pale and deeply convoluted. It has four lobes, along with the wrinkled cerebellum, and two deep grooves.

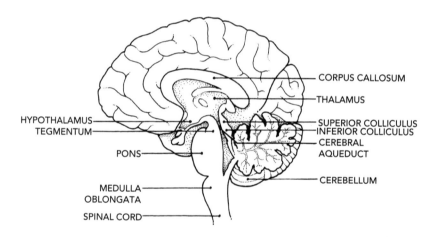

A cutaway view of the brain reveals numerous internal structures central to our consciousness and daily activity.

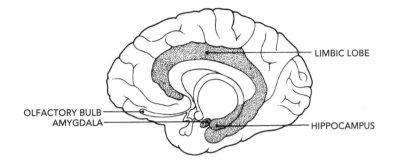

Another sideways view of the brain at a slightly different place exposes the olfactory bulb and some of the structures involved in our emotions.

- Limbic system (including the amygdala), which regulates our aggressions, emotions, and sex drive
- Hippocampus, which helps us learn and remember as well as to handle some visual and spatial information

The huge neocortex, the "gray matter" that covers our cerebral hemispheres and the rest of our brain with deep fissures and convolutions and eventually fills 80 percent of the skull. Our neocortex is divided into five lobes that collectively interpret our sensations, initiate our movements, and enable each of us to think, speak, write, calculate, plan, create, organize, and do all the other things that make us human.

The midbrain region of the human embryo gives rise to:

- Tectum, which includes the superior colliculus, a region that helps us process vision, and the inferior colliculus, which helps us process hearing
- Tegmentum, including a structure called the red nucleus that helps us control our voluntary movements
- An aqueduct that connects two fluid-filled chambers (ventricles) in our brain.

As embryos, we each produce a hindbrain, as well, with three crucial areas:

- Our cerebellum coordinates muscle contraction and tone, allows us to sense our position in space, and assists learning
- The pons (literally, "bridge"), which connects our cerebral cortex and cerebellar cortex and, among other jobs, controls chewing and facial expressions
- Our medulla, a crucial section of the brain stem just one inch long that helps regulate our breathing, blood circulation, tongue movements, and vocal sounds. Our sensations of touch, taste, sound, and others pass through the medulla before they reach the thalamus and then the cerebral cortex and eventually our conscious awareness. Once the cortex is stimulated, we can recognize complex sensations like the feel of a feather tickling, or the sweet taste of a strawberry, or the ringing of a wind chime.

A Ballet of Brain Development

Interpreting sensations like those will come along much later in development. In the meantime, when we are each five-week embryos, our primitive brain with its fore-, mid-, and hindbrain divisions resembles a bulging inchworm. Starting about this time, however, phenomenal cell division in the thin walls of one of our forebrain regions begins to generate the future cerebral hemispheres. The swelling of these half spheres will transform our brain's covering, first into a tiny, smooth lima bean by thirteen weeks, then into a furrowed walnut by twenty-four weeks. The cerebral "bark" layer continues its rapid expansion within the confines of our miniature skull, then the surface begins to bulge, fold back on itself, and dive inward as short springy axons pull some areas inward, and longer, looser axons allow other regions to bulge outward. By the time each of us is a full-term fetus—after sixteen more weeks of this inflation—only one-third of our cerebral cortex lies at the brain's surface in elevated convolutions. The other two-thirds have become tucked inside our brain in elaborate grooves and creases.

The production of the massive human cerebral cortex from the walls of our "inchworm" brain, starting at five weeks' gesta-

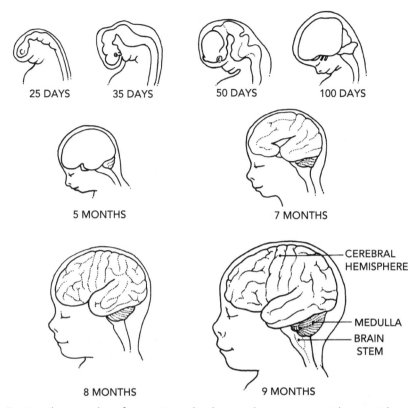

During the months of gestation, the human brain grows with astonishing speed from a segmented tube to an "inchworm" to a smooth orb to a heavily enfolded mass with distinct divisions. (Adapted from art by Tom Prentiss, in *Scientific American*, 1979)

tion, is the most spectacular feat of our embryological development. At seven weeks, our forebrain balloons out into two delicate little bubbles, each a future cerebral hemisphere. At this stage, however, they are no larger than a pea and have two-layered walls no thicker than a human hair, according to physician Richard Restak in *The Infant Mind*. In the vanishingly narrow zone between the two layers of our "bubble walls," a cellular ballet takes place, starring spindly immature neurons. Each spindle elongates gracefully, its nucleus (an encapsulated internal control center) rises then falls, and the cell splits lengthwise to form two new cells. Most of these cells become the neurons that will branch with dendritic antennae and axonal transmission wires. Some, however, will become supporting cells called glial cells or *glia*.

The ballet in the gossamer walls of our embryonic forebrain "bubbles" proceeds night and day at an incomprehensible pace: Neurologists estimate that between 50,000 and 100,000 new brain cells are generated *each second* between the fifth and twentieth weeks of life. As these cells accumulate and our cerebral cortex thickens and folds, a second great drama takes place: "Migration." Nascent neurons begin to slither upward toward the top of our forebrain wall like acrobats shimmying up a rope ladder. In this case, slender glial cells form the scaffolding, and after migrating the right distance, the neurons "hop off" their rope ladder and take up residence in one of the six layers of the neocortical fabric.

"We watched this neural migration in our laboratory in the 1950s," muses Arnold Scheibel, "but I was too stupid to know what was happening. So Pasko Rakic [a Yale University neurologist] was the first to describe what it means. The cells migrate along the guide cells and at the right point, hop off and form a layer. Then the next group comes up and migrates right through this existing layer and forms a new one above it. I tell my students that the cortex develops in an inside-out fashion, much the way the European immigrants slowly pushed westward in North America. We are just learning how this important migration can sometimes go awry," Scheibel adds, "and how it may produce conditions that show up later in the child such as schizophrenia or certain kinds of epilepsy and dyslexia."

The fast-paced narrative of our human brain development begins with the frenetic, proliferative ballet of neurons, their acrobatic migration, and their aggregation into layers of the cerebral cortex and other brain parts. But the story continues in three additional acts of "Connection," "Competition," and "Pruning." As soon as neurons begin aggregating into layers, clusters, tracts, and the myriad brain structures that fill anatomy books, the nerve cells start forming the junctions called synapses. As we've seen, the typical synapse involves a buttonlike ending on an axon from one nerve cell coming into close contact with the flat, bulblike tip of a branch from another cell's dendrite. A synaptic connection, however, can also occur between the axons of two different nerve cells, the dendrites of two cells, one cell's axon and another's cell body, and so on. Together, they create an amazingly dense tangle within the cortical fabric.

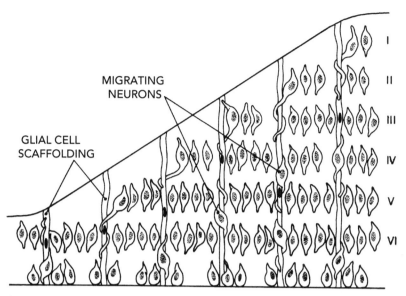

After neurons form in the embryonic brain at the amazing rate of 50,000 to 100,000 new cells per second, a migratory ballet unfolds. The newly formed nerve cells slither up a slender scaffolding, then "hop off" at different levels, forming the six layers of the fetus's cerebral cortex.

Strange as it seems, the growing, connection-seeking branchlets of human axons and dendrites seem to follow a trail of chemical attractants spewed out by the target area on the neuronal landing field to which they are headed. Stranger still, the target cell "feeds" the contacting branchlet with chemical nourishment called nerve growth factor that helps sustain the synaptic "clasps." Finally, and strangest of all, the connection process is so luxuriant that the axonal and dendritic trees become a thicket as impenetrable as the enchanted forest in "Sleeping Beauty," in which every neuron makes virtually every conceivable contact point with its neighbors—upwards of 15,000 contacts *per cell* in many places and in a few, upwards of 200,000! With 85 billion neurons forming in the cerebral cortex, each making thousands of synaptic connections, its not hard to see where neurologists get the figure of 1,000 trillion contact points in the brain. What's harder to envision is how the brain could work smoothly with such an overload of random connections.

Overconnectedness and the Mad Scramble

In fact, it can't. What ensues in the wake of this overconnection is a mad scramble for resources within the brain. The struggle is so reminiscent of Darwinian competition and survival of the fittest individuals that Nobel laureate Gerald Edelman actually dubbed the internal process "neural Darwinism," and wrote a book by that name.

For whole organisms—wolves, let's say—the major contest is over territory, mates, prey, and dominance ("Nature, red in tooth and claw," as Darwin liked to say); for synapses—contact points—between the branches of neurons, the struggle is over nerve growth factor, room on the target cell, and getting enough stimulation in the form of incoming electrical impulses so the "clasp" can become strong enough to permanently establish the connection.

To give one example of how this happens, researcher Carla Shatz and her group at U.C. Berkeley study how the developing retinas in the eyes become wired up with neural connections. They discovered that an initial hooking-up takes place in a somewhat random way that links many nerve cells with many other nearby cells as well as others further away. Following this linking stage, spontaneous bursts of nerve activity flicker through the silent neural groves again and again like ocean waves. The synapses or "clasps" stimulated enough during this extemporaneous "wave action"—all, mind you, taking place long before a baby is born and can begin to see—will tend to survive the Darwinian selection and become hardwired. Those that don't, or that starve for nutrients or for space on a neighboring nerve cell, will probably disappear before they ever experience the light of day. The process may sound chaotic, but only the early individual hookups are random; the processes of wave action and synaptic selection are precisely controlled by genetic instructions and in the end create the orderly neural wiring patterns that allow the newborn to detect light, shape, and movement.

Neurons, with their drive to communicate, need connections so much that if they fail to form enough synaptic contact points, the entire branching treelike cell can shrivel up and die. This so-called *naturally occurring cell death* in the embryo's brain is one way of clearing up developmental mistakes—a cell that migrated to the wrong address, for instance, or that connected up with the wrong targets, or with targets that were already filled. But programmed elimination is more than just a predator of the weak; it is nature's way of shaping each individual brain. Just as Michelangelo's artful chipping and smoothing brought *David* or *Moses* looming out of marble blocks, a form of pruning takes place in the cells and connections of the brain beginning at seven months and continuing after birth for a decade or more. After the brain is outside the womb, the sculpting process no longer depends on spontaneous waves of nerve activity; light, sound, and other input from the environment can now contribute (but more on that later). By the best estimates, natural cell death can eliminate 50 percent of the neurons in the cerebral cortex before the baby is born, and up to 40 percent of the synaptic connections between nerve cells by the age of twenty-one months. Think of it: Your neural heyday came and went before you had your first serious thought!

For the brain, birth is just a momentary pause along the developmental continuum, but ironically, the size of the brain helps determine the timing of our arrival into the world. After nine months' gestation, writes Richard Restak, the human skull is 101.8 percent the size of the birth canal, even though the newborn brain is still only one-quarter of its adult size. (It weights 370 grams at birth and will nearly triple to 1080 grams by age three, and quadruple to 1350 grams by six to fourteen years.) But the protective skull already taxes vaginal delivery to the point of dysfunction. If the fetal brain expanded any further, it could have doomed our species. (Some anthropologists, in fact, have speculated that the Neanderthals were literally squeezed out in their evolutionary competition with the coexisting, smaller-brained, but more easily born Cro-Magnons, our predecessors.)

Our brain size at birth is a balance between extractability and maturity, with the scales strongly favoring the former. More of the latter, producing a not-so-helpless infant, would have altered our family structure and traditional sex roles dramatically, and would continue, even today, to lessen the tremendous challenge of parenthood. But our primitive helpless state at birth has one advantage at least as compelling as family cohesiveness: As the developmental continuum slides past birth into childhood and adolescence, external stimulators can powerfully contribute to brain pruning. This, in turn, helps to sculpt the brain's individuality from the block of excess neural wiring in a way that conforms to the person's needs in his or her own environment and circumstances.

The Slow Spreading Wave

Now, if most of our brain growth takes place after birth but we stopped producing most of our new neurons by seven months' gestation, what exactly keeps growing inside our head to enlarge our brain size as a baby and child? Brain maturation is actually a specialty within brain science, and one of the field's founders, the famous American neurologist Jesse Conel, spent nearly thirty years writing an eight-volume series on, among other subjects, brain fat—the stuff that keeps our brains enlarging. The fancy word for brain fat is *myelin*, sheets of a white fatty material that wrap around axon transmission wires like insulation around a lamp cord. The support cells of the brain, the glia, pump out the makings of these membranous wrappers. As they stick to and ensheathe the axonal wires, layer by layer, the axons are then able to transmit electrical impulses faster and better. In turn, our brain functions—and resulting behaviors—can then start to unfold: babbling, for example, or aiming our hands toward a ball or cookie.

Starting in the 1930s, Conel studied the way myelin accumulates in the human cortex; first in newborns, then in one-month, three-month, and six-month-olds, and continuing in children at fifteen months, two years, four years, six years, and eight years. With meticulous descriptions and photographs filling several thousand pages of his famous series of books on how the brain develops, Conel was able to prove not only that human brain development is a very protracted affair compared to other mammals, but also that the tripling of brain weight after birth comes mostly from accumulating myelin.

About the time Conel finished his last volume, a doctoral candidate in the Diamond lab at U.C. Berkeley, Kathleen Gibson, set out to compare the way myelin accumulates in babies and children with the same process in a close primate relative, the rhesus monkey. She wondered whether our "brain fat" buildup is not only slower than in other animals, but whether it accumulates differently, too, and whether any such difference might somehow explain our unique capacities for language and reasoning.

To test these theories, Gibson obtained brain samples from rhesus monkeys that had died at birth and at various ages up to three years. Those specimens had been treated with a special stain that turns myelin black. Under a light microscope, a thin slice of tissue from one part of the brain or another could look any shade from very pale gray to inky black, depending on how fully the area had become myelinated, and this darkness scale, in turn, served as a maturity index. Gibson, a teacher of anatomy at the University of Texas medical and dental schools for more than twenty years now, draws a masterfully clear portrait of maturing monkey and human brains. The brain of a rhesus monkey, she explains, matures three to four times faster than a person's; at birth, it has the brain maturity of a three-month-old human baby, and by two years, it is equivalent to a six- to eight-year-old child—not in capabilities, of course, just in measures like myelin buildup. Despite this dramatic difference in speed, however, the pattern of fatty buildup in monkeys and humans did not turn out to be different, and is, in fact, remarkably similar.

In both young monkeys and children, axons in the brain stem (which lies at the base of the brain just above the spinal cord) as well as axons in the major nerves running to the face, limbs, trunk, and organs, all receive their myelin sheaths before birth and during infancy. This allows all the infant's basic survival functions—breathing, heartbeat, body temperature, reflexes, sensation, seeing and hearing—to work fairly efficiently early in life. Regions involving more complex motor control such as the cerebellum and areas of the midbrain take longer to mature. They reach adult levels of myelin by six months in the monkey and two years in the human baby. This maturation is reflected in the young child's growing coordination while walking, running, and manipulating objects. Finally, areas of the brain governing the highest functions—awareness, alertness, memory, thinking—take the longest to mature in both monkeys and people. The hippo-campus, the six layers of the neocortex, and the so-called reticular activating system within the brain stem that helps you wake up and stay alert all require between two to three years to mature in the monkey and ten years or more in a child. This long maturation cycle explains why our ability to memorize, to recall information, to generate thoughts, to sing, work math problems, plan strategies, and organize our actions begins to unfold in the toddler but continues to mature well into our teenage years.

Within each major section at the top, back, sides, and front of the brain (also called the parietal, occipital, temporal, and frontal lobes), "myelination presents a picture of a slowly spreading wave," Gibson writes, "that begins at one point and gradually spreads to fill the entire lobe." She added in a recent interview that the trend is toward myelination occurring first in those brain regions that function earliest, as well as in the sequence of brain evolution. Within the neocortex, for example, one of the last layers to evolve is also the last to become fully myelinated. This layer, says Gibson, helps coordinate impulses that arise within the cortex such as thoughts and interpretations, rather than just simple signals from the sense organs.

Gibson's comparison of rhesus young with our own babies and children showed beyond a doubt that our myelin piles up quickly in some places and slowly in others, but that our pileup patterns are not unique: Instead, what sets us apart is our enormous cerebral cortex of recent evolutionary expansion and the astronomical number of neural connections within and between our brain regions.

Myelin, then, is the main matter tripling the size of a baby's brain after birth. But there's another factor in the equation, and it brings us back to the magic trees of the mind—the spine-encrusted dendrites branching inside the cerebral cortex. By twenty-eight weeks of gestation, the phenomenal proliferation of neurons has ceased, and some natural cell death has taken place among unneeded neurons. Depending on an individual's body size, however, and whether they "use or lose" their mental faculties, the number of nerve cells will then remain about the same from seven months' gestation until seventy or eighty years of age.

The branches and spines on those neurons, however, continue right on growing.

Laboring for over twenty years in his laboratory at the University of Chicago, neurologist Peter Huttenlocher has counted and chronicled the dendrites and synapses in the developing human brain. In one series of experiments, he looked at the visual cortex, the part of the cortex that allows a child (or adult) to see. In that one region of the brain, Huttenlocher found a gradual increase in the numbers of synaptic connections from seven months' gestation to birth and then two months after birth. Next he saw a startling tenfold explosion between two and four months of age. This corresponds with a baby's sudden improvement of vision around four months, and his or her ability to form three-dimensional images. During these first few months, new dendritic branches also sprout, and all the branches, old and new, lengthen. The density of synapses in the visual cortex peaks when the baby is eight months old, stays fairly high until age four, then begins a very gradual decline, dropping by age ten to 60 percent of the peak. From there, the density levels off and remains the same throughout adulthood. This synaptic pruning, then, is sculpting the visual cortex between ages four and ten. But the dendritic branches within that cortex layer continue to lengthen and sprout, and new synapses can flourish where the growing branches contact other neurons.

When Huttenlocher looked at the cerebral cortex in the brain's frontal lobes, just behind the forehead, he found a similar narrative occurring but with slightly different timing. In this frontal region, concerned with organization, planning, and reasoning, synapses don't explode over a short period but multiply steadily after birth until they reach maximum density at ten years of age. Then they drop slowly until about sixteen years of age.

The Chicago researcher sees two major phases in a child's brain development: During Phase One, from birth to age one, neurons become less tightly packed as the dendrites grow and branch and push them apart. As this first phase proceeds, the cerebral cortex grows thicker and heavier. During Phase Two, from one year of age to adolescence, the density of synapses declines due to selective pruning of redundant or unused connections, even as the remaining dendrites continue to branch, grow, and form new synapses. As Phase Two proceeds, brain weight goes up about 20 percent, due to myelin accumulation and dendritic branching, then gradually reaches adult weight by about age fourteen. It might sound contradictory, but the gradual loss of synapses reflects not a decline in mental maturity and learning ability but its opposite: Intelligence, physical coordination, language skills, and so on emerge in noble form as the marble block of neural overconnectedness is smoothed, whittled, and shaped by internal competition and by external stimulation.

Peaks, Troughs, and Pruning

The idea that a child's brain development peaks and troughs will surprise some people; a steady, gradual swelling in size and capability better matches our casual observations of how children grow. A fits-and-starts growth pattern, however, receives much corroboration—and coincidentally helps explain the "terrible twos."

Pediatric neurologist and researcher Harry Chugani, raised in Hong Kong and trained at Georgetown University among other places, helped test an ingenious method for studying children's brain development based on the PET scanner. In the mid 1970s, a group of researchers at Washington University in St. Louis, Missouri, built the first PET scanner (Positron Emission Tomography). Unlike an X ray, a CAT scanner (Computed Axial Tomography), or an MRI (Magnetic Resonance Imager), which are best at reflecting structure, PET gives an accurate, detailed view of an organ's activity. PET can reveal the flowing of blood and the body's use of energy, and can even reveal a computer-enhanced lighting up of specific brain circuits during thinking, speaking, or moving. As a result, PET has been a powerful research tool as well as a means of diagnosing disease.

By the early 1980s, Chugani was carrying out PET scans regularly on children with epilepsy. He realized that PET could do more than pinpoint the location of the epileptic seizure site for future drug treatments or surgery; it could also reveal basic information about how the brain matures. Since a PET scan, like an

X ray, exposes a patient to a small but measurable amount of radiation, Chugani could not ethically scan children simply for basic research. This population of young epilepsy patients, however, gave Chugani built-in access to patients already undergoing PET scans for medical reasons. To avoid any possibility that an epileptic brain lesion could affect his data, Chugani later switched to studying children undergoing PET scans for tumors in the limbs or body but no abnormalities of the brain. During each child's PET scan, Chugani injected the patient with a tiny quantity of radioactively labeled glucose, then used the scanner to measure how brain cells burn this glucose along with oxygen for energy. This material allowed him to reveal details of how the human brain matures that were previously obscure. The cellular burning of fuel, whether in the brain, the heart, the muscles, or elsewhere in the body, is called metabolism, and as a rule, the more fuel burned the higher the metabolism, and the higher the activity level in that region.

Chugani now works at Children's Hospital of Michigan for Wayne State University in Detroit, and his portrait of the developing human brain, based on dozens of children, became an instant classic. He found that in newborn babies, the most metabolically active brain regions are those involved in the most basic levels of survival: the brain stem, and parts of the thalamus, cerebellum, and cortex governing vital signs, sensations, and reflexes. These regions are also considered the first to have evolved in simpler mammals. By three months of age, metabolism has increased in the parts of both the cerebellum and the cerebral cortex involved in seeing, hearing, and sensing touch. This heightened activity corresponds to the age in infants when certain automatic reflexes disappear, and when the uncontrolled jerks of the arms and legs subside. The increase in metabolism at two to three months also accompanies the onset, for the first time, of a baby's ability to look at a bright toy and reach for it. By six to eight months of age, brain cells in the frontal and occipital (rear) lobes are burning glucose and oxygen at a furious pace. Since these brain areas are involved in reasoning and vision, among other things, the metabolic upsurge coincides with stranger anxiety in the infant, and with the baby's ability to engage parents, siblings, and surroundings in an increasingly sophisticated way.

Metabolic rates keep rising in most brain structures until the energy use in a two-year-old is equal to an adult's. And then, *the levels keep right on rising* until, by age three, the child's brain is *twice* as active as an adult's. This metaphoric crackling, bristling, sparkling, and glowing of brain cells remains at double the adult rate until about age nine or ten; at that time, metabolism begins dropping and reaches adult levels by age eighteen. Based on his studies and on others', Chugani is certain that the quick rise in brain activity in the first four years, the plateau during middle childhood, and the decline after puberty reflect the same phenomena that Huttenlocher chronicled in Chicago: the overproduction of synapses as well as luxuriant dendritic branching; a period of "transient exuberant connectivity," during which well-used connections are strengthened and unused ones are weakened; and the pruning of these weak links beginning in mid to late childhood and continuing throughout adolescence.

"We've shown," says Chugani, "in the cat, the monkey, and in human children, that glucose metabolism is a very good indicator of the numbers of synapses in the brain." By one estimate, a child's brain—just a small fraction of his or her body weight—uses *20 percent* of the oxygen taken in with each breath.

Why burn so much fuel and oxygen to support an overload of synapses? "The abundance of connections in the brain," Chugani muses, "is because the brain of the individual doesn't know yet what that individual's life is destined to be. I'm getting philosophical here and I don't want to be," he says, smiling, "but it really comes down to the genes.

"It wouldn't be wise to use all of your genes to dictate the precise wiring of the brain except for the functions most essential to your existence. Cardiac rhythms, and so on. Those could be hardwired. But you don't want to waste any more genes dictating what should be connected to what because you don't know what that individual is going to be doing later in life. Why not connect everything to everything?" For the different regions of the neocortex, then, there is a lengthy period of overconnectedness. "When that begins to happen," says Chugani, "is in the child's 'terrible twos'. The child doesn't have the control while in this overconnected state. The discipline is not there and what we see is a highly distractible two- or three-year-old that really doesn't have the discipline to learn or act like an adult but who really absorbs like a sponge all this information."

If people's neural circuits weren't stabilized through use and pruned away when unused, "I think people would continue to be very distractible and I think that might be occurring in some patients with hyperactivity." Chugani quotes one prominent psychiatrist who makes an analogy between a two-year-old and "a fully blossomed schizophrenic." He feels that "the hyperactive, distractible, unable-to-focus schizophrenic" suffers from a lack of synaptic pruning as well as from other changes in the brain.

In the normal sequence, the toddler begins to explore and learn everything from crawling and standing to problem solving, and then the child goes on learning—to play an instrument, to ride a bike, to apply table manners. The child and later the adult "would use specific circuits within the brain to perform each task," Chugani explains. "The way I think about it is that if you use that circuit enough, it becomes strengthened and the brain almost takes it for granted; it is almost hardwired."

By administering PET scans while an experimental subject is solving a mental problem, Chugani explains, researchers have found that "the easier the task is for you—the easier you solve the problem—the lower the signal from the appropriate brain circuit. You no longer have to think about it. It's done very easily. The brain doesn't turn on at all for it. If you have to struggle with something, if the particular task you are dealing with has not been hardwired because of inadequate exposure," then your brain will work harder and this would also show up on a PET scan. "This doesn't mean you can't do it," Chugani adds. Some individuals don't have natural abilities in a certain direction— athletic, say, or musical. "But the nurture part—the exposure and practice over a protracted and reasonably intense period—would certainly bring you closer to having the hardwiring."

Chugani found that the dismantling of unused circuits and connections begins with the earliest signs of puberty in kittens and rhesus monkeys, and he is convinced that the same holds true for children. In people, however, puberty onsets at about ages nine to twelve, so the elimination phase would begin then and continue for a number of years. The pruning of neural connections in adolescence explains why a child under the age of

ten can lose part of the cerebral cortex near the language area—
even the entire right hemisphere (as we saw in the little girl from
Florida described at the beginning of this chapter)—and have no
permanent difficulties speaking or interpreting language. A person like the hod carrier born without a cerebellum can even live a
lifetime lacking a vital brain region and show absolutely no
effects, because other parts of the brain adopted these functions
early on. During childhood, the brain can readily form substitute circuits in other adjacent areas or even across the brain in
the other hemisphere. This ability, however, fades away during
adolescence concurrently with the period of massive synaptic
pruning.

Adults who have suffered strokes or head trauma, or who have
lost limbs, can also recover speech, walking, and other abilities to
some degree, based on cortical shifts away from damaged areas or
zones that have lost input due to a missing body part. With
damage occurring during adulthood, however, the recovery is
usually slower and less complete than in childhood.

Plasticity and Critical Periods

A portrait of brain development has emerged from PET scans;
from the counting of synapses, spines, and dendrites; from the
tracking of myelin accumulation; and indeed, from the study of
enriched environments for rats: It is a view of a vital organ with
plasticity, with the functional springiness, resilience, and pliancy
of living Silly Putty. More than any other organ, the brain can be
shaped by stimulation and use, by disease and trauma, by dull
routine and disuse into a center of thought, sensation, and regulation most appropriate for a given individual's life.

"Appropriateness," of course, is relative, and it changes as a
child grows up, relocates, becomes a parent, takes on a succession
of jobs, learns new skills, falls into middle-aged ruts, and so on.
The dendrites, the magic trees of the cerebral cortex, retain their
ability to grow and branch, and it is this lifetime growing potential that enables us to continue learning and adapting. However,
childhood is a particularly crucial time for the brain because of

the neural sculpting that goes on; for many of our abilities, tendencies, talents, and reactions, those that get "hardwired" in childhood become the collective mental platform upon which we stand and grow for the rest of our lives.

Neurologists call the special time slots of childhood development that seem to depend on neural connecting and pruning *critical periods*. This subject will crop up over and over, particularly in discussions of how we acquire language in our uniquely human way. But there are two physical examples of critical periods for brain plasticity—the development of vision and of hearing—that show both the resilience of a child's brain and the way use, disuse, and the environment mold it.

Back in the late 1950s, just about the time the U.C. Berkeley team was starting to study the environment's impact on the brain, another highly productive collaboration began at Johns Hopkins University in Baltimore, Maryland. Two young researchers, David Hubel and Torsten Wiesel, were interested in how the visual cortex operates. During the 1960s, first at Hopkins, then at Harvard in Cambridge, Massachusetts, they unraveled the miraculous intricacy of the brain's visual machinery and how it recreates whole, accurate images from patterns of light and the millions of individual neural impulses the eyes transmit.

Setting aside for a moment the inherent dangers of boiling down a decade of complicated study into a paragraph, here's essentially what they found, working first on cats, then on primates: The visual cortex, a large section of "bark" covering the back of the cerebral hemispheres, has the standard six-layered construction with the piled-up layers lying parallel to the brain's surface. The visual cortex also has alternating columns or stacks of cells running perpendicular to the surface, each driven by either the right or the left eye. When light hits the retina, an impulse reading either "dim light" or "bright, colored light" travels up the optic nerve to the brain. Neurons in Layer IV of the visual cortex register dots of light corresponding to these impulses, and they, in turn stimulate neurons in Layers V and VI. Here each individual neuron can be turned on only by light of one particular kind—by bars of light, let's say. Or by edges of objects tilted at 40 degrees from vertical. Or by edges at 50, or 60, or 70 degrees, but always just one degree of slant per neuron. By squares or rectangles of light. By corners or other angles of unique degree. By silhouettes or sets of lines that move. Or by simultaneous impulses from both eyes, giving depth to otherwise flat images. As fragmented as this collection of living electrical responders may sound, the visual cortex turns the cacophony of individual impulses into a three-dimensional symphony of moving and stationary lines and shapes. Other parts of the brain can then recognize this coordinated pattern as mother's face, a fluttering moth, or a mountain top bathed in the rosy light of sunset.

Hubel and Wiesel's elucidation of how the brain creates visual images was a milestone. But in the late 1960s, in the flush of the first brain plasticity studies, they wanted to know how vision gets set up in a young animal's brain and how input from the outside world affects it. The two researchers conceived of a way to find out: They took very young kittens and sewed either the left or the right eye shut for a few weeks as the animal was growing up. After about three months had passed, they opened the sutured eye and studied it along with the brain's visual cortex. What they found was stunning in its implications: The eye itself, once opened, was perfectly normal. However, if it was closed from day thirty to day eighty of the animal's kittenhood, the eye was effectively blind; the brain had rewired itself to receive and interpret only the impulses from the eye that had remained open. In a kitten with a newly opened left eye, all the columns in the visual cortex would respond but only when light signals came in through the always-opened right eye. The left eye had been "written off" with an internal brain message, something like "No input coming in from left eye; assign all available resources to remaining eye." Rewiring, here, means that the circuits involved in the right eye's vision were first strengthened, then preserved, then hardwired for that right eyesight, leaving very few circuits available for the left.

The thirty- to eighty-day interval is the critical period for a cat's vision, Harry Chugani points out. And it corresponds perfectly to the surge of metabolism in a kitten's brain at one month of age and the subsequent drop-off during the feline adolescence that begins at sixty to ninety days of age. A kitten's eyes—both of them—must be stimulated by light, shape, and movement during this critical period if the animal is to have normal vision. If that input is blocked from one or both eyes, the brain's plasticity allows for a takeover in the visual cortex and the reassignment of circuits.

Children, not surprisingly, show their own critical period for vision, although it is years longer than a kitten's. A child with a cataract, with a crossed eye, or wearing an eye patch for an extended period will probably lose some vision in the affected eye unless the condition is corrected before ages eight to ten so the eye gets normal input for a period of months before the critical period ends. Without normal stimulation, the child's visual cortex will be hardwired to ignore that eye starting in early puberty, as brain metabolism drops and synapses are massively pruned. Ophthalmologists usually recommend corrective treatment for cataracts or crossed eyes very early in the child's development so he or she will have the best chance for normal vision.

Since the human brain remains plastic throughout life, why do critical periods matter? Why wouldn't the eyesight improve once the stimulation of light, shape, and movement returns, even *after* the critical period has passed? There are two possible answers: (1) The ability to see is so strategic for our survival that the visual cortex is less malleable than brain areas devoted to skills like thinking, planning, or learning new facts. For those latter activities, survival would place a premium on lifelong flexibility, not early maturation. Therefore, they would tend to lack critical periods. Or (2) vision (and the brain's visual cortex) is more plastic than many people think.

One of the biggest advocates of this open-plasticity notion is Helen Neville, a professor at the University of Oregon in Eugene, and director of its Brain Development Lab. Neville brings a healthy "So what?" skepticism to neuroscience, and in conversation tends to turn the focus from esoteric data to the impact of research findings on people's day-to-day lives.

By now, Neville says, all neurologists know about Hubel and Wiesel's work on vision and how one open eye can "take over all the synapses. But what are the functional consequences of that?" she asks. "Does that one eye see better than a normal one? And what happens to the deprived eye? Nobody really knows, and the studies haven't been done, but everybody assumes something."

One researcher at Dalhousie University in Halifax, Canada, repeated the kitten vision experiments twenty years ago, Neville explains. "Initially the reopened eye was blind and it stayed blind for several weeks. Gradually, though, there came some improvement until the researcher actually observed some pretty good function. But the cells in the visual cortex still show a complete takeover by the open eye. So what's going on? The answer is, we don't know!"

For many years, Neville has studied environmental stimulation and the sense of hearing, concentrating on deaf subjects born to deaf parents. Just as Hubel and Wiesel wondered what happens if visual input is cut off from the visual cortex, Neville has concentrated on the parallel issue: "If there is no auditory input, what happens to the auditory cortex? Does it just go lame? Or can it be taken over for another function?"

From the outset, it's more difficult to study hearing than vision. For one thing, most of the critical events in the development of the human ear take place four to five weeks after conception. During this critical fetal period, if the mother catches certain kinds of viral infections or takes certain kinds of drugs, the embryo's delicate aural machinery can be permanently damaged as it is forming and the baby may be born deaf or hard-of-hearing (more on this later). Second, there is no way to temporarily "sew the ears shut" to block off sound during an experiment because the bones of the skull and jaw will continue to transmit sound vibrations anyway. But by using other methods, Neville and her colleagues have discovered that the main hearing part of the brain, the auditory cortex, remains plastic for up to four years in a child, and that input from the ears—and surprisingly, from the eyes, as well—can contribute to how the brain becomes hardwired for hearing and seeing.

In a child born with normal hearing, the ears collect sounds, transduce them into electrical signals, funnel these signals to the auditory nerve and several brain relay stations, and within a split second, they arrive at the auditory cortex. This patch of "bark" lies in the temporal lobe including the region just below each temple, and slightly above and in front of each ear. Scientists have not mapped out the neurons of the auditory cortex as completely as they have the visual, but they do know a few things. They know that just as individual visual neurons become excited by just one kind of light—light from a line slanted at 40 degrees, say—the neurons of the hearing cortex have assignments, too: Some are tuned to brief sounds, some to sustained, some to loud, others to soft, and still others to clicks, bursts, voices, and high pitches or low. They know that just as a normally sighted baby has visual neurons preassigned to each specific kind of light, so a baby with normal hearing has auditory neurons ready to register loudness, pitch, or sound quality. Finally, hearing is sculpted much as vision is: Just as normal input from both eyes before the age of eight or nine strengthens certain visual synapses, weeds out redundant ones, and winnows down the visual circuits to those that will produce the child's three-dimensional color images of the world, so does input from the ears help shape the auditory cortex into its permanent form by about age four.

What happens, then, if a baby is born deaf, or becomes deaf early in life so there is no sustained input from the ears to sculpt the auditory cortex? As Neville asks, does it "go lame" or get taken over? To answer this question, Neville's research group sought out families with an unusual form of inherited deafness in which the auditory cortex and other brain regions involved in hearing are normal, but the cochlea, a snail-like structure in the inner ear, does not form properly. If the gene for this form of deafness turns on while the offspring is still an embryo, the cochlea never develops and the child is born deaf. But in some of the children, the gene is off for a while, allowing the cochlea to form, but the gene turns on at one, two, three, four, or later. The cochlea then stops functioning and deafness sets in. For decades, physicians and others have noticed that deaf people often have particularly acute peripheral vision, but no one understood it. With the help of the rare deaf families with their deleterious gene, Neville figured out why. And it came down, once again, to the brain's amazing plasticity.

Although most of us don't know it, Neville explains, people really have two visual systems, and one is directly linked to our hearing, at least until age three. We have a "*where* visual system," says Neville, concerned with locating objects and events, with focusing our attention, and with perceiving motion. And we have a *"what* visual system," good at picking out forms and colors but not good at motion or location. Our peripheral vision is part of our "where" system, not our "what" system. Neville thinks that after we are born, because of our overpopulation of synapses and connections between brain cells, parts of the "where" visual system are wired to parts of the *hearing* system. If you make a noise near a six-month-old baby, she says, and measure her brain waves, "you get a big response in *both* the auditory cortex *and* the visual cortex." That effect stops at about age three, however, unless a child has been deaf during those years.

In a child with normal hearing, she explains, the extraneous connections from the eyes to the hearing system would disappear as sound input comes in; sounds would compete for the contact points in the hearing cortex, Darwin-style, and beat out the weaker synaptic connections from the eyes. But in a three-year-old child deaf since birth, Neville continues, there has been no competition from auditory input, since no nerve impulses travel from the ears to the brain. Therefore, the visual hookups remain in the hearing brain and give the deaf child a more sensitive "where" visual system, including better peripheral vision. A child that becomes deaf after age four, however, doesn't show this heightened "where" vision and that, says Neville, suggests that the environment's critical shaping of hearing takes place by about age three or a little older.

The crossover between hearing and seeing might seem bizarre, but it is actually among the tamer pairings. One group of researchers produced laboratory hamsters that can "see" through the feeling part of the brain after the animals' visual neurons made unusual inroads into the cortex region that registers the sense of touch. And another research group found that in monkeys who have lost the nerves to one arm, the region of the cortex devoted to sensing touch on the *face* takes over the area that once mapped out feeling in the *arm*.

One upshot of this work, Helen Neville concludes, is that "anything with a long time course of development is more subject to being modified by experience." Another, she says, is that every function of the brain has its own special timetable. "There are multiple critical periods. They are different between different domains such as vision, hearing, and language. And even within vision," Neville adds, the critical period for motion "is not the same as for color." Other researchers, as Nigel Daw notes in his book on visual development, have in fact shown that there are various periods in children between six months and eight years of age for developing sensitivity to dim or bright light and to the direction of light; for sharpness of vision; for the dominance of one eye over the other or a balance between the two; and for the formation of stereoscopic vision so the baby has depth perception. There also seem to be several critical periods for acquiring language, for learning to play music, even for emotional maturity, while certain aspects of these domains, and others, are probably open to lifelong modification.

Our brains are amazingly modular; the dozens of separate regions act in concert to allow us to see and hear and think, but they mature at varying speeds and to varying degrees. When you look at the way a child's brain develops, one thing becomes absolutely obvious: Starting with the swellings and furrows of the embryonic neural tube, and moving on to the branching neural forests of the cortex, the rise and fall of brain metabolism, and the organ's astonishing plasticity when parts or functions are lost, *input from the environment helps shape the human brain.*

Brain enrichment is not an isolated phenomenon of caged lab rats or kittens. It is going on in us as adults, and it is happening in our children day-by-day. Childhood, from conception to adolescence, just happens to be the optimum time for neural development because of the "exuberant connectivity" and neural pruning that takes place in these years. Scientists are still trying to understand the fine details of how synapses are strengthened, weakened, out-competed, and pruned back. If they understood this force of nature well enough, they could harness it and restore plasticity—and with it, perhaps seeing, hearing, speaking, walking—even after a critical period has passed. But that is the province of future research.

For the present, given the special neural nature of childhood and the demands of parenthood and teaching, it is natural to wonder what to do next? Should one try consciously to influence a child's environment and, in turn, his or her brain development? The answer to that, whether you are a parent, teacher, relative, friend, neighbor, or voter, is *"You already do."* Better to ask, "What kinds of environments are we creating for children, and how will these affect their developing minds?" The logical place to start looking is the surroundings we influence most intimately: the environment of the womb.

Chapter 3

Feed My Brain:
Influences in the Womb

And feed my brain with better things.
—G. K. Chesterton, "A Ballad of a Book Reviewer"

• Lisel, born in October, 1992, led what some would consider a charmed life in the womb. Her parents, Tony and Jeannine, had planned for her conception and anticipated their first child's arrival with great enthusiasm. Jeannine kept careful track of the nutrients and vitamins in her diet; she shunned alcohol, caffeine, drugs, and exposure to pesticides, food additives, paints, cleaners, and cigarette smoke. She quit work two months before Lisel was due, avoided stress as much as possible, and took exercise and relaxation classes for expectant mothers.

To their parents' consternation and their friends' amusement, the couple even experimented with prenatal enrichment techniques in the third trimester. They talked, read, and sang to their fetus and delighted as she learned to kick wherever they patted. Her best trick was kicking in a circle; as her parents patted Jeannine's stomach in a clockwise circuit, Lisel learned to trace the pathway from the inside and respond with well-aimed thwacks.

After Lisel was born, she lifted her head three weeks sooner than the average baby, and rolled over, sat up, talked, stood, and walked earlier than other infants her age. Tony credits his daughter's advanced development to the prenatal training they gave her and to Jeannine's careful lifestyle.

• Albert's prenatal experience was more typical. His mother, Denna, was a busy surgical nurse who took good care of herself during the pregnancy, but was under considerable stress. Her job was physically demanding and the operating room atmosphere was occasionally quite tense. Beyond that, Albert's biological father left the relationship five months into Denna's pregnancy, and his mom had to work fifty hours per week to save money. She also remained on the job right up to delivery. And while she wanted to avoid caffeine and nicotine, she found herself drinking coffee two or three times a day to boost her energy, and having an occasional cigarette with friends to "calm her down" during the last exhausting months.

Now, at age nine, Albert is a quiet, sweet-tempered boy. He earns average grades. He likes to play soccer. And he is very devoted to Denna, who is still single and works full-time to support the two of them.

• Jeremy wasn't as lucky as Lisel and Albert. Jeremy's parents, Jack and Joan, were very young, a bit wild, and decided to continue the pregnancy only because they objected to abortion on religious grounds, not because they were happy to be expecting in their early twenties. Joan continued to drink in the first few months of her pregnancy, but stopped after a while as the fetus grew. She thought about eating a better diet than she normally did, but, being an indifferent cook, she still gravitated to hamburgers, tacos, soft drinks, and doughnuts.

Just before the baby was due, Jack gave Joan five grams of cocaine as a birthday gift, and she snorted it over the course of two days. The stimulant drug induced early labor and, at the same time, caused Jeremy's fetal blood pressure to soar. The high pressure burst blood vessels in his brain, and this damaged a portion of his cerebral cortex, including the motor cortex that controls body and limb movements. As a result, Jeremy was born paralyzed on his right side.

Pregnancy and the Developing Brain

There is no period of parenthood with a more direct and formative effect on the child's developing brain than the nine months of pregnancy leading to the birth of a full-term baby. The basic parts of the brain and nervous system originate and grow quickly and in the first weeks and months after conception they are susceptible to permanent damage by a range of things the mother and father may eat, drink, breathe, smoke, pop, sniff, or even carry home on their clothing and hair from industrial exposures. The mother's emotions affect the fetus, and so do her general habits and the parents' physical environment. Finally, many believe that deliberate attempts to communicate with the unborn, such as talking, touching, reading stories, and playing music may directly benefit the developing brain and increase family bonding. It is clear that pregnancy is a special time to foster a baby's healthiest brain development. Statistics, however, suggest that many expectant parents disregard this important opportunity and toss away the role they could—and should—play in safeguarding their child's future potential.

One recent study of American children reveals that as many as one in five have problems with learning, behavior, or emotions stemming from the effects of their physical and emotional environments before and after birth. Nicholas Zill, a psychologist from Child Trends, Inc., in Washington, D.C., an organization devoted to monitoring problems that impact children, estimates that 42 percent of American families with children have one, two, or three socioeconomic factors that contribute to developmental problems: a mother who gives birth to her first child before finishing high school, and/or is under twenty, and/or is not married to the father. As we will see, these and other factors can lead to an emotional climate that actually alters the baby's brain structure. Other factors common to the families that fit Zill's profile— poverty, poor nutrition, drugs, alcohol, and violence—can have a direct physical effect on eggs and sperm even before a child is conceived.

In a perfect world, all women would have "preconception care"—health testing and advice before intercourse and fertilization. They would learn from physicians, nutritional counselors, psychologists, social workers, other professionals, family members, and friends about how diet, smoking, drinking, and taking drugs will affect them and the fetus. They would get help with relationship conflicts, stress, work-related problems, and inadequate housing. They would be screened for overweight, anorexia, anemia, diabetes, vitamin deficiencies, and toxoplasmosis ("cat-box disease"), as well as for AIDS and other sexually transmitted diseases that can affect a pregnancy. They would receive appropriate vaccinations against German measles and hepatitis. They would learn about the risks of genetic disorders that may run in their family, such as Tay-Sachs disease, sickle-cell anemia, or cystic fibrosis. And they would receive family planning advice so they could time pregnancies to provide enough emotional and financial support for their children.

The women who most need preconception services, however, are the least likely to get them, according to a report in the *Journal of the American Medical Association*, because communities lack the money, the social service agencies, the coordination between care providers, the ability, and sometimes the inclination to reach young adults before they make new babies. This is not true for all communities, of course, but for many of them. And no matter where one thinks the costs of preventative care should rest—with individuals, churches, governments, corporations—the benefits are indisputable: Health screening and dissemination of information on drugs, diet, and lifestyle could substantially help protect the fetus—and the fetal brain—from various kinds of damage.

The idea of preconception medical care is fairly new, and has grown out of research into the agents or deficiencies that can cause fetal abnormalities, often very early in pregnancy. A classic example was the discovery in 1989 that a deficiency of the B-vitamin folic acid (also called *folacin*) could lead to brain and spinal cord defects. Tragically, these defects arise during the first two weeks after conception—a time at least a week or two before a woman even knows she is pregnant. Too little folacin in the mother's body can lead to defects of the neural tube, the embryonic structure that gives rise to the spinal cord and brain. One malformation is anencephaly, a fatal developmental flaw in which most of the embryo's brain is absent. The other is spina bifida, a defect in which the lower part of the spinal cord develops outside, rather than inside, the protective bony spinal vertebrae, and sometimes leads to severe disabilities. About one American baby in 1,000 is born with brain or spinal damage stemming from too little of the B vitamin.

It takes a concerted effort for a woman of childbearing age to consume the recommended 400 micrograms of folacin each day from leafy vegetables, wheat germ, beans, brewer's yeast, and other foods, and many women get far too little of the B vitamin. The U.S. Public Health Service estimates that about half of all pregnancies are unplanned, and therefore recommends that all women who might become pregnant should get enough folacin in food or vitamin pills so they have at least a twenty-eight-day buildup in their bodies in case they conceive. Just as with preconception care in general, however, the young women who most need advice on folacin are the least likely to get it and follow it. Fortunately, neural tube defects are far less common in the fetus than folacin deficiencies are in adult women.

Dozens of factors can impinge on the cells and chromosomes of the forming fetal brain and nervous system. Factors like folacin shortage affect the embryo very early in pregnancy. Others harm the fetus in the second or third trimesters. (The developing child is called an embryo from weeks one to seven, and a fetus from weeks eight to thirty-eight.) Because embryonic development is so delicate and precise, many damaged embryos are spontaneously aborted early in the pregnancy. As a result, about 95 percent of babies in the United States and much of Europe are born without identifiable physical or mental defects (although some subtle problems show up only as the child grows). Of the nearly 200,000 babies born in the United States each year with deficits, physicians estimate that 30 to 35 percent either inherit gene or chromosome anomalies leading to disorders like cystic fibrosis or Down's syndrome, or are affected by the mother's diabetes, epilepsy, cancer, or other diseases and associated drug treatments. Of the remaining 65 to 70 percent of defects, at least one-fifth and possibly the majority can be blamed on avoidable exposures to medicinal drugs, recreational drugs, alcohol, tobacco smoke, and toxic agents at work and at home.

Aside from seeking advice for maternal diseases and heritable risks, *avoiding these harmful substances constitutes the simplest, most direct way to assist a child's future neurological well-being, mental and emotional.* Cutting unnecessary stress is a sixth factor, and attention to diet—folacin included—is a seventh.

Because the body harbors and protects the developing young

so beautifully, and because heavy damage is often eliminated through miscarriage, exposures to drugs, alcohol, and toxic compounds can harm cells and chromosomes in only a small percentage of babies. Even mothers who are chronic alcoholics, for example, only deliver babies with fetal alcohol syndrome about a third of the time. Nevertheless, subtle emotional and learning problems that turn up later in childhood are much more common, and these can be equally trying for the family. Fortunately, there are many things prospective parents can do to help build and safeguard a healthy brain in utero.

Medicinal Drugs

Beginning in the late 1950s, a new birth defect swept Europe and America; nearly 6,000 babies were born with shortened, twisted legs and hands that grew directly from the shoulders. Researchers spent more than two years tracing the cause to the drug thalidomide, which doctors had begun prescribing in 1957 to reduce a pregnant woman's anxiety and nausea. It was then discovered that if a woman takes the drug between twenty-eight and fifty-six days after conception, thalidomide can act as a toxin to the cells of the fetal nervous system and developing limbs. Drug agencies quickly cracked down on premarket testing of all new drugs. The tragedy also flagged the dangers of prescription drug use during pregnancy and caused a steep drop in that use over the next twenty years. But not, as it turns out, steep enough.

In 1982, a Swiss pharmaceutical company introduced a powerful new anti-acne drug called Accutane, which they knew from extensive prerelease laboratory research was a powerful *teratogen*, an agent that can cause fetal abnormalities. If taken in the first trimester, Accutane disrupts the developing brain and causes mental retardation, it produces an abnormally small jaw and ears growing below chin level, and it can also cause defects in the lungs, heart, blood vessels, and limbs. Before a doctor will prescribe Accutane to a young woman, she must prove she is not pregnant and sign releases showing that she understands the risks and will not become pregnant while taking the drug. Despite the

strident warnings, the U.S. Food and Drug Administration estimates that more than six hundred women became pregnant
between 1982 and 1988 while taking Accutane and gave birth to
babies with birth defects induced by the drug.

Accutane is an extreme example. But three major surveys conducted in the mid to late 1980s show that as many as *90 percent* of
women still take one or more medicinal drugs during pregnancy.
A separate study by a group of obstetrical researchers found that
the average mother-to-be takes three medications—some over-
the-counter, some prescription—with the potential to alter cells
or cellular function in the developing fetus and to lead to retarded growth, or to malformations or defects. And additional research showed that mothers who used at least one prescription drug
had babies with 30 percent more birth defects than mothers who
took no prescription drugs at all during pregnancy. Some women
mistakenly swallow birth control pills before they know they
are pregnant, and these may cause malformations of the embryo
and fetus. Other women, either before or after their pregnancy is
confirmed, take tranquilizers, antidepressants, narcotic pain relievers (like codeine), antiseizure medicines, antiasthma prepara-
tions, antibiotics, or anticoagulants for high blood pressure—all
of which can damage the developing brain, nervous system, or
sense organs.

Pregnant women take over-the-counter drugs more often than
prescription drugs. Despite warnings on many of the package in-
serts, medical researchers estimate that the majority of pregnant
women take nonnarcotic pain relievers and antinausea medicines
and antacids, and some also take cough and cold medicines, laxatives, and diet pills. Sometimes a woman's medical condition
demands the drug use and her obstetrician recommends or approves it. Much of the time, though, write medical professors
Matthew Ellenhorn and Donald Barceloux in their book *Medical
Toxicology*, women are self-administering drugs from the medicine
cabinet—drugs that are not necessarily safe to take. Safety is of
particular concern during the first trimester when the pharmaceutical compounds could alter the way neurons form, divide, migrate, recognize their proper addresses within the growing brain,
or connect with other neurons. Although major birth defects,
including neural defects, are mercifully rare, drugs can still cause

babies to be born addicted, irritable, hyperactive, or hearing-impaired, or to have other sensory, motor, or cognitive defects, including lowered IQ scores.

The danger of using medicinal drugs doesn't disappear after the first three months of pregnancy: Antidepressants taken late in pregnancy can cause irritability, tremors, and spasms in a fetus, and certain antibiotics can damage the cells of an inner ear (and with it, hearing and balance) that formed perfectly in the first trimester. Obstetricians commonly warn women to avoid aspirin in the third trimester because it can cause bleeding in the fetus and newborn, and at no point to take high doses of acetaminophen (trade name Tylenol) since it can damage or destroy the fetal liver. Ominously, though, even low doses of aspirin might be unsafe to use during the embryo's early formative stages if the theory of physiologist Martha Pierson is correct.

Dr. Pierson, who works at Baylor University School of Medicine in Houston, made an accidental—and so far, unofficial—finding about aspirin. For years, Pierson has been studying audiogenic or sound-induced seizures in rats as an animal model for epilepsy. A tall striking woman who seems at once equally maternal and professorial, Pierson explains that in the rat, the ears, like the eyes, develop almost entirely *after* the pup is born. This makes the critical period for aural development the eighth to fourteenth days of life. On that final day, the ears open and the pup can begin to hear. (The human ear, by comparison, develops in the young fetus at the end of the first trimester and beginning of the second, and the fetus starts to hear in the womb.)

Pierson has found that administering aspirin to a pup on day eleven or twelve, while some of the neural connections are forming between the ear and the brain, can cause the animal to experience sound-induced seizures later on. The same thing will happen if one rings a loud bell next to the rat pup's cage on day fourteen, just after the ears open. The pup's hearing rebounds, but the loud sound deafened the youngster for one day. As a result, its brain was deprived of normal sound input during the critical time period just after ear opening and one sound-processing center in the animal's midbrain gets hardwired incorrectly and permanently.

Pierson compares the ear's faulty hardwiring to an imaginary hotel in the 1940s where a telephone operator sits before a switchboard in a gleaming new lobby, waiting for the first incoming call. "When the first call comes in," Pierson says, "and the caller says, 'I want the upper-floor, northwest-corner room to answer,' " the switchboard operator does the opposite of what you might expect. She does *not* plug a wire in to that particular room. "Instead, she *unplugs* all the other connections in the hotel and leaves the one that's needed." That is how the brain is organized for hearing during the period of synaptic overconnectedness, Pierson explains. "Everything is overwired and when a message comes from the right ear, then the left ear must disengage its connections." Now, by temporarily deafening a pup on the first day its ears open, the unhooking can't take place and the brain is left with an "overly broad and nonspecific wiring pattern," as if all the hotel rooms were wired to ring at once when anyone calls the hotel. In a rat pup, when a sound comes in—usually a high-frequency sound that a human can't hear—the badly wired hearing region of the brain becomes overloaded and generates huge bursts of energy. The animal starts running around in circles or dashing about wildly and then convulses in a seizure that is very reminiscent of human epilepsy.

While Pierson is studying neither human epilepsy nor aspirin exposure during human pregnancy, she has some interesting theories about both. "Physicians deny that humans have sound-induced seizures," she says, "and yet when you talk to a person with epilepsy, they say that sound *can* trigger seizures in people. What's more, many human seizures start with running wildly in circles and then convulsing," and researchers have documented that apes and monkeys definitely do suffer sound-induced seizures. Of every 100 humans who are born deaf, Pierson explains, 74 percent have abnormal brain waves suggestive of epilepsy, and 59 percent have diagnosed epilepsy. "What doctors freely admit," she continues, "is that the causes of deafness in humans are often prenatal," and include a mother's exposure in the first trimester to German measles, to toxoplasmosis from cleaning cat boxes or handling raw meat, to a flulike agent called cytomegalovirus, and to antibiotics such as kanamycin. "Perhaps," adds Pierson, the list should also include "something as crazy as aspirin."

She explains further that sixty-nine percent of women take

some sort of aspirin or aspirin-containing product (including Pepto-Bismol), during the first trimester when the ear is forming. "I don't *know* that aspirin causes epilepsy," she says, and it obviously doesn't affect every mother who takes it, every embryo exposed to it, or even every child with seizures since they can be caused by a range of factors. But if aspirin does harm the human inner ear, she says, "it would be [by a mechanism] similar to one we use to induce temporary deafness and permanent susceptibility to seizures in laboratory rats." Pierson thinks alcohol might also contribute to sound-induced seizures, and points out that children with fetal alcohol syndrome also show higher incidences of both hearing problems and seizures.

In the future, researchers may work out a very complete profile of when it is safe to consume particular drugs during pregnancy. In the meantime, though, it is unwise to take any medicinal drug unless your obstetrician prescribes or approves it.

Recreational Drugs

Baby Jeremy was the permanent victim of his mother's taste for the cocaine high. This high comes from the way cocaine molecules stimulate the brain's pleasure center (the so-called *nucleus accumbens*). Joan's two-day birthday bender probably got her fetus higher than she was herself. That's because the fetal bloodstream carries the same food and drug molecules the mother consumes, but the fetal system breaks them down so slowly that they build up and bathe the brain for a much longer period. The drug dose in Jeremy's fetal brain probably damaged or destroyed cells in the pleasure center, as well as other brain regions involved in emotion, movement, and thought. In addition to the baby's physical paralysis, he may suffer lifelong emotional paralysis as well—an inability to bond with other people, to feel pleasure, to make judgments based on feelings, and to control his own emotional outbursts, according to pediatrician and researcher Jamie Hutchinson in Washington, D.C. Damage to the speech centers in his cerebral cortex may also prevent normal communication and learning. Pediatricians at Yale University found evidence recently that children exposed to cocaine while in the womb are more likely than unexposed babies to feel irritated and to cry at a new experience.

Some find it hard to believe that a mother-to-be would take cocaine and risk both her future child's physical and mental health and a lifetime of caring for a severely disabled dependent. Joan's recklessness, however, was far from rare: Hospitals in some inner city neighborhoods report that up to 50 percent of women use powder or crack cocaine during pregnancy. With 10 million Americans dabbling in cocaine, 5 million using it regularly, and millions more taking amphetamines, synthetic cocaine or "speed," it's hardly surprising that about 425,000, or more than 11 percent, of births are affected each year by cocaine, crack, and amphetamines, as well as heroin and marijuana, according to researchers Lucile Newman at Brown University and Stephen Buka at Harvard.

Marijuana is often seen as a soft recreational drug—so much so that upwards of 40 percent of Caucasians and African-Americans aged thirty-two to forty-four report having used it—10 percent within the last month, according to Newman and Buka. Mothers who regularly smoke marijuana during pregnancy (and even passive "weed" users exposed to someone else's smoke three times per week in a closed room) tend to have characteristic pregnancy problems: slow or painful uterine contractions; less milk after delivery; and babies showing more distress during birth. Many of the babies had bowel movements while still in the womb—an uncommon situation that doubles the risk of the newborn's death from various factors. Like cocaine or crack babies, marijuana babies tend to weigh less, to be high-strung and cranky, and to have disturbed sleep/wake cycles.

Just as recreational drugs sedate or excite the mother's brain, they do the same to the fetal brain as well, but in ways that are exaggerated, negative, and possibly permanent due to the unborn child's inability to break down and expel the drugs efficiently. The one out of ten pregnant women who take drugs "recreationally" apparently either don't know that or don't care. Nevertheless, their children, and their communities must deal with the consequences later.

In the face of so many women taking serious mind-altering

drugs during pregnancy, it may seem trivial to mention a soft drug like caffeine. Nevertheless, many people worry about it, especially given its stimulating effects, and the popularity of gourmet coffeehouses. Each day, the average American consumes the caffeine in a cup and a half of brewed coffee (about 210 milligrams), from coffee, tea, colas, chocolate, cocoa, and/or certain over-the-counter painkillers, stimulants, and appetite suppressants. Researchers have conducted dozens of human and animal studies on caffeine use during pregnancy, and have accused the drug of causing miscarriages and stillbirths, early and late births, low birth weight, cleft palate, irritability, poor nerve/muscle coordination, and even childhood diabetes. The findings have been controversial, however, and news reports tout caffeine's safety one year and its dangers the next. After weighing the evidence on all sides, the American Medical Association agreed with the advice given by the U.S. Food and Drug Administration: "Pregnant women should limit their intake of caffeine to a minimum."

A mother's recreational drug use is obviously a risk factor for her child's developing brain, but the father is not exempt, either. Using cocaine, for example, can drastically reduce the number of sperm a man produces and hobble the swimming ability of the sperm he does generate. Very few researchers have studied how a father's drug use affects the fetus, but some think male cocaine and marijuana use can both lead to an unhealthy fetus. Since sperm have a maximum life span of 90 days, a man can cut his chances of passing on defective sperm by ending recreational drug use (as well as smoking and drinking) more than three months before fathering a child.

Alcohol

It would be tough for a woman to buy a drink or a bottle of wine, beer, or liquor without knowing that it can harm her fetus: Every American supermarket, convenience store, restaurant, and bar is required to post a warning notice prominently at the entrance before selling alcoholic beverages. Women, however, appear to be ignoring these admonitions en masse: The U.S. Public

Health Service estimates that up to 86 percent of pregnant women drink at least once, and 20 to 35 percent drink regularly. And the phenomenon cuts across all socioeconomic levels: In a large study of women with college and postgraduate degrees, 30 percent continued to drink more than once a week during pregnancy.

Researchers think the fetal defects depend on both alcohol dose and timing: Drinking in the first trimester—especially during weeks two to eight when the brain is forming along with the facial features—is more likely to cause malformations; drinking in the last trimester is more likely to reduce overall fetal size. But since the brain develops throughout gestation (and beyond), it can be damaged at any point. Based on the range of cognitive, behavioral, and emotional problems in drinkers' babies, alcohol researchers think alcohol must be damaging cells in the cerebral cortex, the limbic system, and the brain stem. Some physicians fear that even a single drinking binge could damage the embryonic brain, especially in the first two or three weeks of life.

Lucile Newman and Stephen Buka report that at least 4,000 babies are born each year with full-blown fetal alcohol syndrome, and another 40,000 show the milder form called fetal alcohol effect. Alcohol, in fact, is considered a major cause of mental retardation, and 10 percent of the adults confined in mental institutions for very low intelligence may have suffered alcohol exposure during fetal development. A pregnant woman's heavy drinking (forty-five drinks per month or binges of more than five drinks at a sitting) also carries risks beyond fetal retardation. The baby may be born with wide-spaced eyes and other facial abnormalities; low birth weight leading to a very small head and small overall stature; late walking, talking, and other developmental watermarks; and a range of behavioral problems. Difficulties concentrating, paying attention, learning, talking, understanding language, and tendencies toward hyperactivity, impulsiveness, and poor judgment can show up in heavy drinkers' children. One or more of these problems can beset moderate drinkers' children, as well, even when the youngsters are free from the more obvious facial malformations of fetal alcohol syndrome.

One city, Racine, Wisconsin, is trying to do something about maternal drinking in a dramatic way: In August 1996, they charged a hard-drinking pregnant woman with attempted murder. After her bingeing at a bar induced the woman's premature labor, the baby was born with a blood alcohol level of .199 (three times the legal level for drunkenness in Wisconsin) and with the signs of fetal alcohol syndrome. Observers are divided on the wisdom of this legal move, but it did draw national attention.

A man's heavy drinking can lower his testosterone levels to the point of infertility. If a child is conceived, even with a teetotaling partner, it often weighs less at birth. Since no one is sure what level of alcohol consumption is safe for either parent, many obstetricians warn both off alcohol—the father for three months before conception, the mother starting a month before. With persistent alcohol use by pregnant women, this caution is obviously being ignored. And the toll on children's concentration and learning is probably enormous, since researchers worry that even moderate drinking can damage fetal neurons and impede schoolwork and memory during and after a child's growth years.

Smoking

At one time, more than half the adults in America smoked; today, less than one-third do. But women who smoke during pregnancy or breathe in their partner's secondhand smoke can affect their babies' brain development in surprisingly serious ways. Tobacco researchers estimate that burning tobacco releases 2,000 to 4,000 toxic compounds, as well as high levels of carbon monoxide. Together, these can cut the amount of oxygen reaching the fetus by as much as 20 percent, as well as causing facial abnormalities, damaging parts of the brain, and reducing overall body and head size. The toxins in smoke also appear to damage a man's sperm: Besides reducing sperm count, a man who smokes has a higher risk of fathering a child with hydrocephalus, facial paralysis (Bell's palsy), or learning deficits. A mother's direct smoking or her intake of secondhand smoke can damage the fetus's hearing. It can reduce a child's stature, maturation rate, and his or her IQ scores by an average of nine points, according to University of Colorado medical researcher David Olds. And smoking can bring on a host of learning disabilities: difficulty reading, solving problems, interpreting meanings, and staying in school.

Because nicotine is so addictive, quitting is almost impossible for many people, but a pregnant woman has a strong incentive— a smarter child with a higher potential than if she kept smoking. Even a reduction will help; the fewer cigarettes she smokes, the lesser the effects on the fetus.

Environmental Exposures

Nearly half the pregnant women in a given year were working when they conceived, and kept working for the next eight or nine months. But in many jobs, the chemicals encountered daily can damage a developing embryo or fetus. Workers in the medical and pharmaceutical fields, for example, can be exposed to radiation, anesthetics, drug components, viruses, and bacteria. Women who work in agriculture can encounter pesticides, arsenic, dioxin, and other toxics. Textile, garment, and laundry workers breathe in fibers and solvents; hairdressers are exposed to a different set of solvents, dyes, and aerosols; and the list goes on through photography, painting, printing, transportation, and a dozen other fields. Large exposures early in pregnancy can lead to miscarriages and malformations, while lower doses throughout pregnancy can cause more subtle neural defects, low birth weight, and learning problems.

A father's industrial exposure can have a dual effect: Before conception, heavy metals, radiation, and other industrial agents can damage sperm; after conception, particles and odors clinging to hair, skin, and clothing can expose mother and fetus at home. Even a couple living in a pristine mountain environment and commuting a short way to two totally benign work places could still run into trouble on the weekends if they forget about toxic exposures and spray the garden for aphids or strip furniture in a closed garage. And in some parts of the country, the water and soil have been contaminated with enough PCBs that the electrical insulating chemical shows up in human breast milk and can slow a child's later development, memory, and attention.

Stress

Denna, the surgical nurse mentioned at the start of this chapter, had concerns during her pregnancy: She worried about her daily pick-me-ups—coffee, and the occasional cigarette. She was nervous about the anesthetic gases in the operating room. But mostly she worried about the prospect of single parenthood, about her heavy workload, and about stress itself.

She had good reason.

To understand stress in its purest form, picture a zebra stallion, eyes wide and dust billowing up around its hooves as it gallops across the Serengeti with a lioness in ravenous pursuit. The instant the zebra spotted the predator, a signal from the equine brain triggered the adrenal glands sitting on top of the kidneys to secrete stress hormones: adrenaline and noradrenaline (also called epinephrine and norepinephrine), and cortisol. Together, these hormones instantly accelerated the zebra's heartbeat, blood circulation, and breathing so it could escape at top speed. The hormones also shut down processes the zebra didn't need while it was busy running for its life: digestion, growth, sperm production, immune cell responses, and the branching of dendrites and the sprouting of spines on brain neurons. If a zebra runs fast enough to escape the predator, these vital activities can resume later. And that's important, because without them, the animal would die just as surely as if powerful jaws had snapped its neck. Researcher Robert Sapolsky of Stanford University in Palo Alto, California, lays out the dilemma simply: "These getaways don't come cheap!"

Under normal circumstances, after animals in the wild survive periods of extreme fight-or-flight stress, they go back to grazing or napping in the afternoon sun. The mad dash to safety is rough on them, but their stress is acute and temporary. In a person with chronic, long-term stress—an unmarried, pregnant surgical nurse, let's say, such as Denna at the start of this chapter—the body reacts much of the time as if pursued by a smallish, scraggly, slow-running lion, but a lion nonetheless.

In his work at Stanford, Sapolsky has found that during extended periods of chronic stress, cortisol and related stress hormones cause nerve cells in certain parts of the brain to lose their dendritic branches and spines and eventually to die off completely. This can lead to poor memory, fuzzy thinking, and a lack of creativity. Stress also makes preexisting brain diseases like epilepsy, strokes, Alzheimer's, and AIDS dementia even worse. Because of other shutdown effects on the body, an adult's chronic stress hormones can also lead to fatigue, muscle pain, hypertension, ulcers, short stature, fertility problems, and a heightened risk of all diseases.

Just as the galloping zebra experiences temporary reproductive shutdown, a pregnant woman like Denna experiences the effects of chronic stress in her own body and passes them along to the fetus. The cortisol in her bloodstream shunts blood away from the uterus, and this in turn squeezes off some of the fetus's supply of oxygen and nutrients—up to 60 percent in extreme cases. Stress hormones also cross the placenta and raise the fetal heartbeat. While this crossover has not been fully studied, we suspect that stress hormones could act in the fetal brain as they do in the adult—cutting the number of neurons that develop and preventing some of their dendritic branches and spines from forming. Studies have shown that the higher the mother's anxiety levels, the more likely she is to have prolonged nausea, a miscarriage, or extended, painful labor, and the more likely her baby is to be restless, irritable, colicky, and illness-prone.

Ironically, many couples who defer pregnancy until their mid to late thirties, hoping for career and financial stability, find that their stress levels are higher during gestation—because they worry about problems due to the mother's age, because well-meaning family and friends regale them with horror stories about problem pregnancies in older women, and because their own expectations for the long-awaited event are too lofty: perfect pregnancy, perfect baby, perfect family.

In many cultures around the world, pregnancy has for centuries been viewed as a time for deliberate calmness. The ancient Japanese Taikyo tradition, for example, warns pregnant women to avoid loud-voiced vendors arguing in the streets and to seek tranquil gardens and the sounds of wind chimes and bells. In Shakespeare's *Henry V*, Lady Grey worries aloud that her sadness and tears might "blast or drown" her unborn child.

For modern Americans, talk shows and health magazines often

substitute for traditions and superstitions, and the current advice for pregnancy stress is support groups, confidants, guided relaxation, and meditation. Given the very real downside to uncontrolled stress, if these techniques bag the slow-running lion, they are a good way to protect your child's future mental and emotional well-being.

Prenatal Nutrition

A quick visual survey of derrieres and midsections taken in virtually any public place in America proves that over- not undernutrition is our problem. The malnutrition that does exist in industrialized countries tends to show up in children and the elderly, and to be as much a function of ignorance, neglect, and disease (including drug addiction and mental illness) as it is a result of poverty or food shortage. Nevertheless, the National Academy of Sciences estimates that 12 million American children get fewer nutrients than they need each day (although not necessarily fewer calories) and in many cases, this childhood malnutrition follows a pregnancy accompanied by less-than-ideal food consumption. Teenagers are particularly prone to poor prenatal nutrition and if a girl's weight gain is below 25 pounds, if her own normal weight is below 100 pounds, and if she smokes or uses drugs, the risk of an underweight, premature baby is substantial, and with it, the chances of brain impairment.

Researchers have produced mountains of data on precisely how malnutrition harms the fetal and infant brain. Part of their knowledge has come through extensive animal studies, and part has come through history's many accidental and deliberate human feeding experiments. Animal studies confirm that starvation during pregnancy and nursing can cause brain damage. If severe food shortages occur in the first trimester, the result can be neural tube malformations such as spina bifida (unenclosed spinal cord), anencephaly (absent brain), or microcephaly (extremely small brain). Shortages in the second trimester are likely to result in too few neurons, since nerve cells proliferate during this period. Deprivation in the third trimester affects myelination, synaptic connections, brain growth, and the branching of dendrites.

Human researchers confirmed this grim progression—or at least its behavioral readouts—in studies of starving populations in Holland during World War II, in Indonesia, South Africa, Mexico, Guatemala, and the United States. Seriously underweight babies and children starved of protein and calories have small head sizes, lowered IQ scores, and problems hearing, speaking, coordinating hand-eye movements, learning school subjects, and forming normal relationships.

Perhaps the largest and cruelest human "experiment" took place in the Netherlands in 1944 and 1945, when German Nazis prevented the transport of all foodstuffs and produced an artificial but deadly seven-month-long famine. More than 10,000 people starved to death after the average daily calorie ration dropped from 1,500 to 400, and the blockade changed the future for more than 40,000 fetuses. Hospital records confirm that those starved in the first trimester showed the most neural tube defects, while those starved in the third trimester (the time of most rapid fetal weight gain) had the lowest body and head size. More recent studies in Latin America, Africa, and the U.S. have also confirmed that malnourished children earned lower intelligence and school scores than well-fed youngsters from similar neighborhoods. For years, researchers assumed that brain damage alone was responsible for these bleak statistics. Newer research, however, shows that the environment is equally important, and, depending on its stimulation value, it can either help renew the underfed brain or constitute a double jeopardy.

Nutritionists have long posed a major and obvious question: Can a young animal or child damaged by malnutrition ever catch up with peers? The answer is yes, and the best prospects are children who suffered malnutrition *after* the first year of life, when the critical periods of brain formation and neural proliferation had passed and myelination and synapse formation were well underway. But can children deprived during pregnancy be helped later, too?

One of the first pieces of this puzzle came out of the Diamond lab in the early 1980s, when a Peruvian doctoral candidate, Arianna Carughi, carried out a series of experiments on pregnant rats and their pups. All of the mothers ate high-protein pellets during the first part of pregnancy, but half were then taken off this diet and given low-protein pellets. Once the pups were born, Carughi fed half of them high protein and half low. She also split each nutritional group so that half the well-fed pups lived in standard rat cages and half lived in enrichment cages, while half of the poorly fed pups lived in standard cages and half in enriched. In this study, then, pups could gestate and grow under a number of different internal and environmental conditions. Carughi found that pups who were protein-deprived in the womb weighed much less and their cerebral cortex was much thinner than pups well-fed in utero. After weaning, these deprived pups could be rehabilitated with higher-protein food, but Carughi found that those rehabilitated in *enrichment cages* developed a thicker cortex than pups well-fed in the womb but raised in a dull place. The smartest pups with the thickest cortex were still the ones with both proper nutrition *and* a stimulating environment. But their protein-deprived peers could nearly catch up with a combination of better food and challenging surroundings.

Logically, children should react the same way, and studies show that they do. Poor nutrition can put a child's mental development on hold, but if the child gets better nutrition as well as social and educational enrichment before the age of three, his or her brain growth and maturation can nearly catch up. Researchers were startled to discover that some of the learning problems in an underfed toddler stem not from brain damage per se, but from lack of stimulation. Badly fed children are so tired and listless they fail to play with friends or explore their surroundings much. It is this lack of environmental stimulation during years one to three, according to Ernesto Pollitt, a pediatrics professor at the University of California at Davis, that mostly lowers IQ scores and learning ability.

Pollitt teamed up with four other researchers from the U.S. and Central America to study 2,000 children in four Guatemalan villages for nearly a decade. In two villages, they supplied the mothers and children with a hot maize gruel full of protein and vitamins to supplement their normal meals. In the other two villages, the mothers and children received a high-calorie vitamin-filled fruit drink but no extra protein. By tracking the children's progress for eight years, they found that fetuses, infants, and children on the protein supplement grew and developed skills faster, had more energy, and made better social and emotional progress than children the same ages consuming less protein. With an enrichment program of tutors and counselors to help the children learn games, social skills, and preschool activities, both groups did better than without the enrichment. The well-fed youngsters, however, were able to play, experiment, and explore their environment more fully, and this, in turn, promoted their brain growth.

Good nutrition, starting in pregnancy, continuing throughout breast-feeding, and carrying over into a toddler's diet, is clearly a crucial part of promoting a child's healthy brain development, and getting enough protein is obviously a key element. For a pregnant woman, that means at least $2^2/_3$ to $3^1/_2$ more ounces of protein than she would normally eat for her height and weight. Children should be eating at least two servings of protein-rich foods like fish, poultry, lean meat, eggs, nuts, or beans each day, and three to four servings of dairy products, with the serving sizes varying with the child's age.

A child like Jeremy whose mother ate mostly greasy fast-food hamburgers, tacos, and doughnuts probably got plenty of protein and calories as a fetus, but not vitamins; Joan could well have had a severe enough folacin deficiency to cause neural tube defects, not to mention deficiencies of other vitamins needed for normal fetal growth. Baby Lisel's highly conscientious parents, on the other hand, planned for her optimal development by taking vitamin supplements, keeping a food diary, shunning drugs, alcohol, cigarette smoke, and other exposures, and by exercising, meditating, and generally lavishing care on their unborn daughter. Tony and Jeannine wanted to feel assured—and did—that they had not taken unnecessary risks, and had done everything they could to avoid birth defects and to produce a healthy baby with its mental faculties intact.

And then they went a step farther.

Deliberate Prenatal Stimulation: How Much Is Too Much?

Tony had read in *Omni* magazine about a program for teaching a fetus words and sounds. The couple checked with their obstetrician, who had never heard about the techniques, but thought they couldn't hurt. Expectant mothers, after all, have been patting their stomachs and talking to their little ones for centuries. This was just a formalized extension, a way to create a behavioral environment for the fetus as conscientious as the chemical and nutritional one they had engineered. Right?

Tony sent away for a copy of *Prenatal Classroom* by California obstetrician F. Rene Van de Carr and his psychologist coauthor Marc Lehrer. Jeannine was in her fifth month when the book came, and they started right in with "the Kick Game." Following the book's directions, she and Tony would both greet their fetus through a cardboard paper towel roller. "Hi, Mama is here," Jeannine would intone directly at her abdomen through the tube. "Daddy's here, too," Tony would say, taking a turn at the tube. They would wait for the fetus to kick randomly, immediately press on the spot from the outside, then pipe in, "Kick, kick! That's a good baby. Kick here again!" Eventually, their unborn baby girl (they knew her sex from medical tests) learned to respond by kicking wherever they pressed and she could execute circles and fancy patterns with well-aimed blows from the inside.

The lessons went on to introduce different kinds of contact— patting, rubbing, squeezing, shaking, stroking, tapping—and the accompanying verbs, delivered via paper megaphone. Jeannine would stand up, sit down, sway, or rock and say the appropriate words. She would drink hot and cold liquids and label the sensation for Lisel. Tony would turn on a radio speaker ("Music!") or a vacuum cleaner ("Noise!"), or shine a flashlight on and off ("Light!" "Dark!" "Light!" "Dark!"). The couple would read stories or sing songs. They would tap Jeannine's belly in sets of one, two, three, or four pats, and count out loud; and they would perch a small xylophone on her midsection and sound and name the notes, "F!" "G!" "C!" Every ten-minute session, morning and evening, would begin with the "Hi Baby!" megaphone greeting and end with a few minutes of classical music piped in through headphones, just as Richard Dreyfus and Glenne Headley did in the film *Mr. Holland's Opus*. The daily ritual made the couple feel close to each other and to Lisel long before she was born.

This young pair felt good about teaching their child in the womb. *But were they really teaching her?* Is a fetus even listening? Is the brain developed enough in the womb to make sense of words, music, counting, rhythms? Or are these simply random sounds or even irritations to a fetus who then literally tries to kick them out?

Since the late 1970s, researchers armed with sensitive ultrasound and fetal heart monitors, fiber optic cameras, and other high-tech instruments have sketched a picture of life in the womb that was largely blank before. They now know that a human embryo begins to move in the first trimester, and after fourteen weeks, displays most of the movements a full-term baby can make: hiccupping, thumb-sucking, bending, shifting, startling to loud sounds, rotating its trunk, darting its eyes, and breathing (fluid) in and out. Researchers know that a fetus has four activity states: quiet sleep, active sleep, quiet awareness, and active awareness. Before twenty-four weeks, it is rarely still for more than five minutes at a time; after thirty-two weeks, it will rest for up to half an hour. They know that, starting at six months, a fetus can hear. And, they are certain that the fetus is listening. *Carefully*.

Anthony DeCasper, a psychologist at the University of North Carolina at Greensboro, has pioneered a technique for testing the sound preferences of newborn babies less than two days old. Working with psychologist William Fifer and other colleagues in North Carolina and in Paris, DeCasper invented a contraption that allows a baby to suck faster to hear one set of sounds through headphones, and to suck slower to hear a different set. Using this technique, DeCasper discovered that newborns can distinguish their mother's voice from a stranger's, and prefer to hear Mom. What's more, they'd rather hear Mom's voice the way it sounds filtered through amniotic fluid (which DeCasper can produce with a special electronic device) than through air. Newborns would also rather hear Mom speaking in her native tongue than hear her or someone else speaking in a foreign language. They'd rather hear a recording of her heartbeat than hear Dad's voice, and they'll only start sucking harder to hear Dad's voice several weeks after birth, not right away.

Most intriguingly, DeCasper discovered that fetuses are not only listening in the womb, they are learning, too. DeCasper's team instructed sixteen pregnant women to sit down twice daily during the last month and a half before delivery, and read the Dr. Seuss book *The Cat in the Hat* to their fetus. Once the babies were born, he tested them on the sucking device, giving them a choice between *The Cat in the Hat* and a different children's story, *The King, the Mice, and the Cheese*. The babies had obviously been listening carefully to and remembering the rhythm and sounds of their mother's reading, because they voted with their lips: Dr. Seuss please, not a substitute!

In separate research at Oregon State University in Corvallis, Oregon, William Smotherman taught fetal rats to hate the taste and smell of apple juice by injecting it into the mother's amniotic sac, then following that insertion with a dose of lithium chloride, a compound that makes mammals violently sick. After the pups are born, even when they are very hungry, they will turn and run from their mother if her nipples are painted with apple juice! They had clearly learned their chemistry well in uterine preschool. Smotherman repeated the experiment as early as day 17 when the fetal rats were primitive and half formed, but the lesson still sunk in. This chemical confirmation of fetal learning has human implications, some of them ominous: A team of researchers from Cordoba, Argentina, is convinced that when a pregnant woman drinks, especially during the last trimester, the odor and taste of alcohol in the amniotic fluid imprints itself in the fetal brain and increases the chances of alcoholism later in life.

None of this surprises Dr. F. Rene Van de Carr, founder of the "Prenatal University." He has been an obstetrician in Hayward, California, a blue-collar community twenty miles south of Oakland, for more than thirty years, and has observed firsthand what he considers fetal learning. "Fetuses make choices before birth," he says, demonstrated by the distinctly different reactions they show when a father touches a fetus through the mother's abdomen and when, immediately afterward, an obstetrician touches the same spot. "It's a different pair of hands, and instantly the baby—and you can see this on ultrasound—the baby stops responding and freezes. 'Who's that?' You can say that's a conditioned thing," Van de Carr argues, "but it has become clear over my years of working. Perhaps there are differences in the vibratory frequencies of the hands."

Van de Carr is a stocky, white-haired man who looks a bit like the late Burl Ives, and he grows animated when he speaks about how he first stumbled onto prenatal stimulation. "Back in 1979, I had a pregnant patient who would put little animals—a birdie and a kitty—on her stomach, and the fetus would respond by trying to push them off. Also, the mom and dad would play little games with the fetus. I thought this was beautiful." So Van de Carr, a father seven times over, invented techniques to try with willing patients. By the early 1980s, he was offering classes. "Back then—now, too, to some degree—people were tied up in their own experience, the Birth Thing. The baby," he says, shaking his head, "was just a sidecar, just like people focus on weddings and marriage and forget issues like 'How are we going to live together?' I wanted people to consider the fetus an individual, and that pregnancy and delivery wasn't just something you went through to get your hands on the baby."

More than 3,000 patients in Van de Carr's local medical practice have attended his classes. He has lectured in numerous countries and discussed prenatal stimulation on network talk shows and in magazine and newspaper articles. Van de Carr is unambiguous about his objectives in touching, talking to, and playing music for a fetus. "First, we are trying to produce changes that increase the awareness and the perceptive capabilities of the baby. By altering the kind of experiential input, in the vernacular, we teach them to pay attention." Once the fetus and baby are more aware, he adds, "They will be self-generating stimulation. All you have to do is teach the baby to pay attention and then you just turn them loose and they do on their own all of what the Head Start program is talking about."

Second, he continues, "We change the expectations of the parents. If you catch somebody in the prenatal process, especially if it's the first baby, you change the way they relate to their children. You increase interaction and you change the expectation that the baby will respond thoroughly and understand." This, in turn, "increases the kind and content and perhaps even the speed of exchange that's occurring between mother and baby and the father, when present." This prenatal interaction, says Van de Carr, along with the parental awareness and heightened communication, leads to a close-knit family bond and to a baby that is calm, more alert, happier, and talks and walks earlier than babies not stimulated in the womb.

"To me," he says, "the differences between a baby that was *not* stimulated" twice a day for a few minutes and "one that *was* stimulated are startling! Apparent! Major! Mothers bring stimulated babies into the office and at six weeks, you can stand the baby up and he or she will hold your fingers and not fall down and stare at you right in the eye for twenty-five or thirty seconds. So you have persistent attention span, and a child whose muscle control is able to hold them with ease for a substantial length of time." Besides those apparent characteristics, the stimulation program produces teeth that tend to emerge sooner, earlier verbalizing, and the faster appearance of strength and coordination. "We have to warn mothers not to leave these prenatally stimulated babies unattended, because their motor capability allows them in the first week of life to come up on their hands and do push-ups; they can drop one hand and roll—right off the table."

One nurse in Van de Carr's office described her prenatally stimulated four-week-old as "not your ordinary baby." He's more alert, awake, aware, and self-confident than the many unstimulated babies she sees at the office daily. "He never wakes me up crying," she says, and instead makes little "Feed-me" munching sounds with his lips. He babbles during the breaths he takes while breast-feeding, and when he's done, "he wants to be entertained, pampered, and kept clean. I knew this baby before he was born, and he knew me," she says, "and neither of us had any problems adjusting."

Another of Van de Carr's patients, says that playing "the Kick Game" was "fun, strange, and exciting. I had the strangest feeling of knowing Carlton before he was born. Almost like a pen pal." Carlton has always been "very polite, very sensitive, and caring—tuned in to other people's needs," she says, "and has an incredible memory" of incidents that happened before the age of two. When she became pregnant a second time, she began prenatally stimulating this fetus as well. "This child is very active. I can tell already how much more energy he has."

Yet another Van de Carr devotee had an eerily similar story. As a baby, her now six-year-old son invariably grew calm and happy whenever she put *The Sound of Music* on the stereo. This, she explains, was the selection she played to him inside her abdomen each day. He got his first tooth at two months of age. His first phrase was "Daddy bye bye car work." A vocabulary of 227 words followed by age two (his proud mom kept track). He has been identifying trees as "deciduous" and "evergreen" since he was three. And a child psychologist at school thought one of his preschool drawings was made by a third grader. Her son has always said "please," "thank you," and "excuse me," without prompting and is self-confident, sensitive, and popular.

Are these prenatally stimulated children truly advanced? Or is this a case of selective perception by true believers? After years of criticism from skeptics, Van de Carr has grown wary of words like "advanced" or "superior." "The thing that made people the most nervous is that I said right from the start that these kids are able to think better than other people. They just plain can! The first concern of the standard mother hearing this is, 'Are you saying those kids are better than my kids?' It becomes a personal affront." It apparently became a professional affront, as well. In the early 1980s, Van de Carr described his stimulation techniques and the effects he has seen on early speech, early physiological development, and family bonding to obstetricians attending a medical conference. "They were saying that those capabilities we were seeing were impossible. Everybody knew that these things didn't happen, and I was a charlatan and a liar" for even suggesting that they do. "My answer was, why not take the time to do it with your own children, and come to your own conclusions. Over time, they started saying, by golly, these kids *can* do things we didn't think they can do. That's all history now," Van de Carr shakes his head again, "but it was kind of embarrassing."

About the same time, Donald Shetler, an emeritus professor at the Eastman School of Music in Rochester, New York (now living in South Carolina), started a prenatal stimulation program of his own. For fourteen years, Shetler had been in charge of the school's Talent Education Program, designed to spot and encourage children with musical gifts. Inspired by his contact with Shinichi Suzuki in Japan (inventor of the Suzuki method for teaching the violin to children) and by discussions with pregnant music students, he advertised for thirty volunteers willing to play classical music to their fetuses. Each agreed to present the music starting at five months' gestation, for no more than five minutes, twice daily. The morning selection was to be a "stimulative" piece like Handel's *Music for the Royal Fireworks*, or Beethoven's Seventh Symphony. The evening selection was to be "sedative," like Bach's *Air on the G String*, or other Baroque compositions by Bach, Vivaldi, Telemann, or Handel with a heartbeat rhythm of sixty beats per minute.

The mothers-to-be (as well as a control group of mothers who did no prenatal music stimulation) checked in with Shetler every six weeks during pregnancy, then brought in their children every two to three months for more than a decade. At each visit, Shetler would conduct an interview with parent and child, then videotape the youngster's pint-sized musical performance of singing and playing toy instruments. He found that the musically stimulated babies started talking an average of three to six months earlier than the unstimulated babies, and once in school, the former were also ahead of the latter in cognitive development, often skipping grades. Shetler was most amazed, however, by the children's musical ability.

"These kids could memorize musical material quickly and effortlessly," Shetler says, "and they picked up playing and singing remarkably naturally." At twenty-one months of age, one prenatally stimulated little girl could sing a popular hymn in "the correct key with no melodic or rhythmic errors," writes Shetler, and she could sing twelve more songs from memory. She could also play the piano with independent fingering and sing along while playing.

Another thirty-month-old girl from the experimental group could sing fourteen songs from memory in high and low registers, and could play a toy xylophone, the drums, the kazoo, and an electronic keyboard, while simultaneously making up little songs. Several of the children in Shetler's study went on to play the piano and other stringed instruments, and to become "highly motivated musicians. They never need to be coaxed to practice," he says. "In fact, they have to be coaxed to stop and come to dinner."

In his mind, says Shetler, there is "no question about the fact" that prenatal stimulation heightens musical ability and language skills. Although he has amassed hundreds of hours of videotape, he hasn't analyzed it all or pursued further studies. He backed away partly out of financial pressure, partly from public skepticism. "People were always asking, 'Are you trying to create musical geniuses? Little Mozarts?' The answer is 'No!,' but there is a fear in the general public, a suspicion of manufacturing super babies. We were just trying to see if getting the brain to function at a higher level would enhance a child's chances of reaching his or her fullest potential."

Donald Shetler obviously feels that it does, and so does Rene Van de Carr. But is scientific and medical skepticism really "all history now" as Van de Carr claims? Take the doctor's assertion, for example, that a prenatally stimulated child is 160 times more likely than a nonstimulated child to sprout a first tooth by one month of age. Is it even *possible* to cause a forward shift in physical development by playing "the Kick Game" and talking through a paper tube?

The Diamond lab group in Berkeley collected some data on this question in the early 1970s, after placing pregnant rats in enriched environments with plenty of space, companions, and toys, then analyzing their pups. The offspring were heavier and, indeed, they did show accelerated physical development. When these prenatally enriched pups grew up, the experimenters bred them with others, and after two enriched generations each pup tended to have a significantly thicker cerebral cortex at birth as well. Diamond speculates that mother rats actively running around enrichment cages produce more sex steroid hormones, and these, in turn, could cross the placenta and in some way "prime" the fetal cortex.

A highly respected developmental biologist of Stanford University in Palo Alto, Norman Wessells, explains that hormones and growth-controlling factors, ultimately governed by our genes, regulate the speed of an embryo's development. "There is no reason," he says, "that the things that control the timing of teeth eruption couldn't be accelerated." Among mammals, which are all members of the same class of animals, there is already a spectrum of precociousness, he explains. Some mammals, like the elephant, giraffe, and dolphin, are born ready to run or swim off after their mothers, while other mammals like bats and primates (people included) are relatively undeveloped at birth and parents must feed, protect, and teach them for extended periods. "It's not hard to imagine a shift up or down this scale," says Wessells, "but I would wonder whether acceleration might interfere with the normal *sequence* of development."

In the human fetus, as in other mammals and in birds, there is a set order for the onset of the senses, for example. Sensation in the skin appears first, then balance, then taste, then smell, then hearing, and finally vision. Researchers in Virginia designed a test with bobwhite quail to see whether they could artificially change the order with stimulation. They lifted a small piece of shell from hundreds of quail eggs and exposed the chicks inside to bursts of flickering light. The chicks would normally encounter direct light only after hatching and this early exposure seemed to trigger early visual development. It also disturbed the chicks' ability to imprint correctly on their mothers' movements and voice, and instead of following her, they walked around looking dazed.

More evidence comes from premature infants. Babies born too early—sometimes as much as three months too soon—are suddenly removed from the sensory environment in which their brain was designed to mature in a standard developmental sequence over thirty-eight weeks' time. Their early birth thrusts preemies into a world of light, unfiltered sound, direct touch, and general sensory overload. Pediatric researcher Heidelise Als, who studies preemies at Children's Hospital in Boston, notes that 400,000 babies arrive more than a month too early each year, when their brains are growing at the fastest possible rate. Children delivered weeks too early, she says, can (but by no means always) exhibit learning disabilities, lower IQ scores, attention deficits, impaired eye-hand coordination, and speech problems, and they tire and distract easily, lack self-esteem and self-control, and act vulnerable and impulsive. This, writes Als in a recent article, suggests that early sensory stimulation may present unexpected challenges to brain development and may distort it by triggering sensitive periods at a time when the brain can't incorporate visual, touch, or other kinds of stimulation.

Als and two colleagues administered a battery of psychological and academic tests to a group of children born in 1987 from one to three months prematurely. She highlights one eight-year-old child in particular who exemplified the group. Her IQ tested at 115 (an average IQ score is 100), but she ranked in the "dull normal" range for several cognitive categories, including working with numbers and images, while scoring in the "very superior gifted" range for verbal skills, word problems, and a few others. Als concluded that a preemie's early sensory bombardment can lead to "maladaptations and disabilities but also to accelerations and extraordinary abilities." Her work was aimed at discovering the best way for parents and nurses to interact with a premature baby and the best design for a nursery environment so that the brain can continue developing in the best substitute setting for the ideal choice: the dark, quiet, aquatic world of the womb.

To prospective parents wondering whether to try prenatal stimulation, Als's findings might well seem cautionary; they didn't, however, address the question of mild stimulation of a normal-term fetus. Experts who work more directly in that field give a range of opinions from "Thumbs up" to "Jury's still out." French researcher Jean-Pierre Lecanuet, an authority on what a fetus can hear and learn in utero, thinks the fetus "may benefit from prenatal exposure to a variety of sounds, including speech sounds," and that these may help fine-tune the sense of hearing. Psychologist Anthony DeCasper at the University of North Carolina, who sometimes collaborates with Lecanuet, is less sanguine. He worries that scientists know too little at this point and that even moderate prenatal stimulation could change the order of human sensory development. "In the absence of better knowledge of human fetal development," he says, "I wouldn't bet necessarily that the outcome would be wonderful." DeCasper finds Rene Van de Carr's explanations "plausible," but adds quickly that he has not yet demonstrated "that it was his 'prenatal university' curriculum that did the deed . . . the science isn't quite up with the claims. Although you can appreciate where the claims come from—they are not crazy claims," says DeCasper, "but they are still unsubstantiated claims."

Much of the funding for fetal learning studies comes from the National Institute of Child Health and Human Development, and its director of Human Learning and Behavior, Norman Krasnegor, watches the field closely, including the question of prenatal stimulation. "We are not really at a stage yet where we can say that it's either dangerous or helpful," he says, adding half in jest, "I don't think there is any evidence that is credible in the way we snooty National Institutes of Health kind of people wrapped up in our robes of science and our ivory tower can tell you." Very high-decibel sound levels can damage fetal hearing, he says, so you wouldn't want "to take a bullhorn and yell, 'Hey, Fred! How are you doing in there?' I'm being a little facetious, obviously, but we just don't know except to say that mothers always talk to their fetuses and that is to be expected and there is nothing right or wrong about that." At this point, he says, "I would err on the conservative side, simply because with anything having to do with medicine, [the best policy is] 'First Do No Harm.' I'm not suggesting," he continues quickly, "that anyone is doing harm by this. But they just don't know and it may just work out to the detriment rather than the benefits of a developing fetus to do any more than moms do naturally."

Even Van de Carr himself, while convinced his program is safe and valuable, acknowledges that it can be overused. He knows of one mother who exceeded his recommendation to stimulate the fetus no more than five to ten minutes at a time twice daily. Instead, she played chords of music to her fetus "for a minimum of three hours daily from five weeks to term. Sometimes," Van de Carr says, "it was *twelve* hours a day." The boy, by age seven, was living with his parents in Spain and "had played concert piano for most of the courts of Europe." His hands move so quickly while playing his instrument or a computer keyboard that you can't follow them, says Van de Carr, and "his reaction time is hypernormal. If you watch him, you might think he was hyperkinetic and say 'He should be on Ritalin—let's slow him down.' " While visiting with the family, Van de Carr noticed that the boy, in one minute's time, "would be all over the couch, he would have straightened the throw pillows a few times, and checked the phone three more times. But it's not pathological movement," Van de Carr argues, "it's effective movement."

Another group advertising prenatal stimulation claims to have sold 25,000 units of a sonic stimulator device that a pregnant woman wears on a belt. It plays sixteen different audiotapes through a speaker, and the group recommends a woman use it for two hours per day during the fourth through seventh months. Asked about the safety of an approach like this, Philip Cogen, the head of the pediatric neurosurgery team at Children's National Medical Center in Washington, D.C., remarked, "That's probably too much," and joked, "here's a new title for a book: *Drive Your Fetus Crazy!* Fetuses need their quiet, too," he says, just like babies. "If everyone is putting their faces in the baby's and saying 'Coochie, coochie, coo,' it's eventually going to start screaming from too much stimulation." With regards to accelerated development, Cogen suspects that "the development of teeth, motor skills, and that sort of thing are programmed in a biological way that can only be altered minimally."

Some prospective parents will want to try enriching their fetus in the womb, while others will be unwilling to use direct methods until after the baby arrives. Regardless, we think every pregnant woman or couple should monitor excess exposure to stress hormones and to cigarettes, alcohol, legal and illegal drugs, pesticides, and industrial compounds to protect their future child's developing brain. The following program suggests ways both to protect and enrich the fetus.

An Enrichment Program for the Unborn Child

Here are some recommendations for anyone thinking about prenatal stimulation or ready to plan a program to nurture a child's healthiest mental development before birth.

- If you are planning to have a baby, seek out good preconception medical care so you can learn about potential problems with your health, work or home environment, food habits, drug exposures, and stress level before you conceive, and can make the appropriate changes. The Resource Guide (page 307) lists articles, the addresses of health agencies, and other information on preconception care.

- If you are already an impending parent, ask yourself these questions to assess your own behavior toward prenatal care and enrichment.

Does either parent smoke?

Are you exposed to secondhand smoke at work, in public places, or in other people's homes?

Have you consumed alcoholic drinks while pregnant?

Have you taken any potentially harmful over-the-counter drugs?

Have you taken only prescription drugs approved by your obstetrician?

Have you used cocaine, marijuana, heroin, or other "hard" recreational drugs or taken in secondhand smoke from drugs?

Have you consumed caffeinated beverages during pregnancy?

Is either parent exposed to occupational toxins of any kind?

Have you monitored your diet carefully for protein, vitamins, and other nutrients?

Do you experience very little stress, some stress, or high stress?

Do you get regular exercise and relaxation?

Is your life stable with few expected major changes other than the coming child, or is it filled with job changes, moving to a new house or apartment, relationship changes, and so on?

Do you have very little, some, or a great deal of control over your everyday activities and schedules?

Are you often, seldom, or never bored or lonely?

Do you experience mental challenges at least daily?

Do you pay attention to fetal movements?

Do you talk or read to the fetus daily?

- Consider the consequences of everything you breathe in and swallow during pregnancy. Saying to oneself, "A little of this can't hurt," is playing Russian roulette with the most complicated process in the universe. A child's mental and physical growth—before birth and after—presents challenge enough to parents without damaging exposures that can permanently rob potential. The Resource Guide lists informational sources on drinking, smoking, and drug use during pregnancy.

- If you suspect a problem with home or occupational exposures to damaging chemicals, check with the Resource Guide for a list of books and agency addresses to help you track down the source and avoid it during pregnancy.

- Keep a food diary and monitor your intake of protein, vitamins, and calories during pregnancy. Your doctor will probably provide you with nutritional guidelines for pregnant women and for children ages one to ten, as do some of the books and articles in our Resource Guide.

- It is clear from the research we describe in this chapter that a fetus can hear and remember things spoken in a regular, unmagnified voice during the last few weeks before birth. Since your future child is listening anyway, why not—for periods of *no more than five to ten minutes,* morning and evening—speak to it, read stories, play music, touch it gently, and convey your love? Dads and other children can get in on this if they want by speaking in a regular voice near the mother's abdomen. At the very least, this communication will heighten your anticipation, help train you to participate in your baby's cognitive growth, and set the stage for a close family bond.

- Avoid long periods of prenatal stimulation, and any devices that deliver loud sounds, prolonged sounds, or light flashes to the fetus. In our opinion, there are just too many unknowns at this point to go beyond the filtered touch and muffled sound the fetus would naturally encounter.

- Just for fun, keep a diary of the music you played, the stories you read, and voices the fetus heard, and watch to see if the baby calms down or responds happily when hearing the same sounds later.

- Check out first with your obstetrician anything you plan to do, and if following a printed program, show that to your doctor as well.

- Here are some musical selections you can play quietly for the fetus. Since these pieces may calm the baby after birth, it's good to have a small but well-rehearsed repertoire.

These are recommended by Dr. F. Rene Van de Carr and musician and retired professor Dr. Donald Shetler.

Music for the Royal Fireworks, Handel
"Spring," from *The Four Seasons,* Vivaldi
Air on the G String, J. S. Bach
The Brandenburg Concertos, J. S. Bach
Canon in D Major, Pachelbel
Pictures at an Exhibition, Mussorgsky
Slow steady pieces by Haydn, Mozart, Beethoven, or Vivaldi
Popular music by Tom Paxton, Burl Ives, Tom Chapin, and Raffi

Chapter 4

Dreaming Eyes of Wonder:
Nurturing the Very Young

Child of the pure unclouded brow
And dreaming eyes of wonder!
—Lewis Carroll, *Through the Looking-Glass*

• Born in 1993, Willie was a quiet baby. From the start he cried very little and seemed to demand far less attention than did his sister, Beatrice, born seven years earlier. Before Willie was even one year old, it was clear to his mother, Harriet, that he was a shy child: He was sensitive and startled by unfamiliar sounds or sights. He would hang back rather than finger a new toy or pet the family's golden retriever. And it would take thirty to forty minutes for him to warm up to his grandmother even though she came over regularly.

Harriet had worked as a bookkeeper when Beatrice was little, but her husband, Tom, had a better job now, so she decided to stay home and give Willie "lots of love." When he cried, she would hold and cuddle him for as long as he wanted. She'd also pat and reassure him during play, feedings, or diaperings, just so he'd feel her strong, steady presence. She worried about his shyness, but she was determined not to push or criticize him. Her own father had tried constantly to cajole, bribe, and command her shy younger brother into being more outgoing. Harriet and Tom had no fancy strategies for child rearing; they simply loved Willie the way he was and tried to express that every day.

• When Cecilia came along in 1995, Saundra had just begun taking classes for her two-year florist's certificate. Her husband,

Raymond, picked up odd carpentry jobs; for more than a year, a persistent shoulder injury had kept him from working full-time. The couple took turns baby-sitting during the day, depending on Saundra's class schedule, and she thought the arrangement was working out well. She had noticed that Cecilia would scream and cry whenever she left for school, and that the child smiled and played less than her cousin, just three months older. But Cecilia had been colicky, and now had sore gums from teething, and Saundra's sister had advised her not to worry.

One day, Saundra's afternoon class was canceled unexpectedly, and she came home early. As she pulled into her parking space behind the apartment building, she could hear Cecilia crying and started to rush up the back steps toward the kitchen. On a hunch, though, she stopped and quietly descended. She quickly walked around the building, then climbed the front stairs where she could see into the living room window unobserved. In dismay and then disgust, she watched Raymond grab Cecilia roughly by the arm and yell at her to stop crying. Saundra ran up the steps, burst through the front door, and grabbed her daughter. She sped straight through the apartment and down the back steps with Cecilia, then jumped back into the car. Raymond, she noticed, did not get up to follow them and did not come outside as she drove away.

• Max and Amelia were living about twenty miles from the University of California at Davis, when their daughter, Jennifer, was born in 1987. A friend told them about two professors who were looking for babies to participate in a language study. Amelia, on leave from her job as a high school history teacher, felt that perhaps she could make a contribution by taking part in the study, and was pleased when their family was chosen along with 140 others.

During a series of meetings, the research psychologists showed Amelia and Max about sixty simple hand gestures to teach to Jennifer. The study's object was to allow parents to communicate with their one-year-old babies in the months before the youngsters could put their wants and needs into words. Using this gestural language, in turn, promised a happier child, parents aware of their babies' rapid mental development, and a head start toward the infant's speech and language understanding.

When Jennifer was thirteen months old, Amelia took her on

an outing with friends to the San Francisco zoo. Standing in front of the elephant enclosure, Amelia said to her daughter, "Do you see the big elephant?" and simultaneously wiggled her finger from the tip of her nose—the "baby sign" for elephant. Eyes wide and sparkling, Jennifer looked back and flapped her arms at her sides, the sign for "bird." This didn't make sense at first, but then Amelia noticed a tiny sparrow hopping in the dust on the ground next to the elephant. This smaller animal—far easier for Jennifer to take in than a 10,000-pound pachyderm—had caught the child's attention. "Yes, look at the pretty bird," Amelia said smiling, and made a small flapping motion. Jennifer grinned with obvious pleasure at bringing Amelia into *her* world for a moment.

A Child's Early Environment

Although parents have an intimate impact on their child's prenatal environment, that influence deepens and broadens once the baby arrives and the parents establish the physical environment, as well as interact with the child through words, touch, emotions, and visual exchanges.

In the first two years of life, a normal child's senses develop, he or she learns to crawl, walk, run, babble, talk, use a spoon, listen to and understand spoken language, manipulate a range of toys and objects, and interact with other family members and caregivers. The fundamental aspects of personality, temperament, and emotional reactions are also established in this twenty-four-month period. By instinct, babies and toddlers are creatures of learning and of play, exploring every detail of their surroundings with intense curiosity. As a baby's brain matures, his or her abilities to perceive and engage the world bud and flower. These developmental activities, in turn, help shape the developing brain. Through their constant touching, looking, tasting, listening, and moving, babies provide themselves with most of the experiences they need in order for the brain to develop normally. But the parents of babies and toddlers must provide certain kinds of experiences, particularly in the realms of emotional support and language, to foster the child's fullest development at this stage.

Today, more than half of all women return to work before their children are one year old. For women with college degrees, the figure is nearly 70 percent. This means the environment of love and stimulation parents create at home is only part of the child's important experience during development; the child-care situation parents choose makes up the other major part. For 30 percent of parents, the choice is an organized day care center. For 48 percent, it is a relative watching the child. And for about 22 percent, it is a baby-sitter or a nonrelative in another home. In making back-to-work and child-care decisions, it is important to know:

- General elements of an enriched environment
- Milestones for brain development in the child's first two years of life
- Ways that experience can support and expand that growth

Stimulating the Youngest Minds

There is good reason to think that an enriched environment would stimulate a young child's brain. Animal studies carried out in the Diamond lab at U.C. Berkeley revealed that infant rats less than twenty-eight days old and just before weaning show an enlarged cerebral cortex after even a short enrichment period. Diamond's team placed three mothers and a total of nine pups in either a large cage without toys (the control group), or a large cage with toys (the enriched condition), and then compared both to a single rat family housed alone in a small cage sans playthings. In as little as eight days' time, the enriched youngsters developed a cortex from 7 to 11 percent thicker than in the other infants. After two weeks in the enrichment cage with toys, one particular brain region involved in integrating sensory information grew 16 percent thicker in the enriched pups—the biggest increase in any brain region at any age!

Arnold Scheibel and Roderick Simonds at UCLA studied children's brains and made similar observations. They obtained brain specimens from seventeen children who had died between the ages of three months and six years of age. While the researchers had no way of knowing the kinds of learning environments in which the children were raised, they did find out some provocative things about experience and the very young cerebral cortex. Their major interest was the branching dendrites in the cortex layer—the magic trees of the mind we encountered in earlier chapters. They found that at birth, most neurons in the baby's cerebral cortex have only "first-" and "second-order" branches. That means the dendrites, the living antennae that receive incoming nerve signals, usually grow long and split once into two branches then once again into four branches, but stop there. Almost immediately after birth, however, as touch, taste, sound, sights, and other sensory and motor experiences start to pour in from the baby's environment, the dendritic branching resumes. By six months, third- and fourth-order split-offs were abundant in the brain tissue Scheibel's team examined. By the second or third year of life, fifth- and sixth-order branching was common.

Scheibel calls this a "fossilized history" of early dendritic growth. And he was able to read something else in that history, as well: At three to six months of age, before a baby starts talking, the dendrites on the right side of the brain are longer and "branchier" than on the left, especially in the brain areas that control sucking, swallowing, smiling, crying and other expressions, but not speech. As the baby learns to speak between eight and eighteen months, however, the dendritic trees in the left hemisphere (the side of the brain that controls language in most people) grow longer and branch more luxuriantly than the right. This left-side branching, Scheibel speculates, may be not the *cause* but the *response* to the baby's learning and using of words. It is therefore a classic case of dendritic growth in response to environmental stimulation—in this case, presumably, the parents' talking, singing, and reading to the baby.

This work by Scheibel and Simonds is among the most direct demonstrations of how experience and environmental stimulation cause a human baby's brain to grow.

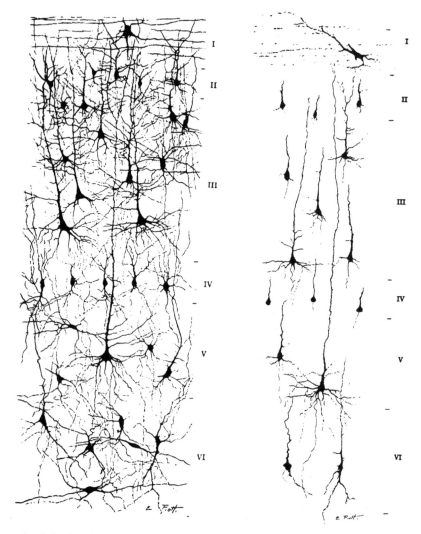

At birth (*right*), the neurons in the cerebral cortex at the front of a baby's brain are smaller and have many fewer branches than they will just a few weeks later. At three months of age (*left*) a baby's dendritic forests are already branching and growing based on the child's genetic program and on just the first 12 weeks of his or her life experience.

Enriched Environments for Kids

Studies like these allow us to identify the common threads in all enriched environments, and allow you to judge whether your child's surroundings are stimulating or not.

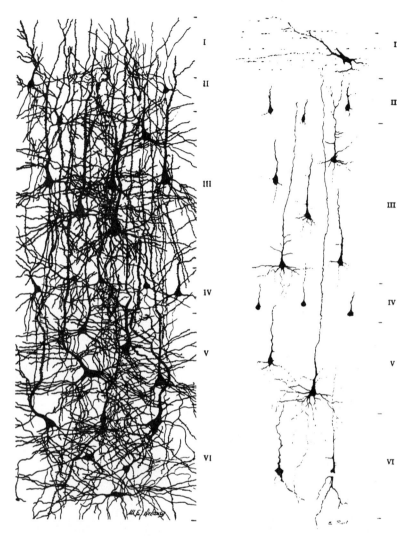

At twenty-four months (*left*), a child's frontal cortex is a true enchanted thicket of neural trees with bushy dendrites and billions of shimmering spines. Learning is nearly effortless, but self-control awaits the sculpting of permanent inhibitory pathways within this overconnected mass.

An enriched environment:

- Includes a steady source of positive emotional support
- Provides a nutritious diet with enough protein, vitamins, minerals, and calories

- Stimulates all the senses (but not necessarily all at once!)
- Has an atmosphere free of undue pressure and stress but suffused with a degree of pleasurable intensity
- Presents a series of novel challenges that are neither too easy nor too difficult for the child at his or her stage of development
- Allows for social interaction for a significant percentage of activities
- Promotes the development of a broad range of skills and interests that are mental, physical, aesthetic, social, and emotional
- Gives the child an opportunity to choose many of his or her own activities
- Gives the child a chance to assess the results of his or her efforts and to modify them
- An enjoyable atmosphere that promotes exploration and the fun of learning
- Above all, enriched environments allow the child to be an active participant rather than a passive observer

A nonenriched, impoverished environment will tend to be opposite in most of these ways, including:

- A diet low in protein, vitamins, and minerals, and too high or too low in calories
- A vacillating or negative emotional climate
- Sensory deprivation
- High levels of stress and pressure
- Unchanging conditions lacking novelty
- Long periods of isolation from caregivers and/or peers
- A heavy, dull atmosphere lacking in fun or in a sense of exploration and the joy of learning
- A passive, rather than active involvement in some or all activities
- Little personal choice of activities
- Little chance to evaluate results or effects and change to different activities
- Development in a narrow, not broad range of interests

It doesn't take the orphanage scene from *David Copperfield* to qualify as an impoverished environment. All it takes is a toddler sitting alone and passive for hours in front of a television set, dreaming eyes of wonder glazed over, imagination shelved, exploratory energy on hold. Then throw in a bowl of potato chips and a soda. . . .

Miraculous Milestones

Watching a baby grow and develop is the most fascinating biological theater in the average person's life—and distinctly more amusing than witnessing one's own body age. Even though the time it takes us to develop is long compared to a dog, cat, or monkey, a human still progresses from newborn to toddler to child with remarkable speed. The obvious expansion of movements, senses, moods, playing, thinking, talking, and socializing during the first and second years reflect the underlying brain growth we discussed earlier: an explosion of synaptic junctions between neural branches; a rocketing of energy consumption and cellular activity; a rapid accumulation of myelin, speeding the impulses along nerve routes; a doubling then tripling of brain weight before the child enters grade school. The inventory of behavioral milestones that follows sets the stage for understanding how the brain matures and how this maturation underlies the joyful signs of growing up.

Newborns. People often refer to newborns as "helpless," and yet a baby is a little ball of animal reflexes, even capable of self-defense to a limited degree. Child development specialists Frank and Theresa Caplan describe these self-defense reflexes in their book *The First Twelve Months of Life.* A baby startles at loud sounds or bright lights. It flings arms and legs outward in response to a sudden noise or touch. When lying down, it lifts and turns its head to prevent suffocating. It will root around for a nipple and suck on it like any nursing mammal. If a napkin falls on a baby's face, he or she will fling it off by flailing arms and head. If stroked, the baby's hands and feet will grasp. And the baby will make stepping movements if held vertically and swimming movements if held horizontally in the water. The rest of a newborn's behaviors are animal-like as well: She jiggles, jerks, and flings her arms and legs randomly, her hands are clenched in tight little fists; she cries and issues soft guttural grunts, smacks, and gurgles; her eyes can track movement, but only within inches of her face; and she sleeps 80 percent of the time.

At one month. Within four weeks of arrival, arm, leg, and body movements are still jerky and random, but the baby is starting to perceive high-contrast patterns, to hear and respond to voices by looking or making thrashing sounds, and to cry intentionally to elicit attention. He recognizes and prefers soft objects, not coarse; gentle handling, not rough; and sweet smells, not bitter or acrid. And according to a panel of pediatricians in the book *Caring for Your Baby and Young Child,* he especially appreciates being talked to kindly.

At four months. A baby's charms are evident now, along with her developing abilities. She can raise her head and chest and prop herself up on her arms; kick and stretch her legs at will; deliberately open and shut her hands; stand when supported; swipe at dangling objects; and grab, shake, and chew on small toys. Her vision is mature by now, and she can track objects at a long distance. She smiles winningly when tickled, talked to, or cuddled, and squeaks, coos, and babbles single syllables—at first vowels, then vowels and consonants. With a bit of support she can sit up, and this frees her to chew on and play with her own hands, fingers, feet, and toes. She spends hours of her now-greater waking time experimenting with how objects feel, taste, move, and fall to the floor. She likes soft music, and usually likes to splash and kick in the bathtub. She has a range of moods and ways of getting and keeping her parents' attention, and responds to their moods as well.

At eight months. A baby is beginning to assert himself now, shouting to get attention, creeping and crawling around the house, pulling himself to a standing position next to the couch, and exploring toys and objects by shaking, banging, scraping, throwing, pounding, or dropping them to see and hear what they do. His aim is good when reaching and grasping and he can now make a pincer out of fingers and thumbs for picking up tiny objects—say, Cheerios or apple chunks off his high-chair tray.

He has a drive to vocalize—to stutter strings of syllables, to babble back and forth with any friendly conversant, and to say his first word or two. His growing alertness and awareness allow him to recognize familiar toys, voices, faces—including his own in the mirror—and as a consequence, to identify and fear strangers.

At one year. By her first birthday, a child's world is getting larger as she perfects lightning-fast crawling, tottering on two feet, and walking a step or two unassisted. Her dexterity has grown so that she can stack a couple of blocks, put small toys into bigger ones and dump them out again. She can drink from a cup, brush her own hair, babble into a toy phone receiver, scribble with a crayon on paper, and she has favorites among her dolls, balls, trucks, and other toys. For the first time, she can watch a small object being hidden beneath a cloth, then reach under and find it. She has started to understand symbols; she can point to a picture of a bird or a kitten and "tweet" or "meow" appropriately. She understands simple commands like "Give me the ball," or "Don't eat that!" and has learned to respond, at times, by vigorously shaking her head and insisting, "No!" She listens intently to spoken words and tries to imitate them, and she has discovered the great fun of testing mom's and dad's reactions when she cries, refuses their requests, or throws something across the room.

At eighteen months. Along the way to eighteen months, a toddler becomes a perpetual motion machine with self-awareness. He gleefully discovers doorknobs, light switches, dials, electric outlets, wastebaskets, and drawers. He learns to climb on low furniture and stairs, first on hands and knees, then on two feet. He can sit himself down on a short chair, but would far prefer to be walking, stiffly running, or hopping; stooping to pick things up, then lugging, pushing, pulling, or rolling them around; or joyfully splashing water or sand. In quieter moments, he can fit blocks and pegs into holes of like shape; he will listen to songs or rhymes for short stretches and hum, sing, sway, bounce, or dance along in an irresistible way.

He usually knows what he likes and points to or drags over what he wants, such as a book to look at or be read to him; a big ball to play rolling catch with on the floor; a record to be played; or a coat to be donned, meaning "Let me out!" He is affectionate, loves attention, and understands dozens of words, including the labels for his nose, ears, toes, and other body parts, and his name and those of other family members. He likes to be helpful, imitating housework, turning book pages, feeding himself with hands, cup, and spoon, and taking off his clothes—sometimes at unfortunate moments. But his self-awareness can veer off into narcissism, temper, or hitting if another child borrows his toy or he disagrees with a parent or babysitter.

At two years. Despite the reputation of the "terrible twos," by a child's second birthday, the temper tantrums can begin to subside if the parents learn to handle them effectively. This helps the toddler to begin learning a measure of self-control. The child's growing vocabulary also helps indirectly, as she learns to express her feelings and needs in words rather than solely with actions and raw emotion. She will probably have a spoken vocabulary of at least fifty words by now, understand most of the object names in her daily life, and know many words for activities (play, sleep, ride in the car), emotions (happy, sad, mad), and states of being (tired, awake, hungry).

The two-year-old is, by nature, self-absorbed and self-centered, wanting her own things, her own way, and to do everything for herself, even if she's not sure how. These expressions of growing independence can be helpful as the child goes into the world of day care, and are usually accompanied by the setting of the current and future temperament: shy, aggressive, outgoing, friendly, distrustful.

The toddler has come a very long way in twenty-four months—from a reflexive baby animal to a walking, talking, thinking being with needs, preferences, and aversions all her own. At this stage, she has the foundations of personality that will influence whom she befriends, how she learns, how she sees herself throughout childhood, as well as much about her adult character. So how do all these changes take place?

Brain Spurts and Spiral Waves

A little more than a decade ago, major medical reference guides on child development talked about how the infant's and toddler's thinking skills and behaviors emerged, *and yet they never mentioned the brain.* Child development was one field, brain research another, and at no point did the two cross over—or so one would have thought.

A few insightful scientists noticed this yawning gap, and launched the new field of cognitive neuroscience to tie the events in the brain to human and animal behavior, including the unfolding march of milestones in a child's life.

One member of this new breed is Kurt Fischer, a Harvard University educator who is a "neo-Piagetian" as well as cognitive neuroscientist. Jean Piaget, a Swiss researcher who studied child development from the 1920s to the 1960s, is that subject's most famous scholar. He is best known for assigning children to four stages of development: the Sensorimotor period, from birth to age two; the Pre-Operational period, from ages two to seven; the Concrete Operational period from seven to eleven; and the Formal Operational period from eleven up (more on these later). Piaget is equally well known for basing his elaborate development theory on observations of his own children, Lucienne, Laurent, and Jacqueline, as they grew up in the family's home in Geneva.

Fischer, an animated, red-haired academic, has built his own updated model on Piaget's framework of childhood stages, matching emerging behaviors with brain changes. He and his colleague Samuel Rose also methodically observed Fischer's son, Seth, starting at birth. This disciplined observation revealed a very startling fact that supports the new, more brain-oriented model of child development. One way to measure a baby's brain growth, they report, is to monitor the size of his head on a weekly basis. Fischer and Rose carefully recorded Seth's head circumference, starting at birth and noting marked growth spurts between three and four weeks, seven and eight weeks, and ten and eleven weeks that coincided with spurts in other babies from other studies. Then, unexpectedly, Seth caught his first major cold from weeks seventeen to nineteen, and instead of another predicted growth spurt, Fischer found that his son's head (and presumably the brain inside) failed to grow at all during the illness. This shows, he says, that organic change and environmental effects work together, and how, during development, "a little environmental input can dramatically change the growth curves" for the brain. "Seth also had problems with his diet at one point," Fischer explains, "and if children aren't getting extra energy because they can't eat or because they are sick, then there is no energy for growth and the system stops for a while."

In Fischer's model, the brain develops by fits and starts throughout childhood, with what he calls "growers" (developing brain functions and behaviors) accumulating and spurring each other's further development. He attributes the growth of particular brain regions—and in turn, behaviors—to mechanisms we've already seen—myelin accumulation, dendritic branching, synaptic formation, and the pruning of weak or unused connections. Fischer's scientific papers feature mind-tangling strings of algebraic equations describing the cyclic action and interaction of "growers" upon each other. The high points, however, are fairly straightforward: Between a child's birth and his twenty-first birthday, his brain exhibits a series of growth spurts, reflected in head growth, brain activity (measured through EEG recordings of brain waves), and the density of synaptic junctions between dendritic branches.

Within the baby's first three months of life, there are three brain growth spurts, each accompanied by new skills related to the infant's simple animal-like survival reflexes. These skills, in turn, feed back as experience that helps shape the brain toward its next growth level. Around the time of the first brain growth spurt at three to four weeks, a baby begins to follow a ball with her eyes and grasp a soft object placed in her hand. At the seven- to eight-week growth spurt, the baby starts to build reflex upon reflex; hearing his mother's voice triggers staring in her direction with his eyes, and seeing a ball triggers reaching with his arm. At the ten- to eleven-week spurt, the reflex chain grows another link longer: Baby hears Mom's voice, looks at her, and responds by smiling or cooing; or sees a ball, reaches toward it, and opens her fingers.

In the next fifteen months of life (from three to eighteen months), the baby experiences three more growth spurts that trigger new *sensorimotor* responses (here Fischer uses Piaget's term)—coordinated actions in response to perceptions of the world. At the fifteen- to seventeen-week brain growth spurt, a sensorimotor response emerges from the simple strings of reflexes: The baby follows a moving ball with his eyes, reaches with fingers wide, and moves his arm once to track the object's path. The spurt at seven to eight months touches off a sensorimotor chain: baby sees a ball, the vision guides her reach, she grabs the ball, then brings it over to examine more closely. Between eleven and thirteen months, another spurt in brain growth brings about a longer chain of sensing and reacting: the baby grabs a rattle, and moves it around so he can see the front, back, and sides. He also hears people speak words, then forms his mouth, lips, and throat in a reasonable imitation of "ball" or "cookie."

In Fischer's model, a toddler by her second birthday has piled up experiences provided by chains of reflexive and sensorimotor actions, and these have helped the brain reach a new level of potential: the ability to represent objects, people, or events through mental symbols. The growth spurt sometime between eighteen and twenty-four months that allows this symbolism in the mind unlocks not just words but short sentences like "Mommy walk," as well as imaginative play, like pretending a doll is the doctor who gives shots or is a mother getting dressed.

Fischer's model goes on to describe brain growth spurts and newly emerging skills at three and a half to four and a half years, six to seven years, ten to twelve years, fourteen to sixteen years, and eighteen to twenty years (all described in later chapters). It's no coincidence that many of the spurts, especially in the first few years, are synchronized with the accumulating myelin in various parts of the brain, the explosion in synaptic junctions, and the booming activity other researchers have seen in very young children's brain cells. To quote nineteenth-century psychologist William James, the brain of the baby and toddler is "blooming, buzzing confusion." In fact, confusion it's not, with its precise sequence of developmental events. But in a metaphoric sense, a baby's brain certainly booms, buzzes, and blooms.

Crawling is a good example of "cognitive bootstrapping" in that busy brain. Bootstrapping is another term for the way brain growth leads to new experience and new experience unlocks more brain growth. The act of crawling, which usually starts between eight and nine months of age, can itself boost other kinds of brain maturation. Take, for example, Alessandra, a normal eight-month-old baby—playful, alert, and ready to touch and gum everything within her sight and reach. Having recently started crawling, now, within a typical ten-minute period, she can explore a doorknob, a window molding, the dog's tail, and a bright plastic toy. By testing babies like Alessandra, each eight and a half months old, give or take a week, two psychologists from the University of Illinois, Roseanne Kermoian and Joseph Campos, confirmed that crawling detonates an explosion of brain development.

The two researchers divided more than one hundred babies into three groups: those that had not started crawling, those that had, and those that could not yet crawl but could scoot around in a plastic baby "walker." They found that the mobile babies could also easily locate keys, toy watches, and other treasures that the researchers had hidden beneath a cloth. In infant terms, this ability equals spatial intelligence—the more mobile the eight-month-old, the more likely he or she will be to find the hidden object. Nonmobile babies, on the other hand, were usually stymied by the test, and failed to find a key or watch concealed beneath a handkerchief.

Joseph Campos in an earlier study with Bennett Bertenthal discovered that babies who crawl are wary of heights, while babies the same age who haven't yet started exploring the three-dimensional world on all fours have not developed a similar fear of heights.

Finding hidden toys and fearing heights are both spatial skills as well as examples of sustained attention, and neuroscientists know more about the baby's development of such skills and the responsible brain regions than they do about any other aspect of early cognitive development. They know many of the details thanks to Adele Diamond, a dark-haired, articulate, fast-speaking psychologist who works at Massachusetts Institute of Technology. Along with a few colleagues, Diamond (no relation to Marian) has studied spatial reasoning in hundreds of infants. One of the methods Diamond has used, is based on Jean Piaget's test from the 1930s, called "A not B." It involves hiding a toy in one of two wells in a tabletop or tray while the baby looks on, then covering both wells with a cloth, waiting a few seconds, then letting the baby choose the correct well, A or B. Diamond found that at seven and a half to nine months of age, a baby will usually make the wrong choice if he or she is delayed from reaching for two to five seconds and prevented from seeing the wells. By the first birthday, with just a few more months of brain maturation, the baby can tolerate a delay of five to ten seconds and still find the toy in the correct well.

In a second test, called "Object Retrieval," the baby must extricate a toy from a clear plastic box open only on one side wall. A baby six and a half to eight months old will reach straight for the toy, bumping into the plastic lid or front-facing wall blocking the path. By nine and a half months, the baby will tip the box or rotate it to find the opening, and reach for the toy with the other hand. By eleven to twelve months, the infant simply sizes up the situation visually and reaches in through the open side to grab the prize. Obviously, something changed in the brain in the second half of the baby's first year, resulting in a better retrieval of objects. But what was it?

The answer to this question came from primate research. It turns out that monkeys can take very similar object retrieval tests and react in similar ways. This fact allowed Yale researcher Patricia Goldman-Rakic to identify particular cells in the front section of the brain's cerebral cortex—the so-called *prefrontal cortex*—that must mature before the animal can find hidden toys in these tests. In the young business of cognitive neuroscience, this is one of the very few links anyone has been able to forge between a specific behavior and the development of particular cells or parts of the brain. Adele Diamond explains that this maturing of the prefrontal cortex "allows us to start to exercise choice and control over what we do instead of just being creatures of habit. It allows us to solve problems in our minds, to hold onto the information long enough to be able to manipulate it in the mind so we can start to plan, and to relate one thing to another."

During the course of a baby's development, connections form between the prefrontal cortex and a midbrain region involved in vision called the *superior colliculus*. Neural signals received across these connections could conceivably inhibit the visual information temporarily. "For babies," says Adele Diamond, "the sight of the toy through this clear box is so overwhelming they want to reach straight for it without a detour. But if you can inhibit the superior colliculus a little bit, then you might be able to attend a bit more to tactile information from the hands and might have a better chance of integrating that [information] instead of just being overwhelmed by the sight of the toy." Inhibitory ability, as well as the capacity to hold information in mind, emerges in a baby between the time he is six and a half and eleven months of age.

Martha Ann Bell and Nathan Fox, researchers at the University of South Carolina and the University of Maryland, proved with EEG brain recordings that the prefrontal cortex of a human baby does become much more active between seven and twelve months of age. In their tests, this area "lights up," particularly during the "A not B" exercise when a baby must hold the image of the hidden toy in her mind during a five to ten second delay. The early maturing of the prefrontal cortex is one of the hallmarks of human intelligence, and even an animal as smart as a chimpanzee never reaches the level of a very young child.

Someday, neuroscientists will be able to match many of a baby's budding behaviors with growth in specific regions of the brain. In general terms, researchers can connect things like the four-month-old's ability to focus and see at a distance for the first time with the surge of synaptic connections in the visual cortex. They can also link the growing coordination between eye and hand movements, like picking up a rattle and bringing it to the mouth, with connections between the visual cortex and its counterpart in the motor cortex. However, measuring a specific connection between one particular column of maturing cells in the prefrontal cortex and success on the hidden toy test are a higher order of association; these will await new ways of studying the child's brain.

In the meantime, one innovative researcher at the University of South Florida has devised a theoretical road map for where other researchers can search in the child's brain and at what ages. Based on EEG studies of over five hundred children, Robert Thatcher has created a model for how a "traveling wave" of a growth-stimulating hormone could "sweep" through the brain in slow spiral waves involving first the left hemisphere, then the brain's center, then the right hemisphere. Each sweep would take approximately five years, he theorizes, then begin again, in the left-center-right pattern. If Thatcher's model is correct, the left hemisphere is stimulated at ages eighteen months to two and a half years (coincident with the language "explosion"); both sides are growing at three years of age, and from four to five years, a period of heightened imagination, the right hemisphere is most stimulated. Another five-year-cycle sweeps from left to right between ages five and ten, another from ten to fifteen, and so forth throughout adulthood. Each wave may stimulate synapses to form, he suggests, and any that are not needed or used are eventually pruned away. Thatcher sees his cycles as the "engine that drives" the growth spurts at the various ages Kurt Fischer outlines.

Curiously, these "traveling waves" might act differently as boys and girls grow. Robert Thatcher's colleague Harriet Hanlon, of Virginia Polytechnic and State University at Merryfield, split the data Thatcher collected into females and males and reanalyzed it for gender differences during development. Based on this work, Hanlon reports that the male brain begins to grow faster than the female at about two years of age. Hanlon thinks that variances in brain growth around ages six and ten (which other researchers have confirmed) lead to separate development rates for different parts of a boy's and girl's brain. She thinks that language, memory, and decision making predominate early in girls, and spatial reasoning, vision, and aiming at a target bloom early in boys. Then, she theorizes, the profiles switch in the two sexes at about age eight and balance out, with faster growth in the brain areas that handle language, memory, and decision-making in boys, and in the spatial, visual, and targeting areas in girls.

If these spurts and spirals are confirmed, we may have a new way to understand the major thinking, learning, and personality shifts of childhood, adolescence, and adulthood. Until they are confirmed, though, there is a delightful wrinkle in the whole orderly Piagetian picture of regularly progressing stages and cycles in the brain's development: Babies appear to be born with certain abilities and knowledge that, at least according to these schemas, they shouldn't have.

What Does a Baby Know?

Does a baby come into the world with a clean mental slate that gets filled only by hearing, seeing, touching, tasting, and manipulating the objects around her? Does she then build upon those experiences to generate the capacity for images, words, and thoughts—at first concrete, and later abstract? Jean Piaget thought so, and most cognitive psychologists still agree. But there's a catch. When tested in certain ways, babies seem to display some very sophisticated knowledge of the way objects, people, and places act and interact that defies Piaget's tidy learning sequence.

From her basement laboratory in a steel and granite fortress called Uris Hall on the Cornell University campus in Ithaca, New York, psychologist Elizabeth Spelke has been discovering all sorts of built-in "initial knowledge" in four- and five-month-old babies. Spelke's baby laboratory is a fairly simple affair. Each lab has a table upon which an infant seat is arranged to face a small "stage." Behind the stage curtains, pointing back toward the baby seat, are a set of video cameras hidden and hooked up to computers. Spelke and her colleagues designed this relatively inexpensive technology to capitalize on a simple principle of human behavior: A quiet, alert baby will stare longer at a novel "unexpected" sight than at an ordinary "expected" one.

Take the example of four-month-old Cynthia, sitting in the infant seat in Spelke's lab with her mother nearby, and both staring at the tiny stage. Spelke and her students have set up a situation to test the baby's knowledge of "object continuity," the notion that an object is solid, substantial, and cannot disappear or pass through other objects. The team shows the baby a ball that falls down onto a table that is mostly concealed behind a small screen (an "occluder"). Then they flip down the occluder to reveal where the ball landed on the table. Simultaneously, an assistant behind the stage videotapes Cynthia's face and the duration and direction of her gaze at the ball. Over and over they show Cynthia the falling ball landing on the table behind the occluder screen, until the infant appears to grow bored. Now they change approach: They show her the dropping ball again, but this time, when the screen flips down, the ball is sitting *below* the table. This is, of course, an impossibility if objects have "continuity" and don't move through solid tabletops. But can a four-month-old baby know this? Being a normal, healthy infant, Cynthia stares longer at the novel "unexpected" situation than she did when the ball came to a rest *on* the table as "expected." This stare demonstrates to the researchers that yes, the child understands "object continuity" in some primal, unspoken way.

Spelke and colleagues have conducted hundreds of different tests like this in which preverbal babies stare longer at novel, improbable, or impossible conditions than at ordinary ones. Much to some people's surprise, the psychologists have concluded that babies are born with innate or "initial" knowledge about physical objects. This, writes Spelke, includes the notion that objects move separately from each other; that they maintain their size and shape while moving; and that one object affects another's motion only if they touch. Sound too complex for a baby? Spelke concludes that it's not, and she also accepts evidence that babies can do simple arithmetic.

Psychologist Karen Wynn, working in a laboratory much like Spelke's at the University of Arizona in Tucson, discovered that five-month-olds have a form of numerical reasoning that amounts to baby arithmetic. As little Jerome, let's say, sits in an infant seat facing the stage, a hand reaches in and places a Mickey Mouse doll on the floor. The occluder screen then goes up to block the baby's view of the small stage, a hand holding another Mickey Mouse reaches in from stage left, and it withdraws empty. If the occluder screen now drops down and the baby can see that there are two Mickeys standing side by side on the stage $(1 + 1 = 2)$, he will stare for a few seconds. But if the screen drops and there is only *one* Mickey $(1 + 1 = 1)$—an impossible outcome given the two separate hand deliveries to center stage—then Jerome will stare much longer, and the videotape of his face and eyes will capture that fascination.

Wynn found that a baby will also stare longer following a "subtraction" problem with the wrong answer: A hand delivers two Mickeys onto the stage one by one, the occluder screen goes up, then a hand removes one toy from stage right. Now, when the occluder screen drops and the baby sees two Mickeys still in the limelight, he "knows" intuitively that the count is off $(2 - 1 = 2)$

and he stares longer than he would at a single remaining Mickey $(2 - 1 = 1)$.

Karen Wynn was not surprised to find evidence of this innate numerical reasoning in human infants because monkeys and even pigeons can perform the same simple "arithmetic," staring longer at "unexpected" answers. Colleague Elizabeth Spelke finds nothing impossible about innate knowledge in people and animals, but acknowledges that the whole idea of initial knowledge is "very controversial. The predominant views of cognitive development," she explains, "are very much what they were three hundred years ago: That no knowledge is innate." Since none of Spelke's tests have been on newborns (who are too sleepy to perform) critics attribute the effect to "very rapid learning in the first four months or so."

Once again, because the study of how abilities arise from the growing brain is itself so nascent, this question of what, exactly, a baby knows is unlikely to be answered anytime soon. But Karen Wynn is philosophical on this point. She feels that even at such an early time in the research, the studies suggesting innate baby physics, geometry, arithmetic, and psychology can give parents "an interesting glimpse into the mind of the infant. It gives them a general sense of knowing that a lot more is actually going on in babies' minds than is obvious on the surface, and that can be fascinating, as long as they don't take it too far—'Oh, my baby can add and subtract. I'd better get out the flash cards!' " The time for that may come later in childhood. But there are much better ways to enrich and support the development of infants and toddlers, based on the way the brain grows and the mind matures.

Temperament and the Brain: More Innate "Knowledge"?

Willie, the shy baby at the start of this chapter, seemed to have been born with a sensitive disposition and a tendency to steer clear of new people and situations. At one time, he would have been viewed and treated negatively by parents, teachers, and other youngsters. "For decades," says Mary Rothbart, a psychologist who studies temperament at the University of Oregon in Eugene, many in her field considered "an introvert to be a failed extrovert." Harvard psychologist Jerome Kagan, for example, "sees the shy child as a problem child," says Rothbart. "He sees individuals as either inhibited or uninhibited," with reticent types like Willie in need of transformation into more outgoing children. Rothbart agrees with Kagan that one's initial dispositions are largely spelled out in the genes and that subtle changes are both possible and desirable for some children. However, she views temperament as more multidimensional, and thinks the child must receive unconditional acceptance as well as certain specific kinds of experiences.

At four months, some babies will become active and distressed when shown a new mobile or other visual stimuli, says Rothbart, and research reveals that by twelve to fourteen months, these same children show fear in new situations. Other four-month-olds may react to the same mobile with activity and smiling, and those, Rothbart explains, "will show extroversion and positive approaching behavior" eight to ten months later. Rather than divide these children into "positive and uninhibited" and "negative and inhibited," Rothbart thinks the two dimensions are separate. "It is possible to have a child who is both highly positive and highly inhibited, and this can be a wonderful set of characteristics, because you can use the sensitive, inhibited side to see when you are making mistakes or need to stop and pull back. I'm really a shyness booster," she continues, "and you may want to even strengthen shyness and inhibition in some people in the sense that [these traits] control aggression, while the positive exploratory side is something that we'd want to strengthen in shy children." Willie's parents reacted to him with love, acceptance, and very gentle encouragement to explore new things.

We believe this approach can draw out a child's natural curiosity and allow his prefrontal cortex to develop new pathways that inhibit his own natural reticence. In a similar way, with age and experience, prefrontal pathways come to inhibit a child's tendency to reach straight toward a toy inside a clear plastic box.

Several researchers have, in fact, measured differences in a baby's frontal lobe, depending on temperament, emotional response, and even his or her mother's mood. Richard Davidson of the University of Wisconsin in Madison, took a group of ten-month-olds and observed their tendency to cry when he asked their mothers to leave the laboratory for a short time. About half of the babies would cry, while the others showed fewer—sometimes no—signs of upset. Davidson and a colleague then measured the babies' brain waves by EEG, and found that the criers had more activity in the right side of the brain's frontal lobe and the noncriers had more activity in the left side. Next, they studied nearly 400 thirty-month-olds, in a different laboratory situation: In this one, the child could explore a tunnel, examine a robot, play with other children, and accept a toy from a stranger. One group of children stayed near their mothers for 78 percent of their time in the lab, and took longer before approaching the new objects. Another group stayed near mom only 1 percent of the time and explored without hesitation. A third group was intermediate for both clinging and exploring. Again, EEGs of the children showed more right frontal lobe activity in the hangers-back, and more left-frontal activity in the explorers.

Davidson has also seen more right-frontal activity when a child or adult is distressed, sad, or disgusted—emotions he classifies as "withdrawal." And he has seen more left frontal activity when people experience emotions of "approach"—feeling joyful, interested, even angry (since this involves active engagement of feelings). A colleague of Davidson's, Geraldine Dawson of the University of Washington, has found, in addition, that the activity patterns in a baby's frontal lobe respond to the *mother's* moods and parenting style. A depressed mother who smiles less, plays less, and makes less eye contact with her baby than does a nondepressed mother will affect her baby's brain waves: Her baby is much more likely to have right frontal activity, associated with inhibitions, even while the two are playing peekaboo, than the baby with the happier mother.

All of these findings on babies' temperaments help us better understand how a child's brain develops and how we can enrich this growth and increasing ability. That is because *the parts of the brain that process emotion grow and mature relatively early in a child and are very sensitive to parental feedback and handling.* For infants and toddlers, an atmosphere conducive to healthy emotional development is probably the most important foundation a parent can provide. Proper nurturing at this stage is a priceless form of mental enrichment that lasts a lifetime, whereas inappropriate or inconsistent treatment, neglect, or outright abuse are forms of mental impoverishment that can also take a lifelong toll. Parenting is a challenge no matter how happy, content, and "easy" the baby and child are by innate temperament. But many children are particularly challenging due to shyness, aggression, slow development, disabilities, or other conditions. Physicians Susan Farrell of the University of North Carolina and Ada Pimentel of the University of Puerto Rico, estimate that 20 percent of all children have special developmental problems that necessitate extra patience, attention, and understanding.

Parents like Harriet and Tom, who are surrounding their shy child, Willie, with consistent love, acceptance, respect, and encouragement, are positively enriching his emotional and physical development in ways we explore throughout this chapter. This best possible enrichment strategy appears to be a simple approach, but it turns out to be both difficult for some parents to achieve and unfortunately, increasingly uncommon.

We've already seen that the maturing of the frontal lobes during the second half of a baby's first year allows the child to begin controlling her own behavior: The growth helps her inhibit certain automatic responses, such as reaching for a hidden toy, or overcoming her initial fear to investigate a strange-looking robot. But the frontal region is just one player in the team of brain structures that help govern emotion. Researchers know that normal emotional responses involve (1) circuits in the frontal cortex, the brain's seat of planning and organizing; (2) additional circuits in the amygdala, hypothalamus, and thalamus—all part of the limbic system that governs emotion and memory; and (3) others in the brain stem's reticular formation, which controls alertness. Students of the brain know a great deal about the roles of these brain regions, and know a substantial amount, as well, about how these emotional structures and circuits unfold as the infant grows.

They know that the reticular system (a set of nerve tracks in the brain stem) is fairly mature at birth, since the baby's brain stem is itself already fully functioning to regulate the newborn's heart rate, blood pressure, body temperature, and calmness or anxiety. The amygdala and other limbic structures mature next; these govern sleep, appetite, alertness, sexual behavior, and emotional reactivity (including aggression and impulsiveness), as well as the ability to form attachments to other people, to feel emotions like joy, anger, and love, and to help regulate one's own reactions. The cerebral cortex, including the prefrontal cortex, does some maturing in the first year, but continues to develop for many years. This longer development allows abstract thought, language, reasoning, decision making, and self-control to blossom—all linked to, and influenced by, the other emotional brain structures. Even in a child with an otherwise normal cerebral cortex, however, if the amygdala were damaged or absent, the child would feel neither fear, nor frustration, nor joy, and would be unable to make appropriate choices, identify and avoid danger, or make friends and feel love for family members. For this reason, in his book *Emotional Intelligence,* author Daniel Goleman refers to the amygdala as "the seat of all passion." Emotional development has a curious and important quality: As tiny infants, long before we have words to describe our feelings, our experiences with parents, siblings, and caregivers—loving or harsh, supportive or destructive—help establish a mental map that will guide our emotional life, and, in turn, its influence on all of our thinking processes.

A child like Willie, held and comforted whenever he cried in the first year of life for as long as he needed, is likely to develop an amygdala and other parts of the emotional brain that are more capable of calming him. As a result, he will tend to be a less-demanding child than one whose basic needs for love and security were not met at that early age. Writes Aimée Liu for the American Academy of Pediatrics, "By helping him establish the sense of security now, you're laying a foundation for the confidence and trust that will allow him gradually to separate from you and become a strong, independent person." On the flip side, consider a child raised without sufficient love, attachment, or attention, given little encouragement for exploring and learning, and punished frequently or severely. Many experts on child development, including Richard Davidson of the University of Wisconsin in Madison, are convinced this youngster will suffer an abnormal process of synapse formation and pruning, leaving her without normal circuitry in emotional brain regions, and without the normal range of emotional responses or their control.

Brain researchers Karl Pribram of Virginia's Radford University, and Deborah Rozman of the HeartMath Institute in Boulder Creek, California, have found additional evidence for how parental behavior may influence a child's brain development. They recorded the effects of love, care, and other positive emotions in creating coherent electrical patterns in children's heartbeat rhythms. They also measured the effects of stress, anger, and negative emotions in creating jagged, incoherent electrical patterns. Heart rhythms, they say, feed back information to the developing amygdala, and this region, along with its connections to the frontal lobes and other areas, comes to register the emotions that feel familiar and comfortable to the child—whether disharmonious and accompanied by jagged heart patterns, or harmonious with coherent patterns. Like many experts, Pribram and Rozman consider the first few years of life to be crucial in this "imprinting" of emotional brain regions.

Abuse, Neglect, and the Developing Brain

Consider Cecilia at this chapter's beginning—a child whose father treated her roughly for months before her mother discovered and stopped his influence. Some children treated this way will show some long-term behavioral problems with trust and self-esteem because her father's rough treatment took place during a period when the amygdala was reaching maturation. At the same time, because her mother worked hard to restore a more stable and nurturing environment after discovering the abuse, Cecilia could recover to a considerable degree.

Or take the case of the John B. Watson family. In the early 1900s, along with B. F. Skinner and Albert Ellis, Watson helped found the Behavior movement, with its belief that normal animal and human reflexes could be altered through stimulus and response. John Watson applied his social engineering theories to his own three children, insisting that to guarantee "minimal fixations," the children should be seen and not kissed, hugged, or touched. In her book *Breaking the Silence*, actress Mariette Hartley,

Watson's granddaughter, describes the devastating emotional and behavioral consequences for her mother and uncles—including school dropout and suicide attempts—from growing up under this antiseptic regimen of emotional deprivation. We can only speculate that the Watson children experienced altered brain development in regions governing emotion. But Bruce Perry, a child psychiatrist and developmental neurobiologist at Baylor College of Medicine in Houston, Texas, has documented many cases of serious emotional abuse and their measurable effects on the brain.

Perry is one of the nation's experts on how emotional trauma and child abuse alter the developing brain. Although his practice is much broader, Perry is perhaps best known for working with the children who survived the conflagration at David Koresh's compound in Waco, Texas, in 1993. From behind his desk in one of the modern towers that dot Houston's immense medical complex, Perry speaks with his curious blend of intensity and informality about a level of mind control in the Koresh community that left children unable to make the simplest decisions.

The shoot-out, fire, and exodus from the compound were "traumatic experiences that impacted the surviving children tremendously," Perry explains. They also "illustrate how the brain develops in a use-dependent way." As happens in a sizable percentage of abusive families, he says, Koresh was a "dominant, domineering male who [told] you who to affiliate with, what you will believe, what you will eat, what you will wear, and how to cut your hair. If every time you make an attempt to make a decision on your own you are punished, the parts of the brain that allow you to develop these independent capabilities don't develop." If the children woke up and ate breakfast while Koresh was still asleep, Perry says, "he'd get enraged. Or if they went to school first, he'd get enraged. So they would literally get up and sit and wait."

After the compound was destroyed and Perry began treating a number of the children at a rehabilitation center, he started to make lunch for them one day and asked a six-year-old girl what kind of sandwich she wanted. "She looked at me and said, 'I don't know.' Then she asked the oldest member of the group, 'What do I want on my sandwich?'" That girl could easily grow into a woman who "gets into battering relationships," Perry says. Ironically, "even though that person mistreats her, she feels rudderless without someone to tell her what to do. And it comes," Perry adds, explaining the link between emotional abuse and brain structure, "from a lack of experiences during a critical period for affective development in the first three years of life when your brain is organizing" and allowing you to function as an independent person.

Perry takes out a stack of magnetic resonance images and points to the frontal lobe of a normal child, then compares the photo to the frontal areas of several children who suffered profound emotional abuse and physical neglect. "We have a kid in the hospital now who was found in an iron crib at age eight, covered with feces. . . . His MRI was read by a neuroradiologist as 'cortical atrophy.' But his frontal cortex didn't atrophy. It didn't grow and shrink. It just never grew!" One of the hardest things to communicate to people in our culture, he says, "is not just that hitting kids and screaming and yelling at them leads to injuries, but that the *absence* of touch, the *absence* of eye contact, leads to something *not* growing."

Recent studies of children in Rumanian orphanages as well as of newborns and premature babies show that a caregiver's soothing touch, voice, and eye contact allows an infant to thrive and grow. The absence of nurturing overtures, on the other hand, can lead to an altered course of brain development, to lowered IQ scores, to small stature, and to abnormal behaviors like chronic, vacant stares and rocking back and forth.

Significantly, infant rhesus monkeys treated in much the same way—deprived of the touching, eye contact, and adult nurturing they need—showed not only very similar types of abnormal behaviors, but also changes in the basic architecture of the amygdala and other parts of the emotional brain.

One volunteer from Seattle who worked in a Rumanian orphanage was shocked when she first arrived to find the babies tightly swathed in blankets and lying in cribs with bottles propped against the railings. "They had very little human contact," Elaine recalls, and because all the windows were closed "to prevent ear infections," there was "an overpowering stench. None of these babies smiled," she remembers sadly. Elaine and other volunteers began to clean, feed, and hold the babies, one by one, and within four days, they noticed the infants responding with some degree of pleasure. Researchers are currently trying to discover how much recovery is possible in orphans and other children deprived of loving contact in their formative infant and toddler years.

In Bruce Perry's opinion, "a year of neglect, if it's the first year, robs a child forever, shifts down their potential along a spectrum. You can have either shorter, earlier periods of profound neglect," he says, "or you can have longer less-consistent attention and come up with the same thing: unattached, emotionally empty individuals. And these kids are highly likely to be violent." When a young child is neglected or abused, he says, he or she tends to have less inhibitory capacity, based, in part, on impaired development in the frontal lobes. The lower the capacity to inhibit antisocial behavior, "the more impulsive, the more aggressive, the more reactive [the child will] be."

Perry sees this reduced inhibitory ability in the children in his practice. "Where there's community violence and domestic violence" in their immediate environment, "their ability to contain themselves is gone." Add alcohol to the equation, and their behavior becomes "literally subhuman. You read about crimes where kids get drunk and go out in packs, find somebody, beat the hell out of them, cut them up, set them on fire, and stab them fifty times. So much of it," Perry sighs, "is facilitated by an affective retardation, an attachment retardation. They never got what they wanted when they were young, so that the value of another human being to them, literally, is about the same as most of us would feel about a squirrel or a toad. It is remorseless violence."

Without actually looking at a person's brain tissues, experts can only speculate on the ways emotional abuse and neglect affected the brain and changed its course of development. But it is easy to find disturbing examples of remorseless violence in the news. Consider this chilling statement from Robert Acremant, a twenty-seven-year-old man charged with the murders of a lesbian couple in Medford, Oregon, in December, 1995. When a newspaper reporter asked him what he liked about murdering people, Acremant replied, "It's not a 'like' feeling. It's maybe a little relieving. It's interesting. It's no different than shooting your chicken that just lost in a cockfight, or putting your sick dog to sleep, or shooting at tin cans. I really haven't cared about people my whole life."

The news, of course, is also replete with stories about children who commit violent crimes: Two ten-year-olds in Great Britain lured a two-year-old from a shopping mall in 1993, beat him, and left him to die alone on a stretch of railroad track. Six- and eight-year-old boys attacked a sleeping six-week-old infant in Richmond, California, in April 1996, fracturing his skull and causing severe brain damage. Two Chicago boys, ten and eleven, dropped a five-year-old out of a fourteenth-story window in October, 1994, because he refused to steal candy for them.

The parade of lamentable stories, month after month, may be just the tip of an enormous iceberg. Bruce Perry estimates that more than 3 million American children experience extreme abuse or neglect each year. If the trauma comes early in childhood, he says, the impact is greater on the brain stem and limbic structures, and upon basic functions like sleep, anxiety, and impulsiveness. If the trauma comes between ages two and five, it is more likely to affect brain regions that regulate mood and thinking. Girls are more likely to react by dissociation—daydreaming, fantasizing, and going numbly inward, while boys are more likely to become aggressive. But in either case, says Perry, their own emptiness and lack of attachment can get passed on to their children. They've never gotten love and attachment, he says, "so they don't feel it. The neglect gets passed on generation after generation, and there is actually a diminution of that capacity across generations."

Perry's experience might seem to suggest that the generational transmission of abuse is absolute, but it's not. While abuse and neglect can leave a terrible legacy, less than half of abused children engage in serious antisocial behavior as adults, and a little more than half suffer long-lasting emotional effects. Psychologist Raymond Starr, Jr., of the University of Maryland, reports that 25 to 35 percent of abused children grow up to abuse their own offspring physically or sexually, while about 40 percent of children who witness either parent striking the other will themselves become spouse beaters. And over half of abused children experience emotional problems in adulthood not severe enough to result in criminal behavior, institutionalization, or abuse of their own families. Nevertheless, some long-term research confirms how children can escape the cycle: Nearly 60 percent go on to lead typical, productive adult lives. And these people tended to have at least one nurturing, supportive adult during childhood who helped them sustain some self-esteem, and/or they had access to psychological counseling, usually after leaving home.

Bruce Perry and his colleagues intervene as early as possible for abused children by trying to educate the people who interact with them at home, along with providing standard social work, educational interventions, and other forms of help. "If we make that group of people 5 percent more psychologically sensitive and build in healthier, more positive interactions with that child, that would be more powerful than his or her coming to see Sigmund Freud every day."

It is not clear how much restoration is possible once a young child has suffered short periods of intense abuse and neglect, or longer periods of lower-level trauma. It is clear, though, that a very young child who is deprived of love, attention, physical affection, and affiliations—heart connections—is living in a deprived environment that may feed back, through direct experience, to produce short- or long-term changes in the brain. It is also clear that one of the best ways to enrich an infant or toddler is through unstinting amounts of affection, to build security and self-esteem that will influence all the child's other experiences, and all further enrichments, throughout life.

When asked for enrichment ideas for infants and toddlers, two brain and behavior researchers gave variations on this same theme. "I would tell people to love their kids," says Adele Diamond of M.I.T., "and most things follow from that. That's what they need most. . . . I think kids are naturally curious, and if they are not in a degraded environment, they are going to find things to explore." You don't have to worry about special forms of stimulation, she adds, "but what they need from you is the sense that they are valuable. That what they say is worth hearing. That somebody cares about them. That it is secure enough for them to explore. That the world is a fun place."

Kurt Fischer of Harvard agrees. "It's the emotional stuff that's really important. . . . Where my efforts go as a parent is into building a good, strong relationship with my twins, now, and with my other two kids so they can trust me to have their welfare in mind, to love them, and to learn whom to mistrust—including when to mistrust me." Adds Fischer, "It's actually the social and emotional dimensions that predict long-term mental health better than most other things."

All You Need Is Love—and Language

Emotional security may be the number one target for enrichment in infants and toddlers, but language is a close second. Attempts to communicate through gestures, sounds, and eventually words are some of the prominent milestones for the child's first two years of life. At birth, the newborn makes small animal-like sounds. This graduates to cooing, trilling, smacking, and clicking. Then the baby begins to converse back and forth with smiles, gurgles, and squeals; to make intense efforts to babble vowels and then consonants; to form syllables and chains of them; to imitate words; to understand word meanings and inflections; to utter single words, then phrases, and finally short sentences.

This sequence is so unerring and ubiquitous that the noted linguist Noam Chomsky considered language acquisition to be an automatic human endeavor. "Language learning is not really something that the child does," he wrote in his 1988 work *Language and Problems of Knowledge.* "It is something that happens to the child placed in an appropriate environment." But why does language learning "happen to" the child? And what is the "appropriate environment"? Steven Pinker, a devotee of Chomsky's and a professor at Massachusetts Institute of Technology, goes Chomsky one better: In his 1994 book *The Language Instinct,* he asserts that language is a human instinct, based on genetic instructions and on the maturing of language centers in the child's brain.

Researchers are using various measures to discover exactly what the brain's language centers might be and how they unfold, and they have outlined a number of possibilities. Some think that the brain's left hemisphere is already specialized for language before a baby is born. French linguist Jacques Mehler and others, using the baby headphones and sucking devices mentioned earlier, reported in 1995 that newborns are better at detecting words through their right ear and left brain, and better at detecting musical sounds through their left ear and right brain.

Using EEG recordings of babies' brain waves, Helen Neville's group at the University of Oregon has found a more balanced pattern. Thirteen- to seventeen-month-olds watching a puppet saying some words they recognized and some they didn't had activity in both right and left hemispheres. At twenty months, however, when most toddlers are speaking at least a handful of words and understanding dozens more, the left hemisphere was decidedly more active. And the larger their vocabularies, the more dominant the left brain was for EEG signals. "When kids learn language," says Neville, "they do so using this left hemisphere processor, and that forces the systems in the right to become specialized for other nonlanguage kinds of things like visual-spatial perception and locomotory information." Mehler thinks that a left-side language specialization is genetically determined and that neural development in this part of the brain is programmed to unfold in the toddler and thus *precedes* understanding and speaking words. Conversely, Neville and many others think that language arises *first* based on an innate drive and that the effort and experience of vocal communication *cause* the left brain to specialize for language. Arnold Scheibel and colleagues at U.C.L.A. have found evidence for this latter position in children's brain tissue.

Regardless, it is clear that the human brain starts preparing very early for its language-learning tasks. At the tender age of two months, a baby is already starting to utter sounds that go together—in other words, to babble phrases—and these lead to the conversational babbling and cooing that teaches a baby the pattern of speaking-listening-speaking with another person. At ten months, a baby can no longer distinguish sounds that are part of other languages but not his own. For example, researchers recording babies' brain waves have found that a Japanese five-month-old who never hears separate "r" and "l" sounds (because they are not part of the Japanese language) still generates a brain response when hearing them. By ten months of age, however, there is no longer brain wave reaction to the sounds. Another study shows that this is already beginning at six months: Both American and Swedish babies will turn their heads toward a loudspeaker making their native "i" sounds more often than non-native intonations of the vowel.

Once the child's full-blown language explosion detonates at eighteen to twenty months, he or she will learn words at the phenomenal average rate of *ten or more per day*, or a new word at least *every ninety minutes* throughout much of childhood. The result, Steven Pinker estimates, is a vocabulary of 13,000 words at age six, and by high school graduation, depending on literacy level, perhaps 60,000 to 120,000!

Returning to Chomsky's assertion that language "happens" to a child, what is the best environment for fostering healthy language development? The answer, as common sense would dictate, is an environment rich in spoken, written, and gestural language. Because the experience of seeing, hearing, and forming words stimulates neural dendrites and circuits in the brain and causes the left hemisphere's language centers to grow and specialize, and because this, in turn, allows the baby to understand and speak more efficiently, the child reaps both brain stimulation and emotional development if he is bathed in communication.

Some people feel silly talking to a baby. An infant can't understand or respond, they reason, so why bother trying to communicate until later? If Jacques Mehler and his Parisian colleagues are correct, however, and the right ear and left brain are predisposed to detecting words, then language heard before birth and immediately after will stimulate this region to grow and develop. Psychologists recently reported significantly higher scores on IQ tests among children whose parents talked to them extensively as babies and young children compared to children whose parents communicated with them less. And some observant parents report that talking with babies promotes their creativity and problem solving, and as they get older, their reading, writing, and decision-making skills. Talking to the baby before he or she starts to form words also helps the child discover ways to focus attention, and to socialize. Babbling and then attempting to form syllables and words both require and build on the brain's language foundation. If parents and caregivers are supportive, the baby's ability to communicate, however small, also provides a sense of accomplishment and control over some aspect of his world.

Let's say that at the age of twenty-two months, a toddler says

"Doggie!" and points out the car window to a policeman's chestnut quarter horse, applying his favorite word to yet another four-legged animal. The parent could laugh and say with mild derision, "That's not a dog! It's a horse. Can't you tell the difference?" Or she could nod absentmindedly, say "Mm-hmm," and keep driving. Or she could say, "Yes! Horse-doggie." Or its expanded version: "Yes, that horse is like a doggie, isn't it? It has four legs and a tail. But a horse is much bigger. See how tall it is?"

Or take the one-word sentence, "Joos!" A parent could reply, "You want some apple juice? Here, I'll pour some in your cup." Or in response to "Put bocks!" Dad might say, "Are you putting blocks on top of each other? What a tall stack—a blue one, a green one. Do you want to put another one on top? Yes! A red one." This kind of relentless language immersion drives some caregivers to search for an adult conversation on politics or philosophy every few hours. But for the child, it is an immeasurable gift, as long as the words and actions relate to the child's immediate activities and interests. As a method of reinforcement, some parents put large-type signs on objects: REFRIGERATOR. TABLE. CRIB. DOOR. Then they occasionally point them out. "I'm putting you in your crib now. See the word for crib?"

Because a young baby obviously can't read, some parents feel just as silly putting up signs or reading to a baby as they do telling it about the weather or the day's menu. But, says Jim Trelease, author of *The Read-Aloud Handbook*, "If the child is old enough to talk to, the child is old enough to read to." Trelease cites numerous studies showing that reading aloud to children builds knowledge about the world beyond the daily environment; expands vocabulary and understanding; stimulates imagination; fosters emotional growth and values through the messages in the stories; brings parents and children together; and is an advertisement for the pleasures of reading. Even for a tiny baby looking at wordless picture books, the experience helps to practice focusing the eyes, distinguishing colors, and parsing the rhythms of speech in his or her native language. Best of all, it's a time to be held, talked to, and given attention.

Educator and writer Colin Greer, who has coauthored with Herbert Kohl a collection of poems and stories designed to teach character and values titled *A Call to Character*, emphasizes these benefits, but stresses, as well, that children learn to like and to value whatever they see their parents doing at home. Trelease also argues that a love of reading starts at home, and notes that most children *never get it.* By age ten, most children spend less than 1 percent of their free time reading, he says, and by high school graduation, 63 percent of American students can't read a tabloid newspaper and 95 percent can't decipher the *New York Times.* He also points to the preponderance of males in remedial reading classes (70 percent). This is proof, he says, that children tend to catch the reading bug from parents, and that the message sons tend to get from dads is not excitement over good literature but "the Giants, the '49ers, and the Kings." Trelease tells parents to read to their children at least twenty minutes per day.

Reading, talking, even singing to your kids are common sense as well as specific stimulation for the brain's language centers, and earn a mention in a book on enrichment only because so many parents do none of these regularly. Some action-oriented parents, for example, value language skills very little. Some busy professionals rely on the nanny, who may or may not share the same native language. And many parents assume that television will fill in the language gaps for them. In fact, however, there is evidence that television fails to help prelingual children learn to understand or speak because it's almost never in "motherese"—the very slow, expressive "baby talk" parents instinctively use for infants and that, according to Steven Pinker, infants instinctively like and need to hear.

There's just no substitute for daily language reinforcement by parents and siblings. There is, however, another medium called "Baby Signs" that may someday become mainstream communication for families with infants and toddlers. Baby Signs were the discovery of psychologist Linda Acredolo when her daughter, Katie, was just a year old, and colleague Susan Goodwyn. Katie, who could say only "kitty" and a couple of other words at that point, was sitting in Acredolo's backyard near some flowers one day. She turned to Linda and sniffed, crinkling up her nose, and the psychologist realized that Katie had just invented her own symbol for "flower." Katie created a couple more signs over the next few weeks: blowing through puckered lips for "fish," and touching the index fingers of both hands for "spider." And of course, she used the universal hand wave meaning "good-bye."

Over the years, Acredolo and Goodwyn have become increasingly fascinated with this gestural language and its implications. "The field of child development is becoming more and more aware of how capable babies are and what they know," says Acredolo, and using these and other gestures was a way to understand Katie's world, to alleviate her preverbal frustrations, and to reinforce her interest in language before she could produce it.

Working with Katie, Acredolo and Goodwyn invented dozens of signs for objects and actions such as:

"Airplane"—arms held out stiffly to the sides
"Bird"—the same, but arms flapping
"Book"—palms hinged and opening like book covers
"Dog"—panting
"Drink"—uptilted thumb to mouth
"Elephant"—finger moving up and down off front of nose
"Monkey"—scratching armpits
"More"—finger of one hand tapping palm of other hand
"Telephone"—fist to ear
"Out"—motion like turning a doorknob
"Up"—upward pointed finger
"Where" or "I don't know"—shoulder shrug

Rather than sitting down to teach or drill Katie, the women would casually slip these Baby Signs in while talking. "Do you want to go out [knob-turning action]?" Or while looking at a book together. "Look, the elephant [finger jiggling from end of nose] is taking a drink [thumb to nose]!" Or during dinner. "Do you want more [finger tapping opposite palm]?"

Katie, who is now a teenager, not only picked up the new signs easily and loved conversing with them, but she also starting talking several months earlier than her playmates, and excelled at reading, writing, and speaking skills throughout school. She was, of course, the child of a university professor in a home environment that treasured both language and learning. That made Acredolo and Goodwyn wonder whether the Baby Signs would work for other children from more average backgrounds, as well as for children with delayed language skills. So from their positions at the University of California at Davis, and California State University at Stanislaus, they obtained a large grant, and advertised for volunteers.

The researchers worked with 140 families with eleven-month-olds. Acredolo and Goodwyn taught Baby Signs to one-third of the families, taught another third to emphasize vocal language interaction with their child rather than signs, and asked the last third simply to participate in a general study of development, remaining unaware of the researchers' interest in language.

Acredolo and Goodwyn found that Katie's facility with signs was not unusual and neither was her language acceleration. The youngsters introduced to Baby Signs started talking and understanding words earlier and at age three were still an average of four and a half months ahead in both. They are currently retesting the children at age seven. The two describe their research in their 1996 book *Baby Signs: How to Talk With Your Baby Before Your Baby Can Talk.*

Some critics were convinced that allowing children to use gestures would *delay* their use of words, assuming they would never make the effort to talk if they could get their needs met by pointing and grunting. Others were sure that the parent's interests and attention were the relevant variable, and not the gestural signs. However, Acredolo and Goodwyn's creation of a control group that encouraged language but did not use gestures proved that the Baby Signs themselves offer a real head start.

Given their findings, what's the benefit of speaking and understanding at an earlier age? "We don't know the long-term consequences for the child," says Goodwyn, "but our goal is not specifically to facilitate language. That certainly is what it does and we're glad. But our primary goal is to help emotionally, to strengthen the parent-infant bond. We're more interested in enriching the parent-child interaction, decreasing frustration, helping day care centers deal with babies that they can't communicate with." In other words, she adds, "We're interested in happier babies."

Continues Acredolo, "When you have a sense that babies can look at the world and pick out things they are interested in, and see how their memory works because they can 'talk' about experiences using Baby Signs, parents develop a new respect for the babies that I think pays off" for the family relationship. The team, in addition to other researchers, is also using Baby Signs as a way to help children whose language skills are delayed for various reasons.

Like many early childhood researchers and just about anyone who spends time with babies and toddlers, Acredolo and Goodwyn have watched what Lewis Carroll called the "dreaming eyes of wonder." "Infancy," they write, "is a time of reveling in the wonders of the world, of discovering how things work, and of sharing with important people the joys and fears that fill each day." Babies are not satisfied with simply staring at an airplane, a bird, or some flowers in awe and curiosity. "They want to *tell* someone about them."

It is clear that a tremendous explosion of dendritic branching underlies the developmental milestones between birth and age two. How parents care for the baby and toddler can help determine the course of that brain development and the child's behavior from animal-like reflexes to walking, talking, and self-awareness. Love, encouragement, a stimulating environment full of places and things to explore, and generous amounts of verbal communication can help a child get the very best start. Here are some specific ideas for enriching a child's earliest environment.

An Enrichment Program for Babies and Toddlers

Because babies under two are so active, curious, and efficient at providing themselves with stimulation, deliberate enrichment at this age is largely a matter of communicating and of providing emotional support, love, encouragement, and opportunities for exploration. This is commonsense stuff, but many parents find it hard to spend the necessary time or are dismayed at the mess that a young child automatically creates while exploring. It's worth the effort.

- Begin by answering these questions to assess the enrichment value of your infant or toddler's physical and social environment.

If you have a one- to two-year-old, have you read books on infant development to learn what behaviors to expect and encourage at the various milestones?

If you have an infant or toddler, do you attend a new parent's support group or club to share experiences and ideas?

Do you allow your young child to explore safe objects and areas of the house and yard?

Does your child spend most waking hours in a baby crib or playpen with roughly the same toys each day?

Do you usually discourage your infant or toddler from making a mess as he or she explores the surroundings?

Do you discourage your young child from crawling to prevent contact with dirt or germs?

Do you think of your young child as having an "empty head," or as having an alert, inquisitive, albeit preverbal intelligence?

Is your child naturally shy, naturally outgoing and adventurous, or somewhere in between?

Do you provide support, love, and praise for your child's basic traits or would you like to change some or most of them?

When your child cries, do you usually hold and comfort him or her until the episode passes, or do you feel children should be discouraged from crying?

Do you make a deliberate effort to give your child love, attention, appropriate physical affection, and consistency?

Do you punish your child with loud threats, slaps, strikes, or long periods of seclusion for being "bad"?

Do you feel adequate to handle the situations that arise in parenting? If not, have you sought help from a social agency or parent-support group?

Do you talk to your young child frequently and encourage his or her attempts at language?

Have you noticed your child using informal gestures that could be reinforced deliberately as Baby Signs?

Do you look through picture books and/or read to him or her daily?

- Within four weeks or so after birth (or perhaps immediately if your child was stimulated prenatally), a baby begins to stay awake for increasingly longer periods and can enjoy visual, tactile, and other kinds of stimulation.

You can stimulate vision with mobiles and posters with strong, clear patterns and, later, with patterns and color.

You can stimulate hearing with soothing music played from a windup box, records, tapes, or CDs.

You can stimulate all the senses by exposing your baby every week or two to interesting objects with different colors, sounds, shapes, textures, and smells. The idea here is not to drill or teach the baby shapes or colors, but simply to entertain her with new experiences. The objects aren't necessarily childproof, so be sure to keep them on a closet shelf and reserve them for parents' demonstration and supervised exploration only.

Your color box might contain large beads (that can't be swallowed), sheets of construction paper, fabric swatches, pictures cut out from magazines, even color chips from paint stores (no chewing allowed!), to show a range of hues, starting with spectral hues then adding subtler shades.

Your texture box might contain a smooth stone, a rough shell, a strip of artificial fur, a piece of leather, a feather, and other objects with distinctive tactile qualities that the baby can touch as you name them.

The smell collection could contain a bottle of perfume, a scented candle, a pinecone, bottles of vanilla, lemon, and almond extract, and other sources of fragrance or pungency. To avoid "odor shock," be sure to hold the source at a distance and waft a small amount of scent toward your baby with your hand, instead of planting it directly beneath his nose.

For a sound box you could collect a small metal clicker, a soft whistle, sandpaper blocks, jingle bells, a small drum, play instruments, and so on. Again, gentle sounds are best to avoid startling the baby, so stand several feet away if you need to.

For shapes, pick balls, cubes, stars, spirals, flat objects, and so on. Show how they move (rolling, sliding, spiraling) as well as what they are called and how they feel.

With a large plastic container and some Ping-Pong balls, you can also demonstrate states like "full," "empty," "in," "on top of," "under," and "upside down."

• When a baby starts crawling, he or she will inevitably find low drawers to pull out, cabinets to open, and wastebaskets to overturn. This can be frustrating and messy—or an opportunity for fun and enrichment.

Dedicate one low drawer to the baby and decorate the front with her name, stars, flower shapes, or other cutouts. Put a few favorite pieces of clothing and small toys in it, then add something new to discover every day or two.

While you are child-proofing all the cabinets, leave one small one unlocked and fill it with plastic containers, wooden spoons, small pots, and other safe, fun objects. Rotate these from time to time and occasionally hide a new object to be discovered.

Designate one small area of the yard—perhaps with a play fence around it—for digging in the dirt or sand. Keep some digging toys there, and a hose nearby. At one exclusive private school near San Francisco, the youngsters are simply hosed off when they get too dirty, are dried with big towels, and then allowed to keep playing!

"NO!" is often a child's favorite word, but the same can be said for many parents. When you say "no" to a child's exploratory drive, is it primarily to keep the child safe and healthy? Or is it usually to spare yourself another mess to clean up? Too many unnecessary "no's" can not only discourage exploration but make a child feel like he is "messy" or "bad" when he is merely doing his job— tasting, touching, smelling, and seeing all the wondrous new things about the world. Some parents redecorate specific rooms so the floors, walls, and furniture are indestructible and easy to clean during the toddler's exploratory years. Even a designated corner with sturdy plastic tarps on the walls and floor can relieve parental stress while giving the child a "mess zone" in which to play.

Consider child-care options where children are allowed to explore openly in a safe, interesting environment. In a recent sociological study, toddlers placed in organized day care centers gained some motor, sensory, and cognitive advantages over toddlers with home baby-sitters because the center care providers had been trained to encourage freer exploration.

• Don't worry about spoiling a child with too much love.

Make contact. Pick up, hug, cuddle, pat, rub, tickle, and invent other new ways to express gentle physical affection.

Comfort a baby whenever she is hurt, frightened, or insecure. Rather then making a perpetual "baby" out of the child, this will create a sense of security and help her to learn to soothe herself.

Read books on child rearing (like those listed below and in the Resource Guide) that help parents differentiate between appropriate and inappropriate responses to various situations. Many of us were raised the old-fashioned "spare the rod, spoil the child" way and need a new model that we didn't ourselves experience. Books can also help you learn what is normal behavior for your child at various ages, so you don't expect tidiness and self-control that aren't possible at given stages. They also inform parents about the milestones the child should be reaching physically, verbally, socially, and emotionally, and what the potential problems might be if the child hasn't reached them. Many communities also offer parent effectiveness courses.

If you have fallen into a pattern of yelling at or striking your children, you can contact one of the organizations listed in the Resource Guide under "child welfare" or read some of the books about young children or about child welfare.

- Starting when your child is born (if not before), create a rich language environment through talking, reading, singing, and gesturing.

  Tell your baby and toddler everything you can think of. Tell her what you are doing. Name everything in her environment. Make up stories. Sing lullabies, kiddie songs, even your favorite opera. In short, bathe your child with spoken language.

  Read to your baby and toddler twenty minutes every day, starting with wordless picture books and graduating to simple readers. The Appendix on page 327 lists the specific books our survey respondents recommended for one- and two-year-old children.

  Babies use gestures as word substitutes, starting at six to eight months of age. Why not expand your baby's repertoire, give him something to feel proud about, and provide a head start on communicating? Linda Acredolo and Susan Goodwyn introduce dozens of signs in *Baby Signs: How to Talk With Your Baby Before Your Baby Can Talk*. They also explain the theory behind the method and give case histories, photos, and exercises.

  Use language to help your child teach herself to see and listen in a more discriminating way. While reading a book to her, point to and name a few extra details. Or with a very familiar passage, stick in a variation like "cat in a vat" or "cat on a mat" and see if she can hear the difference.

  Put large, colorful word labels on furniture and other objects to familiarize your child with written words, and point them out occasionally. Avoid trying to teach or drill them, however.

  Make your language enrichment fun so the child equates learning and communicating with pleasure.

- Surprisingly, some experts suggest that a very young child can learn certain physical activities more easily *before* they begin to walk or run efficiently.

  Many YMCA branches, for example, sponsor swimming lessons to "drown-proof" infants starting as young as eight months old. Because babies make instinctive kicking and paddling movements when placed horizontally in water, moms and tots can take classes together and infants can learn to float to the surface and paddle to the side of the pool. This is especially important for a family with a backyard pool or nearby lake.

In their book *The First Twelve Months of Life*, Frank and Theresa Caplan argue that a toddler with his stiff-legged walk can learn to ice skate more easily than he can learn to run! If properly padded, they say, a very young child can enjoy the mobility and excitement of gliding around on skates while holding the hand of a parent or two. Some parents also find kiddie gym classes to be favorite activities starting as early as age one or two.

- In the enrichment survey we conducted, more than 300 parents responded about the activities of 500 children. Because the families belong to the Lawrence Hall of Science, a children's discovery center on the University of California campus in Berkeley, these adults are clearly concerned about enriching their children's experience and are probably more aware of the cortical growth/stimulation connection than most parents because Hall exhibits and newsletters discuss this topic frequently, and we touched on the highlights of the subject in our survey letter. We asked parents to vote in sixteen different categories for the book; game or toy; model or puzzle; musical instrument; art material; lesson or class; outing or trip; sports equipment; CD, tape, or record; video; and software they found most enriching for their children.

The parents' responses revealed a bias toward simple, classical choices for their one- and two-year-old girls and boys, as the following summaries show. Complete results, including the names of book publishers, toy manufacturers, and so on, appear in the Appendix, beginning on page 330.

Parents consistently voted for time-honored books like
  Goodnight Moon, Little Red Riding Hood, Peter Rabbit, and
  Three Billy Goats Gruff.

They favored games such as hide-and-seek and peekaboo; toys like wooden blocks, stuffed animals, and toy telephones; and large-pieced puzzles of farm and zoo animals and popular cartoon characters.

They preferred toy percussion instruments like cymbals, drums, xylophone, and toy pianos; and classic art materials such as crayons, markers, paper, paints, pencils, and Play-Doh.

Most of the parents who enrolled babies and toddlers in classes chose gymnastics. When they made outings and trips with their very young children, they tended to head for the zoo, for petting farms, or for grandparents' houses.

The sporting equipment they picked for these youngsters included mostly kiddie-cars or bats and balls, especially soft, spongy ones.

There was no consensus on music for tiny children; parents selected CDs, tapes, and records of everything from lullabies to rock artists and movie sound tracks. Videos were more predictable: *Barney, Sesame Street, Winnie the Pooh,* and Disney movies and cartoons.

We were surprised to find parents responding on software for one- and two-year-olds, and wonder whether children this young should spend much time at a computer keyboard. Nevertheless, we list their responses in the Appendix.

Chapter 5

These Become Part of the Child:
Stimulating the Mind in the Preschool Years

> The horizon's edge, the flying sea-crow, the fragrance
> of salt marsh and shore mud,
> These became part of that child who went forth every
> day, and who now goes, and will always go forth
> every day.
>
> —Walt Whitman, *Leaves of Grass*

• In 1994, three-year-old Danny lived in a middle-class neighborhood in Long Beach, California, and attended a parochial preschool near his home. His parents both worked full-time, and placed him in day care when he was less than a year old. This particular school had the standard play materials recommended for two- to five-year-olds: slides, swings, sandboxes, paints, paper, crayons, blocks, puzzles, toys, records—serviceable, but nothing elaborate. Like most young children, Danny loved running, playing, and making things at his school. Then two nice ladies started coming several times each week to teach them songs to sing and to show Danny and a few others how to play notes on a piano. Being adaptable, he loved that too.

This special music program was unusual for a preschool, and it was part of an experiment run by two researchers with an innovative theory: They were convinced that music training for very young children would not only teach singing and instrument-playing, but that it would bolster children's spatial reasoning: their ability, among other things, to fold paper and assemble puzzles in certain ways.

Even before the researchers had finished the study, Danny's teacher was convinced about the technique. She compared the "music kids" chosen at random to receive keyboard and voice lessons with the "nonmusic kids" who went on playing with the school's regular materials. While all preschoolers "are sponges to begin with," she said, "we've already seen big differences [in the music-trained group] in their attention spans, social skills, verbal skills, and how well they retain information." Learning to sing and play music was just a bonus, she said. And all the "music kids"—not just Danny—"absolutely loved it."

• Clara was born in rural North Carolina in the early 1970s to an unwed teenage mother. Children growing up with very young single parents often have marginal diets, few books or playthings, little reinforcement for language development, little attention and guidance, and sometimes outright physical and sexual abuse. Statistics also reveal that children like Clara are at high risk for school failure, truancy, and dropping out before high school graduation, as well as for drug use, delinquency, teenage pregnancy, crime, and dependence on public assistance as adults. Most children born in Clara's neighborhood fit this profile as teenagers and young adults. Clara, however, had a far different outcome: As a preschool child, she attended a special enrichment program designed to change the futures of "at-risk" children, and even to permanently raise their IQ scores. Some observers remain unconvinced that interventions like this have real and lasting effects. But Clara's story is hard to dismiss: in 1995, she finished her graduate work in history, and began a new and very different path from the one she might have had.

• At age five, Skye had yet to start school, but she had been reading books for over two years. She also learned as a toddler how to speak and read some sentences in Japanese and Italian, how to read music and play the violin, how to swim and do gymnastics, and how to work simple arithmetic problems. Skye sounds like a child prodigy, but she isn't. She is one of hundreds of average children whose parents have adopted a set of home-schooling techniques that espouse deliberate enrichment of preschool children—even infants and toddlers—through the use of flash cards and special drills.

Skye's parents, Ellie and Elmer, are dedicated to the idea of "school-proofing" their toddlers—teaching them at home some of the basic subjects like math and reading that many children fail once they enter grade school. Their commitment is so great, in fact, that Ellie quit her career as a business manager to devote full time to enriching both Skye and her two-year-old sister, Kitty. The parents hope their investment of time and effort will pay off in accomplished "Renaissance children" with a wide range of talents and interests. And they take offense at the comments of vocal skeptics who think that instead of helping their children, they are actually robbing them of creativity, self-initiative, and emotional independence.

Preschool Enrichment: An Ongoing Controversy

More has been written about enriching the experience of preschool children than any other age group. Animal studies like those in the Diamond lab prove that the cerebral cortex grows when the environment is sufficiently stimulating, and they inspired researchers to create a number of programs for enriching young children and many experiments (some described here) to test the measurable effects of enriching children.

It's entirely reasonable to think that children in the two-to-five age group might benefit from especially stimulating surroundings and activities. Studies on very young rats and on young children's brain tissue reflected the brain-growth phenomenon. Diamond's team found that in young weaned rats an enriched environment had a mild positive effect on cortical thickness. The more startling effect, however, was the impact of *boredom*: Reduced environmental stimuli had a more powerful effect on cortex-thinning than enhanced stimuli had on cortex thickening. Young rats are obviously very susceptible to losing mental ground when not challenged, and that shrinkage shows up after just four days! And in Arnold Scheibel's study of brain tissue from three-month- to six-year-old children, he found that the dendrites, the "magic trees" that receive incoming nerve signals, continue their fifth- and sixth-order branching throughout this period. Significantly, the neural branches in the left hemisphere grow more and more luxuriantly as the child learns to speak and read new words.

Some people involved in preschool enrichment programs are absolutely certain that deliberate enrichment at this age can increase children's intelligence, improve their educational and life outcomes, and by inference, enlarge their cerebral cortex and mental capacity. Others are less sure that these programs succeed, are safe, and are worth public expenditures. Preschool enrichment is a fascinating story, and you can decide for yourself, based on this chapter, whether it's worth trying. The story starts with the behaviors we see in our high-energy youngsters before their educations officially begin in first grade. It then continues with the events in the developing brain, and how these can explain what we witness day to day.

More Miraculous Milestones

In some ways, the changes we see from ages two to five are less dramatic than the transformation of a tiny, reflexive newborn into a walking, talking, thinking, cuddling, demanding toddler. In preschoolers, walking and running skills become smooth and efficient. A vocabulary of 50 words blooms to perhaps 2,500. Simple thoughts mushroom into towers of fantasy and imagination. And play becomes a vocation, readying the child for ten to twenty years of formal education and free-time pursuits. These developments may be subtler than the baby-to-toddler transition, but they are still exciting. And as Walt Whitman wrote, all the experiences of this age—the color of clouds and sandbars, the smells of the salt marsh and shore mud, the encounters, and adventures of going out into the world for the first time—become part of the child and remain.

From two to three. The appearance of perpetual motion continues in the third year, but developing coordination allows the toddler's wide-set, stiff-legged ambulation to smooth out and to evolve into jumping, climbing, hopping, tricycle riding, and ball kicking and throwing. These abilities far outstrip a child's judgment and self-control between ages two and three, however, and the danger of bumping, falling, and darting in front of cars is ever present. Better hand coordination allows the child to open jars and turn handles, to help get dressed, and to draw or copy lines, circles, and other shapes.

The "terrible twos" still apply at this point, and the adjectives "rebellious" and "obnoxious" spring to some people's minds for the mood swings, tantrums, fears, and anxieties that occasionally overwhelm the child and test the parent's patience and tolerance. Much of this fades by age three, however. By then, the child's vocabulary has broadened to about 900 words and he can verbalize what's bothering him instead of acting out. A lengthening attention span allows him to concentrate on making block towers; molding clay figures; playing with tools, dolls, cloth button-and-buckle books; or listening to rhymes, songs, and stories.

From three to four. Although her self-control and judgment still haven't caught up with her physical skills, the child in her fourth year can now tiptoe, balance on a narrow beam, catch a ball, play tag, operate snub-nosed scissors, build sand castles, and make music on kiddie percussion instruments like the triangle, maracas, bells, or xylophone.

Evidence of problem solving and expanding reason are starting to appear: The three- to four-year-old is developing a sense of time, and a sense of himself as a person with a name, age, address, and family. His vocabulary expands to 1,500 words in this year, his use of grammar is growing, and there is a charming logic to its misapplication ("I eated lunch," "I goed to my room.") Selfishness is giving way to cooperation and sharing, and imagination is so rampant it threatens to overtake reality: This is an age of little fibs, tall tales, and more than half-believing that one really *is* a pilot, a ballerina, a firefighter, or the hunted prey of a fiery dragon under the bed.

From four to five. Motor skills are impressive at this stage: In her fifth year, the child can hop, skip, somersault, dance, and perhaps ride a bike with training wheels, dog-paddle, float on her back, and even ski down a bunny slope. She can also build a structure with Tinkertoys or Legos, solve a simple jigsaw puzzle, work a hand puppet, cut along a line, copy a few letters, and draw a whimsical-looking person.

A four- to five-year-old child can also get bossy and belligerent and be generally hard to deal with. At the same time, however, he can be charming, funny, and talkative, and his vocabulary tends to reach 2,500 words before kindergarten. He can usually count up to thirty or more, name several colors, and understand the meaning of most prepositions (on, in, over, under), and many comparative states (biggest, smallest, tallest). Imagination continues to dominate the four- and five-year-old, including pretend playmates and lively conversations with himself. It is also, however, a social age: Superficial friendships are forged and group activities appeal. And the sense of right and wrong, responsibilities and privileges, grows steadily, based on years of watching and listening to parents.

The Preschooler's Blooming Brain

Neuroscientists would love to have data linking a preschooler's emerging behavior with the precise subregion of the maturing brain that allows each new action. Based on Patricia Goldman-Rakic's work at Yale, experts do know exactly which cells in a monkey's prefrontal cortex must begin firing in order for the young primate (and by inference, a one-year-old child) to find a hidden object in a laboratory test. But this is the best example they have, and it leaves all the child's later milestones more poorly explained. Nevertheless, other, more general measures of brain development allow some educated guesses.

The myelin accumulation we described in Chapter 3—the slow buildup of fatty sheaths around nerves—continues in preschoolers, particularly in the cerebral cortex where myelination goes on until age ten and beyond. As myelin enshrouds each nerve fiber (technically, each axon), electrical impulses can move more quickly and efficiently along each biological "transmission wire." In a growing child, this faster transmission would mean that actions and thoughts become faster, less deliberate, and more automatic. The difference in a child's stiff, wobbly flat-footed walking at age two, and the fluid, heel-to-toe movement of a five-year-old can be credited, in part, to the continued myelination of his nerves.

The young child's explosion of synapses or contact points between nerve-cell branches produces a high density in the visual cortex by age four and in the prefrontal cortex by age ten. The visual cortex is involved directly in vision, of course, but also in visual thoughts and images. Based on this evidence, we think the preschooler's powerful—sometimes runaway—imagination at this age could stem, in part, from the density of synapses in this region. Selective pruning of excess or weak contact points begins in the preschooler's visual cortex, and will continue for half a dozen years. Pruning in the prefrontal cortex won't be in full swing until about age ten, and coincides with a sharpening of language skills, problem solving, and overall intelligence.

The running, playing, chattering preschooler has a supercharged brain, and the measurements Harry Chugani made at Children's Hospital in Detroit of brain cell metabolism in three- and four-year-olds showed that the brain is burning glucose at twice the rate of the adult's brain. Some observers think that this high metabolic rate, supporting the preschooler's overpopulation of synapses, underlies the spongelike, almost effortless learning in children this age.

From his studies at Harvard and elsewhere, Kurt Fischer reports a spurt in head size around age four that seems to coincide with certain other observed changes. Brain-wave measurements by EEG show a dramatic upsurge of activity between ages three and four in two major language regions: Broca's area, which governs speech production, and Wernicke's area, central to understanding speech. This brain-wave activity is reflected in the preschooler's snowballing vocabulary—about 900 words at age three growing to 2,500 to 3,000 before the fifth birthday.

The preschooler also experiences a new level of abstract thought based on what Fischer calls "representational mapping." The child can, for example, invent the personalities for two dolls—one that acts mean, let's say, and another that acts nice—then enact a little scene between them. Some researchers consider this sort of play, emerging around age four, as requiring "theory of mind" skills; that is, the child must have developed an awareness not only of her own mind, but that other people also have minds with memories, knowledge, wishes, and secrets. No one is sure exactly which growing brain regions and connections account for this new awareness of other people's lives of the mind. Robert Thatcher of the University of South Florida, does postulate a big growth spurt around age four to five in the connections between the right and left hemispheres, as reflected in EEG measurements. Perhaps this flowering intracranial "cross-talk," somewhat greater in girls than in boys, helps explain the preschooler's "theory of mind."

At-Risk Enrichment

Fifteen or twenty years before neuroscientists began to link children's burgeoning behaviors with specific phenomena in the brain, psychologists and educators saw this same subject through the lens of intelligence. Many in the field of child development were convinced that a child's early experiences determine her IQ scores to a large extent, and in turn, much of her behavior. The behaviorist tradition was still strong in the early 1960s and it incorporated two basic beliefs: First, that unlike animals, people have no instincts and our behavior and intelligence is unaffected by inheritance. And second, that by changing the educational and social environment, one could radically shift IQ—an indirect but useful measure of mental function. Because there has traditionally been a correlation between lower socioeconomic status, lower-quality schools, and lower IQ scores (as measured by standardized tests) behaviorism spawned a widespread educational movement in the mid 1960s. Funded by Lyndon Johnson's War on Poverty, this movement sought to improve education for disadvantaged students. Many of these so-called "compensatory education" programs were aimed at grade school pupils. There was a conviction in some circles, however, that IQ scores stabilize around age six, and that efforts to bolster intelligence must begin in the preschool years.

In 1965, the best-known of these programs, Head Start, began serving preschool children from economically disadvantaged families. It provided help with language and cognitive skills, nutritious food, medical and social services, and parent training.

Three decades later, the program has reached hundreds of thousands of children, and follow-up studies show that Head Start has improved young people's lives by increasing employment and by reducing rates of school dropout, teen pregnancies, and juvenile delinquency. Most Head Start preschoolers also experience a boost in measured IQ during kindergarten and first grade, but a diminishing of that effect throughout grade school. In their controversial book *The Bell Curve,* authors Richard Herrnstein and Charles Murray facetiously label this "the dreaded 'fade-out.' " (Curiously, their book focuses almost entirely on IQ scores, while passing very lightly over the evidence of vastly improved personal outcomes also documented in the same studies. Further, in 1996, a group of U.C. Berkeley researchers refuted *The Bell Curve*'s main argument that IQ is largely genetically determined and strongly influences adult occupation and earning potential. In fact, the group discovered using their own sociological analyses that America's policies on welfare, housing, taxes, health care, and education help create inferior environments for the poor and these, in turn, lead to diminished IQ.)

The most-often cited intervention for preschoolers is a small-scale experiment that was sponsored by the High/Scope Educational Research Foundation and carried out in the early 1960s at the Perry Preschool in Ypsilanti, Michigan. Child development specialists and social workers taught fifty-eight preschoolers four hours each weekday for two years. Student/teacher ratios were five to one, and IQ scores climbed. As in Head Start, these gains faded by third grade, and the attendees' scores became indistinguishable from neighborhood children who weren't part of the program. Once again, though, follow-up studies years later showed that Perry Preschool graduates stayed in school longer, stayed married longer, earned more money, had fewer arrests, and depended less on social services agencies than neighbors their own age who did not attend the experimental preschool.

Preschool enrichment may or may not permanently alter what we measure as IQ. It clearly changes lives, though. Sometimes the effects take years to show up, and other times they are immediately and dramatically apparent. Social worker Joanne Nurss, writing for *Children Today* magazine, tells the story of a three-year-old who lived with his pregnant mother and younger sister in a shelter for homeless, battered women in Atlanta. When the boy entered the shelter's federally funded preschool, he had a four-phrase repertoire: "No!" "Stop!" "I hate you!" and "Don't touch me!" He refused to participate in activities and was equally and openly hostile to his mother, center caregivers, and the other children. Over the next five months, his vocabulary broadened. He learned to trust his teachers and to participate in games and lessons. He began interacting with other youngsters. And his bitterness changed to enthusiasm.

In one long-running experimental program, the distinction between custodial child care and educational preschool was deliberately blurred. Shortly after child specialists were initiating Head Start and the Perry Preschool program, a group at the University of North Carolina in Chapel Hill had an even more ambitious idea for breaking the cycle of disadvantage: Start children in an enrichment program in early infancy, continue through their preschool years, then go on providing some of them educational support through early grade school. Craig Ramey, James Gallagher, Frances Campbell, Joe Sparling, Isabelle Lewis, Earl Schaefer, and others associated with the University's Frank Graham Porter Child Development Center were involved in the program. Their target population was children at risk of borderline mental retardation and academic failure because of poverty, poor language reinforcement, undereducated parents, and other factors. The Ramey team gave their program the strange moniker "Abecedarian Project" because it means "learning fundamentals, like ABCs."

The Rameys' colleague Frances Campbell, a generous, hospitable woman with a deep Southern accent, recalls the origin of the Abecedarian Project. The team was alarmed, she says, by the frequent application of the term "mental retardation" to children from poor families. "If you looked at most such children," she said in a recent interview, "you couldn't put your finger on anything that was wrong. They didn't have a known syndrome that was associated with retardation. They looked healthy at birth. They were not seen as having problems by their families. But when they entered school, suddenly they couldn't keep up. They were tested and found to have IQs somewhere between 50 and 70, and wound up in special-educational tracks." Based on earlier research, Ramey's team knew that the early experience of children from poor or socially disadvantaged homes "may not support optimal cognitive development" and that the result could be a downward slide toward this low-IQ stigma and removal from mainstream classes. When they designed the Abecedarian Project, they decided to "concentrate on *that* sort of retardation, which accounted for overwhelmingly most of the cases," says Campbell, "to see what could be done about that problem."

Like the other fifty or so babies starting the experimental program at six weeks to six months of age, Clara was picked up each morning, fed, bathed, talked to, and cared for all day, then returned to her mother at night. Another group of about fifty babies of equivalent ages served as the control group; these babies stayed home and received no special enrichment, but their parents got free diapers and baby formula. Some eventually attended other child care programs.

The caregivers at the Frank Graham Porter Center followed an infant curriculum called "Learningames" (a word they coined) designed by Joe Sparling and Isabelle Lewis, also educators at the University of North Carolina. The "learningames" they played with the infants and toddlers helped the children develop language abilities as well as social, self-help, fine-motor, and gross-motor skills. As the children grew to preschool age, they could play in different "interest centers" dedicated to art, building blocks, small play objects, language skills, and special training to help prepare them for reading. Eventually, the children went into public kindergartens and then grade schools. Half the treated children and half of the untreated controls also received visits by home school resource specialists who helped them and their parents in various ways, especially encouraging the whole family's involvement in learning.

Campbell and Ramey tested the Abecedarian children at ages three, eight, twelve, and fifteen and compared the results to the control group of children with no special enrichment. At age three, the Abecedarian children had IQs an average of 16.4 points higher; this declined to 4.5 points higher at age eight, and 4.6 points higher at age fifteen. The reading and math scores of the fifteen-year-old Abecedarians treated in preschool were significantly higher than the control-group children; and fewer

Abecedarian children had been kept back a grade or assigned to special education classes. Most significantly, twice as many of the control-group children were considered "mentally retarded" in grade school as children enriched since infancy. (The students are now over twenty, and an informal follow-up shows that more of the enriched youngsters went on to college.)

Summarizing the overall impact of the experimental program, Campbell says, "It's not huge, but it's there and it doesn't go away. And I think that's important." The Abecedarian study is also significant, she says, because "these children were randomly assigned, so we started with equivalent groups of children." As a result, "we can attribute the differences to our treatment with more confidence."

After the Abecedarian children had gone on to grade school, the research team decided to try another type of early intervention. This time, one group of children would receive only home visits by social workers, who would educate the parents in ways to alter and enrich the home environment and family interactions. A second group would attend the Frank Graham Porter Center and have home visits, and a third group would remain as the untreated control. Interestingly, when the researchers looked at their results a few years later, the children whose parents had been taught to do the enriching at home actually scored *below* the control group in IQ and school achievement. In Campbell's words, "It was not an effective intervention" as their team organized and carried it out. Nevertheless, she says, "what the family does matters a whole lot. You cannot just have a baby and expect that it's going to grow up an intact little kid who's ready to succeed in the big world if you don't help him."

Take a mom, she says, "who says 'Quit it!' 'Stop it!' or even smacks him if he starts to crawl over to the kitchen cabinet and pull out the pots and pans. I think it hurts him very badly right there. Maybe that smack didn't hurt physically, but it hurt his cognitive development." The parenting style called "authoritarian control," adds Campbell, "is linked to lower levels of cognitive function." If the kitchen had been child-proofed for safety but had one cabinet devoted to the child's exploration, says Campbell, the mother could say instead, "Oh, you got the pot! Billy's got the pot! Good boy! What can you do with that? Oh! You're putting clothespins in the pot!" The family has to learn, she concludes, that "if you don't smack a baby's hand when it tries to reach for something, if [instead] you extend his reach, help him to get [the object], praise him for doing it, make new experiences available to him, help him to learn what's out there to be learned, to explore, and get these ideas and constructs into his own little mind, then I think you've given him the foundation he isn't going to lose, to engage in his world the rest of his life. To enjoy learning. And to expect to get something back from doing that."

Family attitudes are clearly crucial. But so is having an effective set of techniques for teaching the infant, toddler, and preschooler. The "Learningames" curriculum that came out of the Abecedarian program is just one example, and is filled with skill-building diversions that require a preschooler's active involvement. Each "learningame" has a rationale. A potato game played with two small spuds, for example, teaches the symbols and concepts of "one" and "two." A game played with lids and blocks gives the child experience in sorting things by color and naming them. And dozens of other games help children learn to make decisions, use grammar, cooperate, share, empathize, and so on.

After nearly thirty years of designing children's enrichments, the Rameys have distilled the "essential daily ingredients" for improving a young child's everyday life. The list is short and it echoes what we suggested earlier for infants and toddlers: Adults must encourage children to explore; show them basic skills; praise their accomplishments; help them practice and expand their skills; protect them from disapproval, teasing, or punishment; and surround them with a "rich and responsive language environment."

Without looking at a child's dendrites and neural connections, no one can say conclusively that enrichment tools like "learningames" and "essential ingredients" alter the course of brain development. Follow-up studies, however, prove that they can affect a ninefold reduction in mild mental retardation among at-risk children. We see this as powerful support for deliberate enrichment and indirect evidence of cerebral growth. Obviously, then, enrichments and interventions should be used for all preschool children, privileged or underprivileged, right? The answer to this depends on the child development expert you consult in the Great Preschool Debate.

Custodial Care, Hothousing, and In-between

Skye, the five-year-old at the start of this chapter who plays the violin, speaks Japanese, works arithmetic problems, reads in two languages, and excels at gymnastics, is the product of the "Better Baby" movement. Her parents read books published by the Better Baby Press, including *How to Teach Your Baby to Read, How to Teach Your Baby Math, How to Give Your Baby Encyclopedic Knowledge,* and *How to Teach Your Baby to Be Physically Superb.* These books have sold hundreds of thousands of copies in the United States and other countries, and the techniques have gotten considerable media attention. Five-year-old Skye is also what many child development professionals call a "hothoused preschooler," a term coined in 1987 by Irving Sigel of the Educational Testing Service in Princeton, New Jersey, and used to refer to a child who is drilled in academic fields such as reading and math long before most children begin such learning in grade school. To Skye, however, her repertoire of subjects is perfectly natural and training in them is the life she's always led: Her mother Ellie began following the Better Baby books when her daughter was just two months old.

As Skye grew and Ellie continued teaching her infant to read, recognize numbers, and absorb what the Better Baby books call "bits of intelligence," she added lessons in "brachiating" or moving hand-over-hand across an overhead, horizontal ladder; swimming lessons starting at six months; instruction in walking a balance beam at one year; and practice in somersaulting. Ellie herself learned Japanese in order to teach Skye to speak and read in another language, and learned to play stringed instruments in order to teach her how to play a tiny Suzuki violin. Before long, she lengthened the list for herself and Skye: French and Italian, running races, handstands, broad jumping, and pirouetting. Skye picked it all up with no effort, she reports, "and *loved* it!"

The "Better Baby" approach is one of the few programs that

promote specific academic skills beginning in infancy, and as such, is one of the most strenuous examples of "hothousing" as child developmentalists use the term. Because the first two years of human life are filled with such natural wonderment and because infants and toddlers are so good at exploring and amusing themselves, many parents see no need to provide special instruction until a child is two and a half or three. Others, however, like Ellie and Elmer, want to use those early years in a more directed way. When the time comes to pick a preschool or child care option, parents discover a spectrum of possibilities. Leslie Rescorla of Bryn Mawr College and colleagues Marion Hyson of the University of Delaware and Kathy Hirsh-Pasek of Temple University discuss these possibilities in their book *Academic Instruction in Early Childhood: Challenge or Pressure?* "Custodial" programs are essentially baby-sitting while the child plays and the caregivers provide encouragement. In a "hothouse" preschool or home setting, they explain, a teacher or parent calls the shots and the child is expected to sit still at least part of the time and practice absorbing words or numbers, memorizing, following instructions, reciting and printing letters, coloring predrawn figures, and using workbooks and flashcards. "In-between" programs tend to balance child-initiated activities with teacher-directed lessons that emphasize hands-on play with blocks, games, puzzles, books, recordings, and activities in art, music, nature, and counting.

For some parents, the "right" preschool experience is unquestionably academic and in a school setting, and is just one step on the path to the right boarding school and the right university. This was caricaturized in a recent box cartoon by a four-year-old character rushing off to school with a briefcase. Other parents want less pressure and more play for their children and deliberately choose intermediate or custodial experiences for preschoolers, whether in school settings, informal child care, or at home.

In the Better Baby materials, parents learn to teach academic subjects at home in a particular way. In the reading course, for example, the parent makes hundreds of large cards bearing words written in big letters. Then, the parent is instructed to sit the child down two to three times a day for a few seconds to minutes and flash these cards past his or her face "very quickly" to avoid boredom. "If you show your child a single card for more than a second you will lose him." As the parent moves each card from the front of the stack to the back, he or she reads off, "Nose." "Spaghetti." "Cucumber." "Petunia." In the math course, the cards hold large red dots and the parent flashes them and calls out, "37." "21." "6." "83." To promote "encyclopedic knowledge," the parent makes sets of cards bearing pictures or magazine cut outs of just about anything: national flags, dog breeds, types of beetles, historical figures, paintings, anatomical parts. Once again, they prop up the infant or child and rapidly run through a stack: "Mauritius." "Portugal." "Nigeria." Or, "Rhinoceros beetle." "Harlequin beetle." "June beetle." "Dung beetle." The Better Baby books warn that the parent and child should be having a "wonderful time" or "you are doing something wrong" and the exercise should stop.

Recently, we watched mothers working on Better Baby materials with their young children. These were casual observations, not a scientific study, but they showed a range of reactions by the children that the child development researchers we consulted considered emblematic: One child seemed excited and engaged by the activities and the other, at least on that afternoon, seemed bored, distracted, and mainly eager to please his mother.

In the first instance, the little boy and his mother were working on math, and sat before the refrigerator door in their kitchen. The woman brought out a box of numbers with magnetized backs, plus two more symbols: the side-pointing arrow heads that signify "greater than" and "less than" in the math world. The mother would stick one of these symbols to the door, and her three-year-old son would then choose numerals and build simple equations like "35 < 72," or "17 > 11." Considering that at age three many children can barely recite the numbers from 1 to 10, this child seemed to have developed a real understanding of numbers, and was delighted by the game of it, giggling and clapping when his mother said, "Yes! 35 *is* less than 72!" or "Okay! 17 *is* greater than 11!"

In the second instance, the mother had pulled out some home-made books with large cut-and-pasted magazine pictures and big hand-lettered words, and sat the child down to "read."

The gaze from the little boy's brown eyes would flicker across the pictures briefly, then wander around the room. Eventually, his mom decided to move on to something more active, and said, "Okay, let's do somersaults!" After rolling forward two or three times on a wide plastic exercise mat, the child stopped and looked up for approval. His mom responded, "Good! Only seventeen more!" and nudged him forward once again. "Come on now, let's go. Okay! Only sixteen more! Only fifteen more!" The day's Better Baby program called for twenty somersaults, morning and afternoon, and so the mother's urging went. After a few minutes and another somersault or two, the child ran off to the corner to grab a toy.

Obviously, some preschool children on some days and in some moods take better to an academic preschool regimen than others. But is specific drilling and training in reading, math, and other disciplines good for a normal, healthy child aged four, three, or younger? And is it the best way to enrich a preschooler's experience and promote his or her healthiest brain development? Several experts in neuroscience and child development offered strong opinions on those issues.

Psychologist Anthony DeCasper, from the University of North Carolina at Greensboro, was not surprised to hear of the young children's divergent reactions to at-home lessons. DeCasper studies fetal learning and is perennially impressed by children's adaptability. Toddlers "will probably adapt to anything you can throw at them," he says, "but whether you would want to or not is another question. Life is long and complicated and has lots of dimensions to it. There is a heck of a lot more to it than being cognitively precocious" at a very young age. "I can imagine that the human variation in responses to these kinds of programs is a bell-shaped curve. The thing you are teaching them is not in and of itself bad; the act is valued by society. You aren't teaching them to be precocious robbers or muggers or anything." But, he continues, "if you've got these toddlers out there memorizing the names of stars and planets or whatever, you can imagine that the effects of that could be relatively more permanent and/or pervasive than they would be otherwise depending on the developmental status of the affected part of the brain."

"I'm sure kids don't think it's weird because it's all they know," he says. "But it's a degree of training and regimentation I'm not personally comfortable with." Resistance such as his, he adds, is not about children learning whatever parents choose to put before them but about "*how* this job is being done. It doesn't set well with the American ideology of freedom of choice, individual freedom, and that whole business. I bet in Japan and Germany, though, there is much less resistance to this approach to rearing a child."

Marion Hyson of the University of Delaware has conducted research confirming that parents' attitudes and actions are central to a child's emotional adjustment to learning at home and school. In a recent study with 125 mothers of four-year-olds, those with what Hyson calls "pro-hothousing" beliefs, i.e., the conviction that academic training is desirable for preschoolers, used significantly more verbal commands, more critical comments, fewer open-ended questions, and exerted more control over their children during at-home instructional activities like making a picture together or assembling a scene with stickers. Not every mother with high expectations brought this kind of pressure to bear, Hyson emphasized, and even " 'laid-back' mothers could be anxious and critical at times." But given the observed correlations between parental expectations and pressures, it is an important caveat that parent and child should be having "a wonderful time," as the Better Baby books state. We wonder how often parents adhere to that standard, however, and even how conscious many are of their approach?

Human brain researcher Arnold Scheibel of UCLA, has been fascinated for decades by the issue of children and enrichment, and takes a very long view of the enterprise. "It seems to me," he says, "that the little mind is hungry for stimulation. We all know parents who are such stern taskmasters of their young people to achieve that it can be negative. But if we exclude that, we think that the young brain, in general, is probably underutilized." At the same time, he says, the demands of the information age may begin to outstrip our average human capabilities. "Maybe what we're expecting is an enormously specialized application of this group of modules up here," he continues, tapping his forehead, "to develop the kind of skills that a highly technologized society seems to demand of everybody. You know, humankind over the centuries has raised itself by its own bootstraps with a fraction of 1 percent of humanity being the one who led the way in the dark in all of this. Then we built the new life to match those insights and raised our own expectations. Aren't we," he sighs, "expecting an awful lot—that the mass of humanity, still hunter-gatherers by brain signature, should be able to do all of this?"

A child neuropsychologist at Harvard Medical School and Children's Hospital in Boston, Jane Holmes Bernstein, also has thought a great deal about hothousing in general and the Better Baby philosophy in particular. "To me," she says with her crisp English accent, "it's a curiously narrow view of education." Children "need the freedom to explore in order to maximize their brain power. It is not maximized by the social group putting stimuli in front of the child." Second, she says, "Brains learn not because they are told that A is A but because they are told that A is A *and* that B is *not* A. A child doesn't learn," she explains, by a parent telling them "This is a cup. This is a cup. This is a cup. But if you say 'This is a cup, but this is a dish,' the brain goes click!"

Like DeCasper, Bernstein thinks that babies and very young children will react individually to flashcards and drilling, some positively, some negatively, but wonders about the long-term effects on any child taught this way. "One of my concerns would be active problem solving as adults," after being in "a very tight school environment [where] people keep giving them information. I would worry about the get-up-and-go component of creative thinking." She also wonders "what their mental health will look like at age thirty." The benefits of drilling small children and infants, she concludes, "is a belief system" that is not supported by scientific data. One of the Better Baby authors, Glenn Doman, responds with his "willingness, and even eagerness" for controlled studies dealing with the benefits of this type of active enrichment in young children.

Psychologist and infant behavior researcher Elizabeth Spelke of Cornell bases her opinion on years of research with infants and young children—she finds it nonsensical to teach certain things to pre-verbal children. "Attempts to train kids in fine number discrimination, for example [distinguishing 59 from 60, let's say] just don't make sense before they have the appropriate level of language" to say and understand the numbers.

To comments like this, Glenn Doman responds, "Suppose we took the same attitude toward speech and said, 'Okay, the kid's not ready to learn language until he's six.' So suppose we all spoke in a tiny voice that the baby couldn't hear. Could you see what would happen? We'd have an illiterate nation. Nobody would learn to talk."

Kurt Fischer of Harvard has been aware of the Better Baby movement for many years, and has this opinion: "I feel like it is actually fairly ineffectual. The research evidence does not support that babies can learn that stuff meaningfully in a way they can build upon." His own research, he says, shows that if a parent tries to force a child's early rapid brain growth, they can be unpleasantly surprised by the outcome. Fischer uses John Stuart Mill as an example: "Mill was reading Latin and Greek when he was a preschooler, and he had a major emotional breakdown in early adulthood that he attributed to this kind of high-pressure childhood."

The biggest critic of early academic training, whether at home or in preschool settings, is surely David Elkind, a professor of child studies at Tufts University. Elkind, in his books *The Hurried Child* and *Miseducation: Preschoolers at Risk*, warns parents and educators about the dangers he sees in teaching academic subjects to young children. Over the short-term, he says, young children stressed by educational pressure tend to show fatigue, decreased appetite, lowered effectiveness at tasks, and psychosomatic ailments. Over the long term, says Elkind, the children can show less interest in learning, less ability to work independently to judge their own progress, and the tendency to worry and compare their intelligence with other children's. As fervently as some parents believe that a child's potential is wasted by letting her play until she reaches school age, David Elkind insists that exposing her to anything other than self-directed activities can be harmful and dangerous.

What's a parent to do?

Here are a couple of things to consider. Education researcher Kathy Hirsh-Pasek at Temple University, set out to study the question of hothousing methodically: What effects do academic pressure really have on a preschooler? She interviewed and tested ninety children ages four to five who attended every sort of pre-school from the babysitting type to the academically oriented, then followed up on their progress after they finished kinder-garten. Hirsh-Pasek found that preschool children sent to aca-demically oriented schools can learn their letters and numbers fairly easily. Other children, however, quickly catch up to their level in kindergarten and erase any discrepancy in performance. In the meantime, academically pressured preschoolers tended to show some performance anxiety, and felt less positive about school after kindergarten than before. What's more, children who attend academic preschools and also happen to have particu-larly hard-driving mothers tended to be slightly less creative than children in nonacademic programs.

As negative as these effects might sound qualitatively, their quantitative degree of risk was "very modest," according to Hirsh-Pasek. She concludes that it's hard to justify choosing an academic preschool on two grounds: First, the benefits are transitory, and second, the child can develop negative feelings about school at an early age.

Also consider this, however. In 1991, the Carnegie Foundation for the Advancement of Teaching asked kindergarten teachers all over the United States whether their pupils are ready to learn the alphabet, numbers, and so on. Depressingly, they replied that *one out of three* incoming kindergartners was *not* prepared to learn the material at that level.

We think there is a balance to be achieved between too much unguided play, leaving a child unprepared to learn academic skills, and too much book-learning too early, leaving them poten-tially less creative and less comfortable in school. And we think it is up to parents to find the right balance for their children.

The National Association for the Education of Young Children (NAEYC) in Washington, D.C., publishes a book on the kinds of learning and teaching they recommend for young children, called *Developmentally Appropriate Practice in Early Childhood Pro-grams Serving Children from Birth Through Age 8.*

For three-year-olds they suggest that adults allow and encourage:

- Play, alone and with friends
- Exploration, indoors and out, with active running, jumping,

chasing, tricycling, or catching balls, and hands-on activities like using construction sets, art materials, puzzles, and so on
- Experimentation with blocks, sand, water, bubbles, seeds, and other objects in the environment
- Language and musical skills through conversation, stories, songs, rhymes, and instruments

For four-year-olds, they expand the list with:

- Field trips to zoos, puppet shows, etc.
- Learning centers in a classroom where a child can choose between puzzles, books, math games, science games, blocks, records, art, and dress-up and dramatic role playing
- Simple problem solving in areas like math, science, social studies, and health; using tools, wood, water, measuring devices, clay, blocks, cooking ingredients, and so on
- More development of language, music, and art abilities through hearing and looking at stories and poems, playacting, drawing, copying letters, singing, and playing instruments

For five-year-olds, NAEYC continues to recommend time for playing, burning off energy and practicing hand skills. But they also introduce the notion of theme learning: taking a topic of interest to local children, say the ocean in coastal towns, or the prairie in midwestern schools, then working reading, writing, math, science, social studies, art, and music activities around this topic.

The great preschool debate will no doubt continue in academic circles. In the meantime, parents must decide:

- Whether they want the intense stimulation of flash-card-style programs for preverbal infants, toddlers, and preschoolers
- How important they feel it is for their preschool child to continue playing freely until kindergarten
- Whether they place a high priority on teaching their preschooler to read, write, and work math problems before entering school
- Whether they are willing to risk what some see as "harmful pressure" to set their child on an early academic path

- Conversely, whether they are willing to risk what others see as "wasted potential" if they don't challenge their child early and fully enough
- Whether a middle-of-the-road option like the kind of guided play the NAEYC recommends appeals to them or seems too bland

Perhaps the ideas in the rest of this chapter will help you achieve a comfortable balance given your own priorities and your child's interests, intelligence, and abilities. One thing to keep in mind is that every choice—even indecision or inaction—has an impact. The environment exerts a strong shaping influence on the young brain, and his or her sensations, mental stimulation, and experiences all become part of the preschool child.

Language and the Preschooler

Most babies begin saying individual words at nine to twelve months, and then slowly build up a vocabulary of about fifty words by fifteen to twenty months. This number fifty seems to represent a critical mass for Baby-Speak, and touches off a veritable language A-bomb. After learning the first fifty words, the child starts accumulating fifty new words *every week or so* and continues at this astonishing pace throughout most of grade school. As the words pile up, the toddler starts stringing them into two-word phrases, then three-, and for a while, they continue to sound like encoded telegrams: "Bernie want apple." "Where Barney?"

A second language explosion—this one involving grammar—detonates around age three, just when the word piles and word strings threaten to become impossibly tangled without some rules for word order, tense, endings, connectors, and so on. Grammar, writes M.I.T. linguist Steven Pinker in *The Language Instinct*, allows a person to sort out the meaning (or its absence) in word groupings. "If either the girl eats ice cream or the girl eats candy, then the boy eats hot dogs," would make no sense without grammar, he says. Neither would "A unicorn that is eating a flower is in the garden."

The ability to pick up grammar appears to be both speedy and innate. By age three, the preschooler is starting to get words into meaningful order—"Why is he leaving?" The verb tenses, Pinker continues, may continue to be a bit rough: "I'm gonna full Angela's bucket." By the time children have reached four, writes Rutgers University psychologist Karin Stromswold, "The vast majority of their utterances are completely grammatical." Even more surprisingly, the children she studied picked up the different aspects of grammar in virtually *the same order* (unaware, of course, of either the linguistic rules or their esoteric labels like "datives" and "preposition-stranding constructions").

Linguists offer even more startling evidence to prove that grammar is both innate and is preprogrammed to appear spontaneously around preschool age and then to become extremely difficult if not impossible to learn after a certain age. Pinker provides a powerful example in the case of a woman with average intelligence who was born deaf in a rural area of California, yet was misdiagnosed as retarded instead of hearing-impaired. Her parents schooled her neither in American Sign Language nor English. Her plight was finally discovered when she was thirty-two, and the woman was fitted for hearing aids. Following a lifetime of silence, she underwent an intensive period of language training, and she was able to pick up two thousand words. She was, however, completely unable to apply any of the grammar linguists tried to teach her in adulthood. She continues to use her vocabulary in sentences like "Banana the eat," "Orange Tim car in," and "The woman is bus the going." Apparently, because she learned no language at all as a youngster, her innate grammar capacity slipped away unused and eventually was irretrievable.

A second example language researchers offer as proof of our innate grammar capacity in childhood is a rare condition called "hyperlexia." In it, a child born mentally retarded nevertheless develops the language capacity of a very bright youngster. Children with a particular type of hyperlexia called Williams syndrome have IQ scores in the 40 to 50 range. Nevertheless, as Pinker explains in *The Language Instinct*, they amass large vocabularies, including words like "ibex," "pteranodon," "remembrance," and "evacuate," and speak in complex, grammatically correct sentences.

Karin Stromswold offers yet another example of the innate nature of human grammar. Parents, she says, may think that by correcting their children's tenses and prepositions, they are playing a crucial role in their youngster's grammatical development. Yet the Rutgers psychologist has studied a four-year-old who disproves this assumption. The boy can say only a handful of words due to an impairment in his brain's speech production area. He can, however, hear and understand thousands of words, and can easily distinguish between a grammatical sentence like "What can Cookie Monster eat?" and one like "What Cookie Monster can eat?" without ever having made his own grammatical errors in speech and having had them corrected.

Linguists like Steven Pinker think humans have grammar genes that are programmed to turn on around age three much the way the genes for permanent teeth rev up around age six. In a similar way, the human ability to acquire grammar may have a specific window of opportunity during brain development. A child who misses out on informal exposure to grammar through other people's talking, reading, signing, or singing will eventually lose the ability to speak grammatically even though he or she can go on absorbing new vocabulary words indefinitely.

To add to this argument, psychologist Elissa Newport at the University of Rochester studied a group of deaf people and the ages at which they were first exposed to language. Infants exposed to American Sign Language starting immediately after being diagnosed as deaf achieved higher fluency in the language than deaf children first exposed at age six. They, in turn, were more proficient signers than deaf teenagers first exposed after age twelve.

Newport and colleague Jacqueline Johnson at the University of Virginia in Charlottesville saw a strikingly similar phenomenon when they looked at how people learn a second language. They studied Korean and Chinese immigrants to the United States who began learning English at various ages between three and thirty-nine. Each immigrant took an English grammar test, and the researchers discovered that the scores depended not on *how long* the subjects had been speaking English, but on *how early in life* they arrived in America: Those who started picking up the language at ages three to seven eventually spoke like natives, with good use of grammar and no detectible accent. If they arrived between ages eleven and fifteen, immigrants achieved only half that proficiency. And if they started learning English after age seventeen, they achieved only one-third.

Whether first language or second, it's obvious that beginning in preschool, there's no time to waste and only ground to lose by missing language exposure during the window of opportunity. Support for this also comes from the sad cases of neurologically normal children who grew up in impoverished and abusive environments that left them deprived of all companionship and, hence, of normal speech. Out of nine well-documented histories of "feral" children, the six children who learned to speak fairly normally after their rescues were all age seven or younger.

What, then, is exposure to the sounds, words, and grammar of a language *doing* in children under age seven? The answer is sculpting the brain by preferentially reinforcing connections within and between certain neural circuits, mainly in the left hemisphere. Helen Neville at the University of Oregon used a type of brain wave recording called event-related potentials or ERPs to learn about where and when language processes arise in the brain. She and her colleagues found that in twenty-month-old toddlers, the more words they knew, the more activity was centered in the left hemisphere. They also found in older children that regular vocabulary words (nouns, verbs, and adjectives) stimulated ERP brain waves in the rear areas of both hemispheres, while grammar words (articles, conjunctions, auxiliaries) stimulated ERPs only *in front of the left temple.* In four-year-olds, the rear of the brain still responds equally to both vocabulary words and grammar words. By eleven years of age, however, only the area around the front left temple fires off ERPs when encountering grammar. This means that the older the children and the more language they have heard in their environment and learned to speak themselves, the more altered the brain becomes, and the more neural circuits are pruned into a left-hemisphere pattern of specialization for grammar. Feral children and deaf children deprived of language stimulation between ages four and seven or eight don't show this brain "sidedness" and also never catch up completely to children their own age who weren't deprived of language.

Parents deciding how to stimulate and educate their preschoolers can take note of these findings as well as take heart: If progressing normally, a preschool child doesn't need special language lessons in order to learn to speak fluently and develop normally. He or she just needs an extension of the same rich language environment required as a toddler—to hear a daily diet of conversations, songs, stories, and rhymes, and to be listened and responded to when speaking. If a child has hearing or language difficulties, however, these should be addressed as early as possible. Says Helen Neville, "If you are the parent of a deaf child, do not delay exposure to the phonology [accent] or grammar of a language. If a child is profoundly deaf, American Sign Language is probably going to be easier than English; he can learn it easily and at the normal age for acquisition. Then he can use his ASL skills to learn English later."

Some parents of deaf children, says Neville, spend years looking for ways to encourage the child to speak English. If this is unsuccessful, as is often the case, an entire elementary education can pass by and the child won't be conversant in any language. Worse still, Neville adds, his or her ability to acquire one will be increasingly hindered as the window of opportunity closes in the brain. "Grammar and phonology are two subsystems of language that suffer enormously with delayed exposure. We don't know why," she says, "but kids below the age of puberty are little language acquisition devices. And after that time, it's really hard." But the good news, she adds, is that once the accent and grammar are in place, people can continue to expand their vocabularies throughout life.

An Early Ear for Music

To Danny, the three-year-old from Long Beach, California, whose story led this chapter, learning to sing and play notes on a Yamaha keyboard were just two more ways of having fun at his preschool. But to Gordon Shaw, a curly-gray-haired, exceedingly cheerful particle physicist from the University of California at Irvine, Danny's lessons were doing something bigger: helping to prove that the mind has an inherent neural language—a language that can be accessed through music and can promote a child's brain development.

This preschool music experiment had a strangely circuitous conception: Several years ago, Shaw heard a lecture on how neural messages are transmitted in the brain. It reminded him of certain aspects of physics, and inspired him to create a theory for how the cerebral cortex organizes impulses into patterns. For most of us, his ten-page mathematical construction, dubbed the trion model, needs a major English translation into something simple like: The neurons in the brain have certain natural firing patterns that act as an internal neural language. These patterns can be mapped and also altered through learning and experience.

While working on the trion model, Shaw and his colleagues happened to encounter a wizard of computer music who gave the mathematic equations a "voice" and a "face." On a computer monitor, the patterns look like brightly colored strips of Native American beadwork with geometric patterns that continually shift and change. And they sound a bit like Mozart. Because the patterns are spatial-temporal (they change in space over time), Shaw made the breathtaking intuitive leap that listening to Mozart might stimulate a person's spatial-temporal reasoning—the cerebral function lurking beneath our ability to mentally rotate and manipulate objects in space.

Shaw and colleague Frances Rauscher set up a three-part test of that intuition. They assembled thirty-six college students, and in the test's first part, played them ten minutes of Mozart's Sonata for Two Pianos in D Major, K. 448. This they followed with an IQ test of their spatial-temporal reasoning. A typical question on this test pictured paper being folded in a particular pattern and then cut and notched while still folded. The student then had to unfold the paper mentally and predict what the geometric "snowflake" pattern would look like with notches and holes in the proper places. For part two of the experiment, Shaw's group assembled the same students, played them ten minutes of a self-hypnosis relaxation tape, and then administered another spatial-temporal IQ test with equivalent but different questions. For the last part of the experiment, the students sat in silence for ten minutes, then took the IQ test for spatial reasoning. The results earned headlines all over the world: Listening to Mozart bumped up the student's spatial-temporal IQ by an average of 8 to 9 points! The architectural genius, however, quickly faded, lasting only about as long as the musical interlude itself.

Now came the final twists in the winding path from trion model to preschoolers and music lessons. Shaw was aware of brain development studies showing that certain abilities, such as acquiring grammar and seeing out of both eyes, had critical periods beginning at a young age. He also knew from work in the enrichment lab at U.C. Berkeley that an animal must *participate* in an enrichment activity for growth to be stimulated in the cortex—just watching won't work. Finally, Shaw knew that Mozart started composing at the age of four, and guessed that the pint-sized prodigy was drawing on his inherent neural firing patterns—his brain's built-in electrical language—to create original music at such a tender age. From the mixture of these notions, seasoned with evidence of the college students' short-term gain in IQ scores, Shaw concocted another experimental design: to teach preschoolers singing and keyboard lessons, then test to see if the experiences bolstered their spatial-temporal reasoning for short or long periods.

Shaw's colleague Rauscher, an accomplished cellist with a doctoral degree in psychology, is herself the product of music training starting in preschool. The two appeared on a classical music radio station in Orange County, California, appealing for preschool volunteers. The principals of several schools called in, and eventually Shaw and Rauscher whittled the list down to the school in Long Beach which three-year-old Danny attended, another school in a middle-class section of West Covina, and a third in a low-income area of Santa Ana. During the 1993–94 school year, two professional piano teachers and one vocal instructor visited the three preschools daily. In all, twenty-two children ages three to four and a half received keyboard training and group singing lessons, while a control group of fifteen children the same ages experienced the identical preschool activities minus the music.

When Shaw and Rauscher tested the children on various tasks including puzzle assembly, an element from the Stanford-Binet

IQ test, they found that the music-trained youngsters were significantly better at spatial-temporal reasoning than their classmates without music lessons. They tested the same children a few days after the program had ended, and found that the boost to spatial-temporal IQ scores persisted long-term in the music-trained children (memory researchers define "long-term" as more than one day).

Gordon Shaw had ideas for other applications of the "Mozart effect": He wanted to see if preschool computer lessons would confer the same IQ-raising advantages as music lessons. A study completed in 1996 showed that of three groups taught either singing, keyboard, or computer skills, only those practicing piano keyboard improved in spatial-temporal reasoning. Second, Shaw is testing the critical-period concept by starting the music lessons in kindergarten and first grade, not preschool. He wants to see if a permanent jump can still occur in spatial-temporal reasoning at ages five and six, or if that's the province of younger brains only, and after preschool, the benefits are short-lived, as in adults. Finally, he'd like to see if Mozart would also benefit chess players: Big Blue beware!

In the meantime, what's the readout for parents trying to select a level of preschool enrichment for their child? Says Shaw, "Get those kids some music training! There are no bad side effects. That's what's really nice about it."

We agree with Shaw's enthusiasm, but would modify it somewhat. Get those preschoolers some music experiences *that emphasize fun, not simply performance and competition.* The benefits for both a lifetime musical foundation and increased spatial-temporal IQ scores are available even without undue pressure, so any lessons at this age should emphasize enjoyment.

Closing the Preschool Math Gap

An impressive and very natural number gap lies between the typical four-year-old preschooler and the typical six-year-old entering first grade. For decades, this gap has been the focus of child development specialist Robbie Case at Stanford University in Palo Alto, California. At four, a child can count the objects in a pile—say, the number of dry kidney beans in a small heap. Or if you show that same young child a pile of four beans and another pile of five, then ask, "Which is more?" she can count the objects and identify the bigger group. But, Case explains, if you don't show any beans and simply ask, "Which is more, four or five?" you're as likely to get a wrong answer as a right one; in other words, the child will guess. A four-year-old can obviously count, but her mind has not yet integrated the words *four, five,* and *six* with the corresponding sequences of quantities. At age six, on the other hand, a child can do this with ease; by then, says Case, counting and quantities are hooked up together in the brain.

You can prove the number gap in other ways. If you show a stack of two $1 bills and one $10 bill to children ages four and six, and ask, "Which is worth more?" the preschooler will go for the bigger pile while the first grader will confidently pick the bigger denomination. Or show the same children two simple circle faces, each with an identical ambiguous expression, one sitting next to a picture of four stuffed toys and the other a picture of five stuffed toys. Then ask, "Who's happier at this birthday party?" The preschooler will go by her interpretation of the facial expression, while the older child will rely on the number of toys.

The math gap between ages four and six, according to Case, is based on the child's "central conceptual structures" for numbers. This is a fancy way of labeling the mental framework the child uses to compare numbers. The typical preschooler has a simple qualitative framework: He knows "a lot" from "a little," "heavy" from "light," and "up" from "down," but can't place values on the shades in between. By first grade, however, the typical six-year-old has a mental number line superimposed on the concepts of "a lot" and "a little"; "a little" might be number 1 in the line, the quantities probably go up in increments of 1, and "a lot" could be 10 or 20 or 100 at the other end of the line. By age six, then, the child could confidently answer questions like, "If you had four chocolates and I gave you three, how many would you have?" or "What number comes two numbers after seven?" or "Which number is closer to five, six or two?" Robbie Case pictures the six-year-old child going off to first grade and, like a water-skier with a tow rope in hand, "popping up" on the force of his mental image of a number line and "gliding across" addition, subtraction, and the rest of math in school.

"Math skiing" is usually true for middle-income children. But as it turns out, there is a second number gap between rich and poor with roots in preschool and potential consequences all the way through a child's education. Studies by Robbie Case and Sharon Griffin in Massachusetts and California confirmed what other researchers have seen in Canada, Europe, and other places: A child's understanding of math tends to vary with socioeconomic level, and it is poorer in inner-city areas.

In one study, Case and Griffin compared first graders whose families live very close to the campus of Stanford University, an expensive private institution in Palo Alto, California, with children the same age living not far away in an economically depressed community. On the question "Which is bigger, five or four?" 97.6 percent of those living near Stanford answered correctly, while in the poorest neighborhoods, only one-quarter got the problem right. Likewise, on the "If you have four chocolates" problem, 70.7 percent of six-year-olds near Stanford answered "seven," the correct response, while only 7.4 percent of children living one mile away could give that right answer. Six-year-olds coming into the public schools with a poor level of math understanding can seldom pop up and glide across math, and instead, will more likely be pulled along, face first, until they eventually let go of the rope.

Case and Griffin created a series of games they call the "Rightstart Program" to deliberately teach four- and five-year-olds the relationship of numerals to words, of numbers to quantities, and of the quantities in a number line so that the children would enter first grade with the appropriate mental framework for understanding math. One of the games, which children can play in groups of four or five, is nothing more than a long narrow board with squares labeled from one to ten. They take turns rolling dice and moving colored game pieces up the number line the indicated number of places. The first child to reach 10 can pour imaginary water on a fire-breathing dragon to put his fire out.

After just twenty hours of playing the Rightstart games, inner-city preschoolers showed *a year's gain* on tests of numerical under-standing, and the gains stayed with them at least through first grade. As simple as it seems, the presence of board games in a child's home is a good predictor of math competence in school. They become part of the child as he or she goes on in grade school and applies math to everyday life. The parent looking for simple ways to enrich a child's mental development for math can stock up on numerical board games (see suggestions below) and occasionally play them as a family at home or on vacation. But the take-home message from Case's work points to *math readiness*—not drilling on addition and multiplication tables—as the way to promote a preschool child's healthy mental development.

Helping preschoolers become ready for grade school skills in reading, writing, and other academic areas is, in fact, the general consensus and is what educators mean by "developmentally appropriate learning." Teaching those specific skills to two-, three-, or four-year-olds is more controversial and can create pressure and anxiety unless the child is precocious enough—and some are—to ask for help with learning to read, work math problems, or play the violin. For enrichment ideas with all this in mind, read on.

An Enrichment Program for Preschool Children

The preschooler's world lies somewhere between the toddler's perpetual wonderment and exploration and the grade-schooler's classes, hobbies, and activities outside the home. The basics—walking, running, talking, understanding words, feeding and dressing—no longer take the child's full concentration. There is room now for imagination, creativity, friendships, and acquiring more complicated skills. If encouraged, the preschooler still generates a lot of her own enrichment. But parents and teachers can help by presenting new challenges and new territory—physical and mental—to explore. The experiences between ages two and five become part of the child, figuratively and literally, as the brain continues its phenomenal metabolism and growth.

- A good starting place is assessing the potential enrichment value of your preschooler's environment:

  If you have a preschool-aged child, do you read parenting magazines or books on what to expect at ages three through five and how best to respond?

  Do you have a support group of other parents with preschoolers?

  Do you know what a preschooler's emotional needs are and how best to fill them?

  If your child attends a preschool, is it a custodial or baby-sitting type, an academically oriented type, or in between? Have you spent time there to see how avidly the children are engaging in its activities?

  Do your preschool and at-home environments fulfill the guidelines of the National Association for the Education of Young Children (page 168)? How about our guidelines for an enriched environment?

  Do you read to your preschooler daily, and look for other ways to support language skills?

  Does your child have toy instruments, records, a radio and/or other forms of music to play and listen to?

  Does your child's preschool or kindergarten teach music? Is there a way to encourage it?

  Do you know what the appropriate developmental levels are for math skills, and where your child stands along that continuum?

  Do you have number-oriented board games at home that children can play?

- Although many of the brain regions responsible for emotion are fairly well-developed by age three, a child needs continued encouragement and emotional support in these years before grade school begins (and of course, throughout life). Just like the infant and toddler, the preschooler needs:

  Regular verbal expressions of love

  Frequent physical contact and cuddling

  Respect and praise for her accomplishments (based on what's appropriate for her age level)

Freedom from harsh criticism, punishment, or teasing
Continued encouragement for exploring and tolerance of
   the occasional mess it creates
Comfort when he is hurt or afraid
As much freedom from stress or pressure as possible.

Since many young children spend time away from the home at day care centers or preschools, parents must be mindful to meet their emotional needs despite having less time together.

- Young children need practice learning to share, empathize, and build other social skills. Providing supervised playtime with children outside the immediate family circle is, at once, both essential and enriching.
- Since youngsters have such active imaginations, the preschool years offer a major opportunity for encouraging inventiveness and the lifelong creativity into which it can blossom. Parents sometimes inadvertently damage their children's development by misunderstanding and discouraging two perfectly normal phenomena: a child's imaginary friendships and her private (although often audible) conversations with herself.

Fantasy friends are common in three- and four-year-olds, and reflect both emotional needs, a healthy effort to fill them, and the product of flowering imagination. Yale University child psychologist Jerome Singer writes that preschoolers with imaginary playmates are "more independent, cooperative with teachers and peers, generally happier, and less aggressive than their peers, and have a richer vocabulary." Fantasy friends are a window into the child's concerns, and sometimes offer a way for them to talk indirectly about uncomfortable things. Parents are advised to accept the "friend" as a natural outlet, but not to try taking it over or controlling it.

In preschoolers as well as in grade school children, "private speech," or talking to themselves, can be more common than conversing with others. Psychologists estimate that one fifth to three fifths of all the remarks children make are "private speech." Parents sometimes see this muttering as back talk or a sign of instability. In fact, though, from ages four to six, children speak out loud to themselves more and more frequently, and it helps them initiate deliberate behavior, acquire skills, and work through unfamiliar situations. Private speech becomes quieter and more internalized by age ten, but for most of us, it never goes away entirely, and reappears throughout adulthood whenever circumstances are strange or particularly demanding. Parents and teachers who understand the utility and normalcy of private speech will be less likely to discourage a child from chattering away to him- or herself, with all its benefits.

Adults can encourage, rather than discourage, imagination and creativity by avoiding judgments and criticisms when the child paints a cubist rendition of the family dog, say, or turns a piece of scrap lumber and the vacuum cleaner into a "lunar lander." Honoring the child's imaginative efforts—if not their products—will kindle more creative activity and a love of the creative process, not just an interest in laudable end results. Parents who pursue creative activities of their own are also encouraging their children by example.

When it comes to providing toys and activities for young children, there is, in general, an inverse relationship between the specificity and elaborateness of a toy and its ability to excite the imagination. A cast-off cardboard box can become a dollhouse, a puppet stage, a school, or an alien planet. Discarded buttons, glue, yarn, string, paper, and paints can become the characters that inhabit these sets. Tools for exploring—a magnifying glass, an old tape recorder, a map—can open doors in the mind, as can the artifacts of make-believe: costumes and props made of discarded hats, shoes, scarves, magazine cutouts, poster board, more empty boxes. The more pressure a parent puts on a child to produce something specific—whether it's a puppet that looks like Rudolf the Reindeer or an "A" for handwriting—the harder it is for the child to express creativity and imagination. Many of the toys, puzzles, and games parents suggested on our survey of preschool enrichment (see Appendix) reflect this emphasis on basic themes for open-ended play. The Resource Guide also includes several books about learning-oriented play for preschoolers.

- The preschooler needs a rich language environment—conversing, singing, being read to, and, if the child wants to learn how, reading itself. Some children can pick up reading just by following along as you read to them again and again from the same simple books such as those our survey respondents suggest (see Appendix). But there are also guides to teaching your child to read, like those listed in our Resource Guide. The key is to wait until the child wants to learn, to avoid pressure, and to make the experience fun. And if you are using an early reading (or math) program, be sure to use short sessions rather than long immersions, and to make these lessons just one small part of a well-balanced enrichment program. Some preschool children like computers, and may find a CD-ROM such as *Reader Rabbit's Ready for Letters* (Learning Company) enjoyable.

- Some parents wonder when their children should learn foreign languages, and as this chapter shows, it makes little sense to wait until high school to introduce a new language, as do so many school districts; students' brains are already on the gradual language-acquisition downslope beginning around age seven. New research employing PET scans of the brain also shows that it takes a little extra mental effort to speak a second or third language, even when a child began learning it early and acquired complete fluency. We interpret these results to mean that subsequent languages represent a special form of brain stimulation. Obviously, the learning materials must be very simple. Packages like the Berlitz "Aladdin" series, for example, in Spanish, French, and German, contain books and tapes for children. Having a bilingual playmate to practice with also helps, and the children's sections of most libraries and large bookstores stock favorite children's titles translated into foreign languages.

- Parents who want their children to "pop up" and "glide across" arithmetic once they start first grade can help their children get ready for math in ways that are both fun and challenging. Board games that are specifically aimed at preschoolers and that foster an understanding of numbers include Number Game, and My First Counting Game (both by Ravensburger) and Fun with Sums (Learning World). At least one recent book addresses preschool math: *Math for the Very Young*, by Lydia Polonsky, Dorothy Freedman, Susan Lesher, and Kate Monison (John Wiley and Sons, 1995). And another excellent resource is *Family Math*, a guide published by the University of California. *Family Math* contains one hundred games for children from ages five to twelve (although three- and four-year-olds could play some of the simplest ones). Parents can gather the household materials needed for the games—paper, colored pens or pencils, scissors, dry beans, buttons, and so on—and make simple game boards based on the book's printed patterns. They can then read directions to small children and/or show them how to play the games. Older children can set up and learn to play the more complicated games on their own. Some young children also enjoy math games on CD-ROM, such as *Math Rabbit* (Learning Company) or *Millie's Math House* (Edmark).
- Young children love making music (or what passes for it) and listening to others do it for them. If you can find a way to provide simple, fun music lessons that emphasize process, not simply progress, you may be able to stimulate the musical-processing portions of the brain as well as the child's spatial-temporal reasoning. But reminders like "Did you practice your flute?" or "No TV until you finish your piano," are best left for elementary school children. Foot-dragging at ages three to five usually means the child is not ready or not interested, and the best remedy is to drop the lessons and return to singing, listening, and free-form music-making with one of the many available percussion toys (more on this below).
- While toddlers are usually too young to appreciate outings and trips, preschoolers often like them, and in urban areas, there are a range of children's venues. In the San Francisco

area, a large population center, a one-week period in July offered this smorgasbord of possibilities: a play at a children's theater, Japanese storytelling, a magic show, a circus workshop, a puppet show, a children's fair, story reading at several libraries, and a teddy bear picnic. And then there are the year-round exhibits and activities at several hands-on science and nature centers, aquariums, zoos, children's art museums, a planetarium, children's symphony performances, several arboretums and botanical gardens, a marine mammal center, and more than one observatory. Older children absorb different things from outings to the same places, so destinations are good for many return visits.

- In general, we're not sanguine about long stints in front of the television because, as we'll see in the next chapter, it is a classically passive way to spend time, substituting for more active mental and physical pursuits. Nevertheless, an hour of educational television or the occasional video can be a respite from more active pursuits.

- Experts view long periods in front of a computer screen as potentially harmful for young children. We'll talk about children and computers in our next chapter, as well. In the meantime, our survey did turn up some educational CD-ROMs and computer programs that parents considered enriching for preschoolers when used in moderation.

- Here is a summary of the "votes" we collected from parents on the most enriching books, games, toys, models, puzzles, musical instruments, art materials, lessons and classes, outings and trips, sports equipment, musical recordings, videos, and software, for children from three to five years old. General trends are indicated here, with the information for girls' and boys' enrichment tools listed together. See the Appendix for more detailed resources separated by age, sex, and category.

As they did for their infants and toddlers, parents found classic stories like *Charlotte's Web, The Three Little Pigs,* and *Treasure Island* to be most enriching for preschool children. They also favored books about words, numbers

and counting, how things work and move, and what
people do.

Parents found surprisingly familiar games and toys to be
most enriching for their young children: action figures;
dolls and dollhouses; stuffed animals; dress-up clothes;
card games; toy cars, trucks, and trains; dominoes,
marbles, and tiddleywinks; and time-tested board games
such as Candyland, Clue, Bingo, Go Fish, Sorry,
Monopoly Junior, Checkers, and Chutes and Ladders.

The adults in our survey found various styles of models and
puzzles to enrich their preschooler's experience. In the
three-dimension category, they voted most often for
Tinkertoys, Lincoln Logs, Legos, Triazzle, and scaled-
down human skeletons. They thought their young
children benefited from tabletop and giant floor puzzles
with a wide range of subjects, from the alphabet and
animals to trains, places, planets, maps and globes, and
familiar story characters like Snoopy, Madeline, and the
animals in *The Lion King.*

Our list of most-enriching musical instruments for three- to
five-year-olds leans heavily toward choices that require
little or no instruction: kazoo, slide whistle, harmonica,
xylophone, maracas, tambourine, ukulele. However,
parents voted for a number of serious instruments, as
well: guitar, piano, electronic keyboard, flute, recorder,
violin.

The parents in our survey provided their young children
with a range of simple art materials: paints, paper,
markers, glue, clay, pens, pencils, safety scissors, chalk
and chalkboard. They reported that their children also
benefited from making dough, collages, puppets, masks,
potato prints, and loom weavings.

Parents enrolled their preschoolers in hobby classes (crafts,
cooking, gardening, woodworking); in active classes and
lessons (swimming, gymnastics, dance, ice-skating, karate,
skiing, horseback riding, bowling); and in more academic
ones (second languages, art, music, science, math,
reading, writing, and computers).

The stimulating outings and trips in our survey included venues similar to those for infants and toddlers—zoos, petting farms, grandparents' house—but went much farther afield, as well, to hands-on museums, nature preserves, amusement parks, campgrounds, and trips to other cities, states, and countries.

Young children are an active lot, and their parents' votes for the most enriching sports equipment reflect that overflowing energy: Balls of all types from soft to hard and small to large were most popular. Next came climbing ropes and structures, then bicycles, skates, skis, swimming gear, and racquets.

Preschoolers like to listen to a wide spectrum of recorded sounds, and our survey parents found stimulating selections across this whole range: sound tracks and show tunes; ethnic and rock music; rhymes, stories, and books on tape; children's sing-along songs; and classical music aimed at youngsters, including *Peter and the Wolf, Mr. Bach Comes to Call,* and *Beethoven Lives Upstairs.*

Most votes for enriching videos fell into two categories: individual classics like *Cinderella, The Sound of Music,* or *The Wizard of Oz*; and popular video series by Sesame Street, Disney, Dr. Seuss, National Geographic, Magic School Bus, Land Before Time, and There Goes A . . .

Although there are hundreds of software packages aimed primarily at entertaining young children, the parents in our survey tended to favor educational software as the most enriching for their preschoolers. Examples include *Dr. Seuss ABCs, Bailey's Book House, Reader Rabbit,* and *Kid Pix.* The full list of software "votes," as well as the detailed responses in all the above categories, appears in the Appendix, page 330.

Chapter 6

Letting the Future In:
The Power of Experience in Middle Childhood

There is always one moment in childhood when the
door opens and lets the future in.
—Graham Greene, *The Power and the Glory*

• At age four, Juliette started attending a preschool gymnastics
class her mother found for her near their home in Michigan. She
learned somersaults, cartwheels, and walking on a low balance
beam, and looked forward to learning more. At age six, Juliette's
mother, Martha, would drive her to a private gymnastics club
where she learned stunts on the parallel bars and flips, spins, and
vaults on the floor mats. At age nine, Juliette's coach took Martha
aside and confided his Olympic aspirations for the child. At age
eleven, Juliette was practicing gymnastics three to four hours
each day after school, and more on the weekends. At age thirteen, she tried out for the Olympic gymnastic team, but didn't
make it. At age fifteen, she again fell short by a few points. At age
sixteen, she slipped while doing a back flip on the balance beam
and crushed a vertebra in her back. After twelve years, she was
forced to "retire" from gymnastics. In the meantime, Juliette had
fallen behind in several school subjects. Her mother got her a
tutor, and she graduated with her class, but her grades were not
high enough to go to college, and she didn't really like studying.
At age eighteen, she took a job at the scarf counter of a large
department store. She was still working there three years later,
trying to sort out her plans for the future.
  • Shawn is at once both as ordinary and as appealing as a

fourth grader can be. The son of a secretary and a hardware store manager, this chubby brunet attends elementary school in a Nebraska suburb, goes to church school on Sundays, and likes to play softball with his dad. Shawn likes his fourth grade teacher, too, but has never been good at reading, and with some embarrassment, must go to a separate classroom every afternoon for remedial reading lessons. He is not very excited about math, either, but he does his homework in front of television each night while his mom cooks dinner. Sometimes a friend comes over and they play Nintendo. But mostly, Shawn watches his three or four favorite nightly TV shows, and makes as many raids as he can get away with on the kitchen cupboard and refrigerator.

• Amber had many interests in grade school—she liked to read, she liked swimming and horseback riding, and she loved science. Her parents wanted her to pursue whatever her interests might be, but they particularly encouraged her love of science and math, since her mother was a chemist and her father a computer programmer. Amber attended a good school in a community dominated by a large university, but she still faced a roadblock if she wanted to follow in her parents' footsteps: In the United States, a girl's chances are extremely small of excelling at math and science in school, then going on to college training and a career in a technical field. Girls have no absence of innate ability; many studies have proven that. But of every 3 million girls entering grade school, only 1 million still like math and science at the end of seventh grade, and only 10,000 will ever get an advanced degree in a technical subject. Of those 10,000, nearly all will pursue some aspect of medicine or psychology. For minority students, whether male or female, the odds become even more remote. There is very little encouragement for girls and minorities to study science. As a result, their chance for sharpening analytical and quantitative brain circuits, as well as for enjoying many types of careers, is greatly reduced.

Luckily for Amber, she grew up near a hands-on science center with after-school classes and clubs. Once or twice a week, she and a friend who also loved science would go to the center and build robots, play on computers, test rats in mazes, and work with teachers who made science and math both fun and accessible. In high school, Amber did well in all her subjects, and in college, she was one of a handful of women who majored in physics and applied mathematics. Today, Amber has passed through the eye of the educational needle: She is finishing a doctorate in computer science. She hasn't given up her other interests, however, and would like to find a way to apply her knowledge of computers to social concerns, including the problems of women and minorities in science.

Middle Years: The Opening Door

In some ways, a child's middle years from ages six to twelve are quieter and less eventful than the preceding baby and early childhood stages—with their dramatic brain growth and behavioral development—and the tumultuous adolescent years with their physical growth spurts and sexual maturation.

In the first thirty months of life, the brain triples in size, enlarging from one-quarter of its adult weight to three-quarters. Between ages two-and-a-half and ten, the brain grows only another 15 percent, reaching 90 percent of adult weight. Growth spurts during the eleventh and fifteenth years then complete the brain's weight gain. The cerebral cortex, of course, that living bark packed with dendritic trees, can go on thickening or thinning for eight or nine more decades, depending on continued mental stimulation or its absence. But more on that later.

The elementary school years may be characterized by subtle, prolonged change and less dramatic development than in infants, toddlers, and preschoolers. But those middle years are nevertheless a crucial bridge from home to school; from dependence to growing independence; from magical thinking to logic, reasoning, and problem solving; from small stature and physical immaturity to the threshold of sexuality; from few skills and activities to many talents; from undefined interests to a unique blend of accomplishments that may well open doors to the future. The abilities we develop in middle to late childhood—proficiency in soccer or tennis or ice-skating, or in self-expression, in constructing things, in working math problems, or all of these—tend to become the framework upon which we hang our later vocations and avocations. While we continue to learn new skills throughout life, there is a developmental state of grace surrounding the preadolescent as neural circuits are sculpted and pruned: The six- to twelve-year-old gains experience and competence in a wide range of endeavors with far less effort than it would take to learn those skills in adulthood.

The cognitive, physical, emotional, and social progress of these years may be less obvious and more gradual than in earlier periods, but viewed through a longer lens, the child's evolution is impressive. He will make the transition to full days of school, and will learn the reading, writing, and arithmetic that form the basics of most subsequent academics. He will start getting his permanent teeth, and increasing physical coordination and control will allow him to walk backward, ride a two-wheel bike, and tie knots. Her imagination will continue to flourish, but she will enter the realm of reason, manipulating ideas and symbols mentally to arrive at solutions rather than needing to touch or move objects literally to work through and solve problems. Her conscience is still in its infancy, but a sense of fairness, ethics, and responsibility will grow steadily, and, points out Marguerite Kelly in *The Mother's Almanac II*, an interest in friendships will intensify (although this year's "best friends" may not be next year's). Self-awareness will mount steadily in the middle years, along with the ability to concentrate and pay fuller attention.

For both boys and girls, conformity in dress and behavior is uppermost, yet despite "dying" to look and act alike, self-motivation, individuality, and competence are on the upswing. Each child develops his or her own set of passions and interests: collecting baseball cards, horse figurines, or dolls in foreign dress; reading comic books, mysteries, or adventures; sewing or tap dancing, playing basketball or video games, learning karate or cooking; excelling at multiplication and division or at reading aloud. Preteen boys and girls share an appetite for food, a curiosity about sex, and often, an overindulgence in television. But a small gap opens between the sexes based on the girls' earlier maturation. On average, American girls usually begin the first stages of puberty around ten-and-a-half (although onset can be somewhat earlier or three to four years later and still within normal

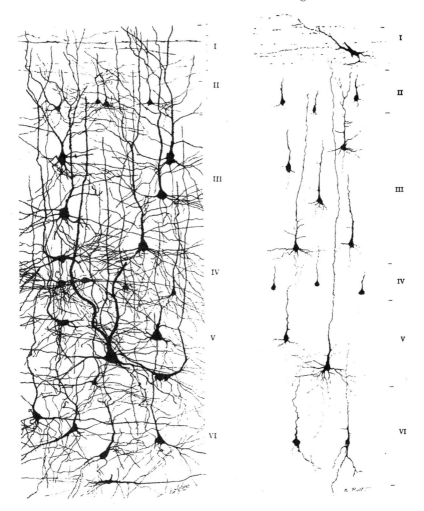

At six years of age (left), a child's neural forests already show some of the pruning that comes with age, experience, and physical maturation. Nevertheless, the dendrites are longer, branchier, and more spine-studded than in a two-year-old, and this expansion can continue throughout life with appropriate stimulation.

range). By age eleven, the average girl will reach 90 percent of adult height and half of adult weight, and begin a growth spurt that continues until one year after menstruation starts, around age twelve. Boys, on the other hand, reach only 80 percent of adult height by age eleven, and the start of their growth spurt is delayed until age thirteen to fourteen. Although preteens hate to stand out or be different, a room full of seventh graders can hold four-footers and six-footers, with varying degrees of sexual maturation, and all still within the bounds of normal development.

The mental, physical, emotional, and social development of the middle years requires brain growth and the bootstrapping effects of experience. These lead to more branching of the neural tree limbs (dendrites), more stabilizing of well-used circuits and connections between neural branches (synapses), and more selective elimination of underused neural networks.

If the brain is stimulated, dendritic branching and growth continue throughout the child's middle years, according to Peter Huttenlocher at the University of Chicago. At the same time, though, excess synaptic connections are more and more heavily weeded. In the visual region of the cerebral cortex, pruning begins at age one and is complete by age ten; in the frontal cortex, more central to thought and self-control, weeding begins in earnest around age seven and continues through adolescence.

Measurements of brain cell activity based on the cell's use of glucose support the idea that a dramatic pruning of weak or unused connections begins in the middle years. Harry Chugani at Children's Hospital of Michigan in Detroit, finds that the brain's metabolic activity peaks around age two, then burns sugar at a high rate until ages eight to ten. At that time, sugar use declines steadily until, at age sixteen to eighteen, it "bottoms out" at adult rates. Chugani thinks the brain of a two- to ten-year-old must burn more cellular fuel to support the huge forests of branching neurons, each with their 10,000 branches synapsing on 50,000 others. Only when the unused connections are pruned away and the cells have smaller "forests" to encompass and support does the fuel-burning slow. But with that pruning and lessened activity, says Chugani, goes some of the brain's plasticity. This is reflected in its slowly fading ability to recover from brain surgery or other traumas without major deficits, and its capacity to absorb grammar and other kinds of information, which we'll get to later.

Kurt Fischer, the well-known child development researcher at Harvard's Graduate School of Education, likes to emphasize the *cooperation* of brain regions and circuits as well as the *competition* between them to be strengthened and selected rather than pruned away. Two brain growth spurts he has documented around ages six to seven and eleven to twelve appear to be associated, Fischer says, with emerging mental capacities. Earlier growth spurts at seven months or at two years, for example, coincided with newfound abilities to track a ball with the eyes and grab it with the hands, or to pretend a doll is walking across the table and to say "Doll walk." At age seven years, a child can, for the first time, make up a scenario in which she assigns one doll to act both nice and mean to a second doll, and the second doll to act in both ways back to the first. The child, in other words, is relating several ideas to each other in her head at the same time. Likewise, along with the brain growth spurt around age eleven comes a new ability for abstract thinking. The child judges her interacting dolls by their "nice" or "mean" intentions rather than their activities. Or she comes, for the first time, to understand the concepts of "honesty" or "arithmetic."

Robert Thatcher, another researcher trying to make sense of how the growing brain evolves new abilities, created the model of traveling waves of growth factor involving first the left hemisphere every five years then the center and the right. Thatcher sees the brain as fairly quiescent and balanced at the start of a cycle—at ages five and ten, for example. He thinks the brain then experiences more growth on one side than the other in the intervening years based on the waves of growth factor. And as his colleague Harriet Hanlon found, the rates of brain growth and the areas of activity are different in boys and girls. Intriguingly, Marguerite Kelly calls seven (a growth spurt year) an "age of reason" tinged with a "patina of sadness." And she calls eleven, the other grade school growth spurt for the brain, "not a vintage year." There is more than coincidence at work here; based on the evidence for brain growth spurts, we think a child's "off year" could very well coincide with major events in brain development.

Kurt Fischer agrees with Thatcher on the notion of a brain growth cycle but thinks it may start with the right hemisphere rather than the left. Regardless, he points out that when neuroscientists take EEG readings of electrical patterns in a child's developing brain, it doesn't matter whether the test subject is asked to read, speak, think, or move his hands, 90 percent of the time connections between the frontal cortex and other brain areas will "light up." Two Dutch researchers found the same high activity in the frontal lobes and their connections while making hundreds of EEG measurements on children ages five to twelve. In one study, they asked five- to eleven-year-old boys to push a button with their left hand when they heard a noise in their left ear, to use the opposite hand when they heard a tone in the right ear, and to refrain from button pushing when the tone sounded in both ears simultaneously. In another study, seven- to nine-year-old girls pushed a button when one or another phrase they had memorized came up on a screen among a series of phrases. The tricky part was waiting for the correct phrase to come up in the *correct color*—red for half of the girls and green for the other half—instead of signaling every time the phrases appeared.

The Dutch team found that the older a child, the faster he or she could respond to tasks like these and the more control he or she would have over spontaneously pressing the button at the wrong stimulus. To the researchers, this kind of control—so-called inhibitory control—was practically synonymous with brain development. And the seat of this inhibitory control is the frontal cortex. The older a child grows, and the more control pathways develop in the frontal cortex, the better able he or she will be to pay attention to one thing selectively, to stay focused on one task, and to keep irrelevant details from intruding. We are certainly more than the sum of our ripening frontal lobes, but many aspects of intelligence—judgment, rationality, mental organization, perseverance—depend on them.

Growing Intelligences

Sometimes a child's special talents are easy to spot from an early age: At eighteen months, Jonathan was taller, stronger, and more coordinated than any child his age in the day care center. Neither his father, a former college football player, nor his mother, a one-time high school basketball champion, were surprised by Jonathan's physical prowess, but he was, in fact, quite exceptional. Most children's individual mixture of capabilities and interests, above average or below, begin to show in their middle years. A teacher, other children, or the parents will notice that this particular son or daughter can carry a tune extraordi-

narily well, or draw realistically, or create a working windmill with
erector-set parts and an electric motor.

In the last two decades, it has become clear to many parents and educators that the traditional IQ test—a test that focuses
heavily on verbal and math ability and leaves other mental
strengths unappreciated—is a woefully poor measure of the many
facets of a child's talent or proficiency. In 1983, Harvard educator
Howard Gardner published *Frames of Mind*, in which he outlined
seven kinds of intelligence. The work has gotten enormous notoriety
and acceptance in part because it confirms our commonsense observations. Each of us can know the world, Gardner says, through
capacities for language, for logic and mathematics, for spatial
representation, for music, for movement, for understanding
others, and for understanding ourselves. Recently, he proposed
an eighth form of intelligence: the capacity to understand and
appreciate nature. Within ten years of Gardner's publication, a
significant percentage of educators had adopted the theory of
multiple intelligences as a foundation for teaching and assessing
children and planning elementary school curricula. Virtually
every child is good in at least one of these areas, and can be
praised for it even if his strengths are not in reading or arithmetic. A school program based on many domains of intellect can
also help children get practice in their weaker areas, whatever
they may be, and develop and discover talents in new realms.

Gardner's theory is one good way to consider out-of-school enrichment efforts as well as those in-school. The facts and ideas that
follow can help you not only assess a grade school child's abilities,
but also think through strategies for enriching the brain during
what is, in many ways, the high point in the brain's development.

Language. Critical period. Sensitive period. Window of opportunity. Whatever you choose to call it, there is a golden age for
acquiring proficiency in speaking, understanding, reading, and
writing that can—but should never be—wasted and can guide
important choices for children and parents. As earlier chapters
discussed, a fetus is receptive to language in the womb, and from
birth to age seven or eight, a normal child seems to absorb
grammar and vocabulary by osmosis: The more exposure to conversation, books, rhymes, poems, stories, and plays, the more the
left hemisphere (in most children) specializes in receiving and

producing words, and the thicker grows the speech areas of the cerebral cortex.

One can actually predict the rate at which the language window slides slowly down. Jacqueline Johnson of the University of Virginia in Charlottesville, and Elissa Newport of the University of Rochester, made a careful study of several dozen immigrants to the United States and their study of English as a second language. Newcomers that arrived and started learning English between ages three and seven scored as high on a language test as native English speakers. Those arriving between ages eight and ten scored an average of 15 points or 21 percent below native speakers; those arriving between ages eleven and fifteen scored an average of 35 points or 50 percent lower; and those arriving at age seventeen or older scored an average of 60 points or 86 percent below the typical person born in America. That steeply descending curve would apply to learning a first language as well as a second language: The cases we saw in earlier chapters of feral children and hearing-impaired youngsters prevented from learning to speak or sign are a poignant demonstration of this principle.

In his book *Seeing Voices*, physician Oliver Sacks writes about two bright children named Joseph and Charlotte who were both born deaf but whose stories were dramatically different based on the closing language window. Joseph entered a school for the deaf at age eleven, unable to sign, speak, or understand anything but pantomime. He had been misdiagnosed as retarded and autistic, and his parents had made little serious effort to educate him. Joseph could draw and appreciate the humor of cartoons, he was a whiz at tic-tac-toe, and he was physically strong and coordinated. But, writes Sacks, "he seemed completely literal—unable to judge images or hypotheses or possibilities, unable to enter an imaginative or figurative realm." A person, continues Sacks, "is not mindless or mentally deficient without language," but is "severely restricted in the range of his thoughts, confined, in effect, to an immediate small world." In his new school, Joseph was hungry to learn, but a considerable chunk of his childhood brain development was already complete—most of the myelination and accumulation of brain weight, most of the period of exuberant synaptic connectivity, and most of the years of revved-up metabolic activity. Without language, his feelings and experiences were limited to the immediate, and many of his neural circuits would have been dismantled or permanently devoted to those tangible, real-time sensations and reactions. Based on the Johnson-Newport scale, his eventual language development would be significantly reduced over what it might have been with earlier training.

Charlotte, a six-year-old first grader, had gotten that earlier start. At ten months of age she was diagnosed as profoundly deaf, and her parents immediately began to learn sign language and to teach it to her. Her older hearing brother, still a young child when he started to learn sign with the family, became completely fluent, as did Charlotte. One of the brightest children in her school, Charlotte was reading well above her grade level, and her mother remarked on her "complex conceptual thought processes," and her use of language "to build complicated ideas."

What's at stake in early exposure to a rich language environment is clearly more than just a big vocabulary or articulateness or speed reading; it is the structuring of the brain's entire cognitive mechanism and the levels at which the child, and later the adult, will interact with and understand the world. As brain researcher Helen Neville of the University of Oregon has stated, it is imperative for the one out of each one thousand American babies that are born deaf each year (as well as the tens of thousands born with hearing impairments) to receive the earliest possible access to language or risk missing the window of fullest brain development from birth to age seven or eight. There is, however, an even larger group of children with language-learning difficulties that may benefit from some innovative new treatment approaches.

For 3 to 6 percent of American children—some 7 million—learning to understand, speak, and read is painfully hard, despite normal hearing, vision, intelligence, and motor skills. These children have a syndrome called language-learning impairment (LLI), and the top expert on the subject is surely Paula Tallal of Rutgers University in New Brunswick, New Jersey. Normal six- to twelve-month-old English-speaking babies can differentiate the phonemes or component sounds of the language they hear—say, the "ba" and "da" sounds of English. Children with the LLI impairment experience a *500 percent delay* in the time it takes to distinguish basic sounds like "ba" and "da." This delay wreaks havoc with hearing and interpreting words, and the LLI children are often unable to understand or say even simple phrases. In school, 80 percent of them also have great difficulty learning to read. Tallal, in fact, thinks the 15 percent or nearly 20 million American children classified as "dyslexic" may actually have the identical or at least a similar underlying delay in differentiating phonemes. While some researchers dispute this idea, Tallal speculates that chronic middle ear infections during the first year or two of life may prevent children from imprinting the "ba," "da," and other language sounds they hear at home.

Working with Michael Merzenich of the University of California at San Francisco's medical school, and other colleagues in California and New Jersey, Tallal created a series of video games and audiotapes to help correct the children's hearing delay. Just as eyeglasses correct vision by changing the signal to the eye and brain, Tallal's games and tapes act as "ear glasses" that alter words electronically to slow down and emphasize the sounds LLI children find difficult to decipher. Over time, the "ear glasses" challenge and gradually train the brain to interpret sounds more quickly. Tallal's team tested twenty-two children with LLI, each about seven years old but with the language skills of a four-and-a-half-year-old. After one month of playing the video games and listening to tapes of "stretched speech" several hours each day, the experimental group had gained two years of language proficiency, and were operating at the six-and-a-half-year level, just six months behind other seven-year-olds. Unlike eyeglasses, these aural techniques made a seemingly permanent correction: The effects remained after several months with no further training. Tallal and Merzenich are planning to test dyslexic children with their video games and tapes, and hope it will help them, as well.

In the meantime, the implications are unmistakable: Children should get treatment for language-learning problems as early as possible. And where learning is normal, children in the middle years should have access to books (to read and listen to), to ballads, poems, and all manner of the spoken and written word. Parents and teachers should act as if their brain development depends on it. It does.

Math. Just as babies are born with a knack for learning how words fit together in sentences, they apparently come into the world understanding simple addition and subtraction at some intuitive level, as Karen Wynn's experiments with the Mickey Mouse dolls seen earlier demonstrate. There is also good evidence that infants have an innate sense of logic. This is exhibited in the one-year-old's ability to collect a stack of like objects from a pool of unlike ones (red and blue X's, for example, from a mixture of colored shapes) and the fifteen-month-old's ability to collect all red X's in one set and all blue X's in another. Logic continues to develop throughout childhood, according to psychologist Jonas Langer of the University of California at Berkeley, becoming more complex between ages four and eight yet remaining concrete, then becoming formal and symbolic between ages eleven and fourteen.

With such innate talent for numbers and logic, one might expect every child to rank high on tests of this intelligence form. Yet we know that many children have trouble with math in school and that only a minority shine in math class, solving problems in their heads faster than most of their classmates can work them on paper. The last chapter gave one explanation for the divergence in math performance that starts to appear in first grade: Many preschool children have had too little basic experience at home with counting, quantities, number lines, and so on, to "get" arithmetic when they reach elementary school. There is, however, still more to the disparity between math-smart kids and everyone else.

Rochel Gelman, an education researcher and professor at U.C.L.A., has documented a natural watershed for children and mathematics beginning with the introduction of fractions. "Kids all over the world have trouble with fractions, and with the mathematics and algebra that follow," she says. "You've got a connected set of learning tasks" that can act like dominoes, collapsing and failing in turn, "and that force us to try to figure out how to get that kind of learning off the ground." Grade school children who are gifted in math "seem to be very good at finding patterns in noise," Gelman explains, "and in helping themselves create some framework" that can support new facts and concepts. When they reach fractions, which are not a natural extension of the number line and counting, she says, gifted children "are probably able to see that they are outside the framework, or at least that there are enough cases that don't fit" to start working on a new framework. Another way to say this is that gifted kids "will give up something that's working and move toward something that produces errors and stay at it long enough for the mind to notice that something's got to change." Since they are old enough to read and ask the teacher for more information, they can then construct a new way of understanding numbers that includes fractions or decimals or algebra or whatever they are presented with.

Neither Amber, the girl who liked math and science in grade school, nor her teachers would have classified the youngster as a math genius with a special gift for numbers or logic. Nevertheless, her science-oriented parents played number and counting games with Amber and her brother at home, and from first grade on, she did well in arithmetic. Despite this proficiency, she still faced much steeper odds than a boy of similar ability if she wanted to pursue math-based subjects as an academic interest and someday a career: Of all the scientists and engineers employed in the United States, only 16 percent are women and only 6 percent are minorities. Observers of science education describe the educational pipeline as "leaking women" between seventh grade and graduate school.

There are several explanations for this "leakage": Math, especially trigonometry, calculus, and other forms of higher mathematics, have traditionally been considered masculine territory, not feminine, and girls are not encouraged to explore them. As a result, they often lack the confidence to take these courses in high school. This, in turn, leaves them less prepared to pursue science and math in college. Many girls and women also see science and math careers as difficult, time-consuming, and incompatible with motherhood, and in fact, women in these fields are much less likely than men to be parents. For example, nearly 40 percent of women chemists over fifty years old are childless, compared to 9 percent of male chemists over fifty. Finally, many girls find math and science classes dry, boring, and not people-oriented, and although they may still like technical subjects, they like other areas more and tend to gravitate toward them.

Amber had two things going for her besides her math and science aptitude: She drew confidence from her parents' strong support, especially her mother's (a recent Wellesley College study emphasizes how crucial that is for a girl's continued success in technical fields). Second, Amber had years of enrichment at the Lawrence Hall of Science, the children's science center on the Berkeley campus. On Mondays after school, Amber would take horseback riding lessons, and on Saturday afternoons, swimming. But at least once a week, Amber's mother or a friend's would take the two girls to Lawrence Hall for classes, programs, and "just messing around with stuff." Amber grew so familiar and comfortable with the facts and concepts of science (as well as unfazed by its male-dominated culture) that she plunged right in to all the math and science courses she could take in junior high and high school. She didn't earn an A in every class—just most of them. Later, as a postdoctoral candidate at Columbia University in New York, she devoted time each week to advising women and minority students about courses and careers in her field. "I seriously considered quitting science," she recalls, "until I found a group of women in physics who met to support each other and a professor who really encouraged me. I still have feelings sometimes of not fitting in, but I want to pass along support to others to help them hang in there like I did."

Spatial intelligence. Virtually everyone has some degree of spatial intelligence—the ability to slide, rotate, or flip imagined objects over in the mind. To get an armchair through a doorway and around a corner, for example, you need to picture its shape and which way to turn it *before* you pick it up. Even animals can reason spatially. One researcher in this field, for instance, reports a telling incident he noticed while watching a German shepherd playing fetch with its owner. Getting a bit rambunctious, the young man threw a long stick over the backyard fence, and the dog bounded up and immediately stuck his head through an opening where a fence slat had fallen off. The dog grabbed the stick horizontally, jerked backward, and one instant before the stick would have rammed the fence and knocked out a few teeth, the dog rotated his head 90 degrees and pulled his prize neatly through the hole in the vertical direction. We'll never know whether the dog's foresight was conscious and internally verbal— "Don't slam the stick into the fence, you meathead!" But, writes the researcher, "Might [there] not have been a preparatory mental rotation of the stick?" A rotation, we could add, similar to the one that lets you picture this whole episode as you read.

Children show this form of intelligence as soon as they start building block towers or putting together puzzles and turning knobs to open doors. But some children go on to fashion castles and dinosaurs out of Lego blocks, or to create original doll costumes, or draw realistic-looking houses inhabited by three-dimensional people. Youngsters with spatial genius often go on to become architects, sculptors, engineers, graphic designers, painters—even neuroanatomists.

It may be difficult to turn a two-dimensional thinker into a spatial whiz, but as we saw in the last chapter, Gordon Shaw and Frances Rauscher in Southern California discovered that Mozart tapes and music lessons can improve a child's or adult's ability to rotate objects in the mind. And as in all things, practice is bound to help. We know a San Francisco architect who had an art tutor in kindergarten teaching him simple perspective drawing. He probably had keen spatial abilities to start with, or his parents would never have noticed his better-than-average doodling and arranged the lessons for him. But the doodling experience itself, at first unguided and then schooled in finer technique, enriched his cortex and fed his spatial intelligence still further.

Grade school children can take part in dozens of fun spatial activities: Climbing on safe, supervised jungle gyms. Designing and building bird- or doghouses. Making papier-mâché masks and puppet heads. Decorating a room or a Christmas tree. Cutting out paper patterns and sewing from them. Practicing origami. Working three-dimensional jigsaw puzzles. Building models. Sculpting clay. Shaping bread or cookie dough. Making potato, wood, fish, cabbage, or linoleum block prints. Even helping parents fix the sprinkler system or miter the baseboard molding or redesign the kitchen. Spatial intelligence is one of the most tangible, practical mental abilities, and one of the many ways for a child to have fun and, at the same time, open a door and let the future in.

Music. Elementary school is traditionally the time most children start music lessons, either at school or with a private teacher, and this is an ideal time according to a group called the National

Coalition for Music Education, made up of music teachers, recording artists, and music retailers. Piano lessons, they say, can start as soon as the child is big enough to sit at the instrument and concentrate—usually ages five to eight. Instruction in Suzuki-style string instruments scaled down from one-half to one-sixteenth size can begin earlier, but for full-sized violins, violas, and so on, they recommend starting no later than ages nine to ten. Lessons on wind and percussion instruments, again, depend on the child's size and ability to concentrate, but, they say, should start no later than age ten or eleven. Are these timetables merely self-serving, coming as they do from the music industry? Or is there a window of opportunity for music as well as language?

Two recent and fascinating studies suggest there is more to this issue than building the largest buying audience. A group of brain researchers from Dusseldorf, Germany, recently tracked down the brain region responsible for perfect pitch—the ability to identify an A-sharp, B-flat, or any other particular note simply by hearing it and not by comparing it to surrounding notes on a scale. Neurologists used to consider music to be processed mainly in the brain's right hemisphere, but the researchers found the seat of perfect pitch in the *left* hemisphere in a region called the planum temporale, which is involved in speech. Perfect pitch may be centered there, one neurologist speculates, because the musician must make a verbal association "to label the tone and say, 'This is middle C. . . .' " But here is the telling part of the study: Using MRI, the German team looked at the planum temporale in thirty nonmusicians and in thirty professional musicians, eleven with perfect pitch and nineteen without. In the musicians with perfect pitch, the planum temporale was twice as big as in either the nonmusicians or the musicians lacking perfect pitch. In this study and several others, 95 percent of musicians with perfect pitch started music lessons before age seven. According to this study, it seems that early music training is associated with more growth in this one particular brain region—and with it, a handy skill. If, on the other hand, training starts later or is absent altogether, perfect pitch rarely shows up.

A second study, by Edward Taub at the University of Alabama and four German colleagues, found that stringed instrument players have a larger area of the cerebral cortex devoted to moving and sensing the fingers of the left hand (which play the notes) than devoted to the right hand (which moves the bow). The nonmusicians they studied had no such variation. Significantly, the differential was much greater for string players who started playing their instruments before age thirteen. After that age, there was almost no difference between their brain representations and those of nonmusicians. Concludes an editorial in *Director,* a magazine published by United Musical Instruments U.S.A., Inc., "If a student of any instrument aspires to be a virtuoso, the chances of succeeding are likely to be far greater if study begins before age thirteen."

Harry Chugani, the Michigan medical researcher who makes sophisticated measurements of children's brain cell activity, tells a personal anecdote to confirm this conclusion about the window for music opportunity. Chugani's daughter started taking piano lessons at age four or five, and, he says, "I decided to start taking lessons with her, and I was starting from scratch." He and his daughter "went to the same teacher, and practiced the same amount. But," he continues, "she made much faster progress than I did. She made good progress; mine was miserable." In time, his daughter shifted to saxophone and voice lessons, and by age twelve, he muses, "she was getting into Italian operas." Chugani got too busy to continue the lessons after a while, and hasn't returned to the instrument for over two years. "When I sit down at the piano now, I am bad! I'm bad at it! I have rapidly lost what I learned." But if children studied then stopped for the same length of time, he says, "They'd be better when they sat down to play."

Unfortunately, fewer children are starting music lessons at any age today, and the National Coalition for Music Education reports that the percentage of high school students taking music classes has dropped by a third since 1950. Cutbacks in school funding combined with flagging church attendance and interest in church choirs has meant that students come to college music departments "with less and less background and a lower proficiency. Many come here," says student affairs officer Bruce Alexander at the University of California at Berkeley, "almost tone deaf and don't know how to perceive notes and scales correctly. It will take them a semester to learn a scale, whereas many students can learn a scale in a week in grammar school."

While far more proof exists for a language critical period than for a musical window in the mind, the general implications are the same: Elementary school is prime time for learning to sing or play an instrument. A child's musical intelligence quotient may be naturally average or low, but experience with music—as long as it is stimulating and fun—can help open the door to future music appreciation.

Physical skills. Juliette, the girl-gymnast at the start of this chapter, had what Howard Gardner might call kinesthetic genius. From an early age, she displayed the balance, coordination, strength, and grace to perform at a high level in her favorite sport. The amount of time she spent practicing in this one intellectual domain, however, created a time imbalance that led some other areas to remain underdeveloped. (We talk about the issue of balancing enrichments in a later section.) Shawn, the chubby fourth grader from Nebraska, is more typical of children in the middle years. His physical intelligence is probably average, and while he likes to play catch with his dad, he likes eating and watching television much more. Sedentary pastimes and high-calorie snacking are causing an epidemic of obesity in young Americans: Whereas 5 percent of children between six and seventeen were judged to be obese in the 1960s, that rate has climbed to 11 percent in the 1990s. The problem is particularly prominent in African-American girls, where 16 percent or nearly one in six is severely overweight, and many more are heavier than average for their height and age. Being overweight doesn't rule out kinesthetic genius, attractiveness, or self-esteem. But it does suggest a tendency to get too little exercise. "Fat camps" are growing in popularity, and when one camp owner recently asked parents what their overweight children like to do, they replied, "Nothing."

It's ironic that American kids are getting plumper at a time when interest in Little League teams is at an all-time high; when the American Youth Soccer Organization reports pressure from parents to move their official starting age from four and a half to four or lower; and when there are four hundred-some ski instructors in the vicinity of Vail, Colorado, certified to teach downhill lessons to children as young as three. One suspects a growing schism between sedentary kids and active ones: The majority of Americans—by some estimates 68 percent—gets little or no exercise, while the minority is pumping iron, climbing stair-steppers, and jogging as never before.

Just as children who grow up watching adults read will tend to become readers themselves, the children of physically active adults will grow up to be more active. All things being equal, though, children love to play and work off nervous energy at everything from hopscotch, jump rope, and kickball to organized soccer, baseball, gymnastics, ballet, horseback riding, swimming, and other sports. Virtually any adult can testify, as well, that it's far easier to develop proficiency at a sport you started in grade school than one you started in your twenties, thirties, or beyond. Regardless of a child's kinesthetic intelligence, physical activity is an enrichment for the motor cortex and other parts of the brain (not to mention the whole body), as long as the play is safe and fun.

And that's a big caveat. Pressure to excel and win not only help drive 75 percent of children who start any given sport to drop out by age fifteen, but they foster self-sabotage and the attitude that playing is not worth it if you can't conquer an opponent. Sports psychologist Chuck Hogan decries pushy parents who over-schedule their children in several sports, verbally abuse coaches, referees, and children alike, and who demand excellence or else. "We need to create ways for children to discover play for the joy of play," he writes, "to enter into it freely and play the game so that the playing is winning." In terms of developing skills, he continues, "there can only be matching the model or mismatching the model . . . the idea of failure has to be removed completely."

Interpersonal and intrapersonal skills. Some children seem to be born negotiators, empathizers, or leaders. They would score naturally high on Howard Gardner's scale of interpersonal intelligence. But virtually all children are concerned—sometimes even obsessed—with being accepted, establishing friendships, and getting along in the society of their peers. "A strong friendship," writes Marguerite Kelly in her almanac for mothers, "teaches children about charity and compassion; honor and honesty; loyalty and discretion; trust and dependability; giggles and good humor." Friendships may need to be refereed sometimes, but seldom encouraged to bloom. Parents who facilitate their children's activities with friends are helping them explore and develop this area of intelligence, as are teachers who set up school projects that require children to cooperate, plan together, and teach each other.

Intrapersonal intelligence is a capacity for self-awareness, morality, responsibility, even spirituality. With church attendance far lower than a generation ago, and with the sense of neighborhood and community eroded by crime, commuting, "cocooning" at home with the TV and VCR, and other factors, the task of raising moral children falls heavily upon parents. The healthiest children, psychologists tend to agree, have parents who are warm and accepting rather than cold and rejecting; who set up firm rules and consequences rather than remaining always lenient; and who support a child's individuality and autonomy rather than exerting heavy control. Parents who act morally and responsibly; who volunteer within the community; and who embody some degree of spirituality are role models their children can emulate. Children can also be directly encouraged to develop these traits by carrying out age-appropriate chores around the house; by taking part in family discussions about current events, movies, or books; and by volunteering alongside their parents. The work ethic, once established in children, can be a source of great satisfaction throughout life.

Martha Pierson, a brain researcher at Baylor University School of Medicine and a mother of teenagers, has strong feelings about raising children, and is philosophical about her own parenting. "At the moment of your child's birth, you say a prayer for a happy human to come from this—a whole, integrated person. And as you work longer with the child, you have other desires. You want them to know the difference between right and wrong, and to act accordingly; to have moral integrity; to have accountability; and to take responsibility, to be heroic." Pierson worked while her children were growing up, "but if I could redo life in a different way," she says (with the benefit of maturity and hindsight), "I would have brought to the fore a basic value I had as a child— self-sacrifice for the good of some other purpose—and I believe I would have stayed home with my children."

Many women would agree with Pierson, while others would disagree for reasons of personal or professional development, or would agree but make the same choice Pierson did out of economic necessity. Nevertheless, as contradictory as it may sound, parents are central to a child's intrapersonal development, and it is important to exercise this form of intelligence in the middle years before a child reaches adolescence.

Knowledge of nature. Just as babies appear to have an innate sense of numbers and how objects move, they can distinguish animate things from inanimate ones. All children, being part of nature, are curious about it, but some home environments promote the understanding of nature—Howard Gardner's last-proposed form of intelligence—more than others. Urban children, for example, may have a built-in disadvantage, although there are good children's books on urban biology, complete with facts and stories about pigeons, rats, roaches, starlings, raccoons, street trees, flower-chomping deer, and window box gardens. Wherever a child lives, though, field trips, vacations, camping, gardening, hiking, tidepooling, birdwatching, reading natural history books, and watching the occasional nature film can all provide experience.

In their book *Kidsgardening*, for example, Kevin and Kim Raftery present dozens of ways children can learn about plants, birds, snakes, bees, butterflies, bugs, and lizards in a small backyard plot. Access to tools like binoculars, a magnifying lens, a microscope, field guides, notebooks, and sketch pads and pencils can encourage a school-age child's interest in natural history, as can clubs and classes and biology units at school, if well taught. Traditional biology lessons that involve memorizing the bones of the feet or reciting the life cycle of slime molds without an inkling of their relevance can squelch a child's interest in nature before it even develops. The object here, as in other realms of intelligence, is fun, exploration, and satisfying the child's own curiosity. In biology, that inquisitiveness can focus on why leaves change color, where frogs go in winter, why people recycle, why birds lay eggs, why deer shed their antlers, and anything else that might bubble to the surface. As the years go on, every walk through the woods, along the beach, or by a lake's edge can lead to more curiosity and reinforce the love for nature.

Children and Free Time: What's the Use?

By the old-fashioned definitions of IQ, centered largely around verbal and math ability, the average child might get all the brain stimulation and enrichment he or she needs just by going to school each day. By the more realistic model encompassing many different kinds of intelligence, a very conscientious school might try to hit all the areas during a given week with a carefully designed program. However, many—perhaps most—children don't attend such enlightened schools. And even if they did, a school day—as interminable as it may seem to a child on a beautiful spring afternoon—takes up just a fraction of his or her waking time. Grade-schoolers sleep close to ten hours per night, and of their fourteen remaining hours, only four-and-one-third or 29 percent are spent in school classes. Children under age eleven spend about three additional hours eating, doing homework, talking to parents, visiting relatives, doing chores, engaging in personal activities, and going to religious services or events. The remaining six hours per day, then, are the child's free time. Since most children aren't in school at all during weekends and summer months, school represents less than 15 percent of a child's waking hours in a calendar year. To a parent interested in enriching a child's environment and experiences, it is important to choose the best school possible based on family resources and location. By using this school time quotient, parents could legitimately devote half again as much concern to the enrichment value of their children's free time as they do to their school time. But do they?

Sociological studies show that for children under age nine or so, parents—by design or default—determine how a child spends most of his or her free time. A working parent might enroll a child in after-school day care with its structured activities. Parents might sign the child up for lessons, classes, or sports teams. They might instruct him or her to go straight home after school and stay there until mom (usually) gets off work. Or they might combine two or all three of these. These frameworks—day care, organized activities, home—account for most after-school time. Evening activities tend to be centered around home and family, with by far the most common events shared by American families being meals and watching television.

Within the framework of parent-directed free time, then, what exactly are grade school children doing? A group at the University of Illinois and Loyola University studied children in almost 1,000 households to answer that question, and what they found may surprise you. On weekdays, grade school children spend the listed average number of minutes on the following activities:

    2 minutes on hobbies
    4 on art activities
    8 out-of-doors
    8 reading
    11 in miscellaneous passive leisure-time activities
    18 engaged in sports (25 for boys, 12 for girls)
    124 watching television
    128 in general play

In this study, children spend about equal amounts of time playing and watching TV. TV alone gets 400 percent more time than hobbies, art, reading, sports, and all other leisure activities combined. On weekends, playing and TV move up to two and one-half hours each. (Many studies, which we describe later, suggest that television viewing takes up closer to four hours a day for the typical child, with the time coming from more active play).

A child's middle years are a bridge from home to school on the younger end and from family to growing independence on the older end. And these two transitions are reflected in how children spend free time. While nine-year-olds devote about half of their free time to family activities, fifteen-year-olds spend only one-quarter of their free time with the family. Boys spend most of the balance alone, while girls tend to spend more of their time with friends. Between ages nine and twelve, time spent playing declines sharply, while time spent watching TV continues to climb to an average of two and one-half hours on weekdays and three hours on weekends (more for boys, less for girls).

After age twelve, television viewing begins to fall off, and is replaced by listening to music. Music on radio, tapes, and CDs becomes a ubiquitous backdrop for teen activities. According to a study commissioned by the Carnegie Council on Adolescent Development and published in 1991, many young teens listen to rock or rap music four to six hours each day. "Hanging out" and "just talking" become serious pastimes during the early teen years as well, with girls spending sixteen hours per week on the phone or with friends, and boys about eight hours.

Our Survey of Children's Time Use

As we mentioned in Chapter 1, we conducted an informal survey of grade-schoolers' use of free time to supplement and update the larger but older surveys we just cited. We wanted to see how closely a study conducted in 1996, during the era of videos and computer games, would resemble the earlier results. And we wanted to see whether a child's socioeconomic status, which we based on his or her parents' education and employment, affected the choice of free-time activities.

We based our survey, in part, on a long-standing relationship between Diamond and school officials in Albany, California, just north of Berkeley. In the mid 1970s, Diamond and public health worker, Bobbie Singer, invented a program called "Each One Teach One," in which anatomy students from the University of California would teach grade school children about the human body: kindergartners about the major organs; first graders about the organs' function; second graders the eye; and so on up to seventh graders and the brain and nervous system. With the blessing of parents, teachers, and school administrators, the program has by now been running for nearly twenty years, and has reached thousands of Albany schoolchildren.

In early 1996, we once again approached that district's cooperative parents and educators, and they allowed us to conduct a survey on children's time use. We administered questionnaires to over two hundred parents and two hundred students in eight classes at three different schools—two second grades, two fourths, two sixths, and two eighths. The children filled out their questionnaires during set-aside class time, while the parents' came by mail. We asked children to tell us how well they liked various school subjects, and to write down exactly what they did on the preceding Saturday morning, afternoon, and evening, as well as after school, before dinner, after dinner, and before bedtime on the previous day, a weekday. We asked parents about their educations and jobs, about their participation in community activities, about their assessment of each child's performance in school, and about their own reading and TV viewing habits.

In total, we collected, matched, coded, and tabulated just over one hundred pairs of surveys from parents and their second, fourth, sixth, or eighth grade child and present that survey's trends here. We use "trends" advisedly, because, for several reasons, the results are less rigorous than serious survey research.

First, Albany residents have a wide range of incomes and educations, and represent a spectrum of racial and ethnic groups, but our survey respondents tended to have higher educations and incomes, on average, than those who chose not to participate or allow their children to.

Second, it is notoriously hard to get scientifically solid data directly from young children, and full-time survey researchers battle over which methods are most reliable. We decided, for example, that second and fourth graders would have trouble judging how many minutes they spent at various activities, so we asked only about blocks of time like "after school," or "before dinner," rather than "3:00 to 4:00 P.M.," "4:00 to 5:00 P.M.," and so on. Even so, we got some answers that were too terse or too detailed. For example, to our question, "What did you do after school?" one seven-year-old responded, "I ate chips," while a nine-year-old girl replied, "Eat cake, popcorn, ice cream, do homework, watch movie." Some of the children had memory lapses, answering, "Nothing," "I don't remember," or "?" to most of the questions. And some of the children weren't exactly spending *free* time, including the fourteen-year-old boy who reported that on Saturday afternoon "I was forced to go shopping for clothes." Nevertheless, most of the responses we received were both useful and relevant.

All things considered, some definite trends were evident from the one hundred pairs of parent/child surveys.

- Most Albany, California, elementary students go straight home from school, or to a friend's or relative's house. A minority of children—perhaps 20 percent—reported going to classes, lessons, or clubs on the day we asked them to document.

- Most parents reported that their children participate in one, two, or three organized activities each month, with weekly participations evenly spread between one and five.

- Children from Albany's middle socioeconomic group were twice as likely as children from high or lower socioeconomic groups to participate in two or three different organized activities per month.

- Most of the children reported doing homework or playing outside while at home between the end of school and dinnertime. Watching television came next in popularity.

- After dinner, television viewing beat out doing homework. The children surveyed were also three times more likely to be watching TV than reading, writing, playing with pets, or pursuing art and music activities combined.

- Before bedtime, reading or being read to was number one, followed by watching television or playing computer games.

- On Saturday morning, a child in our survey was two and one-half times more likely to be watching television than to be doing all other activities combined.

- On Saturday afternoon, playing outside was most popular, but being with friends, watching television, shopping, or indoor play all tied as runners-up.

- One third of the children reported that the television was on "most of the afternoon," one-third that the tube was playing "during dinner," and half said it was on "most of the evening." In our survey, the higher the socioeconomic level, the less likely was the TV to be turned on.

- Our survey also showed that children in middle and high socioeconomic groups were twice as likely to read for pleasure outside of school as children in the lower socioeconomic group.

- Two thirds of all the parent respondents said they read for pleasure daily, but those with the middle and highest education levels were more likely to report this than those with lower educational attainment. That latter group was more likely than the other two to say they "seldom or never" read for pleasure.

- There was an interesting discrepancy in parents' and children's perceptions of school performance and interest. In each of the four areas we mentioned, reading, writing, math, and science, the parents tended to report their child's performance as one level higher than the children themselves did (as "Very good," instead of "Good," or as "Good" instead of "Okay")

- And there was an even bigger discrepancy in answers to this pair of questions: "Do you like school?" and "How well does your child like school?" Only about 25 percent of the children answered "A lot," compared to 60 percent of parents. Fully 75 percent of the children answered either "Some" or "Not Much," while only 40 percent of the parents perceived their children's interest to be so lukewarm.

With their daily homework and reading for pleasure, the children and parents who took part in our survey were more studious than the general population. And even though the television was on in nearly half the homes on Saturday morning and evening and after dinner on weeknights, this percentage is modest compared to the national norm. This suggests that the respondents had a wider range of interests than average and perhaps, also, that the parents are setting restrictions on how much television the children can watch.

Are restrictions a good thing? Is television bad for children? Where does it fit into the subject of environmental enrichment and children's brain development? What about video games—are they better or worse than television? And how should parents approach them?

TV and Computer Games: A Matter of Time

Shawn, the fourth grader from Nebraska whose favorite pastimes are snacking and watching television, is a prototypical American grade-schooler. The average American—both child and adult—watches four hours of television per day. By age eighteen, writes Patricia Greenfield, an expert on how television affects a child's development, "the average American child will have spent more of his or her life watching television than in any other single activity but sleep." And this startling picture excludes the time spent watching videos at home or movies in theaters. Researchers—some funded by government grants, some paid by media organizations—have generated hundreds of studies on the effects of TV upon young children, grade-schoolers, teens, and adults. The conclusions and controversies surrounding them are a book topic in themselves, so we limit ourselves here to a sampling of evidence that speaks to children's mental and physical development in light of TV viewing.

Home visual entertainment, primarily television, is a cultural cornerstone in the United States, and this is more so for certain ethnic groups than others. Based on her study of 349 children in second, fourth, and seventh grades in Chicago-area schools, communications researcher Betsy Blosser reports that African-American and Hispanic children watch more television than Caucasian children, regardless of socioeconomic levels.

In inner-city areas, one family out of three uses television as a constant backdrop to most other activities. Social science researcher Elliott Medrich conducted several studies, including one of 764 sixth graders in Oakland, California, and reports that 35 percent of the households surveyed kept the television on most of the afternoon and evening, as well as during dinner. In the majority of these "constant television households," the mother has a lower-than-average income and educational level, writes Medrich, and the children are more likely to be reading below their grade level in school. The children in these homes, he adds, can usually watch as much TV as they want, and often choose "whatever is on," since they feel they have nothing else to do.

For inner-city children, and others as well, the *kind* of television shows watched can make a big difference. Researchers John Wright and Aletha Huston studied the effects of educational television versus cartoons and adult programming on lower-income preschoolers. They concluded that children who watch shows like *Sesame Street* tend to have better reading and language skills than children who watch only cartoons and adult programming.

Among parents of all socioeconomic levels, worry over television violence has spawned a debate over the "V chip," an electronic device to prevent children from watching violent programs. Experts debate the negative consequences of watching violence; one recent study, for example, showed that the greater the TV-violence viewing at age eight, the higher was a teen's aggression at nineteen. There's little debate, however, about the ubiquity of TV violence.

In February 1996, researchers from four universities led by a team at the University of California, Santa Barbara, reported their findings after monitoring 2,500 hours of programs on network and cable television in 1994 and 1995. They recorded violence on 57 percent of all broadcast programs, with violence on 44 percent of network television shows, 57 percent of cable TV shows, and 85 percent of the movies appearing on HBO and Showtime. They called the violence "psychologically harmful," and they singled out cartoons and children's programming for their frequent "unrealistic" portrayals of violence without consequences or punishments. The American Medical Association blames violence on the screen for part of the huge increase in teen violence (126 percent) between 1976 and 1992. And three-quarters of parents say they have turned off a show or left a theater to spare their children from seeing violence. These statistics helped push the Federal Communications Commission in August 1996 to adopt new guidelines that will force noncable TV stations to begin showing at least three hours of educational programming for children each week.

Beyond the issues of literacy and violence, Harvard professor Robert Putnam sees television as eroding the sense of community in America. Membership in clubs and associations has been declining ever since television viewing became popular in the 1950s, he says. The more television a child or adult watches, he adds, the less they trust other people, the less they vote, and the less likely they are to take part in organized activities outside the home. Putnam recently told a *People* magazine reporter, "it's as if some mysterious X ray zapped Americans who grew up during the 50s and afterwards."

And alienation is not the last of the risks inherent in television viewing at the average American level of four hours per day.

There is an insidious link between diet, obesity, sedentary habits, and television: TV addicts are not called "couch potatoes" for nothing. The federal Centers for Disease Control announced early in 1997 that 35 percent of adults and 14 percent of children ages six to eleven are now dangerously overweight. They also found an obesity rate of 17 percent for teens ages twelve to seventeen. The reason for this increasing girth? Too much food linked with too little exercise—exercise too often replaced, says CDC, by time spent in front of television or computer keyboards and games.

A recent study of ten- and eleven-year-olds in and around Baltimore confirmed that the more television a child watches, the more sugar and fat he or she is likely to eat and the higher is the risk of obesity. Those who watched an average of one hour per day were half as likely to be obese as those who watched three to four hours daily. In a separate study, four-hour-per-day TV watchers had quadruple the risk of obesity over those who watched one hour or less.

A child's kinesthetic ability is a facet of his or her intelligence, and the physical passivity inherent in TV viewing is clearly detrimental to exercising kinesthetic intelligence, not to mention the body! But perhaps television's most pernicious quality is the tendency for even its best shows to encourage *mental* passivity—to dull the imagination and stifle active thought. Communications researchers J. L. and D. G. Singer at Yale University have examined how television affects spontaneous and creative play in preschoolers. They showed three groups of young children two weeks' worth of the most culturally approved shows on network television: *Mister Rogers, Sesame Street,* and nature films. These educational shows promoted a mild degree of creative play in children with the least-active imaginations, say the researchers, but depressed creative play in all the other kids who had livelier imaginations to start with. Researchers found a similar creativity-suppressing pattern with fourth and fifth graders, particularly when they watched programs containing fantasy or violence.

Patricia Greenfield and fellow psychologists at U.C.L.A. wondered whether radio would dampen the imagination as much as television, and devised a clever experiment to find out: They allowed second and third graders in a suburb of Los Angeles to view or listen to two stories, one an African folk tale, the other an adventure involving a boy and a witch. Half the children saw the folk tale on television and heard the adventure on radio, and the other half heard the folk tale and saw the adventure. In every case, though, the researchers stopped the video or audiotape before the story ended, then asked the children to make up possible conclusions. After hearing, judging, and categorizing the endings the children created, the psychologists concluded that they were significantly more imaginative about the new details of the stories they heard on radio (and only saw in their mind's eye) than about the stories they saw on television. When it comes to kids and imagination, they concluded, Marshall McLuhan was right: "The medium is the message."

One family in Columbia, Missouri, got nervous about their two- and five-year-olds' TV viewing when the younger child woke up one day and her first words were "Can I watch *Barney?*" So they unplugged the set for a month to see what would happen. The parents were so impressed by their girls' enhanced creativity, independence, and willingness to do chores, that the unplugging became permanent. They allowed only an occasional program or rented video as a weekend family activity. "Like most things," the mother wrote in *Parents* magazine, "television is neither all good nor all bad. You don't have to kill it; just tame it."

From an enrichment standpoint, time is really the essence with television: Just as the U.S. Department of Agriculture now recommends that our daily provisions include only small amounts of sugar, fats, meats, and dairy products to supplement a diet of fruits, vegetables, and grains, we see television as a "flavoring" to be added in small quantities to a healthy diet of more mentally and physically active pursuits. A little passive entertainment won't hurt a child (or adult, for that matter) and can be a stress-reducer. But most typical American grade-schoolers who watch TV all evening and every Saturday morning for hours at a stretch are getting the mental equivalent of a high-sugar, high-fat diet that weighs down the imagination, clogs the mind, and tends to be accompanied by overweight, apathy, and literacy deficits. Four hours spent daily on passive entertainment is four hours not devoted to more active, energetic pursuits: the trade-off is that simple.

Some people have argued that computer and video games—being less passive and more interactive than television—might benefit children in various ways. And children do like playing them: In 1991, 34 percent of all American homes had a Nintendo game set, and *Nintendo Power* was the largest-circulation children's magazine in the country.

Psychologist Patricia Greenfield and colleagues have studied video game use extensively and conclude that it's "not simply a waste of time." The games act as "cognitive socialization," training the mind of players to adapt to the computers they will probably use as adults. Video games also require the mental rotations that are part of spatial intelligence, and are good practice for the later study of instrument flying, operating radar, and other technical skills.

There are, nevertheless, significant drawbacks to heavy use of video games that, in our opinion, can easily offset those modest benefits:

- Greenfield's team found that video games don't train children in the same process of "inductive discovery through observation" that adults often apply when learning to use new software. Instead, they merely give children practice in recognizing the basic icons or orienting symbols that grace so many computer screens.
- The benefits to spatial intelligence could apply equally to boys and girls. In reality, though, they don't, because girls tend to be turned off by the violent content of most video games and so spend only a fraction of the hours boys spend with a joystick in hand.
- Brain researchers have found that action video games tend to stimulate the brain's visual cortex but to leave unstimulated or actually depress the activity of the prefrontal cortex, with its role in practically all thinking, reading, planning, and organizing.
- And teenagers who play violent video games employing virtual reality experience physiological arousal (faster heartbeat, perspiration, etc.) and more aggressive thoughts than control subjects not playing the games or observers simply watching the players.

Exploring the Internet, which is beginning to replace video games for some children, has much more potential for brain enrichment though the estimated 9.5 million Internet users still represent less than 10 percent of American households, and the typical "Web-surfer" is a man in his thirties, not a grade school child. And many parents worry about inappropriate free advertising on Web sites, sexual predators who pose as children and chat on-line with unsuspecting youngsters, and "cyberkids" who stay up half the night exploring the new medium. Nevertheless, with parental supervision to avoid problems like these, using the Internet seems like an exercise in precisely the kind of "inductive discovery" that Greenfield failed to find with video games, and that characterizes the library card catalogs of old. Navigating through the Internet maze usually requires writing and thinking, and thus is much more mentally active than shooting down alien spaceships or getting to a deeper level inside a video game dungeon. The definitive word on this awaits more Internet experience by children, and studies of the risks and benefits.

In recent years, software developers have begun offering hundreds of CD-ROM titles for children. The CD-ROM's enormous memory allows for animation, music, speech, interactivity "hot spots" on the screen, and for a variety of problem-solving pathways and levels of complexity. One might suppose that the interactivity feature guarantees an enriching level of mental involvement and therefore that any CD-ROM would be a good choice. Some of the programs, however, are little more than glorified video games varnished with a patina of educational information; the child has to quickly shoot down flying objects rather than grasp concepts or analyze situations.

Children's temperaments and mental habits will dictate their taste in CD-ROMs: Some are happy to learn from fairly static programs that are essentially books on screen, while others need cartoon characters and video game elements to keep them interested. A guidebook such as the American Library Association's *Best of the Best for Children* (Random House, 1992) or *The Computer Museum Guide to the Best Software for Kids* (HarperPerennial, 1995) can help you sort stimulating CD-ROMs from the shoot-'em-down varieties. A good guide can also help you find programs that automatically progress to higher levels of challenge after the child has mastered the previous level, or allow parents to do the adjusting. And as in all matters-of-the-screen, moderation is the key; even the most stimulating, educational CD-ROM is still a two-dimensional replica and no permanent substitute for real-world experiences.

For now it's clear that video games, virtual reality, web-surfing, and CD-ROMs can be just as seductive as television, but their benefits are variable and depend in large measure on whether they are used for hours daily and to the exclusion of a wider variety of more active pastimes. Finding the right mix and balance is really the heart of any deliberate enrichment plan. But what's the best way?

Pressure, Motivation, Entropy: Finding a Balance for Enrichment

The name Jessica Dubroff may not sound familiar to you now, but in April 1996, this seven-year-old girl was headline news every day for a week. The child of a New Age spiritual healer and a management consultant, Jessica lived and died a nontraditional life: Her mother, Lisa Hathaway, educated her and her siblings at home; Jessica never watched television; and her mother and father, Lloyd Dubroff, encouraged her to pursue whatever interested her. Jessica worked a paper route in the small seaside community of Pescadero, California. She took music and horseback riding lessons. She built furniture with power tools. She shoveled manure off stable floors. But above all, she flew planes. Her biggest joy in life was the flying lessons her father was providing through an experienced pilot, Joe Reid, at a small local airfield. Jessica started the lessons at age six, and after a year, her father came up with an idea: Jessica, standing just 4 feet 2 inches and weighing 55 pounds, could set the record for the youngest pilot to fly coast to coast in a small plane. He proposed this to Jessica and she jumped at the chance.

Dubroff rented a single-engine Cessna for a week, set up a flight plan with Reid, including four rest and refueling stops, and he alerted news media to the upcoming story. With the plane carrying hundreds of pounds of luggage, food, water, and souvenir baseball caps to distribute along the route, Reid, Dubroff, and his daughter taxied out of Half Moon Bay airport on April 10, heading east-northeast. After two brief stops, they landed in Cheyenne, Wyoming, to spend the night. Reid had taken over the controls along part of the route because Jessica grew sleepy, and so the record-setting opportunity had already been eliminated. Nevertheless, with media representatives awaiting their arrival in Ft. Wayne, Indiana, and Falmouth, Massachusetts, the team pushed on, leaving Cheyenne just after 8:00 A.M. the next morning in a rainstorm with strong wind gusts and temperatures just above freezing. Within five minutes, the overloaded plane was in trouble. With Reid at the controls, the Cessna went down, narrowly missing a house and killing all three aboard on impact. The National Transportation Safety Board determined in early 1997 that the fatal mistake of taking off under such poor weather conditions was Reid's.

Thousands of news outlets, formerly eager to publicize the flight, quickly ran editorials condemning Dubroff and Hathaway for pushing Jessica into a self-aggrandizing stunt that was far too difficult and risky for a child. Other pundits defended both adults; these were not pushy "stage parents" shoving their child into the limelight, went a common theme, but parents devoted to providing their children with real-life experience, and whose daughter was lost in a tragic accident no different in essence than a drowning at camp or a bicycle crash on the child's own street.

We were particularly struck by a quote in the *Times* of London, just before the plane crash. In its coverage of Jessica's attempted record, the paper reported Dubroff as saying, "I think I finally got my job description in order as a parent. I used to think being a parent meant teaching things. Now, I feel my job is to help them learn by exposing them to new experiences." Though Jessica's case may be an extreme one, it highlights a dilemma facing every parent: What is a parent's role in directing or shaping a child's free time when he or she reaches grade school and has his or her own preferences and aversions? How does one find a balance between a laissez-faire attitude that could lead to a pint-sized TV-viewing couch potato; a pushy "gourmet" approach that could produce an overscheduled, stressed-out, irritable young dilettante; or a narrowly channeled child "star" of the gym, court, field, or stage who develops highly in one realm at the expense of school and friends?

Juliette, the young gymnast we saw earlier, risked her future on the Olympics, and like so many in full-time sports, injured herself and could no longer compete. Juliette may have been what child psychologists call a "prodigy," a youngster with superior talents who is internally driven to develop that gift as fully as possible. David Feldman, a developmental psychologist at Tufts, is quoted as saying, "You'd almost have to kill that child to keep him or her from doing what he or she wants." On the other hand, Juliette was very young when her gymnastics career started, and pleasing her mother and coach may have been equally compelling—or more so.

A more common scenario is the grade school child who is forced to practice piano or clarinet every afternoon, and who is none too pleased about it. Is "forcing" a child to pursue a particular free-time activity ever a good idea? When brain researcher Harry Chugani started piano lessons with his young daughter, she made steady progress but occasionally rebelled against the discipline of daily practice. "She could be an obstinate child," Chugani says smiling with obvious paternal pride, and "if my child doesn't want to practice the piano, well, 'No, I'm sorry, you've got to do it.'" Many people who hated music practice "are thankful they got it when they start playing again after ten or fifteen years and find it easy and enjoyable. Their parents did them a big favor, even though they took some flack for it." But, Chugani adds, "You don't want to push the child too much, and different kids are going to break at different points. If the child rebels and says, 'I don't want to do this anymore!' then Okay, [at least] you got five good years in."

Elizabeth Spelke of Cornell University, who is both the mother of two and a renowned infant cognition researcher, takes a somewhat softer stance. "I'm not one for forcing kids to do things they don't want to do. When our son didn't want to practice the piano, I took that as a cue that maybe it wasn't being taught in a way that he liked, and we changed teachers. Now he is really happy." He's probably not destined to be a concert pianist, she says, "but if the goal is not to have a little Mozart but to have a happy, well-rounded kid with a wide, rich variety of skills, then it seems to me they don't have to practice for two hours. You set up situations where it is fun and there is still plenty of room for creativity in the situation—finding bilingual playmates [if the child is learning a second language], finding the right music teacher—things like that."

One of America's foremost survey researchers, Reed Larson of the University of Illinois in Urbana/Champaign, has discovered that finding structured leisure activities a child will like is more than just humanistic parenting. Music, sports, hobbies, and crafts, he finds, are invaluable for a child's mental development. One of the many bridges a school-aged child must cross takes him or her from impulsiveness and distractibility to the capacity for "voluntary attention." Inherent in this transition, writes Larson, is "the transformation by which whimsical, impulsive, and periodically indolent children become motivated, directed, and energetic adults." Larson and his colleagues studied this transformation to see if it happens automatically with age, or if the unfolding ability to direct one's thoughts toward a chosen task needs some help from parents and children themselves.

Larson's group and other researchers have identified various states of motivation and attention in children. A typical play session, for example, represents *high intrinsic motivation*, since the child wants to do the activity and does it freely, but *low attention*, since playing with toys or playmates usually presents little or no challenge. For most children, sitting quietly at a school desk working arithmetic problems on a warm afternoon represents the opposite state: *high attention* since the work requires concentration and effort, but *low intrinsic motivation*, since the teacher is "making" the child work the problems. Teachers have traditionally used both rewards and punishments to get children to comply with school tasks. But, Larson believes that over time both external rewards and punishments erode whatever self-generated interest the child can muster; rewards lead to interest only in the reward itself, not the activity, and punishment leads to frustration, dependence, and hopelessness.

Only when a child is engaging in an activity that elicits intrinsic motivation *and* high levels of attention does he or she reach the state of self-absorbed enjoyment psychologists refer to as "flow." When in this state, the child's own internal drive to work at the activity is balanced with his or her skill level and the challenge the task represents. And the best way for a grade school child to move toward the motivated, directed, energetic attention of the teen-ager or adult is through the "flow" that comes with structured leisure activities—cooking, building models, working puzzles, sew-ing clothes or toys, playing basketball, practicing the flute, or do-ing any of the thousands of hobbies and activities available to youngsters. While "wrapped up" in a favorite pastime, children report feeling excited and forgetting their problems. The high internal motivation accompanying those feelings linked with con-centrated attention is a form of reinforcement for directed effort, learning, and accomplishment that can't be achieved in any other way quite as successfully.

The key to the parent's dilemma of "When to force?" is to avoid the whole problem by helping the child find active pastimes he or she will turn to spontaneously and with pleasurable con-centration. Because television and video games induce forms of intellectual entropy—sinking to the level of greatest energy conservation and lowest mental output—they could easily out-compete most kinds of effortful activity, at least for some children and at least in the beginning before they get "hooked" on the new hobby. Unplugging the television set or Nintendo for a month might help and so might limiting electronic time to week-ends. Some find they have to banish the "plug-in drug" (as author Marie Winn calls it in her book by that name) altogether to redi-rect children to more mentally active pursuits. But as Reed Larson has documented so clearly, the result is likely to be a hap-pier child and a more motivated, energetic adult. Given the tem-porary vacuum left by the unplugging, parents might cultivate some new interests of their own; with enrichment, the amazing dendritic trees of the mind continue to branch and grow in adults as well as in children.

"Unplugging," of course, is just one way to redirect a grade school child's energy toward mentally and physically challenging activities. Consider the ideas we offer next, along with the results of our enrichment survey.

An Enrichment Program for Grade School Children

- The best place to start planning an enrichment program for school-age children is to assess the enrichment value of your child's current environment.

  Does he or she like school? Does the school address and reinforce multiple forms of intelligence or just the traditional academic subjects?

  How much of your child's awake-time is devoted to school and homework, how much to necessary tasks around the house (eating, chores, etc.), and how much to free time?

  Is your child overscheduled with teams and groups outside the home and underscheduled on quiet time devoted to hobbies, reading, music, and projects that can build motivated attention?

  Of your child's free hours, how many are spent watching television? If your child is overweight, can you see a link between TV, sedentary free time, and his or her weight problem?

  How much time is spent playing computer games?

  How much is spent on reading, hobbies, music, art, sports, gardening, cooking, and other activities capable of inducing the pleasurable challenge and concentration called "flow"?

  Does your child like all or most of these activities, or do you force him or her to attend and practice?

  If television and computer games are your child's main interests, the long list of specific toys, games, classes, and outings in the Appendix may provide other ideas for fun projects that stimulate the body and brain.

  Does your child get "exercise" for all his or her facets of intelligence? The Appendix may also supply you with ideas for areas of the intellect that have gotten too little attention—language skills, math and logic, movement and exercise, spatial skills, music, interpersonal and intrapersonal skills, and appreciating nature. Howard

Gardner's *Frames of Mind* (Basic Books, 1983) may help you judge the performance of your child's school, as well as his or her free-time activities.

- Children continue to need support, encouragement, and attention throughout their middle years. Parents of very young children often read books on childhood development and parenting, but this is less common in the parents of grade-schoolers. Reading books on parenting techniques such as those listed in the Resource Guide under "Books About Older Children" is a good way to learn communication and discipline skills with preadolescent children. These books can also help parents understand the wide range of capabilities that are normal for youngsters of this group—a knowledge that can reassure both parent and child. Many parents find help in parent support groups such as those listed in the Resource Guide.

- The bulk of the survey responses we gathered and present in the Appendix focus on boys and girls age six to twelve, since most of the children who spend time at the University of California's Lawrence Hall of Science (and whose parents we contacted) are of grade school age. In the following pages, we summarize the responses about enrichment tools for this age group. The middle years are prime time for learning to do anything from weaving and throwing pots to playing cello and riding a unicycle. Our results are certainly not all-inclusive, and with ingenuity, you are likely to find dozens of choices that fit comfortably within the constraints of your child's talents and interest, your budget, your time, and your transportation options.

   For children six through nine, parents find enriching books in several categories: nonfiction books on how the body works; books on animals, especially dinosaurs; mysteries; science fiction and adventure stories; and old favorites like *Anne of Green Gables, Charlotte's Web, Huckleberry Finn,* and the *Little House* books.

   In the ten-to-twelve age group, the categories are similar, but the nonfiction books include "how the world works"; and the classics shelf is filled with more complicated works: *Fahrenheit 451, Joy Luck Club, Little Women, Pride and Prejudice, Old Yeller, The Lost World,* and *Watership Down.*

For children in the early grade school years (first through fourth), our survey parents report a wide range of toys and games that expand on earlier themes: dolls and action figures; stuffed animals, puppets, and puppet stages; Nintendo, Sega, and Gameboy video games; Legos and erector sets; electric trains, race car track sets, and remote-control cars; board games like Mancala, Scrabble, Yahtzee, and Stratego; card games like hearts; instruments like microscopes and toy microphones; and collections of stones, shells, matchbox cars, horse figurines, and baseball cards.

For youngsters in the later grades (fifth through seventh), parents report benefit from many of the above-mentioned games and toys, but add to the list: diaries; computers; telescopes; flash cards, harder card games like pinochle and gin rummy, and more complicated board games like Concentration, Cribbage, Medical Monopoly, Risk, Life, Rook, and Go.

Grade-schoolers love models and puzzles, and the older the child, the more complicated the subjects they like. Six- to nine-year-olds like to make models of anything that moves—airplanes, battleships, wooly mammoths, helicopters, the space shuttle. They like two- and three-dimensional jigsaw puzzles with lots of pieces and they like a range of products to build and manipulate: K'Nex blocks, Legos, Rubic's Cube, Triazzle, Geo Blocks, IQ cube, and others. Ten- to twelve-year-olds are challenged by jigsaw puzzles with 1,000 to 2,000 pieces, by 3-D puzzles of complicated buildings, and by practical projects using carpentry tools, electric motors, and sewing machines.

Our survey suggests a progression in how grade school children use musical instruments. Some parents of six- and seven-year-olds report that their youngsters find fun and stimulation from simple-to-play instruments like wood blocks, whistles, harmonica, drums, and marimba, while their peers are already pursuing harder-to-play

choices such as piano, violin, guitar, and recorder.
Starting at age eight, however, parents reported only
band and symphonic instruments such as these last four
and other strings, woodwinds, and horns. Perhaps
musical experimentation falls away by age eight or so and
children (and their parents) tend to see themselves as
either serious musicians or nonmusicians.

Children's use of enriching art materials shows a
progression as well. For six- to nine-year-olds, parents
voted for a mixture of fine arts materials—like paints,
pencils, clay, pastels, sketchbooks, and watercolors—and
crafts materials—beads, glitter, origami paper, scented
markers, cardboard, yarn, and wood. By ages nine to
twelve, however, the emphasis was on fine arts: painting,
drawing, and sculpting supplies.

Elementary school is prime time for taking lessons and
classes, and our survey respondents reported that their
six- to twelve-year-olds pursued a wide range of subjects,
from popular sports, hobbies, and academics to hip-hop,
learning a foreign language, even making glow-in-the-
dark goop.

The families in our survey also traveled with their grade
school children, now old enough to learn from and
thoroughly enjoy new places and experiences: Local,
regional, and national parks. The aquarium, planetarium,
or even serpentarium. Amusement parks and sporting
events. Dramatic and musical performances. Outings and
field trips to nature preserves, the mountains, the
seashore, camping, fishing, boating, skiing, rafting,
birdwatching. And vacations, from nearby towns and
historic sites to around-the-world excursions.

Parents' votes for most enriching sports equipment for their
six- to twelve-year-olds reveal a transition similar to that in
musical instruments. Six- to eight-year-olds were
stimulated by a mixture of tools for play, such as swing
sets, jump rope, tricycles, tetherballs, Nerf balls, and
monkey bars; and tools for more serious sports, like skis,
skates, riding and gymnastics equipment. In older
children, sports seem to eclipse pure play, with the

addition of basketballs, volleyballs, soccer balls, and archery and rock climbing equipment. Nevertheless, some items are popular at every age: bicycles, swimming gear, tennis racquets, and Rollerblades.

Audio selections seem to defy categorization in our survey. Parents report that children from six to twelve are enriched by lullabies, children's songs, movie scores and show tunes, classical music, recorded stories, historical songs, Christmas carols, nature sounds, language tapes, oldies, rock, rap, jazz, and easy listening.

When asked about enriching videos, the parents of grade school children seemed to favor classic stories like *Little Women* and *The Secret Garden*; musicals like *Fiddler on the Roof* and *The Sound of Music*; and nature shows like *National Geographic* specials. They also, however, included a number of comedies, adventures, and science fiction videos in their list.

Parents saw dozens of CD-ROMs and software packages as enriching for their six- to twelve-year-olds. But we noticed that these titles show up most often regardless of age: *Gizmos and Gadgets, Fine Artist, Kid Pix, Magic School Bus* series, *Mario Teaches Typing, Math Blaster, Oregon Trail, Reader Rabbit, Sim* series, *Thinkin' Things, Treasure Math Storm, Treasure Mountain,* and *Where in the World Is Carmen Sandiego?* For the full list, including publishers and manufacturers, see the Appendix starting page 330.

Chapter 7

Plant Another Tree:
Continuing Mental Development in Adolescence

If a tree dies, plant another in its place.
—Carl von Linne, Swedish naturalist

• Twelve years ago, a pregnant teenager named Darnella came to
the Living Stage Theatre Company of Washington, D.C., a nonprofit arts project founded by actor/director Robert Alexander.
"I wanted to help people exercise their most important organ,"
Alexander says, "their imagination." This philosophy terrified
Darnella her first day on the improvisational stage. In time, however, it helped unlock her mind and change her life.

When Darnella arrived, she was fourteen and had dropped out
of high school after learning she was pregnant, along with half
of her neighborhood friends. School was not only a frightening,
violent place, but the school district's resources were minimal, the
student truancy rate was high, and less than 5 percent of the students went on to college. Darnella suffered from very low self-
esteem, recalls Jennifer Nelson, director of the theater program at
that time. The teenager's physical health was also poor, she had a
short attention span, her attitude toward the future was fatalistic,
and according to her mother, she was "an abject failure in English." She even sucked her thumb occasionally, Nelson remembers, and hid behind other teenagers like a shy three-year-old.

Afternoons at the Living Stage were a bright contrast to Darnella's normal routine of isolation and watching television. As a
participant in the program, she learned to sing and beat a drum.
She took part in "living sculptures" and in improvisational skits.

She learned photography, painting, and clay sculpture techniques, and she was expected to write daily. "Nobody ever told me before," she confided in Alexander, "that you could write to tell your *feelings*." So she wrote about her life, her baby, and her hopes for the future. Although she failed English in high school, she eventually passed her high school equivalency exam and went on to junior college. In 1995, reports Alexander, Darnella is "a magnificent young woman, working in the community" in social programs for children and seniors.

• Malcolm is such a fan of rock and rap music that, while he likes one or two of his high school subjects, he tends to see the hours in school as a long, unjustifiable separation from his Walkman, his car radio, and his CD player. Malcolm likes an occasional basketball game with other teens at the park, but he mostly likes to hang out with friends, male and female, and just talk, smoke, and of course, listen to Smashing Pumpkins, Boys II Men, and his other favorite groups.

Malcolm's mother, Sandra, is divorced and works in Alexandria, Virginia, forty miles from their home in suburban Maryland. Her long commute keeps her away from the house much of the time, and that suits Malcolm. Sandra worries about her son constantly—about his disinterest in school, about his sloppiness, and about his fast-food diet. His father died of a heart attack at age forty-seven, and Sandra read that 40 percent of American children have high cholesterol levels, and that most teens can't pass the President's annual fitness test administered in gym class—not to mention read their high school textbooks! Malcolm appears to be one of those typical teens, and no matter what Sandra says, she can't seem to influence him much.

• Wendy attends a private college-preparatory school in the state of Washington and is a straight-A student, interested mostly in English and history. She plays tennis, studies every evening, and is a vegetarian like several of her friends. Her major passion, however, is volunteer work, which she does in a variety of community child care and tutoring programs. Every day after school, she drives to one of five program centers and tutors, baby-sits, and plays with children. "She's one of our best volunteers," says one of the program directors. "Wendy has a great way with kids." One of Wendy's best friends volunteers at an AIDS hospice, and the two support each other through the sometimes difficult work. Neither is interested in a social work career, in personal recognition, or in gratitude. "I care about the kids," says Wendy, "and in doing something interesting before I go off to college."

Teenage Rap

A random sampling of recent newspaper and magazine articles about adolescents suggests that the passage from puberty to adulthood is a cultural minefield that many have difficulty navigating safely.

- More than one-third of seventeen-year-olds smoke cigarettes, and most of them smoke daily, according to the U.S. Department of Health and Human Services. As a group, 3.1 million adolescents smoke 1 billion packs of cigarettes per year, and nearly 80 percent smoke the three most heavily advertised brands: Marlboro, Camel, and Newport. This, says a researcher at the University of British Columbia, shows that teens are three times more likely than adults to be swayed by cigarette ads. In August of 1996, President Clinton established tough new Federal Drug Administration rules to limit tobacco sales to minors: These include showing a photo ID when buying cigarettes, removing most cigarette vending machines, and curbing various kinds of advertising. Most adult smokers, antismoking advocates point out, started as teenagers. And tobacco firms, these critics continue, specifically attempt to lure teens with promotions, insignia merchandise, and event sponsorship to fill in the ranks of older smokers who quit or die from their habit. A recent $368.5 billion settlement between four tobacco companies and the attorneys general of nearly 40 states would also impose additional regulations and require funding for campaigns to curb teen smoking.
- At least two million teens have serious drinking problems. Ninety-two percent report using alcohol despite being legally

underage, and one in every four adolescents gets drunk at least twice a month.

- Illicit drug use by teenagers has risen by nearly 80 percent since 1992 after a decline in the late 1980s and early 1990s. More than one-third of eighth graders and nearly half of all high school students have used marijuana, cocaine, heroin, Ecstasy, or another illegal drug. Eighteen percent of teens say they now use illegal drugs at least once per month—the highest level ever recorded.

- The United States has the highest rate of teen births in the industrialized world: 60 births per 1,000 females aged fifteen to nineteen. In 1993, nearly 514,000 women under twenty gave birth, three-quarters of them unmarried. While this is down 22 percent from the peak year 1970 (before abortion was legalized in most states), some observers fear a coming epidemic of unwed births as the number of fourteen- to seventeen-year-old girls climbs by 1.2 million between 1995 and 2005.

- As adults debate whether or not to educate teens about sexually transmitted diseases and condoms for fear that the knowledge could promote promiscuity, teenagers are contracting AIDS at frightening rates: Nearly one-quarter of new HIV infections are occurring in thirteen- to nineteen-year-olds. That represents 10,000 to 20,000 new infections per year. *Newsweek* magazine cites a 1990 study showing that 1 in 500 college students carried HIV at that time. A rate that high would translate to nearly 100 single, dating, HIV-positive students at any given time on a large college campus.

- Youth crime is climbing, and increasingly, teenagers carry guns to school. First Lady Hillary Clinton writes in her 1996 book *It Takes a Village and Other Lessons Children Teach Us*, that "homicide and suicide kill about 7,000 children every year" and "135,000 children bring guns to school each day." More than 26,000 juveniles were arrested for murder between 1984 and 1994, and most were carrying firearms. While overall crime rates in the United States have dropped since 1989, this could be "the lull before the crime storm," according to Princeton University professor of politics and public affairs John Dilulio, Jr. Nearly 40 million children ten and under will become teenagers by 2005, with a 14 percent increase in the fourteen- to seventeen-year-old group.

- Divorce claims about half of all American marriages, and nearly half of teenagers live in single-parent households. Like Sandra, the working mothers who head most of these families tend to have limited incomes and only modest amounts of time to spend at home with children.

Adolescence is no longer the carefree extension of childhood it once was, but press reports like these leave the impression that nearly all teens smoke, drink, and toy with heavy drugs, sex, and violence. In fact, a Northwestern University professor who studied hundreds of Chicago-area teens believes that only about 20 percent have serious problems. The rest are more successful—or at least less destructive—in their experiments with independence and self-identity. Nevertheless, even today's untroubled teens and children are adrift, says author Mary Pipher, quoted in an April 1996 issue of *Newsweek*, because they are being socialized not by their parents but by television and other electronic diversions. The author of popular works on American culture and the family, Pipher says children's manners, social skills, and ability to cope with frustration and sadness have all been affected by a media culture that teaches kids to be "self-centered, impulsive, and addicted" and focuses on a single-minded materialism that isolates people.

Even with strong family support, the teenage passage is never entirely smooth. Starting at puberty, the body undergoes rapid growth and sexual maturation that causes most eleven- to fourteen-year-olds to feel painfully self-conscious and to shift their self-image repeatedly. This period is usually characterized by strict conformity to peer standards, a pulling away from the family, and intermittent attempts at assertiveness. While these behaviors are a necessary part of growing up, teenagers often come across as surly, rebellious, and egocentric. Partly because their sex hormones are surging, young teens feel emotions with an unparalleled intensity, and some researchers think that for many people, this period is the most difficult in the entire human life cycle (more on that later).

By ages fifteen to sixteen, the painful self-consciousness is starting to lift, and teens are beginning to express a unique self-image, more independence of thought, and more ability to make decisions. Their values and morals are solidifying, and they are forging more permanent friendships. Yet at this age, they also are more willing than ever to take risks and experiment with anything that seems adult. Exceptional fifteen- and sixteen-year-olds can win Olympic medals, graduate from college, or end up in treatment programs or in jail, depending on the paths they followed earlier in life and the success of their risk taking.

By ages seventeen to eighteen, an adolescent is crossing into adulthood. He or she is likely to be deeply involved with school, work, and/or relationships—often sexual. Idealism is high at this age, self-reliance is growing steadily, and the late teen probably has plans underway for leaving home and starting an independent life of travel, college, career training, marriage, or a full-time job.

Hormones are central to adolescent changes, but the maturing behavior that turns a pubescent wiseacre into a near-adult also depends upon the final development transition from a child's brain to an adult's.

The Adolescent Brain

The teenage years are filled with physical change, emotional Sturm und Drang, and the emergence of identity. Yet the brain's developmental heyday—its time of seemingly effortless learning and of sculpting original neural circuits in response to experience—is starting to trail off in some ways. Throughout childhood, the brain's large but thin cortex layer was a thicket of dendritic trees with branches and spines crisscrossing and touching billions of times in every cubic centimeter of tissue no bigger than a grape. The density of these synapses or contact points rose meteorically between birth and age two, and remained at 50 percent above adult levels until puberty.

Most of the synaptic connections arising after birth were random hookups awaiting the taming and modifying influences of stimulation. The child's collective and specific experience—

everything that she has seen, heard, tried, said, learned, thought, tasted, felt—brought order to the neural chaos and created a landscape of functioning neural networks. Sets of connections she used repeatedly became stabilized into functional circuits. And connections rarely used and not welded into permanent circuits became cortical dead wood to be pruned away. Most of the pruning takes place between ages ten and sixteen, and this unseen, unfelt process brings the density of synapses to the adult level.

The cortex still supports an enormous number of synapses, the junction points between dendritic and axonal branches, which act, respectively, as receiving antennae or as transmission wires for neural messages. Thirty-three percent of those synaptic contacts are chipped and smoothed away to sculpt the brain's adult neural contours. The carving and chiseling is actually gradual and silent: The synapses and sometimes the spines and branches supporting them simply wither and disappear. But without so many to support, the brain's metabolic load declines, and its energy use drops by one-third. The natural pruning in the adolescent brain is reflected in the windows of opportunity for learning grammar, for acquiring perfect musical pitch, and so on. Nevertheless, Harry Chugani, who studies how the brain's energy-use peaks and falls during childhood, is careful not to discourage anyone who misses such a window. "It's never too late to learn a second language or a musical instrument," he says. "But I don't think you have maximized the way nature intended for you to be able to learn within that certain time if you don't take advantage of that. If you haven't done it and you want to do it later, that's okay. But," he adds, "it will just become more difficult."

As the adolescent years pass, you can't actually see a slowdown within the brain or its billions of cells (unless you count how long teenagers can sleep on the weekends!). But you may notice a gradual fading in the youngster's ability to pick up new skills with magic ease—the classic golf swing, the perfect tennis serve, French spoken like a Parisian. Even if you observe this, though, you will probably also notice continued psychological and cognitive development, based on additional spurts of dendritic growth in the brain.

Researchers William Hudspeth and Karl Pribram at Radford

University in Virginia studied EEG (brain wave) data collected from 561 Swedish subjects ages one to twenty-one. They identified three peaks of brain maturation during adolescence: one at age twelve, one at fifteen, and one at eighteen and a half. These, they say, coincide with the development of what Jean Piaget called "formal operational" thinking processes, or logical reasoning. The peaks are accompanied, as well, by a maturing of moral judgment, and of psychological and social skills around those same periods.

At Harvard's Graduate Department of Education, Kurt Fischer registered growth spurts at ages ten to twelve, and at ages fourteen to sixteen, and eighteen to twenty. Along with the spurt around fifteen (usually sophomore year of high school), Fischer sees the emerging ability to relate one level of abstract information to another. He gives two examples: A fifteen-year-old can relate addition to subtraction and understand why they are opposite functions. He or she can also learn to blend kindness and honesty (or its absence) in the social lie. At the end of high school (around age eighteen), a teenager can usually relate two sets of abstractions to two more, says Fischer. An eighteen-year-old can, for example, understand how addition and division are alike and different. And he can offer constructive criticism, which entails judging and pointing out mistakes, but also applying directness, kindness, and tact all at the same time. The brain's frontal lobes are increasingly active during adolescence, Fischer explains, enabling the teen to hold several items in mind while comparing or interrelating them.

Given this complicated picture of solidifying circuitry, pruned "misconnections," and growth spurts in cognitive ability, one might wonder: Are there any prospects for brain enrichment in a teenager? The answer is an unqualified "Yes." Despite the natural synaptic pruning taking place at this age, dendritic trees in the cerebral cortex can still branch and grow in response to new experience. The Diamond laboratory group used enriched, impoverished, and standard cages to house sixty- to ninety-day-old rats, a period after the rodents are weaned to the onset of full sexual maturity. Just as in younger animals, the cerebral cortex grew in the "teenage rats" that were provided a stimulating environment. In fact, measurable brain change appeared after just four days of rearing in the cages full of ladders, play wheels, and playmates.

Significantly, the cortex also grows thinner just as quickly in a bored teenage rodent with too few interesting new toys. The take-home message for teenage and young adult brains is startling: An impoverished, unstimulating environment has as much or more impact on the adolescent brain as does deliberate enrichment. The nearly adult brain needs a variety of inputs just to hold its ground. Human teenagers are typically bored with school and homework and spend almost all of their free time hanging out with friends, dating, listening to pop music, watching TV, or working at low-paid part-time jobs. We'll see later whether or not these can collectively be considered "enrichment." In the mean-time, though, there is little doubt about the erosive effects of smoking, drinking, and taking drugs—common adjuncts to "hang-ing out."

Mind-altering substances can have a devastating effect on the developing fetal brain, as we saw earlier. But what about their impact on the adolescent brain, itself still maturing? Despite the well-publicized Just Say No! and D.A.R.E. antidrug campaigns, there is surprisingly little data on how drugs affect the teenage brain. Nevertheless, an impression does emerge from the avail-able research, and it is cautionary.

- The U.S. Department of Health and Human Services esti-mates that one-third of teens smoke, while the National Cancer Institute sets the figures somewhat lower at 27.9 per-cent of white, 12 percent of Hispanic, and 4.4 percent of African-American teens. Smoking is clearly "cooler" in some circles than in others. Regardless, it has dramatic effects on the brain.

  At an average dose of 30 cigarettes per day, the norm in America, a smoker will inhale 110,000 times in a year, and deliver over 150 grams of carbon monoxide to the lungs. This onslaught reduces the oxygen-carrying capacity of the blood by 3 to 9 percent, and measurably reduces mental capacity. Psychologist George Spilich, working with col-leagues at Washington College in Chesterton, Maryland, presented mental exercises to nonsmokers, active smokers, and deprived smokers suffering nicotine withdrawal after enduring several hours without a puff. They tested subjects on how fast and well they could: (1) recognize one target letter among dozens of others; (2) scan twenty letters and detect when one transformed into a new letter; (3) remember and detect a sequence of letters; (4) read a paragraph and answer questions about it; and (5) operate a simulated car. In every case, nonsmokers performed significantly better than deprived smokers, who in turn, outperformed active smokers. Ominously, deprived smokers caused rear-end collisions in the video-simulated driving test 67 percent more than nonsmokers. But the crash rate for active smokers was *350 percent* higher! People who claim that a cigarette "clears their head and helps them think" may feel sharper but they aren't. We can only speculate that regular nicotine and carbon monoxide exposure during the brain's final formative years could leave permanent reductions in mental capacity.

- Virtually all teens (92 percent) use alcohol, reports child researcher David Elkind in *Psychology Today*, and 25 percent get drunk at least once every two weeks. What, if anything, is this drug exposure doing to their brains? A high dose of alcohol—enough to make a person drunk—dramatically changes his or her thinking, speech, coordination, balance, and reflexes. By affecting the prefrontal and temporal lobes of the brain, alcohol slows or impedes the ability to remember facts, to recall and pronounce words, to plan out activities, and to control walking and the use of arms, hands, and fingers. All of these factors explain why drunk driving is so dangerous, especially for teens with their paucity of practice at the wheel. Heavy drinking also carries a less obvious risk for young adults and teens: a large number of drinks within twenty-four hours (based on body size) can trigger blood clots in the brain. Researchers aren't sure whether getting drunk can permanently affect the brain or thinking of a young nonalcoholic, but in testing teens who abuse alcohol, they have detected some significant problems with focusing and maintaining attention. This, again, suggests an impact on the brain's frontal lobes.

- In 1995, a group of Australian researchers studied selective attention—a person's ability to focus on one thing and block out irrelevant details—when under the influence of marijuana. They discovered some curious effects: The *longer* you use cannabis, the less able you are to filter out useless details, indicating a negative effect on the frontal cortex. And the *more often* you use cannabis, the more slowly the brain processes information. The team members speculate that cannabinoids, the active compounds in "dope" smoke, build up in the brain and cause short and long-term cognitive impairments.

  In another cleverly designed study, a group of scientists at the University of Iowa judged the brainpower of 72 adult marijuana users by giving them a standardized test and comparing the results to each individual's own test scores when they were in fourth grade. They also gave the same tests to and made the same grade comparisons with 72 occasional users and nonusers. The team found that people who smoke marijuana daily scored far lower than light users and nonusers on math and verbal tests, and on tests of memory retrieval. Neither team mentioned whether marijuana's effects were permanent; a "toking" teenager would discover that answer the hard way—through self experimentation.

- A new drug called MDMA or Ecstasy started to appear in the 1980s, and by the early 1990s, teens, especially in Great Britain, were dosing themselves up to seven or eight times a night during dance parties called "raves." Users say the drug gives them a feeling of love and oneness with other people, and banishes normal inhibitions. Ecstasy appears to do this by interfering with nerve cells in the brain that produce the chemical messenger called serotonin, which helps regulate sleep, mood, and learning. In a recent study of MDMA, medical researchers at Johns Hopkins University in Baltimore found that the drug can permanently damage these serotonin-releasing nerve cells and warned that people who use high doses of MDMA "may be putting themselves at significant risk for brain injury."

- Cocaine use is so common among teens and young adults that it has been characterized as an "epidemic." Fully half the people between ages twenty-five and thirty have tried cocaine, as have 20 percent of those eighteen to twenty-five. While "coke" is considered a party favor in many circles, the neurological risks from powder or crack cocaine make a staggering list: Elevated blood pressure. Blood clots in the brain. Blood vessel spasms or inflammation. Areas of brain bleeding. Strokes. Seizures. Death.

When a cocaine user comes to an emergency room with neurological symptoms such as seizures, delirium, dizziness, drooling, lethargy, or lack of muscle coordination, physicians will often order an MRI, CT scan, or other imaging test. A terrifying 80 percent of the time, the tests reveal abnormalities in the brain such as bleeding or blood clots. Chronic cocaine users often have partially blocked blood vessels scattered throughout the frontal and temporal regions of the brain, as well as an area or two of bleeding. But the most frightening aspect of cocaine use, say drug researchers, is that "the worst complication"—seizure, stroke, death— "can occur the first time a person uses cocaine." One of the saddest examples of this phenomenon involved Len Bias, a promising young basketball star drafted by the Boston Celtics in 1986. Bias, according to friends, celebrated signing his lucrative contract by snorting cocaine for the first time. Within a few hours, he was dead from seizures and cardiac arrest.

- Some teenagers have one favorite drug, but most use a variety of psychoactive substances such as alcohol, cocaine, and marijuana. Some even sniff gasoline or glue along with their beer, crack, and other drugs. In a pair of studies on how teenage drug abusers process information, researchers found that mixed drugs clog your thinking and fog your awareness. One research group found that teenage girls who used drugs regularly scored lower in language skills, sustained attention, perception, intelligence, and academic achievement than nonusers. And another group studying mainly teenage boys found that drugs impaired language, memory, perception, and the ability to learn and repeat an action. The researchers were surprised that the effects were

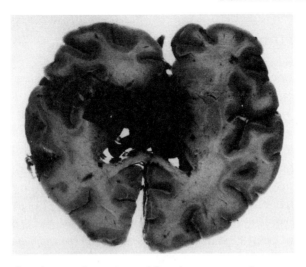

The brain of a deceased cocaine addict shows a massive zone of internal bleeding, brought on by the stimulant drug.

mild rather than strong, and hypothesized that the drug abuse might be slowing the teen's brain development more than altering it permanently.

The data so far on drugs and the brain suggest that:

- Long-term use can easily damage the brain and impair thinking.
- Certain very powerful drugs like Ecstasy and cocaine can wreak their havoc much faster.
- Drug use by teens may slow brain development or change it in unknown ways.

Even if a teen grows out of his drug phase with an entirely intact brain, however, there could still be a toll on his mind's enchanted forests: Days, weeks, or months spent in a drug haze are not devoted to stimulation, varied experience, and enrichment of the brain with its multiple intelligences. Given how quickly the branches and spines of the mind's magic trees can disappear in the idling adolescent cortex, drug use is clearly a potent form of deprivation, both direct and indirect.

Sex and the Teenage Brain

Every generation of teenagers thinks it discovered sex—and if you go back far enough in our species history, teens did. Today, with good nutrition and medical care, puberty starts at age ten to twelve for girls, and twelve to fourteen for boys. For unknown reasons, the pea-sized pituitary gland at the base of the brain starts to release priming hormones early in adolescence, and these begin to "wake up" a girl's ovaries and a boy's testes. These organs release estrogen and testosterone, and the sex hormones take aim on targets all over the young teen's body, creating the changes in bones, skin, muscles, nerves, brain, and internal organs we call secondary sex characteristics. Together, these turn a small androgynous child body into a young woman with breasts, hips, and a menstrual cycle, or a young man with abundant body hair, bulging muscles, a low voice, and an enlarged sex organ.

Physical change is the adolescent's core experience, and the growth spurt, maturing body, and nascent sex drive take some self-redefining as well as just getting used to. For many teens— especially white girls inculcated with media notions of thinness and beauty—the normal fat deposition that creates breasts and hips at sexual maturity can trigger an identity crisis. Researchers at the University of Arizona found that 90 percent of white junior high and high school girls were dissatisfied with their bodies; they defined the "waif look"—5 feet 7 inches and 100 to 110 pounds— as the perfect feminine physique. Coveting a largely unattainable standard like this one contributes to the spate of adolescent eating disorders. By some estimates, one in four teens—mostly girls—suffers from anorexia, bulimia, severe dieting, or some other eating ailments. Before puberty, these conditions are rare. They are also far less common in African-American teenage girls; in contrast to the nearly universal dissatisfaction among their white counterparts, black teens like their bodies 70 percent of the time. Clothes, grooming, and attitude, they agree, are much more central to attractiveness than weight.

Body image, budding sexuality, and gender-specific behavior consume large amounts of adolescent mental energy. But despite the look of it, masculinizing and feminization are only *accentuated* at puberty: Sex hormones stamped the brain and future behavior years earlier in the womb. From the moment of conception, the presence or absence of a Y chromosome establishes the biochemical environment for the fetal brain and sex organs and dramatically shapes them. The contrast in genitalia is easy enough to see in most children, but the effects on brain structure are subtle and took decades for researchers to confirm.

There appear to be at least four gender-based differences in the human brain's basic architecture:

- In one region of the temporal lobe, males have 11 percent fewer neurons than females.
- Some researchers have found evidence that the corpus callosum, a bundle of fibers connecting the brain's two hemispheres, is larger in females, especially in the posterior (back) region.
- The anterior commissure, which also connects the hemispheres, is larger in females.
- Males have a thicker cerebral cortex in the right hemisphere than the left, while in females both hemispheres have a "bark" layer of equal thickness.

Researchers don't agree on whether and how these small structural nuances affect male and female behavior. But some credit the female's generally greater facility for language, melody, and speech tones to the temporal lobe differences, and her greater tendency to sense and talk about emotional states to the larger hemispheric connections.

Experimenters have confirmed a number of male-female differences in brain activity, as well as quiet distinctions in how girls, boys, men, and women act. Using a technique called functional magnetic resonance imaging (fMRI) that visualizes the brain at work, researchers found that when male and female brains are idle (alert but thinking about "nothing"), two distinct regions remain active, depending on sex: Various structures in the male's limbic system, which governs emotion, sex, and aggression, light up during an fMRI session, as does the part of the female's brain involved in sensation, grooming, pleasure, and emotion (the cingulate gyrus).

Thinking about nothing was just the first task. Experimenters also asked males and females to judge whether pairs of nonsense words like "lete" and "jete" and "loke" and "jote" rhyme. When a teenage boy or man thinks about the pairs, his left hemisphere is activated. But when a female contemplates "loke" and "jote," parts of both the left and right hemispheres glisten. When asked to work math problems, males gifted in mathematics showed intense activity in their right and left temporal lobes. Gifted females working the same problems, however, showed less neural activity and appeared to be operating with more cortical efficiency and less overall effort within the brain. When researchers asked women to recall sad memories, their limbic regions sparkled across a far larger portion than men dredging up depressing items. And when asked to decide whether photographs showed faces with happy expressions or sad ones, males were good at recognizing sadness on men's faces but not as adept at telling when a woman was downhearted. Females, on the other hand, were equally good at spotting joy or sadness in either sex, and their brains did it with less effort.

It takes a multimillion-dollar imaging machine to pinpoint fleeting gender differences in brain function. However, variations in outward behavior are easier to document, as Canadian psychologist Doreen Kimura reported in a recent *Scientific American* article. Little boys engage in rough-and-tumble play much more often than little girls. And as early as age three, boys are better at aiming and catching objects. This simple skill blooms into an entire constellation of distinctions in spatial ability: Boys and men are generally better at rotating objects mentally and at navigating. What's more, they use geometric cues (angles, shapes, compass points) to solve spatial problems. Girls and women are better at recalling landmarks and they tend to use these remembered cues when navigating or solving spatial problems. And there are other gender-based proficiencies, as well. Males tend to excel at mathematical reasoning; females are better at arithmetic calculations, at manual dexterity, at verbal fluency, and at perceptual speed, quickly seeing small differences between people, places, or objects.

Two education researchers from Chicago analyzed the scores from over 150,000 students aged thirteen to seventeen to look for variations in how the sexes perform on standardized academic tests. After sifting this massive pile of numbers, they found sexual disparities, but only slight. Teenage boys scored a little better on math, science, and social studies questions. Teenage girls were slightly stronger in reading comprehension, perceptual speed, and remembering associated facts and concepts. The Chicago team found just two notable differences: Males had a wider spread of scores, that is, more boys scored higher and more scored lower than did girls. At the top of the math scale, for example, males outnumber females 7 to 1. But females performed "substantially better" than males at writing, and, the researchers concluded, "males are, on average, at a rather profound disadvantage" for this basic literary skill.

Are sex hormones, operating first in the fetus and later in the teenager, to blame for all these diverging brain structures, behaviors, and abilities? Is nature, in other words, more important than nurture? Or do the expectations of parents and teachers channel boys and girls into these mental grooves?

The old nature-versus-nurture dichotomy may have made sense thirty years ago before we learned how profoundly experience shapes the brain. Today, though, we see the influences as more circular: Genes influence behavior, and behavior, in turn, can influence how the genes function and how the child grows and develops. Males are encouraged to take more math and science courses, their experiences in these classes stimulate and shape the brain, and not surprisingly, their test scores tend to be higher in these areas. Beginning in junior high school, girls often lose confidence in their math ability, take fewer courses, get less experience, and score somewhat lower. On the other hand, girls tend to develop verbal skills at an earlier age than boys, and the praise they receive as well as the experience they accumulate feed back into verbal capacity, heightened experience, expanded receptivity to words, and still greater fluency.

One of the true mysteries of gender and the teenage mind is the self-esteem tailspin many girls experience around the time of puberty—a plummeting confidence that carries down with it feelings of attractiveness, social ability, health, positive personal qualities, and self-worth. Worries over math and science ability are practically a footnote. In a study of 3,000 children aged nine to sixteen, boys as well as girls experienced an adolescent drop in self-esteem: 67 percent of nine-year-old boys liked themselves the way they are, but only 46 percent of fifteen- and sixteen-year-olds reported feeling this way. Fewer girls liked themselves to start with: 60 percent of girls were happy with their basic traits at age nine. But this crashed to 29 percent by age fifteen to sixteen. The declines for white and Hispanic girls were sharper than for African-American girls; nearly half of black teenage girls retained their self-esteem in the transition from grade school to high school.

Why do some girls suffer such a setback in self-esteem? One theory holds that as girls mature sexually, they feel a strong sense of connectedness to and caring for others, based both on brain differences and on society's expectations. These feelings may clash with the competitiveness and self-focus it takes to succeed in school and at work and they may rob girls of self-confidence. Another theory suggests that a young teen's mental development allows him or her, for the very first time, to clearly imagine what other people think of them. This sudden awareness may undermine self-confidence and heighten feelings of awkwardness and incompetence.

Many parents blame the surging sex hormones that initiate puberty and reconfigure a child's mental landscape for the sweeping emotional swings adolescents are heir to. The emotional roller-coaster is certainly real enough, says researcher Reed Larson of the University of Illinois: Larson and colleague Maryse Richards issued beepers to hundreds of Illinois teens and their parents and interrupted them at random moments over a period of days to ask for a reporting of their immediate mental state. Both boys and girls reported feeling "very happy" five times more often than their parents, and "very unhappy" three times more often. "Teens," write Larson and Richards, "live life with less epidermis" than their experience-hardened parents. Raging hormones may be involved, they conclude, but so are "the pileup of transitions and life events" teens face: Physical maturation. The passage from grade school to junior high school and then high school. Peer pressure to experiment with drugs and alcohol—not to mention clothes, food, hair, music, and slang. The thrills and shattered feelings connected with falling in and out of love and initiating first sexual relationships. And the demands, both personal and parental, to study hard, choose an educational or career path, and to plan for an independent life outside the family.

Teens clearly deserve their emotional ups and downs. By fifteen, say Larson and Richards, teens felt much less in control than they did at age ten, and their level of motivation "appeared to be a low point for the entire life span." The biggest sources of negative emotion teens reported were schoolwork and grades, followed by relationship difficulties with friends and family. In good moments, though, friends supplied support and understanding for their naturally intense feelings about life. And the secret sanctuary most adolescents found behind a closed bedroom door gave them a place to let down and shut down for a while each day.

Perhaps Malcolm, the Maryland teen whose rock music-listening swallows most of his waking hours, feels out-of-control and unmotivated and can cope with these sensations best when hanging out with teenage friends or relating to the lyrics of Smashing Pumpkins. His mother's fears for her son's future are not misguided. American high school students score rather poorly in math and verbal skills compared to teens in most other industrialized nations. Not all teens do, of course—students like Wendy have time for straight A's and community volunteer work on top of a social life. But the reason for the generally lower scores is simple: American teens spend fewer hours at school or doing homework than adolescents in many other countries. What are our teenagers doing instead? The answers are intriguing and help inform the issue of teenage enrichment: What's possible in the synaptic pruning years?

Teens at Play and Work

After the elementary school years are over, a teenager's major occupation is studying for junior high or high school classes, right? In Russia, that's true. Also in Japan, Taiwan, and many populous industrialized countries. In the United States, however, if you judge by hours and effort, the teen's highest calling is free time.

In Russia and Japan, behavior researchers report, adolescents spend 50 percent of their waking hours at school or doing homework. By contrast, American junior-high-schoolers spend 22 percent of their time studying at school or at home. This goes up a bit in high school, but Japanese teens still spend 30 to 40 percent more time on academics than Americans. Parents and educators in the U.S. sometimes lament our teens' low math scores, which trail those of most other First World countries. But there's no great mystery behind them. In a country like Taiwan, 27 percent of eleventh graders take a math class as an after-school activity on top of their longer school day; that makes the enterprise 27 times more popular than in the U.S.!

Several hundred American teens in one survey sample found class time "boring" at least one-third of the time, and saw homework as generally "dull" and "unpleasant." Malcolm, plugged in to pop music, turned off by school, and seeking the company of his like-minded friends, is a thoroughly typical American student.

American teens, in fact, spend 80 percent more time hanging out with friends after school (an average of eighteen hours per week) than they spend studying outside of class (ten hours per week). Socializing takes up nearly 20 percent of an average adolescent's waking time, whether in a group, or in one-on-one activities, including dating. Dating is relatively unimportant to Taiwanese and Japanese high-schoolers; only one-third of those teens spent time on it. In the U.S., however, 83 percent of teens are dating someone, and this fact may help explain another anomaly of American teenage life.

Dating means dressing up, looking good, and going places, and all of these require money. Nearly 80 percent of American high school students hold part-time jobs—usually minimum-wage service sector positions. Compare this to Japan and Taiwan, where only one-third as many adolescents work. Children and teens are particularly susceptible to advertising, and the underlying message of consumerism has obviously taken hold in America: Teens want clothing, fast food, car stereos, cosmetics, compact disks, tapes, and a thousand other things, and they are willing to work for the millions of dollars they spend annually on these items. When combined, part-time jobs, hanging out, and dating account for nearly as much of an American teenager's time as school and study. It doesn't take an Einstein to see why our teen pop culture is so vibrant and globally infectious while our academic rankings flag behind so many other equally prosperous countries. Just wake up a teenager and watch what he does with his time.

For young teens, sports is a fairly important pastime, consuming about 6 percent of waking time or about six hours per week. Nearly three-fourths of this is devoted to informal sports like biking, skateboarding, swimming, or shooting baskets, while organized team sports—baseball, tennis, gymnastics, track, and so on—account for about 11 percent. Gym class fills in the remaining 17 percent. Even this modest investment in physical activity, however, shrinks by junior year in high school: 80 percent of all teens who sign up for organized sports drop out by age seventeen. Even if you toss in dancing at parties and clubs, physical activities take up only 3.4 percent of a late teen's free time.

Ironically, teenagers frequently report that sports are their most enjoyable outlets. And sports can create the kind of "flow" that matches inner motivation with skill level and challenge, and promotes the development of focused attention. Those who stay with organized sports throughout high school tend to earn higher grades and have plans for a college education, and many of those teens thrive on self-discipline and competition. Says one seventeen-year-old girl from suburban Los Angeles, "I love my coaches. I love winning. And I feel happier on the baseball diamond and basketball court than anywhere." She is hoping to win a rare women's baseball scholarship to help finance her higher education.

For most of the teens who drop out of organized sports, demanding coaches are a drag. So are sitting on the bench, being pressured to win, and feeling like dead weight on the team. Fair enough. But why do most teens drop out of *informal* sports, too? This is less clear, but sports may be a victim of the same growing self-consciousness that leads to a teen's plummeting self-esteem. "I got sick of being embarrassed," laments one fourteen-year-old girl who dropped out of an after-school softball club in suburban

St. Louis. "I was horrible at softball, and I'm glad I'm not playing it anymore. I might try tennis; I don't know."

Just as sports can be a source of psychological flow for good athletes who have the skills to compete well and enjoy themselves, hobbies, art projects, playing musical instruments, and belonging to clubs and organizations can be absorbing for teenagers. Unfortunately, they spend on average only 1.8 percent of their free time or about two hours per week pursuing structured leisure activities—one-tenth as much time as they spend hanging out with friends. Socializing builds important skills, too, but realistically, some of this large block of "hanging" time is spent experimenting with sex and drugs. From the viewpoint of brain enrichment and development, these time expenditures are out-of-kilter.

Media use—listening to music, playing video games, or watching music videos, television, or rented movies—also consumes about 10 to 15 percent of a teen's free time. These can be relaxing and help a teenager get over powerfully felt emotional hurdles. For the most part, though, they are mentally passive and probably contribute little to neural development relative to the time most teens invest in them. By contrast, writing music for a small rock group, creating the lyrics for rap songs, making one's own videos, or writing media reviews for the school newspaper can be sources of challenge and stimulation, and some mentally active teenagers do engage enthusiastically in these pursuits.

Teens and Enrichment: Plant Another Tree

At age fourteen, Darnella felt as if her life were over. She had dropped out of junior high school, and her boyfriend stopped seeing her as soon as he heard she was pregnant. Many teens in her situation require public assistance, lack basic literacy skills, and bear the dead-eyed look of children with too many cares and too few dreams. Darnella, though, was among a handful of teen mothers who got a second chance from a group whose work proves as well as any scientific study that the teenage brain can respond to enrichment, even after years of deprivation.

It is true that during the adolescent years, synaptic connections are steadily pruned within the brain's thin layers of cerebral cortex. The "exuberant connectivity" of the two-year-old—that is, the overabundance of random neural connections—gives way to more orderly circuitry in all parts of the cortex based on the repeated experiences of early and middle childhood—visual, auditory, tactile, gustatory, kinesthetic, emotional, lingual, and so on. By age ten to twelve, the strong circuits begin to inherit the brain and the weak or unused ones to dissolve away over a period of years. Despite this survival-of-the-fittest scenario, however, Darnella's cortex—like other teens'—still has plenty of room to grow, based on the mind's magic trees—the luxuriating forests of dendrites.

Throughout adolescence and all during adulthood, the dendrites continue to branch, grow, and form new synaptic connections as a person learns and experiences more of the world. Underused synapses will go on disappearing, even after the major pruning years are over at sixteen to eighteen. But as long as new ideas, sensations, and experiences continue to stimulate the brain, the growth and loss of connections is at least a zero-sum game. At best, lifelong enrichment will promote continued branching and growth of dendrites and with that, continual thickening of the cerebral cortex. Carl von Linne, the eighteenth-century Swedish naturalist who invented the naming system for all plants, animals, and microbes we still use today, once wrote, "If a tree dies, plant another in its place." This is an apt slogan for the business of brain enrichment in teens and adults: If a connection, a branch, or an entire dendritic tree withers from lack of use, plant another through stimulation of the senses and multiple intelligences. Childhood's sculpting of major brain tracts may be over, but the etching of subtle lines, textures, and details can go on for a lifetime in the dendrites and synapses. And this plasticity begets more of the same as the brain, constantly remodeled by experience, soaks up additional stimulation and experiences ever more easily.

This is how Darnella came to plant a new tree—actually, an entire grove. She lived in one of Washington, D.C.'s, gritty inner neighborhoods not far from the Living Stage Theater and its resident company. This part-school/part-dramatic playhouse/part-encounter group resides now in a brick building that once housed the Club Bali. In the 1940s, performers like Billie Holiday, Duke Ellington, Louis Armstrong, and Charlie Parker played there, but the club eventually closed, and by the 1970s, the building was boarded-up and used only by junkies looking for a "shooting gallery." In the mid 1980s, the creator of the Living Stage, former New York actor Robert Alexander, along with his small cast of actor/educators and technical supporters, worked to get funding for a new venue. With help from Washington's well-known Arena Stage and other local and national sources, they bought the old Bali and renovated the building into a big airy space with stages on two levels. After years of renting school cafeterias, church basements, and multipurpose rooms, they moved into the Living Stage Theatre in the late 1980s. Their unusual mission, however, continued as it had for twenty years: to improve the lives of people like Darnella and create social change through improvisational theater.

Robert Alexander, now retired due to an illness, brought several powerful philosophies to the Living Stage: He believed that the human birthright is "to think, learn, and create," and that only during the instant of creation is a person vibrantly alive and reaching his or her fullest brain potential. He also believed that the imagination is like a muscle that must be regularly exercised to keep it operative. Improvising songs, poems, and dramatic scenes is, to Alexander, the best way to encourage children and adults to use their "bodies, voices, minds, imaginations, hearts, and souls to express and communicate what is most important to them."

The first day Darnella came to the Living Stage Theatre, as she and seven other equally nervous teen mothers greeted each other in the lobby, they heard lively music coming from the stage in the next room. They could see through a one-way mirror that several adult actors and musicians were warming up on a set of multilevel platforms beneath a huge rainbow, playing electric piano, conga drums, and guitar, and singing impromptu phrases and verses about courage as they danced wildly about. The teenagers started clapping and moving to the driving Calypso rhythm, and eventually they were led into the big stage room. Their timidity faded as the adults invited them to join in; the collective group shouted, sang, swayed, and danced for nearly an hour.

Later that day, and on subsequent days, the adults, including veteran actor Oran Sandel, now directing the theater, would initiate exercises involving the teens. They created living sculptures and enacted scenarios around themes like drug abuse, suicide, conformity, pregnancy, sexism, racism, education, courage, and dreams for the future. The teen mothers' group named themselves Teemot, and through improvisational song writing and acting, they explored a theme of their own choosing: "All men are dogs."

Theater work like this, says Sandel, practically guarantees "life-enhancing changes" in the participants. Sandel is a slender man with long, dark hair pulled back from his mobile, expressive face, which he uses, along with his arms, hands, shoulders, torso, and even his feet to emphasize points. "Sexism was a big, big dynamic in their lives," he explains, "so we tried to mess around with this stuff. We tried all kinds of scenes of different qualities of relationships. 'Freeze it! Whole group now! Where does [the interaction] need to go? What does he need to say? [How] does she need to [respond]?' Real methodical stuff. We did all of that with them," he continues, "and then we trust that the human being is a learning being and will start making healthy choices in their lives."

Besides the weeks of acting, singing, and other impromptu exercises, Darnella and the other Teemot members wrote poems, plays, and diaries. They worked with clay and cameras, drums and maracas. They took field trips to art museums to see other forms of artistic expression. And they heard talks on child development—"on what," says Sandel, "a three-year-old needs, a one-year-old, a four-year-old"—along with ways to handle difficult child-care situations.

"We don't hit them over the head or force them to do anything," says Sandel emphatically. "We offer them information and give them the freedom to do whatever they want with it." One member of Darnella's group had an extremely kinetic child labeled "hyperactive" by his schoolteacher and principal and "a good candidate for Ritalin" (a behavior-modifying drug). The boy's mother decided, "No drugs for my son," says Sandel. "She struggles with his behavior; she's embarrassed by it. . . . But she doesn't step in and hit him. I mean," Sandel says, eyes widening, "that's a major victory right there." Little by little, "through the generations, we'll have some improvement. A revolution does not happen overnight; health progresses if we consciously attend to making that happen."

Funders constantly ask Sandel, and before him, Robert Alexander, for empirical evidence, such as high school diplomas and college enrollments, that the improvisational program improves lives. "I'm not convinced that going to college is necessarily something that makes a human being more productive or more intelligent," Sandel argues. But "across the board, we see enhanced self-esteem. Expanded perception of self in relation to the environment, to the society, to the culture. Yes! Enhanced ability to articulate feelings and concepts, no question about it. And that's documented repeatedly in their own words. 'I used to be so shy, now I'll just talk to anybody.' Or, 'I used to not be able to put my feelings into words because I didn't even know what my feelings were. Now I do.' "

Darnella never liked to write in school and had failed English, but at the Living Stage, "She wrote and wrote," Alexander confided. "We asked her, 'how come here, but never in school?' and she answered, 'Nobody ever said to me that a reason to write is to tell your feelings. Now I know that and the feelings are coming out.' " Whether a meaningful measure or not, Darnella did finish her high school equivalency, go on to college, and become a "magnificent young woman," in Alexander's words, and a continuing friend of the Living Stage.

As dramatically as this creative work affected Darnella and so many other teens, the Living Stage has been returning to its original focus thirty years ago: young children. "You can impact them the deepest," says Sandel, "because they are so much closer to the root of what it's all about. They are close to grace. The muse is still in them; it hasn't been reasoned or beaten out of them yet. Every person is an artist," Sandel says, with such conviction that it raises goosebumps in the listener. "And to teach a child on a fundamental level about the power a song, poetry, movement can have is to strengthen their backbone in a way nothing else can. They'll carry that," he concludes, eyes wide again, "their whole life."

Even after years of stress and largely passive mental activity, it was not too late for Darnella to "plant another tree," and the same would be true for many adolescents. Even though a massive pruning campaign eliminates our little-used dendrites in the teen years, neurons in the cerebral cortex can still branch and grow profusely and, say many experts, help establish the permanent inclinations and abilities of adulthood. Because parental influence wanes in junior high school, and because adolescent culture propels older children toward dating, hanging out, working for pocket money, and experimenting with drugs, sex, and alcohol, teenagers must be committed to their own enrichment and mental development. Here are some additional ideas.

An Enrichment Program for Teenagers

Carl von Linne's message about "planting another tree" is an apt one for teenagers because environments impoverished by routine, apathy, drug use, or socioeconomic conditions may lead to shrinking dendrites and a reduced cognitive potential. It's not too late, of course, for a teen (or a person of any age) to stimulate the brain in new ways through new experiences: classes, hobbies, sports, volunteer work, and so on.

But there is another relevant perspective on this, as well. In July of 1944, Anne Frank wrote in her diary: "[Daddy] said: 'All children must look after their own upbringing.' Parents can only give good advice or put them on the right paths, but the final forming of a person's character lies in their own hands." Teenagers, especially late-teens in high school, are their own mental masters and must decide for themselves if they want to pursue less passive, more active experiences. If they want to limit or avoid potentially brain-bruising drugs and alcohol. And if they want to seek out a series of enjoyable challenges, both recreational and educational. Parents and teachers can stay informed and provide various kinds of encouragement and support for their choices.

But by and large, enrichment lies in the teenager's own hands, perhaps inspired by some of the following ideas.

- Parents or teens can use the following questions to help analyze their environment's current enrichment value:

   Are his or her high school classes challenging?
   Do they require daily reading and writing in school and out of school?
   Does the student do at least one to two hours of homework per night?
   Does the teen's peer group reinforce or denigrate good performance in school?
   Does he or she use successful peers and adults as role models?
   Do local opportunities exist for volunteer work or interesting paid work for teens?
   Has the teen already formed a dislike for math, science, reading, or any other basic subject?
   Has he or she developed skills in several physical activities and does he or she enjoy doing them regularly?
   Does the school offer classes and clubs in art and music, even if an older student is a beginner in those areas?
   Does sports practice cut too deeply into academic time and the pursuit of other hobbies and activities?
   Does the teen spend hours listening to one form of popular music like rap or rock?
   How much time does he or she spend watching television, playing computer games, and talking on the phone?
   Does he or she smoke, drink, or take drugs that could interfere with normal adolescent brain development?
   What percentage of his or her activities are mentally passive or observational versus mentally active and participatory?

- Teens can exercise their imaginations, as well as build self-expression and self-confidence, by taking speech, poetry, or writing classes, or joining a theater group. Even a non-joiner can get the same effect by following Robert Alexander's Daily Recipe for the Imagination: Make up and say aloud three stories and three poems each day for the rest of your life!

- Teens can continue developing language skills by

  Taking school courses that assign frequent writing assignments
  Keeping a daily journal
  Reading fiction, plays, literature, biographies of successful people, mysteries, history, and science fiction
  Using a daily vocabulary-building calendar
  Writing to a pen pal or e-mailing friends on the Internet
  Continuing foreign language study
  Working on the school newspaper or yearbook

- Teens can build math and science skills through:

  School classes and special projects
  Enrichment classes after school or at science centers in subjects like higher math, animal conservation, astronomy, ecology, robotics, or physics
  Tutoring younger students in basic math skills
  Learning applied math such as beginning statistics and beginning computer programming
  Using math- and science-oriented CD-ROMs

- Teens can continue expanding their music appreciation and performance skills through:

  Musical instrument lessons and/or choral singing
  Writing music or lyrics for rock, rap, or other music groups
  Classes sponsored by local symphonies
  Deliberately expanding musical interests beyond rock and rap to classical, bluegrass, jazz, New Age, musicals, gospel, and others

- Teens can develop existing physical skills through lessons or team participation, and learn new ones such as tennis, golf, skiing, snorkeling, dancing, football, basketball, aikido, soccer, dressage, karate, surfing, boogie boarding, skating, gymnastics, or swimming.
- Volunteer work, hometown environmental efforts, and part-

time jobs can help adolescents expand relationship skills, social responsibility, and practical skills.

- Teenagers can reinforce artistic skills or learn new ones with materials, books, and classes on caricature and animation, photography, video, drawing, watercolor, landscape, pottery, ceramics, costume design, and art appreciation classes at local museums and galleries. Our survey respondents had other ideas, as well. (See the Appendix for specific suggestions for honing skills in all these areas.)
- A motivated teen can turn off the television or computer games after a limited time per day.
- Traveling with family and organized groups can be enlightening and stimulating; see our survey respondents' ideas for trips and outings.
- Most of the parents who answered our mail survey suggested enrichment tools for preschool and grade school children, since they use the exhibits and classes at U.C. Berkeley's hands-on science center most actively. Nevertheless, our survey does cover two dozen 13- to 16-year-olds and might contain some useful hints for teens and their parents and teachers. As in earlier chapters, those results are summarized here, and provided in more detail in the Appendix.

The kinds of books our parents and teen respondents find most enriching include mysteries, science fiction, adventure stories, and women's literature.

Teen "toys" and games tend to be sophisticated: electronic equipment such as computers, CD players, boom boxes, and Nintendo and Sega sets; and intricate card and board games that adults often play, such as Chess, Parcheesi, Uno, Monopoly, and Clue.

Our survey teens still enjoy puzzles, models, and other three-dimensional teasers, but of the most complex types: Rubic Cubes and 1,000- to 2,000-piece jigsaw puzzles of cars, ships, rockets, engines, telescopes, airplanes, and historic buildings.

Teens play a range of instruments from the more popular flute, piano, guitar, drums, and voice, to the cello, trumpet, and other strings, woodwinds, and horns.

Favorite art materials include the supplies for origami, calligraphy, and candle and costume making, as well as fine arts projects using clay, charcoal, pastels, watercolors, and oils.

The teens in our survey take lessons and classes in several areas, including arts and crafts, music, dance, and drama; various kinds of sports; and languages, math, science, and other academic fields.

Outings and trips are to the same rich collections of venues as grade school children, but teens tended to go on many of them with groups of peers and adult chaperons instead of with their parents.

Sports equipment for teenagers reflects the same broad selection we saw among preteens, but also includes body- and stamina-building tools such as weights, punching bags, rowing machines, and cross-country running shoes.

Teens report feeling enriched by all kinds of recorded music—rock, rap, classical, opera, movie sound tracks, as well as by recorded humor, stories, and foreign language drills.

Adolescents find a range of science fiction, drama, humor, and adventure videos enriching, from *Goonies* to *Henry VIII.*

And in our survey, four software titles got repeated votes for most stimulating to adolescents: *Oregon Trail, Where in the World Is Carmen Sandiego, Myst,* and *Sim City 2000.*

Chapter 8

Learning Not by Chance:
Enrichment in the Classroom

Learning is not attained by chance, it must be sought
for with ardor and attended to with diligence.
—Abigail Adams, in a letter to her son,
John Quincy Adams, May 8, 1780

• "One child in our district," says Claudia Pogreba, principal of
Woodway Elementary School in Edmonds, Washington, "well, his
story gives me goosebumps." The boy, whose mother had been a
heavy drinker during his fetal development, had "a very negative
attitude toward school and was making poor decisions." These
"decisions"—to misbehave with teachers, start fights with other
children, and to cut classes—were landing him in the principal's
office regularly. He and Pogreba were developing a relationship—
one desired by neither party—based on his disruptive behavior.
Just as the situation was growing worse, Pogreba explains, the boy
"got hooked on the newspaper." Woodway schoolchildren publish their own newspaper, complete with advertisements from
nearby retailers. "He started designing ads for local businesses,"
says Pogreba, "using graph paper to figure out space and area. He
was good at what he did and took it very seriously. He also started
conducting interviews for stories." Soon, she recalls, "he was making appointments with me to lay out ads and plan sales campaigns. Our relationship went from troubled to very positive."
The boy, now in middle school, remains enthusiastic. He still
values his applied experience on the newspaper, but, more gener-

ally, he has come to see reading, math, and formerly abstract school subjects as practical tools for his own success.

• Sue Preckwinkle's fourth grade reading class at Dubois Elementary School is doing better than ever. The school is part of District 186 in Springfield, Illinois, and its staff has been teaching reading a particularly successful way for nearly ten years. In the mid 1980s, an education professor from the University of Illinois contacted the district's reading coordinator with a bold new idea for reading instruction. The idea was called "reciprocal teaching," and in it, a group of children help each other learn to read.

At that time, Springfield grade school students generally sat in rows, read an entire assigned story like *The Chocolate Touch* by Patrick Catling, then tried to write out or say answers to questions in class. Nearly half the children struggled with that approach, Preckwinkle recalls, but "reciprocal teaching really helped, and today, we are getting much better results."

Now, Dubois schoolchildren sit in small "literature circles" and read a passage from a story. Then they discuss it together in ways peculiar to the "reciprocal" method. In the past, says Preckwinkle, "the children had much more trouble with reading comprehension." Now, they can read *The Chocolate Touch*, follow the escapades of boy protagonist John Midas as he turns everything he touches to chocolate—from his toothpaste to his trumpet to his mother—and build reading skills at the same time. "Working in a group is nonthreatening," she says. "The slower readers have better models to follow and they all have the thrill of sharing a story with someone their own age."

Education Meets the Brain

These educational success stories would have been impossible without recent research into the brain and its thinking process—or so say proponents. In a field noted for buzzwords and bandwagons, some educators have in recent years been touting the science of deliberate enrichment, including discoveries from the Diamond lab at U.C. Berkeley, to stimulate their students' development. They call many of the new educational theories and techniques "brain-based education," and this approach is generating some real benefits, as well as a lot of dollars for a few entrepreneurs. Certain teachers swear by "brain-based" methods, while others see them as time-tested techniques with new labels. Still others choose a different approach and dismiss "brain-based" as so much hooey. Regardless, there are excellent reasons for teachers, school districts, and parents to jump on *some* bandwagon: Traditional American school approaches seem to work poorly for a large percentage of students, and nationwide, the majority of graduates are facing employment in the new millennial information age without the requisite skills. Can the lessons from deliberate enrichment experiments and other kinds of brain research be successfully applied to mass education? If not, what else can educators do to address the gap between what most graduating seniors know and what society expects of them?

Education in a Fix

The days when confident parents sent carefree children off to the public schoolhouse in search of a fine education are long past in many communities. Most people will agree that American public education is in trouble without being able to cite any of the facts that prove it:

- In 1983, the National Commission on Excellence in Education sent out an alarm call with its report *A Nation at Risk.* Among its conclusions were these: American students ranked in last place in seven of nineteen international achievement tests, and ranked below second place in each of the other twelve. Thirteen percent of U.S. teens are functionally illiterate. And three-quarters of recent recruits to the Armed Services read below the ninth grade level.
- After a decade of sweeping and costly educational reforms following that 1983 report, the picture had changed only slightly. More students were taking rigorous course loads, but science and math scores had barely inched upward after a precipitous fall in the early 1970s and a nearly fifteen-year

depression. History scores have continued to fall; on the history section of a recent exam called the National Assessment of Educational Progress, only 40 percent of high school seniors could show a basic knowledge of American history, including why the Pilgrims emigrated to New England.

- Educational goals set in 1990 for the coming decade by then-President George Bush and fifty state governors have gone largely unmet: Drugs are more prevalent in the schools now than in 1990. There now are fewer teachers with undergraduate or graduate degrees in the subjects they are teaching than in 1990. And there has been no increase in the percentage of students graduating from high school (86 percent). Schools do, however, seem to be a bit safer, judging by the percentage of tenth graders accosted or injured at school (40 percent in 1991 versus 36 percent in 1994).
- Executives from the nation's largest corporations told a governors' conference in April 1996 that American high school graduates lack the skills they need to succeed in business. Large corporations can train graduates in specific vocational skills, an IBM executive said at the conference, but "What is killing us is having to teach them to read and to compute and to communicate and to think."
- When math researchers tested American preschool children against their counterparts in Japan, they detected virtually no difference in the children's understanding of numbers and counting at ages three and four. By the end of grade school, however, according to UCLA educational researcher James Stigler, the *lowest-scoring* Japanese children are solving arithmetic problems with more success than the *highest-scoring* American elementary school pupils.
- The largest state in the union, California, has more than 10 percent of the nation's enrolled elementary and high school students. Within ten years, the current 5.8 million California schoolchildren are expected to be replaced by 6.8 million, and will require nearly 100,000 extra teachers, 6,000 new schools, and an additional $15 billion just to provide education at the current level. That level, unfortunately, is far from adequate, at least if you judge by student performance: A state-administered test of fourth, eighth, and tenth graders

in 1995 showed that six out of ten California students scored below the "basic" level in reading. This tied with Louisiana for the worst grade school reading scores in the nation. Writing and math scores were nearly as low, according to State Superintendent of Schools Delaine Eastin, who called the results "alarming."

- The National Association of Scholars (NAS) reports that the top fifty U.S. colleges and universities have slashed their basic "liberal arts" prerequisites. In 1964, the NAS reports, 60 percent of these top schools required history courses, 90 percent required physical or biological science courses, and 82 percent required math. Today, only 2 percent require history, 34 percent require science, and 12 percent require math. The college school year has also shrunk by 20 percent from 191 days to 156 days.

- Understandably, many Americans have lost confidence in their schools. Fully half of those polled no longer trust the public schools and think private schools do a better job at maintaining discipline in class, keeping students safe, upholding high academic standards, and teaching honesty, reliability, and other traditional values.

The question "What's wrong with American education?" has been addressed and answered hundreds of times by school boards, special commissions, federal studies, educators, and authors. A much more fascinating question concerns "Why?"—why do American schools fail to provide most children with a real understanding of basic facts, and the ability to apply standard literacy skills to real-world situations?

We saw one primary explanation in the last chapter: American students spend far fewer hours in school than their counterparts in Europe and Asia, and far more time watching television, hanging out, dating, and working part-time jobs. Typical fifth graders in Taipei, for example, do thirteen hours of homework per week compared to the four hours per week on average that fifth graders perform in Minneapolis. Some American parents keep close tabs on their children's schoolwork and homework, but more do not; this lack of concern itself erodes school performance by suggesting that homework is the child's prerogative and is unimportant.

Wherever educational researchers have looked, however, it's been clear that homework pays off, even for struggling students, and even for a subject like math. A researcher from the University of California at San Diego, Julian Betts, recently reported his findings on a study of extra math homework. After tracking 6,000 junior high and high school students for over seven years, he discovered that an additional thirty minutes of math homework per night in grades seven through eleven raised the students' scores by the equivalent of nearly two letter grades. What's more, extra homework produced results far more effectively than hiring more teachers with math degrees or reducing class size. And the homework could even go ungraded; the benefits accrued from the student's mental efforts alone, regardless of feedback. (Returned homework papers were all the more helpful, however.)

Another reason for the American educational system's relatively poor showing is the diversity of the collective student body: Japanese teachers usually address racially and economically homogeneous groups of students in a single national language. Some American teachers have that luxury, but here diversity is the rule, not the exception. Taking just one medium-sized school system as an example, San Francisco Unified School District serves nearly 64,000 students of nine "ethnicities": Hispanic, Caucasian, African-American, Chinese, Japanese, Korean, American Indian, Filipino, and "other," including mainly Europeans, Middle Easterners, and Southeast Asians. San Francisco teachers deliver their lessons primarily in English, Chinese, and Spanish, but a visitor can hear Tagalog, Vietnamese, Cambodian, Russian, and several other languages spoken in the schools, depending on the children's native tongues. Students and their parents speak at least fifty-seven languages in their homes, says Dr. Roger Brindle, Program Evaluator for the San Francisco schools, and this informal tabulation may actually underestimate the diversity. "There are one hundred spoken dialects of Chinese, alone," he says, and many of these are represented in San Francisco households. While San Francisco is admittedly one of America's most multicultural cities, other Pacific Rim municipalities, including Los Angeles and Seattle, have similar patterns, as do New York, Miami, Houston, and cities in many other regions.

Not only are millions of American children studying their

school lessons in English as a second language, but they are simultaneously learning about a mainstream American culture they may not be part of. Despite our democratic ethos, a child's home life is strongly correlated with his or her achievement in school. Research shows that students tend to score higher on standardized tests:

- When the family is intact (parents not divorced)
- The more education their parents attained
- The higher the family income
- The smaller the family's size
- The older the mother at the child's birth
- The more the parents talked to them as infants and toddlers

Since nearly half of all schoolchildren have divorced parents and less than one-third have parents with college degrees, these correlations predict an uphill battle for the majority of students, and in fact, this matches the statistics. All of this said, biology is not destiny and neither is family background; many students do well despite gender, family income, native language, parents' educational level, and the rest. The maverick variable is *motivation*, and some students have it in abundance. Motivation is itself central to a third explanation for the American education system's relatively poor showing: Many of our traditional teaching methods depend on a child's inner motivation to pay attention and complete assignments. Yet they often do little to bolster that inner drive and, in fact, in some ways actively erode it.

James Stigler, an educational scholar at the University of California at Los Angeles, has compared the way Japanese and American math teachers operate in their classrooms and has discovered startling differences. (The American approach is familiar to most of us, and encompasses most academic subjects, not just math, Stigler's focus.) The American math teacher stands at a podium or near the chalkboard, lectures and demonstrates how to work a particular kind of problem—say, simple one-digit subtraction—then assigns a sample problem for the students to solve in class. After a few minutes, the teacher will lead the class through the problem they just attempted, and pose questions about each step in the solution as students try to guess the right answers and say what the teacher wants to hear. The American teacher acts as an authority, a source of knowledge, a supplier of right answers, and a corrector of wrong ones.

The Japanese math teacher, by contrast, works in a very different way, according to Stigler. He or she will begin by posing a new kind of problem—double-digit multiplication, let's say— then wait for a "painfully long time" while students struggle with 43×57, or whatever the sample problem may be, on their own. Eventually, the teacher will solicit ideas from the group on how to solve the problem, acting as a discussion moderator to draw out the students' own explanations, rationales, and supporting arguments. Japanese teachers refuse to be authorities in the classroom, Stigler observes, even when students present blatantly wrong solutions. Instead, they steer the discussion toward a collective agreement of what makes sense to the students and how to relate it to earlier procedures like addition or subtraction, and not toward a single correct answer.

Stigler recently borrowed a day's math lesson from a Japanese teacher and presented the material to two American fourth grades: one in the classic Japanese style and one in the typical American style. He then tested both classes for how well they understood the lesson he taught. Both groups were equally good at picking out the relevant events—the tips and steps needed to work the problem. The American students taught Japanese-style, however, could also distinguish and discard irrelevant events, while the students taught American-style could not. This shows, says Stigler, that the Japanese-style lesson required *thinking* while the American one required mostly memorization and guesswork. Guessing-what-the-teacher-wants is a motivating game only when you play it consistently well. After a few wrong answers, it's safer to clam up, whether you understand a lesson or not.

Methodological differences like these help explain why American grade school students have fallen so far behind their Japanese counterparts by the end of elementary school. But there is more. Not only is learning collaborative in Japan, teaching is, too. American teachers choose their own lesson plans and teaching methods and use them autonomously and largely unobserved. All Japanese teachers, on the other hand, observe and are observed by their colleagues, Stigler says. Classroom teachers in that nation have daily meetings and publish thousands of articles to discuss *what works best* for teaching students. Their philosophy, Stigler explains, is that you can't improve a process by inspecting the products. If you ran an assembly line, you could sort out and throw away 20 percent of the widgets as defective, but still not know which mechanism was stamping out the defective products unless you searched for it directly. In the same way, only by looking at what goes on in the classroom, say Japanese educators, can you separate what works from what doesn't. (Despite their students' high productivity, Japanese educators are not entirely satisfied with their system. A 1996 report in *Science* magazine states that the majority of Japanese teachers worry about their schoolchildren having too little free time and exhibiting too little creativity.)

In the U.S., several factors predispose our traditional methods using the teacher as an autonomous authority: (1) An ethos of intellectual freedom combined with the democratic notion that all teachers are equally competent. (2) A workday packed with monitoring lunchrooms and playgrounds as well as educating students. (3) Very little time allotted for teachers' meetings and collaborations. Add to these, says Stigler, our nation's small, poorly funded educational research effort, and the result is too often classroom lessons based on memorization and "regurgitation" that fail to teach real understanding to any but the brightest and most highly motivated.

Our American system of mass education from kindergarten through senior high school year imposes a heavy expectation: that every child will spend at least twelve years successfully following an academic path. In England, Europe, and many other "First World" industrial societies, students are tested as young teenagers and channeled toward either a rigorously academic college-preparatory high school or a trade school with fewer intellectual demands. Since a high school diploma is considered the minimum entry credential for most American jobs, it seems reasonable that our nation would develop teaching methods that successfully motivate our diverse population to stay in school, to learn effectively, and to remember what they learned.

According to many American educators, however, including James Stigler and John Bruer, president of the James S. McDonnell Foundation in St. Louis, we spend far too little trying to invent and test new ways of teaching, and what we do spend is often focused on producing educational theory (of the sort that procures tenure) rather than innovative new classroom methods. Both of these, they say, help explain our students' poor academic showing. The foundation Bruer heads is one of the few private groups that fund research into better teaching methods, and for years, their role has been growing as federal research dollars have dwindled. Yet school enrollments are climbing beyond the 50 million mark, Bruer points out, and the average instructional investment is $5,000 per child. This makes K through 12 education "a $250 billion business. If you took 5 percent of that figure [to devote to research], it would be $12 billion," Bruer says, "but that dwarfs what we actually spend on educational research now." It would be hard to name any $250 billion industry that devotes less money than education to developing improved techniques, he observes. Plus, Bruer adds, successful new ideas often fail to reach classroom teachers. "Dedicating a small percentage of the total educational budget to disseminating good ideas to teachers in the field could have a huge impact."

Bruer's foundation has funded some remarkably successful projects (described below) that increase students' real understanding and motivation. Other techniques lumped under the rubric of "brain-based education" are also exciting students and teachers across the country. But the reform of such a giant enterprise proceeds ponderously, and for now, because of America's relatively restricted hours of school and homework, our diversity of student backgrounds, and our traditional teaching methods, test scores continue to reflect our problems as much as our solutions.

A Fix for Education

Some astute educational historian probably predicted that in the 1990s—the government-proclaimed "Decade of the Brain"—we would see an educational reform movement based on brain research. Democracy and mass education have been interlocked for most of American history, and the impetus for changes in public education spring from the same social and scientific movements that have shaped democracy's changing form.

Thomas Jefferson tried in 1779 to establish free elementary school education for colonial children. He was defeated, though, by elitist foes who saw schooling as the responsibility only of the church or of wealthy private families. By the 1840s, as state governments solidified and carved out their authorities, "common schools" (public elementary schools) cropped up in Massachusetts, Connecticut, Rhode Island, Pennsylvania, New York, and Michigan, and in a flood of states thereafter. Along with the nineteenth-century push toward democracy came the earliest public high schools and universities and the demand for enrollments by females and African-Americans.

In the early twentieth century, the juggernaut of industrialization brought wave after wave of educational reform: John Dewey's progressivism, with the founding of experimental schools and softer discipline. Maria Montessori's child-centered education, freeing children from "adult suppression" to explore their own interests and creativity. Robert Hutchin's antivocationalism—a back-to-the-classics retro movement, followed in the 1930s by the plain cloth of "essentialism," with reprises in the 1950s and 1980s.

Educational movements have also mirrored the social reforms of the mid- to late-twentieth century: The push for equal education regardless of sex, race, ethnicity, or physical disabilities. The storm over bilingual instruction. School prayer and creationism. Busing. Compensatory education. Tracking versus "mainstreaming." Finally, the massive educational enterprise has reflected society's love-hate relationship with science and technology. This started in the 1950s with Sputnik and the scare over our international competitiveness in those areas. And it progressed through the anti-science backlash of the 1960s, the surge of interest in environment and ecology in the 1970s, the demand by women and minorities for better access to science education and jobs in the 1980s, the upsurge of computers in education in the late 1980s and early 1990s, and today, the ascendancy of the Brain.

Teachers—especially those laboring during the social and scientific turmoil of the last half century—have shown a tendency to jump on ideological bandwagons. And with good reason. Teachers are an overworked, underpaid, highly dedicated lot, discouraged by the sievelike memories of many students and the obvious absence of true subject understanding despite everyone's hardest efforts. They are as disturbed as parents and administrators by lagging scores and half-baked literacy, and they are understandably searching for the key, the method, the Right Answer. In the late 1960s and 1970s, for example, there was a flowering of excitement around so-called "right-brain, left-brain" studies. These suggested new ways of differentiating and reaching artistic, intuitive right-brained learners from analytic, verbal left-brained types.

When shoehorning a seamless spectrum of students into these two categories didn't work overly well, teachers looked for something better. By then, the "triune brain" theory was catching on. This is the idea that humans have a primitive reptilian brain wrapped with an emotional mammalian brain and encrusted with our convoluted neocortex, seat of human intelligence. The interactions of these three cranial species, according to triune theory, can help explain learning and behavior.

By the early 1980s, Howard Gardner had published in *Frames of Mind* his theory about the seven different kinds of intelligence we all possess in large or small measure, and that seemed to many to be an even better way of categorizing students, fathoming their scholastic foibles, and helping them absorb information. In a more recent book, *The Unschooled Mind: How Children Think and How Schools Should Teach,* Gardner described a school curriculum he developed with colleagues at Harvard—a program based heavily on apprenticeships and practical, hands-on training for youngsters. Other educators spun entire school designs off their own interpretations of Gardner's theory, including the Key School in Indianapolis.

By 1990, a pair of education professors from Southern California, Renate Nummela Caine and Geoffrey Caine, published a book on "brain-based" learning called *Making Connections: Teaching and the Human Brain.* This work laces together various theories and bits of research on behavior, cognition, and brain function into a prescription for educating today's students. It starts with brain anatomy and the Diamond lab's work on plasticity, then touches on gender and hemispheric differences in the brain; human memory research; the triune brain; stress, emotions, and learning; and multiple intelligences. Along the way, it shows how all of these threads can be stitched into a detailed strategy employing hands-on, active involvement and promising better motivation, better retention, and better understanding for students. Within a few years, brain-based education had become a lucrative enterprise for some, complete with competing authors, videos, consultants, in-service training seminars, toll-free 800 numbers and operators waiting to take your order. One can't help but wonder whether education comes in any variety other than "brain-based," whether this is a well-meaning fad that will help a few students in a few places; leave the majority at approximately the same level of confusion; and be replaced in time by some other catchphrase like "whole-body" or "whole-spirit" education; or none of the above?

The school principal who led this chapter, Claudia Pogreba of Edmonds, Washington, has seen educational bandwagons roll in and out during her twenty-some years in the field. Pogreba is well-versed in the "brain-based" tenets, having read the books, heard the consultants, attended the seminars, discussed the ideas with her staff, and presented them to local parents. And she happens to believe quite firmly that they work, *really work*, and represent an educational movement that will last. The story of the troubled boy who found meaning on the Woodway school newspaper was just one of the examples Pogreba offered over lunch on a frigid Seattle day in 1996, when the schools were shut down by icy roads.

Pogreba, a soft-spoken woman with powerful conviction, explains that "another boy was really struggling in class with reading, and was extremely discouraged by school. He signed up—the only boy—to take part in a school drama production and won the role of the king in Cindrella. He had to learn to dance the waltz with a girl who played Cinderella, and he did a really nice job. Everyone was impressed by his effort, and most importantly, his attitude toward school became positive, not negative." Still another boy, a native Spanish-speaker, she recalls, refused to speak much English at school and was not learning very effectively. "After he signed up to work in our commercial art venture," Pogreba says, "he started taking school more seriously and believing that it had a purpose. Before long, he was using English more and starting to learn more in class."

The newspaper, dramatic workshop, and commercial art venture Pogreba described are part of a program she and the teachers on her staff call the Woodway Elementary Micro-Community. Two afternoons per week (perhaps three or more in the future) children in grades four to six leave their normal classrooms and take part in one of seven "micro ventures" taught by Woodway teachers, counselors, and experts from the community:

- An illustrated monthly newspaper
- A multimedia production team that creates slide shows and video features
- A dramatic arts group that stages plays
- A team that tutors other students, mediates student conflicts, and learns about stock market investing
- An art venture that generates flyers, posters, programs, and other graphic designs
- A team devoted to improving school life
- An economic team that learns about how to start and run small businesses

Pogreba was instrumental in organizing this set of "immersion" workshops to help children apply academic skills to simulated life situations. She learned about grade school microcommunities in part by visiting an elementary school in Lowell, Massachusetts, which had operated a similar program since 1982. "The microcommunity model hasn't caught on widely," Pogreba says, "because it's a philosophy, not a kit you order, and it is developed through the interests of a school's individual staff members." Planning the Woodway workshops took the staff hundreds of hours, and convincing skeptical parents took many more. One of Pogreba's fellow principals in the Edmonds district, Harriet Green from Lynndale School, who also lunched with us on that cold Seattle Monday, explained further. Both parents and teachers are "very reluctant to give up what they have always done. 'Drill and practice and memorizing did it for me,' they say, 'so why change?' " But once Woodway school launched a pilot microcommunity program, "The parents overwhelmingly supported it," Pogreba added. "They said their kids were talking about it and making connections between math and other topics."

Some of the fear of math learning was lessened in the Edmonds district even before they introduced the microcommunity plan. "Math is very hands-on and developmentally appropriate, as we teach it. Lots of applications of math concepts," Pogreba explains. "An integration of materials to develop number sense, lots of emphasis on seeking out patterns, and what I think is phenomenal, an emphasis on journaling."

Green explains "journaling." The child "will jot down, 'How did I figure this out?' 'What was I thinking when I did it?' 'How did I get my answer?' 'What did I do in math today?' " and the result is an understanding of the subject that also incorporates visualization and language development. "How could that be more aligned with brain research?" Pogreba joins in, rhetorically. In fact, in Edmonds, Washington, as in many districts around the country, elementary education barely resembles the classroom experiences of most adults raised in the 1930, 1940s, or 1950s.

"You don't see many desks in rows anymore," says Green, "and you seldom hear a teacher say, 'That's the wrong answer.' " Instead, she says, "You'll hear, 'Tell me why you think that.' Or, 'What made you give that answer?' What's more," she goes on, "instead of saying, 'I'm going to have all the kids reading on the same page of the same book,' the planning goes more like, 'We're going to be reading such and such a story and I'm going to want a lot of activities that build on it. Some will appeal to some kids' learning styles and interests and some will appeal to others. So I am going to put puppet making on one table to go with the story, and on another, a series of questions where the kids have to write answers. And I'm going to put a tape of the story over here, and paints over there for making a mural about the story.' "

Pogreba credits some of the changeover to a paid consultant from California who presented "brain-based" education theory to the Edmonds district several years ago. The teachers there were already using many innovative techniques, Pogreba explains, and the seminars "substantiated that our focus was developmentally correct." Harriet Green, however, a serious woman with strong opinions, is more skeptical. "We had to make some leaps to put things together between brain research, education, teaching, and the community. Simply to say that the brain research we just learned about—dealing with rat studies—means that you should react to your children this way and do this kind of stimulating environment stuff is a leap!"

There is a tendency, Green says, "to want to have a research base for what we've already known were great teaching practices. Kids learn and retain things when they are actively involved . . . that's how I define 'brain-based education.' You could call it 'teaching to the multiple intelligences,' or before that, that 'everybody has their own unique learning style,' and when teachers teach the same ways to everybody, they're not reaching some students."

Green uses a personal anecdote to explain learning styles. "I was the model student," she says. "I went through high school as a great memorizer and I gave teachers back exactly what they wanted. . . . I got A's on my tests. I made maximum honor roll. And I went to college and played the same game and graduated magna cum laude." Green's husband, by contrast, "was a self-taught learner. He read what he was interested in but he didn't care much to read what was assigned unless he happened to be interested in it." Today, she goes on, "He and I talk history, and for all the A-pluses I got in my history courses, I remember nothing. And furthermore, I remembered nothing the day after the test! But my husband remembers everything there is to know about history and can talk about it intelligently because it was driven by his own interest. I think that tells you a lot about what we are trying to do in education now. Yeah, the old way worked, sort of. I learned a process—put down the two and carry the one. But I had no idea what I was doing: If I forgot to move one number over, I had an absurd answer and didn't even notice! Those stellar teachers along the way that we all remember—they may not have called what they were doing 'brain-compatible' or using 'multiple intelligences.' But they knew how to grab a kid's learning style . . . and they did it intuitively."

While the labels may not impress Principal Harriet Green, the learning strategies that are being called "brain-based"—hands-on, collaborative, open-ended, applied—certainly do. When we asked whether these innovative approaches produce better learners, better prepared for life, she was quick to respond. "I don't have a doubt in my mind, but it depends on what your measure is. If it is how successful they are going to be in the real world, definitely. If it's how well they perform on standardized tests, not necessarily. If your measure is how turned-on they are to what they are learning, absolutely. But if it's how well they can spout back information, probably not."

A Science of Learning Based on Classroom Results

For some educators, like John Bruer of the James S. McDonnell Foundation, "brain-based" education is not just a label, it's a "huge leap." Bruer's organization reviews and funds educational research, and while he thinks "how the brain works to support cognitive function is a very interesting question, we are decades away from having any understanding of brain function that would contribute to classroom learning." Right now, he says, "there is a lot of bad neuroscience being peddled in the educational marketplace." In spite of the powerful evidence showing that experience changes the brain, Bruer insists the link with classroom performance is missing. "I don't know of a neuroscientific result that one can implement in the classroom and show that it is *for those reasons* that children's educational outcome was improved." Some of the techniques being recommended under the "brain-based" rubric, Bruer continues, do work, "but what it's got to do with the brain is a leap of faith."

Bruer criticizes educators who think that "doing something different is by definition doing something better. And it's just not true!" When a physician is confronted by a drug company salesman with a new product, "He should ask, 'Okay, how much better will my patients do if I buy this drug from your company than they are doing now?' A good physician will think that way," Bruer insists, "but educators seldom do." As a result, he says, teachers are susceptible to "the guru of the week who goes in to a school on a Wednesday afternoon or a Saturday morning to talk to teachers for three or four hours and it's wonderful and pleasant," but fails to "amount to any significant change in teacher behavior."

Bruer advocates a new "science of learning" based on how learners process and use information, not on "synapses and arborization and neurotransmitters." Rather than focus on "cellular, molecular things," he argues, educational researchers—at least for now—should stick to techniques with a proven foundation in the science of cognition (how we think) and with verifiable results in the classroom.

The number line games developed by Robbie Case and Sharon Griffin are prime examples in Bruer's recent book *Schools for Thought: A Science of Learning in the Classroom*. Teaching these games, he says, is an educational technique with a quantifiable outcome in student test scores as well as in a real understanding of the subject that they can apply in other situations. Another example is "reciprocal teaching," the approach to reading instruction Sue Preckwinkle uses for her fourth graders in Springfield, Illinois. John Bruer also cites a seventh-grade boy named Charles with an IQ of 70 and a third-grade reading level. After three weeks of reciprocal reading lessons, the boy had advanced nearly two years on standardized reading tests, and the gains lasted long after the remedial lessons ended. In the reciprocal technique, children work together in groups to summarize a short passage they just read, to create questions about the subject matter, to clarify any misunderstandings and talk about the gist of the story (with the teacher's guidance), and then finally to predict what the next part of the story or book will say. Charles and Sue Preckwinkle's fourth graders are just a few of the beneficiaries; the new technique is now widely used in Springfield, Illinois, and in a number of other school districts nationally. Everywhere it's applied, reading comprehension and retention seem to go up dramatically.

Bruer points to a third example of an educational technique with proven results based on cognitive science—how the mind learns. A physics teacher named Jim Minstrell working at Mercer Island High School in Washington State created a new way to teach physics concepts so that students could absorb, remember, and apply them. Minstrell sets up an experiment such as placing a ten-pound bag of sugar on a scale beneath a glass dome. Next he asks students to predict whether the weight will change if he pumps all of the air from the dome. By doing this, Minstrell discovered that all students come to physics with preconceptions about what objects weigh and how they move, fall, and behave in various circumstances based on their own observations throughout childhood. Minstrell also found that these preconceptions are not highly individualized and instead, fall into just a few groupings.

In the weight-in-a-vacuum experiment, every one of his students predicts one of just four outcomes: that the weight will double; stay at ten pounds; fall to zero; or fluctuate by an ounce or two. Minstrell leads a discussion during which students defend their guesses. Then he pumps the air from the jar, reveals that the weight remains at exactly ten pounds, and explains why. Using this approach (which is, coincidentally, very similar to the Japanese method for teaching math), Minstrell allows each student to discover his or her own beliefs and amend them based on new observations of the physical world (during the experiment). Other approaches Minstrell has tried leave the students' naive misconceptions in place; when they finish the physics course, they quickly forget the thin veneer of memorized concepts and fall back on their original guesses. Minstrell calls his method the "Cognitive Approach," and reports that Mercer Island students taught this way scored substantially higher on math and physics tests than similar students at a sister school who learned science and math with traditional techniques.

John Bruer, a leader in the funding of educational research (and whose foundation supports Minstrell's work) comments, "The challenge for the educator is to make a bridge from a child's informal learning that occurs outside of school to the formal demands that school presents. I don't think that brain research and glucose metabolism or whatever has a whole lot to say about that." But, he concedes, "I don't want to discount [brain research] because eventually we will know much more. In twenty years, it's conceivable we will understand the brain circuitry involved in reading, for example, and how learning to read changes neural circuitry as the skills mature."

Since today's students and teachers can scarcely wait twenty years for a neuroscience of learning to emerge with proof enough for the highly meticulous, what's the best alternative? The behavioral strategies of cognitive education researchers for teaching math, reading, science, and other subjects are surely an important start, and the McDonnell Foundation in St. Louis is trying hard to spread the word to teachers. But the enthusiasm Claudia Pogreba, Sue Preckwinkle, and many other educators feel about techniques based on brain research cannot be ignored, even if the "brain-based" label and the notions behind it seem like a great leap to some.

Ironically, the student involvement and motivation at the core of the "brain-based" model is decades, even centuries old. The microcommunity Pogreba helped organize at Woodway School in Edmonds, Washington, is based on a similar ten-year-long experiment at Lowell School in Massachusetts. It, in turn, drew ideas from Peninsula School in Menlo Park, California, which began an "open participation plan" in the 1930s, following John Dewey's philosophies. For many years, Howard Gardner and his colleagues at Harvard have been applying the multiple intelligences idea in a student-participation program based on the apprenticeships employed since antiquity in societies all over the world. And English educator John Abbott of the Education 2000 Trust seconds the idea of apprenticeships in a recent article. Students want "more contact with adults other than parents and teachers," Abbott writes, and society does young people "a grave disservice by separating the world of learning from the world of work." Students need "interaction with ideas and the environment," he concludes, "if they are to develop a sense of general purpose, self-esteem, and an understanding of the essential interconnectedness of all forms of human endeavor."

Call this educational movement "brain-based," if you like; the key factor is motivation. And that is also what deliberate enrichment is about: Pursuing activities that are fun, interesting, even exciting to a child and that provide challenge and stimulation while requiring active involvement.

Abigail Adams had no inkling of future controversies when she wrote that "learning is not attained by chance" and must be "sought for with ardor and attended to with diligence." It is obvious from the disputes surrounding modern education, however, and from the disappointing performance of most American students, that a successful learning environment cannot be attained by chance or tradition, and that the lecture-memorization-drill-test model of the past is largely unsuccessful for children. We adults may have learned our numbers that way, our reading, vocabulary, history, and science. But it was surely our own ardor and diligence, our own inner drive to learn that propelled us. How much better it would have been for us to have had these immersion-participation-application approaches, these apprenticeships, collaborative learning groups, and microcommunities! And how much better it will be for arousing motivation in our children—regardless of intelligence and learning type—and at building contexts for true understanding. We can hardly continue educating "by chance" and then expect young people to perform in a rapidly evolving information era.

Students must see a reason for applying their ardor and diligence beyond college entrance exams and future earning power. These may work for older children, but will seldom motivate youngsters just starting to learn basic subjects. A participatory school where children see a direct application for their learning tools—like the boy designing newspaper ads or the child learning about commercial art in English—is a place for fun, motivation, and enrichment. Since we know how to do this from working models like the Peninsula, Lowell, and Edmonds schools, why wait twenty years? With the chance to create more enchanted minds and with the terrible costs of mental deprivation, perhaps a leap is justified while other kinds of educational research continue. To return to medical metaphors, a physician might know that researchers are testing a new and highly effective drug and that it will be available in a few years. But he or she would rarely, if ever, withhold the best available alternative in the meantime. Should we do any less for our children?

Chapter 9

As Morning Shows the Day:
How Social Factors Shape Future Minds

The childhood shows the man,
As morning shows the day.
                    —John Milton, *Paradise Regained*

. . . People often ask me, "After such a long, full career, aren't you planning to retire and enjoy yourself?" At age sixty-five, when I took on the new challenge of directing the Lawrence Hall of Science on top of full-time teaching and research at U.C. Berkeley, I was living out my answer. After my family, my twin priorities have always been contributing something worthwhile and pursuing creative endeavors, and the directorship presented both, as well as the chance to add another level of enrichment to my own experience.

When I was asked to direct the Hall starting in 1990, it was an ideal time to leave my hands-on research and spend most days at the public science center. I had several doctoral students who were very independent souls and whose research was going exceedingly well with only weekly consultations. I tried to provide an enriched environment for the staff at the Hall so they could do their best work at creating new science and math programs and exhibits, and it was very rewarding. After a five-year term, though, I was getting tired. I didn't think I could hold up for another term working seven days a week, sixteen hours a day. More than that, though, my graduate student Gary Gaufo had completed some beautiful data on the immune system and the brain, and if I was going to follow a lifetime dream of studying this subject, this was the time to go back to it.

The terrible autoimmune disease called lupus erythematosus runs in my family and took hold of my brother's life at age forty-one, my sister's at age twenty-six, and my niece's at age thirty-two. A nephew has it now, and at age forty, he's already had a stroke and a hip replacement. One of my greatest desires has been to find a relationship between the cerebral cortex—always my area of focus in the brain—and the immune system. Based on work done in France, we knew that removing the left half of a mouse's cerebral cortex would result in a falling number of the white blood cells called T-cells. So we tried to find the exact region associated with those immune cells. Using a wrinkled, hairless lab animal called the nude mouse, we located regions in both hemispheres, including one just behind the eyes and in front of a mouse's ear (the dorsal lateral frontal cortex) and even succeeded in stimulating the areas to grow by giving the animal a new thymus that produces new T-cells.

Having found this link between the brain and the immune system, we want to continue now with people. We would like to learn how to stimulate the equivalent region of the human brain (the dorsal lateral prefrontal cortex) to see if that stimulation can increase a person's T-cell count. We know from PET scans of the living human brain that sorting playing cards in a particular way will stimulate that exact brain region. So we want to find more practical everyday activities—playing bridge, perhaps—that will stimulate the dorsal lateral prefrontal cortex with its basic involvement in planning, short-term memory, and sequencing information. Our hope, in turn, is to induce a normal, healthy person to make more T-cells. Perhaps through deliberate enrichment and stimulation of this and other brain regions, we can eventually help people with diseases like the lupus that runs in my family.

Just as enrichment stimulates the cortex, stress affects the brain and, I believe, it may also contribute to the onset of lupus and its ugly path. We may someday find that enrichment could counter the onset of lupus by working through the cortex to stimulate the immune system in a positive way.

A second doctoral candidate who worked in my lab during the past five years, Seth Brooks, made another terrific discovery—this one about genes and enrichment. Before Seth joined our lab, during our thirty years of research, we had shown that you can see a thickening of a rat's cerebral cortex—an actual, structural change in its brain—after the animal lives in an enrichment cage for eighty days. We also found a change in the brain after thirty days, fifteen days, seven days, and just four days of enrichment. Seth, being very bright, zeroed in on the four-day effect to search for genes that might be altered or turned on in brain cells when an animal is enriched and that could somehow contribute to learning and memory as well as to the branching and growth of dendrites, to more spines and synapses, and to cortex thickening. Seth spent some time in my lab, then collaborated with Professor Joe Martinez at U.C. Berkeley (now at University of Texas, San Antonio), who has long studied the genetic processes that underlie memory and learning.

It has been clear to Joe and other researchers in that field that in order for any of us to learn new facts and remember new experiences—some for a lifetime—there must be a physical change in the brain. Well, working in collaboration with Joe's team in Texas, Seth found that a rat housed in an enriched environment for four days will produce higher levels of a particular protein in neurons in the brain—a protein associated with "long-term potentiation." This term refers to the fact that after very frequent or very active stimulation, a neuron will change physically and respond more strongly for weeks or even years. Seth's finding means that enriching an animal can turn on a gene associated with long-term potentiation (the *lag* gene), and the protein it makes, in turn, helps alter the neurons so they can retain new memories. They also found evidence that active mental stimulation causes portions within the *lag* gene to permanently rearrange themselves; this could allow learning to be literally inscribed in the DNA, not just in the structure of the neurons.

This discovery is terribly exciting. In one sense, it is a scientific vindication of our work; some biologists have looked upon enrichment research as a "soft finding" with too many uncontrolled variables. This new work traces the effect right to the genes and proteins, and helps explain the cortex thickening we first saw over thirty years ago.

For the person on the street, of course, this finding could

have a much more practical implication: Most of us have noticed that it's easier to relearn something than to learn it the first time, including skills learned in childhood and picked up again later. Perhaps the *lag* gene may explain this. The discovery certainly underscores the idea of sampling a wide range of experiences and skills in childhood and adolescence, as well as of returning to some childhood pleasures and activities in adulthood. Of course, it might also apply to the old "college try"—if at first you don't succeed at something, give it another chance; maybe learning will be easier the second time.

It's gratifying to see these important new molecular findings about immunity and the brain and about genes and enrichment stemming from our original work on rats and deliberate stimulation. But a part of my work will always be trying to spread the basic underlying message. In 1988, nearly twenty-five years after our first work was published, my husband and I were in Kenya having dinner at the home of a physician who was the head of the anatomy department at the University of Nairobi. We could hear a noise in the background and asked, "What's that?" This learned man replied, "Well, that's our child. He has experienced brain damage, and we have hired someone to sit with him." We replied immediately, "But you should be stimulating him! That's what we've learned from years of work." We explained our research and provided papers, and before we left Africa two weeks later, our host had set up a little school for thirteen brain-damaged children and had begun working with them. It was very impressive. And even so, I can talk to my colleague next door here at the university and he'll ask, "What are you doing now?" and when I reply, "Continuing with the brain change work," he'll remark, "What? The brain can change?"

The message is such a crucial one, yet so counterintuitive, that it may take generations before people routinely enrich their children. And when they do . . . well, the results may surprise them. With our four children, we carefully laid out guidelines for manners, ethics, morals, and the amount of TV allowed. We provided a reasonable number of games, books, lessons, home experiences, physical activities, and trips. We tried never to overload them. And most important, we wanted to avoid imposing our specific fields of interest onto their explorations so they could express themselves in unique ways. That strategy certainly worked, considering the diverse paths branching off in one family with a nuclear physicist father and a neuroanatomist mother.

Catherine, now forty-three, asked for piano lessons as a child. She switched to classical guitar, playing for hours and hours in her own room every day. She's now a professor of theater in Taiwan, writes books about culture and dance in East Asia, and for fun does flamenco dancing, which she went to Spain on her own to learn. Rick, now forty-one, asked to play the violin when he was four years old and practiced without ever being told. Today, he plays in the Berkeley symphony part-time when he's not working in his professional field of energy and architecture. Jeff, who's thirty-eight and the father of a newborn son, was always fond of people and animals. He took up bird-watching, went scuba diving off the Great Barrier Reef in hopes of seeing a great white shark, and traveled to El Salvador as a teenager to learn about the revolution there. He now teaches at Boston University. And Ann, thirty-three, loved every kind of sport from scuba to skydiving. At one point, she couldn't even walk because of juvenile rheumatoid arthritis. But she recovered and went on to play varsity women's soccer at Harvard. Although she majored in geology, she eventually became a family M.D.

Some might say, "Well, of course your children did well; they inherited genes for intelligence." No doubt genetics does play a role. But enriched environments very definitely add to it. We truly believed in enriching heredity. We tried to make choices as parents based on love and on our intuition of what was best for the children, and we also tried to keep those young brains stimulated in a healthy way. One time, I got a call from the school psychologist saying that Ann was disrupting her first-grade class and no one could reason with or control her. I went right down to the school and learned that the teacher was having the children draw 3's for half an hour. Ann had made her row of 3's in a few seconds, then started playing with the kids around her. That was the disruption! We got her into a different, more challenging class as soon as we could. This kind of attention to the child and to the young developing brain pays off. We were lucky to be able to make the changes we thought necessary as the children grew up. Some parents either can't, based on their situations, or just don't have enough energy to try. In either case, I think it's a loss to the young person, to the family, and to society. . . .

Enrichment and Society

When English poet John Milton wrote in the late 1650s that "The childhood shows the man/ As morning shows the day," he was speaking about Jesus of Nazareth as a child, teaching the rabbis in the temple. He might, however, have been describing his own classical education at the finest schools in England, and the greatness he achieved as a writer. Naturally, Milton had no formal knowledge of child development, enrichment, and the brain. But through literary insight, built upon observation and common sense, he arrived at a truth that twentieth century scientists are still working to document: Our childhood experiences help shape and predict our character, our intelligence, and our interests.

This book has related the considerable evidence for brain changes based on experience, and it has shown the devastating consequences of deprivation. People born to poverty, neglect, drug exposures, or restricted experience usually have a life outcome influenced by this deprivation. Even the minority of those from a deprived background who escape and transcend it still prove Milton's rule: Some positive influence upon the child—the steadfast support and encouragement of a teacher, a counselor, or relative, for example—was usually present to help shape the person's expectations, goals, and abilities.

We've seen that each child and each adult has multiple forms of intelligence, and consequently, brain-shaping influences come in many forms:

- Some are chemical: Infants and toddlers can be exposed to nutritional deficiencies, and to drugs, alcohol, stress hormones, or toxins that stunt brain development.
- A child's emotional climate—whether of love, nurturance, and attachment, or of abuse, neglect, and rejection—powerfully shapes the youngster's developing personality. It also influ-

ences his or her ability to pay attention, to learn, to control him or herself, to mature, and to bond with and nurture others.

- The educational milieu—starting with informal exposure to language, numbers, and reading, and progressing through all the experiences of preschool, grade school, and high school—make an enormous difference in a child's total sensory, motor, and intellectual exposure. This, in turn, helps determine how stimulated the brain's cortex is to grow and how able it is to absorb and respond to additional stimulation. The quality of schooling largely molds a child's attitude toward future exploring and learning, and ultimately, helps channel him or her toward career paths and stations in society.
- Finally, the child's vocational realm—sports, hobbies, activities, and other free-time options that are so often eclipsed by television and/or video games—dramatically sculpt a child's coordination, dexterity, skills, and interests.

Parents face an awesome responsibility, starting at a child's conception, in steering away from chemical privations and toward emotional, educational, and vocational enrichments. But as First Lady Hillary Clinton argues, "It takes a village to raise a child," and parents are joined in their developmental influence by teachers, relatives, neighbors, children's peers, employers, police, religious institutions, government agencies. What is society's responsibility, if any, in encouraging children's mental enrichment and preventing chemical, emotional, educational, and vocational forms of deprivation?

Some of the strongest voices in the enrichment field have equally strong opinions about society's role in enrichment and in turn, about its potential impact upon society.

F. Rene Van de Carr, the California physician who created the "Prenatal Classroom" exercises to teach to an unborn fetus, worries about the economic stratification in American society and sees an important role for enrichment in lifting the underclass from poverty. "We are building a very dangerous segmentation," he says, "between the people who can make a living and the people who can't. When the population grows large enough in that latter group, they are going to rebel; our society is going to have a heck of a problem and there won't be enough police to solve it." Van de Carr is convinced that "All you have to do is teach babies to pay attention," through prenatal stimulation, "and they will do all of what the Head Start program is talking about. . . . What *we* are talking about," he says, "is a method of *self-generating* stimulation that doesn't require vast expenditures. Anybody speaking any language and with essentially no equipment in their own dwellings can make the changes necessary to add 10 to 15 points to the IQ of every living human on the planet."

Van de Carr readily admits that prenatal stimulation "is my religion," and that many physicians and educators disagree with him. Even some who agree that experience and deliberate stimulation are important to the developing brain might question whether prenatal stimulation *alone* is sufficient to influence the entire course of a child's brain maturation. But Van de Carr is undeterred by such objections, and offers a personal anecdote as evidence. "One of my sons was trained with prenatal guitar music. It was an accident, really. We were just playing the guitar on his mother's stomach out of silliness." Van de Carr was separated from the boy some for years, but "suddenly, at age twelve, the boy told his mother he'd like to take guitar lessons. He had sufficient tonal capabilities to learn very, very quickly and to become successful at it. He formed his own group, cut some records, and sold them commercially, all on his own."

To Bruce Perry, the Texas child psychiatrist who worked with David Koresh's children after the Waco incident, as well as other cases of extreme child abuse, the prenatal period is notable for its beginning organization of the personality. This, he says, the mother can indirectly or directly influence, and her habits, even her role in society, play a part. "Temperament," he says, "is probably determined by intrauterine experience. If you have a distressed, overwhelmed, traumatized pregnant woman, the fetus's brain stem, which is organizing at that time, is going to come out hyperreactive. Instead of organizing to a heart rate of 80 beats per minute, it's organizing to 100 beats per minute, let's say, and that child will be more difficult to soothe. You know what sensation seekers are?" Perry asks. "Well, the warmest you ever were, the most contained, and never hungry, was in utero. If that state, when you [were laying down] all these primitive memories, is associated with a heartbeat of 100 or 120, then after birth, as a child, you will feel soothed when your heart rate gets to 120 instead of 80."

Perry has observed what he calls "a whole variety of settings that are extremely destructive to children but are still culturally acceptable. If you really do understand that the brain develops as a reflection of experience," he says, "you just can't help but make all the connections between the way we treat our children and the way we are." Perry fears a coming "social cultural devolution" in the least-privileged segments of society if resources continue to shift toward the more privileged. "I think there will be a very wealthy, very protected, but very small upper class, a middle class that is increasingly disaffected, and a large chaotic underclass that will be angry and feel shut out of the American dream.

"Our culture needs to reorganize to appreciate that the way we treat our children and the way we provide consistency, predictability, and nurturance is what determines the health of our society." We need to do things like changing the workplace, he says, to make it "more female friendly and child friendly." Perry also favors less age stratification in the educational system so that children of mixed ages learn together. "If you are five, you can teach a three-year-old and you get something positive from that. The better you are at teaching and sharing 'down,' the easier it is for you to accept from 'up.' " (Diamond's Each-One Teach-One program in the Albany, California, elementary and junior high schools worked on the same principle.) Schools, he says, should integrate child development issues throughout the curriculum at all levels "so that people understand affective development the same way they can understand algebra and geography. Once people know about these things, they will be better parents, whether they get pregnant at twenty-five or fourteen."

Our only chance to address some of the enormous societal problems we face, Perry says, "is if there is a social cultural transformation in our attitudes and expectations about raising children. . . . We are dramatically underrealizing the true potential of human beings, so that if you took random selections of one hundred humans at conception and looked at their potential in areas of anxiety regulation, emotional connectivity, and cognition, these would be far greater, far higher than the average you see when they grow up. Even in the best settings, in many healthy families in very healthy communities, there are a whole host of unrealized experiences that leave portions of our population underdeveloped in every domain of brain function." The human mind has enormous capacity, he points out. "Kids in the eighth grade now learn concepts and facts that got people the Nobel Prize fifteen years ago—concepts that were completely foreign to the brightest brains on earth." Since experience impacts the organization of the brain, we can literally evolve or devolve, depending on how we value and treat the learning and stimulation of children.

Some parents intuitively understand the value of enrichment and take pains to insure their children get plenty of it. Recalls Harriet Green, elementary school principal in Edmonds, Washington, "I've worked in communities where the joke was, 'If you put up a billboard that said Lessons: 555-1234, you'd get a thousand calls.' We had second graders who on Monday went to dance followed by soccer practice, and on Tuesday went to gymnastics followed by Hebrew school followed by French lessons, etc., etc., through their week. Of course, they were way overprogrammed, overstimulated, and bombarded, and had no time to play in the kinds of ways that kids need." Adds Green, "But then we also get parents who say, 'My kid doesn't want to do anything; he's not interested in sports. He only wants to come home and watch TV and play Nintendo.' " And to that we would add the sizable strata of parents that aren't even interested or involved enough to worry about whether their child "cocoons" or plays in the park. Considering that the average mother spends less than thirty minutes per day interacting directly with her child and the average father less than fifteen minutes, the What-me-worry? group is certainly very, very large.

If the parents don't worry, should society? Physician and researcher Harry Chugani of Detroit, Michigan, an outspoken advocate of deliberate enrichment for children before puberty, is concerned that "there are vast segments of the population missing out on a good opportunity. It is society's role," he insists, "to pick up where parents are leaving off.

"There has to be a societal commitment to an enriched environment for every child," he elaborates. "There are just too many wasted minds, and I think that it is society's task. Maybe it doesn't all have to be totally intervened by the Feds, but I think that certainly there could be volunteer organizations of older retired people coming and doing things with underprivileged children all day long. Take a child between one and four or five, prior to school. Then, maybe volunteers could be involved in the schools to provide that rich environment after school all the way through adolescence. Then," he concludes enthusiastically, "you've got the framework; that rich endowment for each individual that's happening already for many kids in the suburbs. Wouldn't that be nice? And why just the United States? Why not the rest of the world?"

Societal Impact and Enrichment Programs

A book like this, outlining how experience impacts the brain and how adults can help nurture a child's healthiest mental development, is destined to reach different groups in different ways.

For the minority of readers already pursuing their own enrichment plan, this book may provide a technical rationale for what they have been doing all along. It may also lend support in the form of success stories and statistics, and supply some ideas for fine-tuning their current approach. Those readers may not have known much about prenatal stimulation, for example, or about Baby Signs, Learningames, preschool music lessons, number line games, or the proven benefits of sports, hobbies, and other child-motivated leisure pursuits for the development of attention. They may not have encountered the multiple intelligences idea and how it can serve as a framework for encouraging enrichment in diverse areas. And they may actually decide to tone down their enrichment efforts if the child is overprogrammed with organized activities.

For a majority of readers, this book may inspire specific changes in child-rearing decisions. They may:

- Decide to aggressively avoid prescription drugs, caffeine, and alcohol during pregnancy.

- Be more cautious about the protein and vitamin content of their prenatal diets and of their child's diet after birth.
- Decide to try some mild prenatal stimulation, such as reading or music, and to provide a rich language environment of reading, speaking, and singing after birth.
- Be inspired to learn more about emotional support for infants and toddlers, as well as how to encourage a child's safe but unimpeded exploration of the home environment.
- Analyze preschool differently and consider the issues of reading and math *readiness* versus *academic training* for small children.
- Look upon the role of homework differently, and decide to encourage their children's maximal effort by banning television during homework time. They could also create a positive family activity around schoolwork by doing some "homework" of their own alongside the child: bill paying, reading, or catching up on office paperwork.
- Decide to restrict television time for both themselves and their children in the interest of more mentally and physically active pursuits.
- Pick up some new sports, hobbies, and activities for themselves, and encourage their children to fill leisure time actively.
- Invent new family traditions to encourage active mental pursuits, like weekly Scrabble night, or Sunday museum visits.
- Take more seriously the threat of cigarettes, drugs, and alcohol for their child's developing mind and for their own mental clarity.
- Perhaps decide to increase their efforts to prevent teen pregnancy, with its associated risk of premature delivery and fetal drug and alcohol exposures.
- Step up their efforts toward curricular reform in the local school, and begin volunteering classroom or after-school time.
- Begin to encourage a teenage child to choose activities, classes, or stimulating volunteer work instead of a repetitive low-wage part-time job.

For those two groups of readers, who are either modifying a preexisting enrichment plan or starting an effort in earnest for their children, society offers support in the form of programs funded by federal, state, and local governments and by private groups, religious organizations, and corporations. These include antidrug efforts, AIDS prevention, maternal and child health programs, parent training and support groups, crusades for better children's television programming, job skills training for teenagers, and campaigns for improving schools and public recreational facilities.

Society clearly has at least a modest enrichment ethic to begin with, and a stronger one, based on the evidence in this book, might inspire an even more decisive effort to back these kinds of programs. Why are greater efforts needed on behalf of programs like these? Take, as just one example, the history of a city recreation and parks department such as San Francisco's. Prior to 1978, the city operated several dozen clubhouses that provided supervised after-school activities for thousands of youngsters. The department also operated an extensive list of tuition-free classes in everything from painting and jewelry making to languages, open to city residents of all ages. Swimming pools and sports fields were free to use, and golfing, boating, horseback riding, and many other hobbies were available for a minimal charge.

These extensive offerings, however, all came before the California voter rebellion of 1978, also known as Proposition 13. This statewide reform rolled back property taxes and greatly benefited home and business owners. It also, however, simultaneously deprived local city budgets of hundreds of millions of dollars per year. Public schools suffered a major blow as local funding dropped by half—a blow that led in many schools to the reduction or elimination of "frills" like art, music, sports, and some if not all after-hours activities. But the cutbacks were even more devastating for local recreational programs.

The San Francisco Recreation and Parks Department, for example, was forced to close the clubhouses, according to assistant general manager Ernie Prindel. Besides cutting many of their classes, the recreation department began looking for ways to generate revenue, and started charging for the pared-down list of classes and for use of the swimming pools. It also steeply increased user fees for golfing, riding, boating, and the photo and art centers. And for the first time, it began charging for entrance to formerly free tourist attractions such as the Japanese Tea Garden in Golden Gate Park.

By deferring or foregoing maintenance that was once routine, by firing staff, doing with less, shifting priorities to the city's neediest groups and neighborhoods, charging the middle class, and inventing creative financing solutions, the department has gotten along for twenty years. Only recently, with the help of advocacy groups and some budgetary alchemy, were they able to reopen many of the after-school clubhouses. With just one voter initiative, a diverse recreational program that had evolved over decades to serve San Francisco's half million children and adults had shrunk dramatically. (Inflation and additional fiscal cutbacks in the following two decades also impacted the department's resources.) Surrounding the remaining programs was a pay-per-enrichment climate that retained the middle and upper classes but left behind many poorer residents without discretionary income for hobbies, activities, and costlier forms of recreation.

Identical belt-tightening has occurred across the country in the past twenty years in the schools and in virtually every type of public program. The rising cost of living, massive job cutbacks, and growing financial insecurity has fueled a triage mentality for public expenditures. And there is an equally fundamental demographic explanation: Families are becoming the exception in America, not the rule. The U.S. Commerce Department finds that by a slim 52 percent majority, most American households have no children under eighteen living at home. By the year 2010, they predict this will increase to a 60 percent majority. All-adult households are less motivated to vote for public programs that benefit children. And beyond that, parents tend to disenfranchise themselves: Only 39 percent of parents with dependent children at home voted in the last national election, compared to 61 percent of the elderly.

The constituency for children is clearly dwindling, and the upshot of the sweeping economic and demographic changes we've been describing here is that a third group of potential readers—our country's least privileged 20 percent—would benefit most from enrichments of all types but are the least likely to do so.

The gap between haves and have-nots has never been wider in

America, and children make up a disproportionate segment of the poor. In California, 47 percent of those living below the poverty level are children. (In 1995, that level was officially defined as $15,455 per year for a family of four.) Nationally, more than one of every four children is living in poverty! Among children under age three, 1 in 10 lives in "extreme poverty" or less than $7,700 per year for a family of four. By 1993, half of all household income went to the richest 20 percent of Americans, while the poorest 20 percent received only *one-fourteenth as much,* or 3.6 percent of all income. The richest 5 percent of Americans, in fact, earns more than the bottom 60 percent.

Besides the sheer misery and inequity of such realities in a country as rich as the United States, there is a future cost for allowing one-quarter to one-half of our children to live below the poverty line in households with incomes less than $15,455 for a family of four: Poverty is the biggest risk factor for teenage pregnancy, for school failure and dropout, and for violent crime. Other risk factors for what author Lisbeth Schorr labels "rotten outcomes" in her book *Within Our Reach,* include poor maternal and infant health and nutrition, abuse and neglect, poor housing, and having a poorly educated or impaired mother, particularly one that lacks access to social services.

As we've seen in other chapters, poor prenatal care, malnutrition, inadequate emotional nurturing, and an unstimulating home environment can all influence brain development dramatically. It is safe to conclude, then, that poverty is also an important risk factor for failing to reach the brain's potential. For this reason, deliberate enrichment could be seen as one powerful way to help break the generational cycles of poverty and despair. But a fourteen-year-old single mother, let's say, is much less likely to seek out and buy a book like this than a thirty-year-old suburban woman with top-notch reading skills, expendable income, and leisure time.

Underprivileged parents need society's help in escaping poverty through enrichment programs for themselves and their children (among other types of assistance), and luckily, numerous programs have proven effective at changing "rotten" outcomes. Head Start is the largest and best known; but interventions such as the Abecedarian program in North Carolina also changed the lives of

most participants; as have the Resource Mothers of South Carolina; Avance in San Antonio, Texas; the Parents as Teachers program in Missouri, and others.

One of the founders of Head Start, Edward Zigler, has helped
form year-round schools in Mehlville, Missouri; Norfolk, Virginia;
and Bridgeport, Connecticut; and inspired others in additional
states. Each has an all-day preschool for children three and older,
and enrichment programs for grade school pupils during school
vacations, and before and after regular school hours. These all-
day schools attempt to provide as many of children's physical,
emotional, and social needs as they can—like nurturing homes
away from home. Although Lisbeth Schorr has concluded that
Americans are better at creating small, successful pilot programs
than at scaling up to massive public ones, the lessons of Head
Start show that with federal funding, interventions can reach
large numbers of needy children.

Unfortunately, the climate for supporting underprivileged
youngsters is anything but expansive. Despite a nationwide Stand
for Children march on Washington in June 1996, and the intense
lobbying efforts of the Children's Defense Fund and other advocacy groups, both houses of Congress passed bills ending federally funded welfare, including Aid to Families with Dependent
Children. Two months later, President Clinton signed it into law.
For over sixty years, poor families had the right to federal assistance under an act signed by Franklin Roosevelt. Now, states will
receive block grants to distribute aid under their own rules, con-
strained by strict federal guidelines. Among them, the welfare
umbrella closes over a family after two years if the head of the
household has not found work. In addition, no family can receive
benefits for more than five years in a lifetime. The emphasis will
be on "a second chance, not a way of life," the President said
upon signing, and on assistance with day care, transportation,
and job hunting. A pregnant teenager must stay in school or lose
her benefits, and if she has additional children while on welfare,
states have the right to deny them any assistance.

If what *Time* magazine writer George Church calls "this vast
and risky experiment" succeeds, perhaps the suffocating poverty
so many endure will begin to be lifted and replaced by jobs and
better education. Some observers, however, are not sanguine

about the prospects. Children's Defense Fund president Marian Wright Edelman called the legislation a "moral blot" on Clinton's presidency, and Ralph Nader called it a "betrayal" likely to throw one million more children into poverty. Whatever the results, our nation ignores or further deprives the poor at its own peril. Every year, over 700,000 teenagers drop out of school and fail to return; *this represents 1 in 7 students who never get a high school diploma or equivalency degree.* The dropouts from a single class—say, the Class of '98—will cost America over $80,000 per individual in lost taxes during their work life at low- rather than higher-paying jobs. Premature babies born to young mothers with poor prenatal care cost an average of $400,000 per child over a lifetime for medical and social assistance. Head Start costs $3,000 per child per year, but if it keeps a child from later committing a crime, it would save the $20,000 we spend per year to support a prison inmate. Can we really afford not to help children growing up in impoverished environments to a better, more enriched childhood experience?

Sociologists, politicians, authors, and activists have suggested dozens of remedies. David Hamburg, president of the Carnegie Corporation of New York, a large charitable foundation, recommends a number of interventions for parent training, home care visits, education, and teen programs in his book *Today's Children.* Activist Lisbeth Schorr adds family planning, parental and child health care, family support services, and child care interventions. In 1992, then-presidential candidate Bill Clinton proposed a number of programs for improved child care, AIDS and drugs education, expanded Head Start, and a youth corps for school dropouts—most of which he still supports. In October 1996, President Clinton also proposed a tutoring program wherein 100,000 college students would help young children learn to read. And author Ruth Sidel, among others, argues in her book *Keeping Women and Children Last* for an all-out mobilization—a domestic Marshall plan for blighted inner-city and rural areas— that would provide jobs and rebuild dilapidated schools in addition to helping children.

If we could add one recommendation to this list, it would be this: to create a Constituency for Enrichment. This block of parents, teachers, and other citizens would believe that we've disenchanted too many minds already, and that families, schools, recreational organizations, and all the elements of our culture that can influence and stimulate young minds must see enrichment as a necessary part of child development—just as fundamental as good nutrition, good exercise, good hygiene, avoiding strangers, or wearing bicycle helmets and safety belts. Growing brains must be protected and "exercised" so that new generations of bright, inquiring minds will see us, and themselves, through the twenty-first century.

We propose to build this constituency the same way advocacy grew for wildlife and wildlands in America: by experience. Visiting a national park, watching moose, antelope, or wild geese, and smelling the fragrance of pine forests and wildflowers has turned many an urbanite into a staunch protector of wilderness. We believe that in the same way, parents, teachers, grandparents, neighbors, and friends who implement the ideas in this book will see substantial, lasting benefit to their children and will adopt an enrichment ethic—a different lens for viewing prenatal care, child care, education, recreation, and the political issues that surround them. With this large advocacy block, legislation, propositions, and elections that hinge on enrichment issues may start to swing away from our current miserly stance toward public schools, impoverished children, and troubled teens, and toward a more caring, generous position. It's never too late to begin enriching the brain; the magic dendritic trees can branch and grow, enlarging the cortex, throughout life. But as we've seen, childhood is a magical time for brain development that we must carefully protect and nurture.

The Future at Hand

What would the future be like with a powerful constituency for enrichment and an ethic supporting the healthy, active mental lives of children and adults? One could envision pregnancies free of cigarette, drug, and alcohol use. Babies bathed in love, language, and gentle sensory stimulation. Children free to explore, imagine, and create. Schools that motivate students to learn so they understand and remember what they study, think for themselves, and reach higher for a brighter future. Children and teenagers who value and nurture their own developing brain by avoiding long stints of television, physical inactivity, and harmful drug exposures, and who look for new ways to stimulate their own multiple intelligences. Parents who model for their children an interest in reading, creativity, and participating in sports, hobbies, and organized leisure activities.

Sound utopian? Perhaps. But for most individuals, these elements would require not money or advanced degrees but simple information, awareness, motivation, and effort. And some families have been operating in just this way for years. Take, for example, a couple from San Diego, California, named Robert and Rochelle, and their son, Allen. Robert is an eighth-grade science teacher at a year-round school serving a largely Hispanic population. Rochelle teaches blind children how to move around freely in their environment. And Allen is a bright, well-adjusted fifth grader.

When Rochelle was pregnant, she avoided all drugs and alcohol, and ate an exemplary diet, planned for maximal fetal nutrition. She and Robert also began a prenatal stimulation program during the third trimester. They read to the fetus daily and played classical music, then continued both stimulations after he was born. Since Allen was very small, they have traveled extensively, providing the child "a lot of exposure to a diverse experience base. He was also reading fairly early," Robert says, "and when he read, we read along with him. Not only was he a good reader, but he developed an incredible oral memory" for stories, songs, and dialogue. "He could watch a movie once and afterwards, act out scenes, quoting the script verbatim."

In third grade, Allen started showing an aversion to reading, which surprised the parents because he'd received "such a rich introduction and so much support." Rochelle suspected that Allen might have an eye-tracking problem that showed up when the reading material for his age group shifted from large-print words to smaller ones. The couple consulted a reading specialist, and after a few months of intensive work with their son, his problem turned around rapidly. "By the end of third grade," boasts the proud father, "he received a reading prize from the state." Now, at age eleven, Allen has played golf for nearly a decade (since he was eighteen months old), he recently took up the viola, he is an exceptional runner, and he is charismatic and popular with both his peers and adults.

Robert's direct experience with enrichment inspired him to join a special "brain team" in his school district, and to begin applying "brain-based" education techniques in his science classroom. He starts each class with music the students select—Led Zeppelin, Foreigner, Beatles, Jimmy Buffett, White Snake, Green Day, Freddie Fender—to "get them engaged so they bring a positive mind-set to the work." He teaches them memory techniques like "chunking" and using "silly monikers" to help them learn science facts such as the elements of the periodic table. "In one week," he says, "we learned the first thirty elements, this way, from hydrogen to xenon." For that unit, he went on to demonstrate some "kitchen chemistry" to illustrate some of what the students had learned about the elements. "We burned peanuts to create Number 6, Carbon. We created 'kitchen froth' with baking soda and vinegar, popped corn to see an exothermic reaction at work, and the students are now building their own molecules using computers."

Robert says he knows of "forty or fifty kids who would have given up if it hadn't been for some of these 'brain-based' teaching techniques. For one kid in particular, my class was the only one he had success in. He had been labeled a special education student, and was having real difficulty. But we worked hard with him on his organization skills, his behavior, and on staying current with his homework. This boy is now making A's and B's in his first year in high school," Robert says, again with obvious pride, "and he tells me, 'You saved my bacon; you kept me on track enough to pass.' " Robert uses "brain-based" techniques to "create a positive emotional set," he says, "then to key in on the students' strong points to build in success. My personal sense," he concludes, "is that the number one factor is positive experience in the classroom. It keeps them in the ball game like nothing else will."

Robert has influenced hundreds of students—"a hundred and twenty per year," he estimates—with his educational enrichment techniques. And he and Rochelle have created a home environment that bolstered Allen's reading skills, oral memory, music ability, sports talents, and has no doubt stimulated his brain development in other significant ways. Theirs is an enrichment ethic at work. Creating enchanted minds is not some twenty-first-century idea to them; it's how they have lived for the past decade. With their quiet determination, they took a leap of faith based on science. And they are altering their children's futures in a priceless way.

Childhood enrichment is not just the province of professionals like Robert and Rochelle. Our goal has been to show the way a child's brain grows and matures, the consequences of stimulation and active involvement versus boredom and passivity, and the myriad ways of enhancing environmental input without overloading the child's "mind full of enchantment." We hope you have discovered and perhaps already tried some specific approaches herein, and that they will, over time, help your children reach their fullest and healthiest mental development. The Resource Guide and Appendix that follow are designed to provide you with still more ideas.

Resource Guide:
Additional Tools for Enrichment

This section provides additional resources for deliberately enriching a child's home environment or school experience. It includes suggestions for reading; support groups and organizations; on-line resources; catalogs and other ways to find specific commercial products; and miscellaneous information about the ideas, classes, activities, and playthings discussed in this book. While many people live in large urban areas that offer a wealth of opportunities for increased enrichment, others live in less-populous areas with fewer resources. This listing is designed to help people locate the materials they need by mail, phone, or Internet.

Articles

About the brain

"Brain Food: How to Eat Smart," by Randy Blann. *Psychology Today,* May/June 1996, pp. 35–37.

"Building a Better Brain," by Daniel Golden. *Life,* June 1995, pp. 63–70.

"Einstein's Brain," by Gina Marento. *Discover,* May 1985, pp. 29–34.

"Fertile Minds," by J. Madeleine Nagh, *Time,* Feb. 3, 1997, pp. 48–56.

"How to Build a Baby's Brain," by Sharon Begley. *Newsweek,* Spring/Summer, 1997, pp. 28–32.

"How to Stand for a Child," by Michael Ryan. *Parade,* Feb. 9, 1997, pp. 8–11.

"How Would You Raise a Brilliant Child?" by Ponchita Pierce. *Parade,* April 13, 1997, pp. 10–11.

"A Love Affair with the Brain," by Janet L. Hopson. *Psychology Today,* November 1984, pp. 61–73.

"Marian Diamond Wants to Know All the Pill's Side Effects," by Barbara Rowes. *People,* March 28, 1977, p. 31.

"New Evidence Points to Growth of the Brain, Even Late in Life," by Daniel Goleman. *New York Times,* July 30, 1985, "Science Times," p. 1.

"Secrets of the Brain," by Earl Ubell. *Parade,* Feb. 9, 1997, pp. 20–22.

"You Can Raise Your Child's I.Q.," by Edwin Kiester, Jr., and Sally Valente Kiester. *Reader's Digest,* October 1996, pp. 137–142.

About pregnancy

"Eating for Two," by Pamela Von Nostitz. *Parents,* April 1995, pp. 44–46.

"Enhancing Early Speech, Parental Bonding, and Infant Physical Development Using Prenatal Intervention in Standard Obstetric Practices," by Rene Van de Carr and Marc Lehrer. *Pre- and Peri-Natal Psychology,* Vol. 1, pp. 22–30. Spring, 1986.

"Preconception Care: Risk Reduction and Health Promotion in Preparation for Pregnancy," by Brian W. Jack and Larry Culpepper. *Journal of the American Medical Association,* September 5, 1990, Vol. 264, No. 9, pp. 1147–1148.

See issues of *All Babies Count* newsletter; Scott Newman Center, 6255 Sunset Boulevard, Suite 1906, Los Angeles, CA 90028.

About young children

"Infant Health and Development Program for Low Birth Weights, Premature Infants," by Craig T. Ramey, et al. *Pediatrics,* Vol. 3, March 1992, pp. 454–465.

"On Raising Moral Children," by Robert Coles. *Time,* January 20,

1997, pp. 50–52. Excerpted from *The Moral Intelligence of Children,* by Robert Coles. New York: Random House, 1997.

"Terrific Twos," by Bernice Weissbourd. *Parents,* March 1993 pp. 111–114.

"Ready or Not: What Parents Should Know about School Readiness," a brochure from the National Association for the Education of Young Children, 1834 Connecticut Avenue, NW, Washington, DC 20009; 800-424-2460.

"Help Your Child Learn at Home," a brochure from the National Parent Teacher Association; send a self-addressed envelope to National PTA, 700 North Rush Street, Chicago, IL 60611-2571; 312-787-0977.

"Helping Your Child Get Ready for School," a brochure from the U.S. Department of Education; many large cities have government bookstores, and you can find this under catalog number S/N 065-000-00522-1, or call 202-783-3238 and order it with a credit card.

About older children

"Gender and the Culture of Science." *Science,* April 16, 1993, pp. 393–432.

"Great Science Museums." *Discover,* November 1993, pp. 78–113.

"Playthings of Science," by Fred Guterl. *Discover,* December 1996, pp. 54–61.

"The Best Software for Kids," by Warren Buckleitner. *Parade,* November 24, 1996, p. 13.

"Underdog Days," by Jeff Giles. *Newsweek,* November 27, 1995, pp. 82–85.

About education

Early Childhood Today; Scholastic, Inc., 730 Broadway, New York, NY 10003; 212-505-4900.

Education Today; Educational Publishing Group, Statler Building, Suite 1215, 20 Park Plaza, Boston, MA 02116; 800-927-6006.

Young Children; National Association for the Education of Young Children, 1509 16th Street, NW, Washington, DC 20036; 800-424-2460.

About child welfare

Child Welfare, a bimonthly publication of the Child Welfare League of America, 440 First St., NW, Suite 310, Washington, DC 20001; 202-638-2952. Internet address: http://ericps.edu.inc.edu/ npin/reswork/workorgs/cwlamer.html

Books

About the brain

The Brain: A Neuroscience Primer, by Richard F. Thompson. New York: Freeman, 1993.

The Brain: The Last Frontier, by Richard Restak. New York: Warner, 1979.

Brain Development and Cognition: A Reader, edited by Mark H. Johnson. Cambridge, MA: Blackwell, 1993.

Brain Maturation and Cognitive Development: Comparative and Cross-Cultural Perspectives, edited by Kathleen Gibson and Anne Peterson. New York: Aldine de Gruyter, 1991.

Brain Plasticity and Behavior, by Bryan Kolb. Mahway, NJ: Erlbaum, 1995.

The Conscious Brain, by Steven Rose. New York: Vintage, 1976.

Discovering the Brain, by Sandra Ackerman for the Institute of Medicine, National Academy of Sciences. Washington, DC: National Academy Press, 1992.

Enriching Heredity: The Impact of the Environment on the Anatomy of the Brain, by Marian Cleeves Diamond. New York: Free Press, 1988.

Human Behavior and the Developing Brain, edited by Geraldine Dawson and Kurt W. Fischer. New York: Guilford, 1994.

The Human Brain Coloring Book, by M. C. Diamond, A. B. Scheibel, and L. M. Elson. New York: Harper and Row, 1985.

Human Embryology, by William J. Larsen. New York: Churchill Livingstone, 1993.

The Infant Mind, by Richard M. Restak. Garden City, NY: Doubleday, 1986.

The Three Pound Universe, by Judith Hooper and Dick Teresi. New York: Putnam, 1992.

About pregnancy

The Complete Book of Pregnancy and Childbirth, by Sheila A. Kitzinger. New York: Knopf, 1994.

Education and Counseling for Childbirth, by Sheila A. Kitzinger. New York: Schocken, 1979.

Fetal Development: A Psychobiological Perspective, edited by Jean-Pierre Lecanuet, William Fifer, Norman Krasnegor, and William Smotherman. Hillsdale, NJ: Erlbaum, 1995.

Planning for a Healthy Baby: A Guide to Genetic and Environmental Risks, by Richard M. Goodman. New York: Oxford University Press, 1986.

Planning for Pregnancy, Birth, and Beyond, by the American College of Obstetricians and Gynecologists. New York: Dutton, 1996.

The Pregnancy Cookbook: Easy Recipes for Nine Months of Healthy Eating, by Marsha Hudnall and Donna Shields. New York: Berkley, 1995.

Prenatal Classroom: A Parent's Guide for Teaching Your Baby in the Womb, by F. Rene Van de Carr and Marc Lehrer. Atlanta, GA: Humanics Learning, 1992.

The Well Pregnancy Book, by Mike Samuels and Nancy Samuels. New York: Summit, 1986. The discussion on stress, relaxation, and the fetus is particularly relevant to prenatal brain growth.

Why Zebras Don't Get Ulcers, by Robert M. Sapolsky. New York: Freeman, 1994.

About the home environment and pregnancy

Cleaner, Clearer, Safer, Greener: A Blueprint for Detoxifying Your Environment, by Gary Null. New York: Villard, 1990.

The Natural House Book, by David Pearson. New York: Simon & Schuster, 1989.

Well Body, Well Earth, by Mike Samuels and Hal Zina Bennett. San Francisco: Sierra Club Books, 1983.

Your Home, Your Health, and Well-Being, by David Rousseau, W. J. Rea, and Jean Enwright. Berkeley, CA: Ten-Speed Press, 1988.

About children of all ages

Betty Crocker's Cooking with Kids. New York: Macmillan, 1995.

Classics to Read Aloud to Your Children, by William F. Russell. New York: Crown, 1984.

Cooking with Children, by Marion Cunningham. New York: Knopf, 1995.

Family Math: A Book of Fun Number Games and Exercises for Kids and Their Parents, by Jean Kerr. Regents of the University of California; to order, call 510-642-1910 or send a check for $23 made out to "Regents of the University of California" to Equals Publications, Lawrence Hall of Science, University of California, Berkeley, CA 94720-5200.

French, German, Spanish for Children. Berlitz courses published by Aladdin Books and available at quality bookstores; language tapes included.

How to Raise Avid Readers in the Video Age, by Mary Leonhardt. New York: Crown, 1996.

Let's Learn French (Spanish, etc.) Picture Dictionaries. Published by Passport Books and available at quality bookstores.

The New York Times Parent's Guide to the Best Books for Children, by Eden Ross Lipson. New York: Times Books, 1991.

Parenting for Dummies, by Sandra Hardin Gookin. Foster City, CA: IDG, 1995.

The Parent's Handbook, by Don Dinkmeyer and Gary D. McKay. Circle Pines, MN: American Guidance Service, 1989.

The Parents' Resource Almanac, by Beth DeFrancis. Holbrook, MA: Bob Adams, 1994.

The Parent's Resource Manual, by Beth DeFrancis. Holbrook, MA: Bob Adams, 1994.

P.E.T. Parent Effectiveness Training, by Thomas Gordon. New York: Plume, 1975.

The Plug-in Drug, by Marie Winn. New York: Penguin, 1985.

Positive Discipline, by Jane Nelson. New York: Ballentine, 1996.

Positive Discipline for Parenting in Recovery, by Jane Nelson, Riki Intner, and Lynn Lott. Rocklin, CA: Prima, 1996.

Practical Parenting Tips, by Vicki Lansky. Deephaven, MN: Meadowbrook, 1992.

Teaching Your Children Responsibility, by Linda Eyre and Richard Eyre. New York: Simon & Schuster, 1994.

Teaching Your Children Values, by Linda Eyre and Richard Eyre. New York: Simon & Schuster, 1993.

365 TV-Free Activities You Can Do with Your Child, by Steve and Ruth Bennett. Holbrook, MA: Adams Media Corp., 1996.

What Are We Feeding Our Kids? by Michael F. Jacobson and Bruce Maxwell. New York: Workman, 1994.

What Should I Feed My Kids? by Ronald E. Kleinman and Michael S. Jellinek, with Julie Houston. New York: Fawcett Columbine, 1994.

About young children

Academic Instruction in Early Childhood: Challenge or Pressure? edited by Leslie Rescorla, Marion C. Hyson, and Kathy Hirsh-Pasek. New Directions for Child Development, No. 53.; San Francisco: Jossey-Bass (Fall 1991).

Active Learning for Fours, by Debby Cryer, Thelma Harms, and Adele Richardson Ray. Menlo Park, CA: Addison-Wesley, 1996.

Active Learning for Fives, by Debby Cryer, Thelma Harms, and Adele Richardson Ray. Menlo Park, CA: Addison-Wesley, 1996.

Baby Signs: How to Talk with Your Baby Before Your Baby Can Talk: Building a Bridge with Baby Signs, by Linda P. Acredolo and Susan W. Goodwyn. Chicago: Contemporary Books, 1996.

Deafness in Infancy and Early Childhood, by Peter J. Fine, M.D. New York: Medcom, 1974.

Developmentally Appropriate Practice in Early Childhood Programs Serving Children from Birth Through Age 8, edited by Sue Brodekamp. Washington, DC: National Association for the Education of Young Children, 1987.

The Early Childhood Years: The 2 to 6 Year Old, by Theresa Caplan and Frank Caplan. New York: Bantam, 1984.

Early Schooling: The National Debate, edited by Sharon Kagen and Edward F. Zigler. New Haven, CT: Yale University Press, 1987.

Educating the Infant and Toddler, by Burton White. New York: Lexington, 1988.

The First Twelve Months of Life, by Frank and Theresa Caplan. New York: Bantam, 1995.

Infants and Mothers; Differences in Development, by T. Berry Brazelton. New York: Dell, 1983.

Getting Ready to Read, by Toni S. Gould. New York: Walker, 1988.

Kidsgardening: A Guide to Kids Messing Around in the Dirt, by Kevin and Kim Raftery. Palo Alto, CA: Klutz, 1989.

The Language Instinct: How the Mind Creates Language, by Steven Pinker. New York: HarperPerennial, 1994.

Math for the Very Young, by Lydia Polonsky, Dorothy Freedman, Susan Lesher, and Kate Monisor. New York: Wiley, 1995.

The Mother's Almanac, by Marguerite Kelly and Elia Parsons. New York: Doubleday, 1992.

The New Parents Source Book: Information, Products, and Services for You and Your Baby, by Hilory Wagner. New York: Citadel, 1996.

Parenting Young Children, by Don Dinkmeyer, Gary D. McKay, and James S. Dinkmeyer. Circle Pines, MN: American Guidance Service, 1989.

Ready or Not: What Parents Should Know About School Readiness, a brochure from the National Association for the Education of Young Children, 1834 Connecticut Avenue, NW, Washington, DC 20009; 800-424-2460.

Ready, Set, Explore, by Marlene Barron. New York: Wiley, 1996.

Ready, Set, Read and Write, by Marlene Barron. New York: Wiley, 1995.

Ready to Learn: A Mandate for the Nation, by Ernest L. Boyer. Carnegie Foundation for the Advancement of Teaching, Princeton, NJ, 08540, 1991.

Seeing Voices: A Journal into the World of the Deaf, by Oliver Sacks. New York: HarperPerennial, 1990.

The Superbaby Syndrome: Escaping the Dangers of Hurrying Your Child, by Jean Grasso Fitzpatrick. New York: Harcourt Brace, 1988.

Teach Your Child to Read in 100 Easy Lessons, by Phyllis Haddox and Elaine Bruer. New York: Simon & Schuster, 1983.

Touchpoints: The Essential Reference, by T. Berry Brazelton. Reading, MA: Addison-Wesley, 1992.

Your Child's Growing Mind, by Jane Healy. New York: Doubleday, 1987.

About older children

Adolescence: The Survival Guide for Parents and Teenagers, by Elizabeth Fenwick and Dr. Tony Smith. New York: DK, 1996.

Amazing Grace, by Jonathan Kozol. New York: Crown, 1996.

The Best of the Best for Children, edited by Denise Perry Donavin. From the American Library Association, reviews of books, magazines, videos, audio, software, toys, and travel. New York: Random House, 1992.

The Best Toys, Books, and Videos for Kids, by Joanne Oppenheim and Stephanie Oppenheim. New York: HarperPerennial, 1995.

Caring for Your School-age Child, Ages 5 to 12, edited by Edward L. Schor, the American Academy of Pediatrics. New York: Bantam, 1995.

Computer Museum Guide to the Best Software for Kids, by Cathy Miranker and Alison Elliott. New York: HarperPerennial, 1995.

Decoding Your Teenager: How to Understand Each Other During the Turbulent Years, by Michael DeSisto. New York: Morrow, 1991.

Living with Teenagers, by Jean Rosenbaum and Veryl Rosenbaum. New York: Stein & Day, 1980.

The Parent's Guide to Teenagers, edited by Leonard H. Gross. New York: Macmillan, 1981.

School's Out: Now What? Afternoons, Weekends, Vacations; Creative Choices for Your Child, by Joan M. Bergstrom. Berkeley, CA: Ten-Speed Press, 1990.

Surviving Your Adolescents, by Thomas Phelan. Glen Ellyn, IL: Child Management, 1993.

About education

Frames of Mind, by Howard Gardner. New York: Basic Books, 1983.

The Hurried Child, by David Elkind. Reading, MA: Addison-Wesley, 1981.

Making Connections: Teaching and the Human Brain, by Renate Nummela Caine and Geoffrey Caine. Menlo Park, CA: Addison-Wesley, 1994.

Miseducation: Preschoolers at Risk, by David Elkind. New York: Knopf, 1987.

Schools for Thought: A Science of Learning in the Classroom, by John Bruer. Cambridge, MA: MIT Press, 1994.

Schools That Work: America's Most Innovative Public Education Programs, by George H. Wood. New York: Dutton, 1992.

Smart Schools, Smart Kids: Why Do Some Schools Work? by Edward B. Fiske. New York: Simon & Schuster, 1991.

The Unschooled Mind: How Children Think and How Schools Should Teach, by Howard Gardner. New York: Basic Books, 1991.

About child welfare

Breaking the Silence, by Mariette Hartley and Anne Commire. New York: Putnam, 1988.

Child Abuse and Neglect: Cross-Cultural Perspectives, by Jill E. Korbin, editor. Berkeley, CA: University of California Press, 1981.

Child Abuse Prevention Handbook. Crime Prevention Center, Office of the Attorney General, California Department of Justice, P.O. Box 944255, Sacramento, CA 94244-2550.

Childhood's Future, by Richard Louv. Boston: Houghton Mifflin, 1990.

It Takes a Village and Other Lessons Children Teach Us, by Hillary Rodham Clinton. New York: Simon & Schuster, 1996.

Keeping Women and Children Last, by Ruth Sidel. New York: Penguin, 1996.

101 Things You Can Do for Our Children's Future, by Richard Louv. New York: Anchor, 1994.

There Are No Children Here, by Alex Kotlowitz. New York: Doubleday, 1991.

Today's Children, by David A. Hamburg. New York: Times Books, 1992.

The Way We Never Were, by Stephanie Coontz. New York: Basic Books, 1992.

Within Our Reach, by Lisbeth Schorr. New York: Anchor, 1989.

Organizations

Relating to the brain

Dana Alliance for Brain Initiatives
1001 G. Street, NW, Suite 1025
Washington, DC 20001
202-737-9200
http://www.dana.org
(publishes *The Brain in the News*, articles about the brain and neu-
    rological research)

The Harvard Mahoney Neuroscience Institute
Harvard Medical School
220 Longwood Avenue
Boston, MA 02115
617-432-1000
http://www.med.harvard.edu
(publishes the newsletter *On the Brain*, articles about recent brain
    research)

Relating to pregnancy

National Fatherhood Initiative
1 Bank Street, Suite 160
Gaithersburg, MD 20878
301-948-0599
(literature and other resources promoting fathers' involvement
    with children)

Natural Resources: A Pregnancy, Childbirth, and Early Parenting
    Center
1309 Castro Street
San Francisco, CA 94114
415-550-2611
(information and catalogs on pregnancy and childbirth issues)

Parent Action (part of the National Association of Parents)
2 North Charles Street
Baltimore, MD 21201
410-727-3687
(information on child care, self-esteem building, and other parenting topics)

Planned Parenthood
810 Seventh Avenue
New York, NY 10019
212-541-7800
(information on birth control and family planning)

Relating to young children and parenting

Action for Children's Television
20 University Road
Cambridge, MA 02138
617-876-6620
(information on nonviolent and educational programming for children)

American Association of Retired Persons Grandparent Information Center
601 E Street, NW
Washington, DC 20049
202-434-2296
(information on effective grandparenting)

American Psychological Association
1200 17th Street, NW
Washington, DC 2000
(202) 336-5500
(information on parenting issues, mental health, learning disabilities, referrals)

Boys Town National Hot Line
800-448-3000
(counseling services, pamphlets, and videos on parenting)

Center for the Education of the Deaf Infant
1810 Hopkins Street
Berkeley, CA 94708
510-527-5544
(information and referrals on childhood hearing impairments)

Civitan International Research Center
University of Alabama at Birmingham
P.O. Box 313
UAB Station
Birmingham, AL 35294
205-934-8900
(early educational and intervention programs)

Family Research Council
700 13th Street, NW, Suite 180
Washington, DC 20005
202-293-2100
(publishes the newsletter *Family Policy*)

Family Resource Coalition
200 South Michigan Avenue, Suite 1520
Chicago, IL 60604
312-341-0900
(offers parenting information and help finding and starting sup-
    port groups for parents)

Moms Offering Moms Support Club (MOMS)
814 Moffat Circle
Simi Valley, CA 93065
805-526-2725
(information on support for nonworking moms, and local con-
    tact numbers)

National Association of Child Care Resource and Referral Agencies
PO Box 40246
Washington, DC 20016
202-393-5501
(information on finding quality child care)

National Center for Family Literacy
401 S. Fourth Avenue, Suite 610
Louisville, KY 40202
502-584-1133
(publications promoting family literacy)

National Coalition for Music Education
1806 Robert Fulton Drive
Reston, VA 22091
703-860-4000
(information on benefits of music education for children)

National Parenting Association
65 Central Park West, Suite 1D
New York, NY 10023
800-709-8795
(books and information on parenting skills and issues of concern
    to parents)

National Parenting Services
900-246-6667
(fee per minute for expert parenting advice)

Relating to older children and parenting

EQUALS Program
Lawrence Hall of Science
University of California
Berkeley, CA 94720
510-642-1823
(math and science ideas for children, parents, teachers)

Full Option Science System
Lawrence Hall of Science
University of California
Berkeley, CA 94720
510-642-8941
(ideas for science teachers)

Gifted Child Society, Inc.
190 Rock Road
Glen Rock, NJ 07452-1736
201-444-6530
(information and workshops on identifying and helping gifted
    children)

Kidsnet
Consumer Information Center
6856 Eastern Avenue, NW, Suite 208
Washington, DC 20012
202-291-1400
(coordinates reading materials with current broadcast programs)

Living Stage Theatre Company
6th and Maine Avenues, SW
Washington, DC 20024
202-554-9066
(information on improvisational community theatre)

National Association for Gifted Children
1155 15th Street, NW, Suite 1002
Washington, DC 20006
202-785-4268
(publishes *Gifted Programming Today: A National Sample*, with state-
    by-state listings of schools and local organizations)

National Center for Family Literacy
401 S. Fourth Avenue, Suite 610
Louisville, KY 40202
502-584-1133
(publications promoting family literacy)

National Center for Service Learning in Early Adolescence
CASE/CUNY Graduate Center
25 West 43rd Street, Room 612
New York, NY 10025
(information on programs for teens teaching younger children
    to read)

National Coalition for Music Education
1806 Robert Fulton Drive
Reston, VA 22091
703-860-4000
(information on the benefits of music education for children)

Operation SMART
Girls, Incorporated
30 East 33rd Street
New York, NY 10016
(math and science opportunities for girls)

Project Discovery
420 McGuffy Hall
Miami University of Ohio
Oxford, OH 45056
513-529-1686
(math and science for girls)

Women in Science Program
Center for Education of Women
The University of Michigan
330 E. Liberty
Ann Arbor, MI
313-998-7080
(educational opportunities for women)

Relating to child welfare

Childhelp National Child Abuse Hotline
800-4-A-CHILD (800-422-4453)
(help for adults in crisis and literature on child abuse)

International Society for Prevention of Child Abuse and Neglect
PO Box 94253
Chicago, IL 60604
312-644-6610
(literature and referrals for help preventing child abuse)

National Association for the Education of Young Children
1500 16th Street, NW
Washington, DC 20036
800-424-2460
(offers Childhood Resources Catalog for teachers, parents, and child
    care providers, and publishes books on age-appropriate learning)

National Committee to Prevent Child Abuse
800-556-2722
(free brochures and information on preventing child abuse, par-
    enting, substance abuse)

Parents Anonymous
800-339-6993
(information hotline to help parents in crisis and to locate local
    chapters)

Relating to education

Alliance for Parental Involvement in Education Inc.
PO Box 59
East Chatham, NY 12060-0059
518-392-6900
(publishes materials for parents, including *Alternatives in Educa-
    tion: Choices and Options in Learning,* by Mark Hegener and
    Helen Hegener. Home Education Press, 1992)

National P.T.A.
700 North Rush Street
Chicago, IL 60611
312-787-0977
(information about child safety, education, health, advocacy,
    parent involvement in schools)

Parents as Teachers National Center
9374 Olive Boulevard
St. Louis, MO 63132
314-432-4330
(publishes material for parents, including *Be Your Child's Best First
    Teacher*)

On-line Resources

About the brain

This site on the World Wide Web discusses *Brain Plasticity and Behavior* by British researcher Bryan Kolb, one of the most complete treatments of this subject now available.
http://www.erlbaum.com/626.htm

The Dana Alliance for Brain Initiatives, a nonprofit organization that promotes public awareness of brain discoveries, maintains a web site with information about various neuroscience subjects, about brain health, and about two dozen neurological diseases and conditions.
http://www.dana.org/dana/www/aunc.html

Restorative Neurology is a Swedish web site (published in English) with a good description of brain plasticity, especially following stroke, brain tumors, and other neurological disorders.
http://www.wnc.lu.se/restoneu.html

About pregnancy

Baby Web. This web site provides literature, answers to frequently asked questions, services, and products for new and expectant parents.
http://www.netaxs.com/~iiris/infoweb/baby.html

New York Online Access to Health has a web site called Ask Noah providing discussions of several dozen topics related to pregnancy and childbirth.
http://www.noah.cuny.edu/pregnancy/pregnancy.html

The Parents Place web site lists products and information for parents and features a bulletin board.
http://www.parentsplace.com

About young children

The David and Lucile Packard Foundation maintains a web site from the Center for the Future of Children, listing articles on

various subjects, including several on the outcomes of early childhood programs.
http://www.futureofchildren.org/lto/06_lto.htm

An article presented by Unicef on preparing children for school.
http://biz.map.com/~ecdgroup/prepari.html

Newsweek Parent's Guide to Children's Software lists over 600 software titles with recommendations.
http://www.newsweekparentsguide.com

National Institute on Early Childhood Development and Education lists news about recent research in this area.
http://inet.gov/offices/OERI/ECI/

About older children

Children's Software Review lists articles and opinions about computer programs and CD-ROMs for kids.
http://www.childrenssoftware.com

Internet information on parenting teenagers. The "Parenting Teens" offers conflict resolution techniques, tips, books, and resources for parents as well as links to three dozen other web sites on teens, parents, and families.
http://www.commnet.edu/QVCTC/classes/conflict/parents.html

Newsweek's Parent's Guide to Children's Software lists over 600 software titles with recommendations.
http://www.newsweekparentsguide.com

The Book World web site lists books on parenting older children and teens.
http://www.bookworld.com/subjparenting.html

The Positive Parenting online newsletter lists products, expert referrals, and professional resources for parents and teachers.
http://www.positiveparenting.com

About education

The Association for Supervision and Curriculum Development lists upcoming conferences on brain-based education.
http://www.ascd.org/develop/97conf2/part2.html

The Eclectic Education web site is an index of many education web sites, including "Brain-based Education," "Brain and Behavior," and "Genes and Behavior."
http://nature_art.simplenet.com/tech.htm

The Association for Supervision and Curriculum Development (ASCD) maintains this web site with information about accelerated learning, including brain-based education, early childhood education, and minority education issues.
http://www.ascd.org/cr/network.html

The Learning Theory Funhouse web site gives principles of brain-based learning, its implications for students, and a reading list on the subject.
http://www.funderstanding.com/brain.htm

The Knowledge Network's Education Exchange has a web site on brain-based learning with addresses for specific topics within the subject.
http://www.nhptv.org/brain.htm

Annotated bibliography of books on brain-based learning and teaching.
http:www.ascd.org/services/eric/ericbra.html

About child welfare

The Child Welfare League of America's home page lists recent legislation relating to child welfare.
http://www.handsnet.org/handsnet2/cwla/cwla.alerts.html

The Filmmaker's Library web site lists sociological films and programs dealing with families in crisis, child welfare, and adolescents, among other topics.
http://www.filmakers.com/FAMILY/FAMILY.html

The Children, Youth and Family Consortium Electronic Clearing-house is a University of Minnesota web site that provides a list of child welfare-related resources and web addresses.

The National Clearinghouse on Child Abuse and Neglect is a search service containing a link to the Good Health Web, which has information and further addresses on abuse and neglect. http://www.social.com/health/nhic/data/index.html

Catalogs and Commercial Sources

Enrichment products for children of all ages

Alcazar Music
P.O. Box 429
Waterbury, VT 05676
800-541-9904

Art Institute of Chicago
The Museum Shop
Michigan Avenue at Adams
   Street
Chicago, IL 60603
800-621-9337

Books of Wonder
132 Seventh Avenue at 18th St.
New York, NY 10011
800-207-6968

Nature Company
P.O. Box 188
Florence, KY 41022
800-227-1114

Signals, for Fans of Public
   Television

WGBH Educational Foundation
P.O. Box 64428
St. Paul, MN 55164-0428
800-669-9696

Smithsonian Institution
7955 Angus Court
Springfield, VA 22153-2846
800-322-0344

Troll Learn and Play
100 Corporate Drive
Mahwah, NJ 07430
800-247-6106

Wireless, for Fans of Public Radio
Minnesota Public Radio
P.O. Box 64422
St. Paul, MN 55164-0422
800-669-9999

Enrichment products for young children

Back to Basics Toys
305 Sunset Park Drive
Herndon, VA 20170
800-356-5360

Childcraft
250 College Park
P.O. Box 1811
Peoria, IL 61656-1811
800-631-5657

Creative Parenting
Parenting Press, Inc.
P.O. Box 75267
Seattle, WA 98125
800-992-6657

Hearthsong
6519 N. Galena
P.O. Box 1773
Peoria, IL 61656-1773
800-325-2502

Enrichment products for older children

The Brain Store
Turning Point
11080 Roselle Street Suite F
San Diego, CA 92121
619-946-7555

Complete PC (IBM-type home
computer products)
W226 N900 East Mound Drive
Waukesha, WI 53186
800-544-6599
http://www.sharbor.com

Computerware
605 West California Avenue
Sunnyvale, CA 94086-5020
800-725-4622
http://www.macsource.com

Cuisenaire: Materials for
Learning Mathematics and
Science
P.O. Box 5026
White Plains, NY 10602
800-237-3142

Dick Blick (art materials and
books)
P.O. Box 1267
Galesburg, IL 61402-1267
800-723-2787

Edmund Scientific
101 East Gloucester Pike
Barrington, NJ 07410
800-222-0224

Egghead Software
P.O. Box 7004
Issaquah, WA 98027-7004
800-344-4323

Exploratorium to Go!
3601 Lyon Street
San Francisco, CA 94123
800-359-9899

Great Explorations in Math
and Science
Lawrence Hall of Science
University of California
Berkeley, CA 94720
510-642-7771

Heinemann Art Education
361 Hanover Street
Portsmouth, NH 03801
800-541-2086

Heinemann Math and Science
361 Hanover Street
Portsmouth, NH 03801
800-541-2086

Mac Zone
707 South Grady Way
Renton, WA 98055-3233
800-248-0800
http://www.maczone.com

Museum of Fine Arts, Boston
P.O. Box 244
Avon, MA 02322-0244
800-225-5592

National Wildlife Nature
National Wildlife Federation
1400 16th St., NW
Washington, DC 20036
800-245-5484

PC Connection
P.O. Box 100
Milford, NH 03055
800-800-0014
http://www.pcconnection.com

Public Television, Videofinders
    Collection
National Fulfillment Center
P.O. Box 27054
Glendale, CA 91225
800-799-1199

Science News Holiday Gift
    Collection
1719 N. Street, NW
Washington, DC 20036-2088
800-544-4565

SEPUP, Science Education for
    Public Understanding
    Program
Lawrence Hall of Science
University of California
Berkeley, CA 94720
510-642-8718

The Time-Warner Sound Ex-
    change (CDs, recordings,
    audiotapes, etc.)
45 N. Industry Center
Deer Park, NY 11729-4614
800-521-6177

Educational products
(including educational toys)

Environments, Inc. (early
    childhood development)
P.O. Box 1345
Beaufort Industrial Park
Beaufort, SC 29901
803-846-8155

Growing Child
P.O. Box 1100
22 North Second Street
Lafayette, IN 47902
765-423-2624

J. L. Hammett Company
30 Hammett Place
Braintree, MA 02184
800-333-4600

Lakeshore Curriculum Materials
2695 E. Dominguez Street
Long Beach, CA 90807
800-421-5354

Learning Materials Workshop
58 Henry Street
Burlington, VT 05401
800-336-9661

Toys to Grow On
2695 E. Dominguez Street
Long Beach, CA 90807
800-542-8338

Nasco Learning Fun
NASCO
901 Jamesville Avenue
Ft. Atkinson, WI 53538-0901
414-563-1700

U-R Special (language
development)
P.O. Box 17104
Milwaukee, WI 53217
414-353-0062

Opportunities for Learning
941 Hickory Lane
Mansfield, OH 44905
419-563-2446

World Wide Games
Mill Street
Colchester, CT 06415
800-888-0987

Parent-Recommended Enrichment Tools

Our primary goal in *Magic Trees of the Mind* is to present portraits of brain development at each stage of childhood along with the latest research findings on how experiences sculpt the living brain. We also, however, wanted to provide our readers with a wealth of specific ideas for particularly enriching toys, books, art materials, and the like. Since our own children and stepchildren are grown, we needed a reliable, up-to-date source of children's enrichment tools. That need inspired us to conduct an original survey for our book.

In January 1996, we contacted Ian Carmichael, interim director of Lawrence Hall of Science, about using that institution's mailing list of family members for our survey. The Hall is a hands-on discovery center on the University of California campus in Berkeley, with a membership of three thousand families and another two thousand individuals. Marian Diamond had served as director of the Hall for the five previous years, and was well acquainted with the members' enthusiasm about enrichment and the brain. These were favorite exhibit and newsletter topics, and in the three thousand mailers we sent out to those with family memberships, we recapped the subjects briefly.

We asked a parent from each family to tell us the age and sex of one or two of their children. More to the point, we also asked the parent to provide a set of information for each youngster, describing the items they thought had been *of greatest benefit for the child's development* in sixteen different categories: books, games, toys, models, puzzles, musical instruments, art materials, lessons, classes, outings, trips, sports equipment, CDs/tapes/records, videos, CD-ROMs, and software.

Of the families we contacted, about three hundred wrote back with information on over five hundred children ages one to sixteen. If parents and relatives ever needed a holiday gift list, it is here in voluminous splendor, along with ideas for hundreds of hobbies, classes, destinations, and pastimes. Significantly, the information comes from parents who are concerned enough about their children's enrichment to join a science center with exhibits and classes in everything from bubble-ology to ecology and physics.

Naturally, we wondered whether the survey answers would be skewed toward books, games, and toys with a scientific slant. Our analysis showed that they weren't. We also wondered whether we'd get more answers for boys than for girls, but the sexes were fairly evenly represented. We display the survey findings by children's sex and age. This is just as we collected it from the responding parents, and does not suggest a view that a puzzle for a seven-year-old girl is wrong for a nine-year-old boy, or vice versa. Our approach aimed at impartiality; no sexism implied and we hope none taken.

Our intention in presenting the families' responses was to give readers the widest possible selection for their own children and students, not to recommend a "Best Ten" list for books, toys, or other enrichment tools. Each item we include represents one family's vote for "Best in Its Class"—best book, best puzzle, best CD-ROM, or what have you. After reading the list, you can then make your own choices based on your children's or students' ages, interests, and preferences. In the one-to-five and thirteen-to-sixteen age groups, the lists of "votes" are rather short, reflecting the child population served by this (and most other) discovery centers. By far the biggest sets of "votes" were for enrichment tools to excite six- to twelve-year-old children since most of the child members of Lawrence Hall of Science fell into those age categories. Youngsters are so individual and their development proceeds within general parameters but at such a unique pace for each child that we thought it better to let readers harvest tips from three hundred families and five hundred kids rather than to preselect items based on our own tastes and preferences.

We do issue one caveat regarding our enrichment survey: The "Outings" and "Trips" categories are somewhat West-Coast-centric; one could expect such bias to appear in any survey conducted regionally rather than nationally. These can at least show the *types* of destinations children like, if not specifics relevant to your area. Exceptions are generic venues like "Grandma's house" and the spectacular Western national parks, which virtually any child would enjoy.

Finally, we superimposed one additional level of organization on the survey results. We separated the answers into "general" and "brand name" selections so that readers can differentiate between those tools our respondents recommended with specific brand names from the more general tools other respondents favored. For example, some parents felt that the brands of blocks, or modeling clay, or gymnastic lessons didn't matter to their child's enrichment. In other cases, parents found a particular type to their liking: Duplo blocks, or Fimo clay, or Gymboree. We set these apart so that readers could see the range of opinions and make their own selections without a confusing mix of responses. Now, onto the survey answers themselves.

Selections for Babies and Toddlers

BOOKS (Girls)

One Year Old

The Big Red Barn, Margaret Wise Brown (Harper Trophy, 1993)
Goodnight Moon, Margaret Wise Brown (Harper & Row, 1947)
Moo, Baa, La La La!, Sandra Boynton (Simon & Schuster, 1995)
Piggies, Don Wood (Harcourt Brace, 1996)
Where's Spot? Eric Hill (Heinemann, 1984)

Two Years Old

Chickens Aren't the Only Ones, Ruth Heller (Grosset & Dunlap, 1993)
Go, Dog, Go!, P. D. Eastman (Random House, 1992)

Goodnight Moon, Margaret Wise Brown (Harper & Row, 1947)
The Honeybee and the Robber, Eric Carle (Putnam, 1981)
Jamberry, Bruce Degen (Harper & Row, 1985)
Jim Henson's Muppet Babies in Kermit's Ball, Tom Brannon (Western, 1993)
Kate Gleeson's Mary Had a Little Lamb, Sarah Josepha Buell (Western, 1994)
One, Two, Three!, Sandra Boynton (Workman, 1993)
Owl Moon, Jane Yolen (Philomel Books, 1987)
The World of Christopher Robin, A. A. Milne (Dean with Methuen Children's Books, 1991)

BOOKS (Boys)

One Year Old

Goodnight Moon, Margaret Wise Brown (Harper & Row, 1947)
In the Small, Small Pond, Denise Fleming (Bodley Head, 1995)
Shapes, Shapes, Shapes, Tana Hoban (Mulberry Books, 1996)
Trucks, Byron Barton (HarperCollins Children's Books, 1986)
Who Said What: Over 7,000 Quotations from Earliest Times to the Present Day (Chancellor Press, 1993)

Two Years Old

Big Pumpkin, Erica Silverman (Scholastic, 1993)
Goodnight Moon, Margaret Wise Brown (Harper & Row, 1947)
Little Red Riding Hood, Carolyn Magner (Book Club of America, 1993)
On the Day You Were Born, Debra Frasier (Harcourt Brace Jovanovich, 1995)
Stellaluna, Janell Cannon (Design Farm, 1994)
The Tale of Peter Rabbit, Beatrix Potter (Madison, 1993)
Three Billy Goats Gruff, Ted Dewan (Hippo, 1995)

GAMES AND TOYS (Girls)

One Year Old

gymnastics
hide-and-seek

peek-a-boo
toy telephone
playing with siblings
stacking cups

[playing with] teddy bear
Duplo Blocks (Lego)
Magna Doodle (Tyco)
Squishy Fish (Manhattan Toys)

Two Years Old

[playing with] baby dolls
blocks
hide-and-seek
playing kitchen
peek-a-boo
playing doctor
[playing with] stuffed animals
tea party
toy telephone
Barney (Playskool)
Don't Wake Daddy (Parker
    Brothers)
Four First Games
    (Ravensburger)
Lotto (Plan Toys)
Tinkertoys (Playskool)

GAMES AND TOYS (Boys)

One Year Old

balls
chase games
peek-a-boo
shape-sorter toys
wooden blocks with or without
    hammer
Duplo Blocks (Lego)
Playskool Go Round (Play-
    skool)
Squishy Fish (Manhattan Toys)

Two Years Old

balls
finger play games
playing with siblings
shape-sorter toys
toy cars
toy train
[using] puppets
wooden blocks
Brio Train (Brio)
Duplo Blocks (Lego)
Little People Neighborhood
    (Fisher Price)
Memory (Milton Bradley)
Mouse Trap (Milton Bradley)
Simba pool toy (Disney)

MODELS AND PUZZLES (Girls)

One Year Old

word puzzles

Two Years Old

geography puzzles
models of bats or insects
toy kitchen model
wooden puzzles
Barney puzzle (Playskool)
Foam Animal Floor Puzzle
    (Berk)
Maggie the Moody Bear (Small
    World Toys)
Sesame Street puzzle
    (Playskool)

MODELS AND PUZZLES (Boys)

One Year Old

nesting cubes
puzzles of farm animals, zoo
    animals, and balloons
Rhomblocks (Tensegrity)

Two Years Old

airplane models
puzzles of oceans, animals, and
    vehicles
Duplo blocks (Lego)
Lincoln Logs (Playskool)
Magnetic Activity Blocks
    (Playwell)
Montessori School puzzles
    (Montessori)
Sesame Street puzzle (Play-
    skool)
wooden puzzles (Small World
    Toys)

MUSICAL INSTRUMENTS (Girls)

One Year Old

cymbals
toy piano

Two Years Old

flute
piano
plastic horn
xylophone

MUSICAL INSTRUMENTS (Boys)

One Year Old

drums
flute
harmonica
maracas
recorder
toy radio
voice

Two Years Old

drums
piano
recorder
toy piano
xylophone

ART MATERIALS (Girls)

One Year Old

crayons
markers
paper

Two Years Old

beads
fabric scraps
felt pens
finger paint
markers
paints
paper plates
safety scissors
Play-Doh (Playskool)

ART MATERIALS (Boys)

One Year Old

crayons
markers
paper

Two Years Old

clay
crayons
markers
paint
paper
pencils
Play-Doh (Playskool)

LESSONS AND CLASSES (Girls)

One Year Old

Tot Drop

Two Years Old

crossing the street
dance/movement
geography
gymnastics
making books
playing music
tumbling
Gymboree

LESSONS AND CLASSES (Boys)

One Year Old

gymnastics
swimming
Gymboree

Two Years Old

baseball practice
language classes
Gymboree
Kindergym

OUTINGS AND TRIPS (Girls)

One Year Old

beach
grandparents' house
petting zoo
trips on airplane
zoo

Two Years Old

amusement park
bank
beach
children's museum
children's park
grandparents' house
hiking/camping
seashore
zoo

OUTINGS AND TRIPS (Boys)

One Year Old

art museum
car trip
children's museum
hands-on science museum
miniature steam train
mom's office
ocean
outdoors
sandbox

Two Years Old

airplane trips
amusement park
animal farm
animal museum
mountains
train trips
zoo

SPORTS EQUIPMENT (Girls)

One Year Old

balls
Nerf paddle and ball (Kenner)

Two Years Old

balls
bat
hop-ball
kiddie car
skates
slide
swing

SPORTS EQUIPMENT (Boys)

One Year Old

balls
basketball
bicycle side car
running stroller

Two Years Old

ball
basketball hoop
bat and ball
Nerf ball (Kenner)

CDs/TAPES/RECORDS (Girls)

One Year Old

Wee Sing, Wee Sing: Silly Songs

Two Years Old

Story tapes
Beauty and the Beast sound track
Salty tapes
Sesame Street tapes and CDs

CDs/TAPES/RECORDS (Boys)

One Year Old

Lullabies
Best of Richard Scarry
Dancin' Magic
Gil Scott Heron
Keiki Hawaiian Songs

Two Years Old

Baby Beluga
David Grisman
Disney sound tracks
Everything Grows
Jerry Garcia

VIDEOS (Girls)

One Year Old

Baby Songs
More Baby Songs
Even More Baby Songs
Lullaby Video by Judy Collins

Two Years Old

Barney
Beauty and the Beast

Big Bird in China
Dink the Dinosaur
National Geographic videos for
    kids
The Sound of Music
Winnie the Pooh

VIDEOS (Boys)

One Year Old

Barney
Peter Rabbit
Sesame Street
Thomas the Tank Engine
Wee Sing series

Two Years Old

101 Dalmatians
Big Bird in China
Disney Sing-A-Long series
Gymboree video: *Zoo Safari*
Mighty Morphin Power Rangers
Pooh Bear Videos
Richard Scarry's Busytown
Thomas the Tank Engine
The Wizard of Oz

Note: We don't think infants and young toddlers should spend lots of time at a computer keyboard, but some parents do, so we report their preferences.

SOFTWARE (Girls)

One Year Old

none reporting

Two Years Old

Berenstain Bears (Living Books)
Just Grandma and Me (Living
    Books)
Lion King Storytime (Disney)
Millie's Math House (Edmark)

SOFTWARE (Boys)

One Year Old

Just Grandma and Me (Living
    Books)
Sammy's Science House
    (Edmark)

Two Years Old

Bailey's Bookhouse (Edmark)
Dr. Seuss's ABCs (Living Books)
Paintbrush (Microsoft)

SELECTIONS FOR PRESCHOOLERS

BOOKS (Girls)

Three Years Old

Alf 'n Bet Learn Their ABC, M. Twinn (Child's Play, Swindon, 1992)
Best Friends for Frances, Russell Hoban (Harper & Row, 1969)

Cinderella, Dorothea Goldenberg (Publications International, 1993)

The Gunny Wolf and Other Fairy Tales, Duane Hutchinson (Foundation Books, 1992)

The Paper Princess, Elisa Kleven (Dutton Children's Books, 1994)

Peek-a-boo, Michael Evans (Ideals, 1992)

Richard Scarry's Best Word Book Ever, Richard Scarry (Western, 1995)

The Runaway Bunny, Margaret Wise Brown (Harper & Brothers, 1972)

We're the Noisy Dinosaurs, John Watson (Candlewick Press, 1992)

Four Years Old

The Jolly Pocket Postman, Janet Ahlberg (Heinemann, 1995)

Madeline in London, Ludwig Bemelmans (Hippo, 1996)

Need a House? Call Ms. Mouse! George Mendoza (Grosset & Dunlap, 1981)

The Rainbow Fish to the Rescue! Marcus Pfister (North-South Books, 1995)

Voyage to the Bunny Planet, Rosemary Wells (Dial Books for Young Readers, 1992)

Where the Wild Things Are, Maurice Sendak (Puffin Books, 1980)

Where's Waldo?, Martin Handford (Grolier, 1991)

The Wonderful Wizard of Oz, Lyman Frank Baum (Houghton Mifflin, 1993)

Five Years Old

The Big Book of Questions and Answers: The Bible As Told in the Old Testament, David M. Howard, Jr. (Publications International, 1992)

Charlotte's Web, E. B. White (HarperCollins, 1980)

Cloudy with a Chance of Meatballs, Judi Barrett (Aladdin Books, 1988)

The Foot Book, Dr. Seuss (Random House, 1968)

Goodnight Moon, Margaret Wise Brown (Harper & Row, 1947)

Goosebumps, R. L. Stine (Hippo, 1994)

The Indian in the Cupboard, Lynne Reid Banks (Doubleday, 1980)

Laura Ingalls Wilder's Little House Books, Laura Ingalls Wilder (Harper Trophy, 1994)

A Light in the Attic, Shel Silverstein (HarperCollins, 1981)

Lunch with Aunt Augusta, Emma Chichester Clark (Dial Books for Young Readers, 1992)

The Magic School Bus Inside a Beehive, Joanna Cole (Scholastic, 1996)

Miss Spider's Tea Party, David Kirk (Callaway, 1994)

Misty of Chincoteague, Marguerite Henry (Houghton Mifflin, 1991)

Pippi Longstocking, Astrid Lindgren (Buccaneer Books, 1978)

The Polar Express, Chris Van Allsburg (Houghton Mifflin, 1995)

Ramona Quimby, Age 8, Beverly Cleary (William Morrow, 1994)

The Random House Book of Fairy Tales, Amy Ehrlich (Random House, 1985)

Richard Scarry's Best Story Book Ever; Richard Scarry's Best Word Book Ever, Richard Scarry (Western, 1995)

Stellaluna, Janell Cannon (Design Farm, 1994)

Trouble with Trolls, Jan Brett (National Braille Press, 1994)

The Wheels on the Bus, Harriet Ziefert (Random House Books for Young Readers, 1990)

BOOKS (Boys)

Three Years Old

Charlotte's Web, E. B. White (HarperCollins, 1980)

Chato's Kitchen, Gary Soto (Putnam, 1995)

Choo Choo: The Story of a Little Engine Who Ran Away, Virginia Lee Burton (Children's Choice Book Club, 1937)

Frog and Toad Together, Arnold Lobel (HarperCollins Children's Books, 1972)

Goodnight Moon, Margaret Wise Brown (Harper & Row, 1947)

Mike Mulligan and His Steam Shovel, Virginia Lee Burton (Houghton Mifflin, 1939)

The Mixed-Up Chameleon, Eric Carle (Mantra, 1994)

Richard Scarry's Cars and Trucks and Things That Go, Richard Scarry (Golden Press, 1975)

Richard Scarry's What Do People Do All Day?, Richard Scarry (Random House, 1968)

Tell Me a Mitzi, Lore Segal (Farrar, Straus, & Giroux 1991)

Things That Go (Western, 1995)

Where's Waldo?, Martin Handford (Grolier, 1991)

Four Years Old

At Midnight in the Kitchen I Just Wanted to Talk to You, Shuntaro Tanikawa (Prescott Street Press, 1980)

The Berenstain Bears Say Good Night, Stan Berenstain (Random House, 1991)

Best Stories from the Indian Classics (Roli Books, 1994)

Blueberries for Sal, Robert McCloskey (Lakeshore Learning Materials, 1994)

The Cat in the Hat, Dr. Seuss (Random House, 1994)

Charlie and the Chocolate Factory, Roald Dahl (Knopf, 1964)

Curious George Goes to the Circus, Margaret Rey (Scholastic, 1987)

Effie, Beverley Allinson (Harcourt Brace, 1995)

Electricity, Terry Jennings (BBC, 1995)

Frog and Toad are Friends, Arnold Lobel (Harper, 1970)

Goodnight Moon, Margaret Wise Brown (Harper & Row, 1947)

Horton Hatches the Egg, Dr. Seuss (Collins, 1979)

June 29, 1999, David Wiesner (Clarion Books, 1992)

The Jungle Book, Rudyard Kipling (Smithmark, 1995)

The Little Engine That Could, Watty Piper (Platt & Munk, 1986)

The Magic School Bus, Joanna Cole (Scholastic, 1991)

My Very First Number Book, Angela Wilkes (Dorling Kindersley, 1993)

One Morning in Maine, Robert McCloskey (Troll Associates, 1980)

Quick as a Cricket, Audrey Wood (Lakeshore Learning Materials, 1993)

Richard Scarry's Cars and Trucks and Things That Go, Richard Scarry (Golden Press, 1975)

Stellaluna, Janell Cannon (Scholastic Books, 1994)

The Three Little Pigs, Paul Galdone (Lakeshore Learning Materials, 1994)

Treasure Island, Robert Louis Stevenson (Globe, 1980)

Five Years Old

The Big Book of Questions and Answers: The Bible As Told in the Old Testament, David M. Howard, Jr. (Publications International, 1992)

Charlotte's Web, E. B. White (HarperCollins, 1980)

Cloudy with a Chance of Meatballs, Judi Barrett (Aladdin Books, 1988)

The Foot Book, Dr. Seuss (Random House, 1968)
Goodnight Moon, Margaret Wise Brown (Harper & Row, 1947)
Honest Abe, Edit Kunhardt (Greenwillow Books, 1993)
Jost Hochuli's Alphabugs, Jost Hochuli (Agfa, 1990)
Laura Ingalls Wilder's Little House Books, Laura Ingalls Wilder (Harper Trophy, 1994)
The Little Prince, Antoine de Saint-Exupery (G. K. Hall, 1995)
The Magic School Bus Inside a Beehive, Joanna Cole (Scholastic, 1996)
Misty of Chincoteague, Marguerite Henry (Houghton Mifflin,)
My Very First Number Book, Angela Wilkes (Dorling Kindersley, 1993)
Paddle-to-the-Sea, Clancy Holling (Houghton Mifflin, 1969)
Patrick's Dinosaurs, Carol Carrick (Houghton Mifflin, 1983)
Pirates and Buccaneers, Tillie Brading (Wayland, 1979)
Richard Scarry's Best Story Book Ever; Richard Scarry's Best Word Book Ever, Richard Scarry (Western, 1995)
The Star Wars Question and Answer Book About Space, Dinah L. Moche (Random House, 1979)
Stellaluna, Janell Cannon (Scholastic Books, 1994)
Thirteen Bears, Sir Charles George Douglas Roberts (Ryerson, 1947)
The Wheels on the Bus (Western, 1994)

GAMES AND TOYS (Girls)

Three Years Old

animal figures
baby dolls
dinosaurs
dollhouse
dolls
dress-up clothes and jewelry
go fish
matching games
playing with parent
pretend
tea set

Candyland (Milton Bradley)
Cootie (Milton Bradley)
Don't Wake Daddy (Parker Brothers)
Duplo Blocks (Lego)
Kids on Stage (University Games)
Legos (Lego)
Madeline doll (Eden)
Memory (Milton Bradley)
Mickey and Friends Dominoes (Disney)
Polly Pocket (Mattel)

See's Candies' Playhouse
(See's Candies)
Sesame Street Dominoes
(Tyco)

Four Years Old

dollhouse
dolls
dress-up clothes and jewelry
go fish
paper doll refrigerator
magnets
Which hand is it in?
Barbie doll (Mattel)
Bingo (Pavilion)
Clue (Parker Brothers)
Cootie (Milton Bradley)
Dominoes (Pressman)
Duplo Blocks (Lego)
Elmo doll (Tyco)
Fisher Price toys (Fisher Price)
Geosafari Junior (Educational
Insights)
Hi-Ho Cherry-O (Parker
Brothers)
K'nex (K'nex)
Legos (Lego)
Little Smart School Yard (V-
tech)
Madeline and Her Puppies
(Eden)
Memory (Milton Bradley)
Monopoly Junior (Parker
Brothers)
Playskool toys (Playskool)
Polly Pocket (Mattel)
Ravensburger toys
(Ravensburger)

Scrabble for Kids (Milton
Bradley)
Tinkertoys (Playskool)

Five Years Old

animal figures
bears to dress up
building blocks
cards
dinosaurs
dolls
dress-up clothes and jewelry
electric toys
five little piggies
jump rope
make-believe
markers
remote control car
running games
stuffed animals
Baby Born doll (Zapf
Creations)
Barbie doll (Mattel)
Candyland (Milton Bradley)
Chess (Pavilion)
Clue (Parker Brothers)
Concentration (Hasbro)
Duplo Blocks (Lego)
Guess Who? (Milton Bradley)
Jenga (Milton Bradley)
Kirby (Nintendo)
K'nex (K'nex)
Legos (Lego)
Memory (Parker Brothers)
Monopoly (Parker Brothers)
Monopoly Junior (Parker
Brothers)
My First Loom (Hearthsong)

Playmobil toys (Playmobil)
Playmobil Covered Wagon
    (Playmobil)
Pretty Pretty Princess (Milton
    Bradley)
Scrabble Junior (Milton Bradley)
Sorry (Parker Brothers)
Trouble (Milton Bradley)

GAMES AND TOYS (Boys)

Three Years Old

action figures
cards
go fish
hide-and-seek
tiddleywinks
toy horses
one potato two
plastic hammer
scooter car
toolbox
Animal Dominoes (Golden)
Brio train set (Brio)
Candyland (Milton Bradley)
Concentration (Hasbro)
Excavator with Small People
    (Little Tykes)
Fisher Price people (Fisher
    Price)
Geosafari (Educational
    Insights)
Hot Wheels (Mattel)
Legos (Lego)
Mario Brothers (Nintendo)
Matchbox cars (Tyco)
Not So Scary Things
    (Educational Insights)
Thomas the Train (Ertl, Tomy)

Four Years Old

blocks
car track
cardboard bricks
cards
cars
cash register (solar powered)
crane
dinosaurs
dominoes
five hundred rummy
go fish
hard rubber animals
hide-and-seek
marbles
pump gun
remote control car
stacking boxes
wooden blocks
wooden train
Batman figures (Kenner)
Big Bird (Tyco)
Brio train set (Brio)
Busy Gears (Playskool)
Candyland (Milton Bradley)
Connect Four (Milton
    Bradley)
Cozy Coupe (Weedo Toys)
Duplo Blocks (Lego)
Four First Games
    (Ravensburger)
Hi-Ho Cherry-O (Parker
    Brothers)
Hot Wheels (Mattel)
Hungry Hungry Hippos
    (Milton Bradley)
Labyrinth (Pavilion)
Legos (Lego)

Lincoln Logs (Playskool)
Memory (Milton Bradley)
Pirate Ship (Playmobil)
Power Rangers (Ban Dai)
Rivers Roads and Rails
    (Ravensburger Games)
Thomas the Tank Engine train
    set (Ertl, Tomy)

Five Years Old

blocks
bow and arrow
cars
mazes
pretend
puppets
rubber animals
self-made games
stuffed animals (bunny, dog,
    teddy bear)
trolls
trains
war
Air Hockey (Carrom)
Batman Forever 3-D board
    game (Kenner)
Batman Returns (Nintendo)
Brain Quest (Workman)
Brio train set (Brio)
Candyland (Milton Bradley)
Checkers (Pavilion)
Chess (Pavilion)
Chutes and Ladders (Milton
    Bradley)
Clue Junior (Parker Brothers)
Dinomite (University Games)
Duplo blocks (Lego)

Fish Four First Games
    (Ravensburger)
Guess Who? (Milton Bradley)
Jumanji (Milton Bradley)
Kids on Stage (University
    Games)
K'nex (K'nex)
Legos (Lego)
Lincoln Logs (Playskool)
Little Tykes car (Little Tykes)
Mancala (Great American
    Trading Corp.)
Memory (Milton Bradley)
Monopoly (Parker Brothers)
Monopoly Junior (Parker
    Brothers)
Playmobil Horses (Playmobil)
Playmobil toys (Playmobil)
Sega (Sega)
Sorry (Parker Brothers)
Star Trek (Playmates)
Star Wars figures (Galoob)
Stratego (Milton Bradley)
Stretch Armstrong (Cap Toys)
Toobers and Zots (Kenner)
Transformers (Kenner)
Uno (Mattel)
Z Bots (Galoob)

MODELS AND PUZZLES (Girls)

Three Years Old

animal alphabet puzzle
animal-shaped puzzle
dolphin puzzle
ocean puzzle
ocean life floor puzzle
Barbie doll puzzle (Mattel)

jigsaw puzzles (Frank Schaffer)
Lincoln Logs (Playskool)
Mudpuppy Press puzzles
   (Mudpuppy Press)
Playmobil puzzles
Sesame Street puzzles
   (Playskool)
Simba puzzle (Disney)
Tinkertoys (Playskool)
Triazzle (DaMert Company)

Four Years Old

animal puzzle
castle made out of blocks
dinosaur puzzles
dot to dots
floor puzzles
USA puzzle
baby animal puzzle
First Puzzles (Galt Toys four in
   one box)
Lego models (Lego)
Lion King puzzle (Disney)
Madeline puzzle
   (Ravensburger)
Mickey Mouse puzzle (Disney)
Playmobil Victorian Wedding
   (Playmobil)
Ravensburger two-layer puzzle
   (Ravensburger)
Sesame Street puzzle
   (Playskool)
Triazzle (DaMert Company)

Five Years Old

African savannah puzzle
dolphin model
giant floor puzzles

human skeleton model
mazes
solar system floor puzzle
troll puzzle
USA puzzle
whale model
wildlife puzzle
Aladdin puzzle (Disney)
dinosaur puzzle
   (Ravensburger)
Fantastic Crystal Creations
   (Kenner)
Lego Pirate Set (Lego)
Legos (Lego)
Playmobil house (Playmobil)
Pocahontas puzzle (Disney)
Ravensburger puzzles
   (Ravensburger)
Snow White and the Seven
   Dwarfs puzzle (Disney)

MODELS AND PUZZLES
(Boys)

Three Years Old

airplanes
giant nature puzzle
ocean puzzle
railroad engine models
simple jigsaw puzzle
trains puzzle
USA puzzle
wooden puzzles
Ocean Life floor puzzle (Frank
   Schaffer)
World Map floor puzzle (Frank
   Schaffer)

Four Years Old

100-piece puzzles
alphabet puzzles
bats puzzle
dinosaur models
floor puzzle
giant rain forest puzzle
homemade mosaic puzzles
human skeleton model
insect models
nature puzzle
paper train station model
planets mobile
solar system puzzle
USA puzzle
visible house model
wooden puzzle
world map puzzle
airport puzzle (Ravensburger)
Beauty and the Beast puzzle
    (Disney)
desert scene puzzle
    (Ravensburger)
Disney characters puzzle
    (Disney)
fire truck (Ravensburger)
garbage truck (Playmobil)
Inside/Out Airplane
    (Ravensburger)
jungle puzzle (Frank Shaffer)
Legos (Lego)
Power Rangers Mega Zord
    (Ban Dai)
Sesame Street puzzle
    (Playskool)
Thomas the Tank Engine
    model (Ertl, Tomy)

Five Years Old

castle puzzle
dinosaur puzzles
dinosaur skeleton (plastic
    model kit)
endangered species puzzles
house model (cardboard)
model cars
Napoleon puzzle
Noah's Ark puzzle
pinewood derby car
small model cars
solar system puzzle
USA puzzle
wooden puzzle
Castle puzzle (Ravensburger)
Erector sets (Meccano)
F-14 Tomcat (Lego)
Humpty Dumpty puzzle
    (Ravensburger)
K'nex (K'nex)
Legos (Lego)
Lion King puzzle (Disney)
Lionel Electric Train (Lionel)
Pirate Ship (Playmobil)
Star Wars puzzle (Parker
    Brothers)
Triazzle (Da Mert)
Unicef six-way cube (Feber)
Visible Man (Skilcraft)

MUSICAL INSTRUMENTS (Girls)

Three Years Old

kazoo
piano
toy piano

toy trumpet
voice

Four Years Old

electronic keyboard
flute
maracas
piano
toy trumpet
voice
Chimalong

Five Years Old

drums
glockenspiel
kazoo
keyboard
keyboard in treehouse
mandolin
piano
recorder
rhythm instruments
toy flute
ukulele
violin
voice

MUSICAL INSTRUMENTS (Boys)

Three Years Old

drums
harmonica
keyboard
piano
talking drums
toy guitar
ukulele

Four Years Old

drums
flutaphone
guitar
harmonica
kazoo
keyboard
piano
pots and pans
slide whistle
tambourine
toy flute
violin
voice

Five Years Old

drums
electric piano
flute
guitar
harmonica
homemade guitar
kazoo
piano
violin
xylophone

ART MATERIALS (Girls)

Three Years Old

acrylic paints
beads
blackboard
buttons
chalk
collage materials
easel
finger paint

glitter marker
glue stick
markers
paints
paper
watercolors
Play-Doh (Playskool)

Four Years Old

clay
colored pencils
markers
paints
paper
pencil crayons
puppet- and mask-making
    materials
scissors
stickers
Play-Doh (Playskool)

Five Years Old

art brushes
beads
chalk
clay
colored pens
crayons
glitter
glue
loom
markers
paint
paper
pastels
pattern scissors
pencils
stencil

watercolors
artist materials set (Art Worx)
Play-Doh (Playskool)

ART MATERIALS (Boys)

Three Years Old

chalk
chalkboard
clay
collage materials
crayons
glitter
glue
markers
paintbrushes
paints
paper
scissors
stamps
watercolor
white glue
Play-Doh (Playskool)

Four Years Old

colored pencils
construction paper
crayons
easel
glitter
glue
homemade play dough
markers
paint
paper
pencil
potato prints
scissors

staples
stickers
tape
Play-Doh (Playskool)

Five Years Old

art supply kit
boxes
chalk
class
clay
coloring supplies
construction paper
crayons
easel
finger paints
glitter
glue
markers
paint
paper
paper towel tubes
pencils
rubber bands
scissors
string
tape
wood scraps
Crayola Model Magic
Fimo clay (Eberhardt Faber)
Play-Doh (Playskool)

LESSONS AND CLASSES (Girls)

Three Years Old

animal class
art

ballet
circus
crafts
dance
gymnastics
matching shapes
petting class
preschool
swimming
tap dance

Four Years Old

art
ballet
bear puppets
cooking
dance
drawing
gymnastics
ice skating
karate
language classes
making crystals
music
gymnastics
science activities
sign language
sports
swimming
writing

Five Years Old

animal homes
art
baby animals
ballet
bowling
carpentry

ceramics
cut-out clothes for dolls
early dance technique
environmental yard gardening
gingerbread-house baking
gymnastics
how the body works
judo
kindergarten
math
reading aloud
science activities
sign language
springtime biology
swimming
violin
Montessori preschool

LESSONS AND CLASSES (Boys)

Three Years Old

animal babies
birdwatching
gymnastics
music
puppets
skeletons
sports
swimming
toddler swimming
tumbling
Kindergym
Montessori lessons

Four Years Old

animal birthday party
ceramics

computers
electricity
gymnastics
growing plants
horseback riding
music
physical science for pre-
    schoolers
piano
reading
science activities
science experiments at home
singing
skiing
sock-puppet making
Sunday school
swimming
toy making
tracing

Five Years Old

animals and their young
art
button art
carpentry
circus
computer
cooking
drama
gymnastics
horseback riding
karate
kindergarten
language
martial arts
math
music
paperweight making

physics for preschoolers
prekindergarten
preschool
sand painting
science experiments
sharing
singing
slime making
soccer
speech
sports
stargazing
swimming
symphony music listening
woodworking
Gingerbread Man class
Gymsters
Kindercooking

OUTINGS AND TRIPS (Girls)

Three Years Old

bat exhibit
camping
grandparents'
hiking
marine preserve
mountains
park
playground
pony rides
ranch
science center
Discovery Museum
Marine World
San Diego Zoo and Wild Animal Park

Four Years Old

beach
cove
commuter train
feeding ducks
grandparents' house
Halloween
hiking
lake
animal museum
science center
skiing
snow
tide pools
Discovery Museum
Marine World

Five Years Old

aquarium
beach
backpacking
beach/ocean
bike riding
camping
children's museum
farm
garnet mine
mom's work
park
science museum
skiing
visiting relatives
zoo
Discovery Museum
California Academy of
    Sciences
Disneyland
Exploratorium

Fairyland
International Museum of Folk
    Art (Sante Fe, New Mexico)
Marine World
Nutcracker performance
Pixie Playland
San Diego Zoo and Wild Animal Park

OUTINGS AND TRIPS (Boys)

Three Years Old

animal farm
aquarium
beach
cabin
camping
camping in national parks
children's museum
construction sites
dinosaur dig
driving cross-country
grandparents' house
movies
seashore
relative's house
zoo
Discovery Museum
Exploratorium
Fairyland
Marine Mammal Center

Four Years Old

aquarium
bats exhibit
beach
camping
commuter train

farm
friend's house
grandparents' house
lake
marine preserve
miniature train rides
nature walks
park
skiing
symphony
science center
sea shore
zoo
Discovery Museum
Discovery Zone
Disneyland
Exploratorium
Fairyland
Museum of Natural History
    (New York City)

Five Years Old

animal museum
bats exhibit
beach
bike riding
cable car
camping
canoeing
co-op nursery school
grandparents' house
hiking
mountains
movies
museums
railroad
park
pumpkin patch

train museum
science center
snow
miniature steam trains
tide pools
zoo
Discovery Museum
Disneyland
Exploratorium
Fairyland
Little Farm
Marine World

SPORTS EQUIPMENT (Girls)

Three Years Old

balls
bike
football
swimming pool
swing
trampoline

Four Years Old

baseball
basketball
bike
ice skates
in-line skates
leotard
monkey bars
slides
swings
trampoline
tricycle

Five Years Old

ball
bicycle
climbing rope
climbing structure
Hula Hoop
hop ball with handle
jump rope
monkey bars
scooter
skis
soccer ball
swim goggles
tennis racquet
tire swing
trampoline

SPORTS EQUIPMENT (Boys)

Three Years Old

balls
bat and ball
bicycle
football
roller skates
skis
street hockey equipment
tricycle

Four Years Old

balls
basketball
bat and ball
bicycle
bicycle with training wheels
football
Frisbee
giant ball

in-line skates
rollerskates
skis
soccer ball
tetherball
tricycle
Nerf bat and ball (Kenner)

Five Years Old

balls
baseball
basketball
bat and ball
bicycle
canoe
football
hockey set
in-line skates
soccer ball
tennis racquet
tricycle
Nerf crossbow (Kenner)

CDs/TAPES/RECORDS (Girls)

Three Years Old

Children's music
Barney
Child's Celebration of Showtunes
Elephant in the Bathtub
Lion King cassette and book
Nancy Raven
Postman Pat
Raffi's Bananaphone
Reggae for Kids

Four Years Old

Books on tape
Beatles

Beethoven
Beethoven Lives Upstairs
Gary Lapow
Goldilocks and the Three Bears
The Lion King sound track
The Nutcracker
Pocahontas sound track
Pooh Bear Stories
Singing Rainbows
Wee Sing Songs from Around the World

Five Years Old

Books on tape
traditional children's songs
Chanukah at Home
Gary Lapow
Heidi
Kid's Song series
Kindermusik
Lambchops
Lion King sound track
Little Thinker Tapes
Make Believe
Mozart's Magic Fantasy
Mr. Bach Comes to Call
Mrs. Robinson
Old Yeller
Raffi
Rainbow Palace
Santa Claus
Swan Lake
Tim in the Trees
Vivaldi's Ring of Mystery
You'll Sing a Song and I'll Sing a Song

CDs/TAPES/RECORDS (Boys)

Three Years Old

Chinese rhymes
traditional children's songs
Bananaphone
Children's AIDS Benefit tape
Hushabyes
Lion King sound track
Madeline
Riders in the Sky
Robert Meunch stories

Four Years Old

Spanish language tapes
Ace of Base
Awesome Adventures (vacation
    bible school)
Barney's Volume I
Classical Kids
Disney tapes
Fifty Ways to Fool Your Mother
Gary Lapow
Jose Luis Orozco
A Midsummer Night's Dream
Peter and the Wolf
Raffi at Carnegie Hall
Remembering John Coltrane
Renaissance Knights music
Wee Sing Dinosaurs
Wee Sing series
Wee Sing Together

Five Years Old

Books on tape
nursery rhymes
Bach Lives Here
Banana Slug String Band

Beethoven Lives Here
Down By the Bay
Ghostbuster sound track
Jason songs
Jimmy Buffett
The Lion King sound track
Little Ant
Lyle Lyle Crocodile
Nho Lobo folktales
The Nightmare Before Christmas
    sound track
Teach Me French
Teach Me More French
Wee Sing Dinosaurs

VIDEOS (Girls)

Three Years Old

Barney
Barney's Imagination Island
Big Bird in China
Cinderella
Fantasia
The Indian in the Cupboard
Land Before Time III
Lion King
Muzzy (BBC in Spanish)
Sound of Music

Four Years Old

cartoons
Barney
Bill Nye series
Franken Pooh
The Grinch Who Stole Christmas
Land Before Time series
The Lion King
Mrs. Tiggy Winkle

See How They Grow: Wild Animals
Sesame Street
The Swan Princess
Winnie the Pooh

Five Years Old

Benji
Big Bird in China
Disney Sing-A-Long
Geo Kids
Land Before Time III
Little Women
Magic School Bus series
Red Riding Hood
Return of Jafar
Richie Rich
The Secret of Roan Inish
Shalom Sesame series
Totoro
Toy Story
Wee Sing series
Wishbone
The Wizard of Oz

VIDEOS (Boys)

Three Years Old

Cowboy Pooh
Doctor Seuss
Kids Love Trains
The Lion King
The Little Engine That Could
There Goes a Bulldozer
There Goes a Fire Truck
There Goes a Train
There Goes a . . . series
Thomas the Tank Engine
Wee Sing Train Video

Four Years Old

Child-care videos, train videos
Barney
Bill Nye the Science Guy
The Brave Little Toaster
Dink
Dinosaurs (clay animation)
Disney movies
Great Indian Railway
Land Before Time (I, II, and III)
Let's Go to the Farm
Little Big League
Lorax
Magic School Bus
National Geographic Wild Animals
Road Construction Ahead
Rugrats
Storytime Sesame Street
The Tale of Samuel Whiskers
There Goes a . . . series
Thomas the Tank Engine

Five Years Old

about music-making
Bill Nye the Science Guy
cartoons
Clive James' Postcard from Cairo
Fantasia
House Construction
The Jungle Book
Land Before Time
Land Before Time III
The Lion King
The Little Engine That Could
Little Rascals
Magic School Bus
The Marx Brothers Go West
Mask

Muppets at Disney World
National Geographic Nature
   series
Pagemaster
Road Construction Ahead
Shining Time Station
Thomas the Train
Timmy's Special Delivery
Winnie the Pooh
The Wizard of Oz

SOFTWARE (Girls)

Three Years Old

The Backyard (Broderbund)
Just Grandma and Me (Living
   Books)
*Madeline and the Magnificent
   Puppet Show* (Creative
   Wonders)
Paintbrush (Microsoft)
The Playroom (Broderbund)

Four Years Old

Allie's Playhouse (Opcode
   Interactive)
Bailey's Book House (Edmark)
Crayola Art Studio (Micrografix)
Dr. Seuss' ABCs (Living Books)
Kid Pix (Broderbund)
Living Books series (Living
   Books)
Macdraw (Macintosh)
Magic School Bus series
   (Microsoft)
Putt Putt (Humongous)
Putt Putt Goes to the Moon
   (Humongous)

Putt Putt Saves the Zoo
   (Humongous)
Sammy's Science House
   (Edmark)
Thinkin' Things (Edmark)
Thinkin' Things II (Edmark)

Five Years Old

A.D.A.M. (Mindscape)
Aladdin Activity Center (Disney)
Arthur's Birthday
Bailey's Book House (Edmark)
Dinosaur Adventure (Knowledge
   Adventure)
Kid Pix (Broderbund)
Kidsworks 2 (Davidson)
The Lion King Activity Center
   (Disney)
Math Blaster (Davidson)
Math Rabbit (Learning Co.)
Millie's Math House (Edmark)
Reader Rabbit (Learning Co.)
Ruff's Bone (Living Books)
Sammy's Science House
   (Edmark)
Scooter's Magic Castle
   (Electronic Arts)
The Playroom (Broderbund)
Treasure Mountain (The
   Learning Company)
Trudy's Time and Place House
   (Edmark)

SOFTWARE (Boys)

Three Years Old

Bailey's Book House (Edmark)
Dr. Seuss' ABCs (Living Books)

Kid Pix Studio (Broderbund)
Living Books series (Living Books)
Millie's Math House (Edmark)
Putt Putt Saves the Zoo (Humongous)
Ruff's Bone (Living Books)
Sticky Bear Early Learning (Phillips Media Software)

Four Years Old

Dr. Seuss' ABCs (Living Books)
Gus Goes to Cyberopolis (Modern Media Ventures)
How Things Work in Busytown (Viacom New Media)
Kid Pix (Broderbund)
Kids on Site (Digital Pictures)
Mickey's ABCs (Disney)
Pantsylvania (Broderbund)
Playroom (Broderbund)
Reader Rabbit (Learning Co.)
Sammy's Science House (Edmark)
Thinkin' Things (Edmark)
Where in the World Is Carmen Sandiego Junior (Broderbund)

Five Years Old

Allie's Playhouse (Opcode Interactive)
Backyard (Broderbund)
Clarisworks Paint
Kid Cuts (Broderbund)
Kid Pix (Broderbund)
The Lion King (Disney)
Magic School Bus series (Microsoft)
Math Rabbit (Learning Co.)
Math Workshop (Broderbund)
Playroom (Broderbund)
Putt Putt (Humongous)
Putt Putt Checkers (Humongous)
Reader Rabbit (Learning Co.)
Sammy's Science House (Edmark)
Science Adventure (Knowledge Adventure)
Science House (Edmark)
Treasure Galaxy (The Learning Company)
Treasure Mountain (The Learning Company)
Troggle Trouble Math (MECC)
Trudy's Time and Place (Edmark)
Where in the World Is Carmen Sandiego? (Broderbund)

SELECTIONS FOR GRADE SCHOOL CHILDREN

BOOKS (Girls)

Six Years Old

The Amelia Bedelia Treasury, Peggy Parish (HarperCollins, 1995)
Body Detectives: A Book About the Five Senses, Rita Golden Gelman (Scholastic, 1994)
The Cat in the Hat, Dr. Seuss (Random House, 1994)
Dancing with Manatees, Faith McNulty (Scholastic, 1994)
Draw Me a Star, Eric Carle (Puffin, 1995)
Fox in Socks, Dr. Seuss (Beginner Books, 1993)
Karen's Softball Mystery, Ann M. Martin (Scholastic, 1996)
The Little House in the Big Woods, Laura Ingalls Wilder (HarperCollins, 1953)
The Little House on the Prairie, Laura Ingalls Wilder (HarperCollins, 1991)
Mother West Wind "How" Stories, Thornton Waldo Burgess (Grossett & Dunlap, 1973)
The Mouse and the Motorcycle, Beverly Cleary (Houghton Mifflin, 1996)
Mrs. Piggle Wiggle, Betty Bard MacDonald (HarperCollins Children's Books, 1957)
My Book About Me, By Me Myself: I Wrote It! I Drew It!, Dr. Seuss (Beginner Books, 1969)
Ready—Set—Read!, Rose Zertuche Trevino
Teaser and the Firecat, Cat Stevens (Scholastic, 1972)

Seven Years Old

Children Just Like Me, Susan Elizabeth Copsey (Dorling Kindersley, 1995)
Cloudy with a Chance of Meatballs, Judi Barrett (Aladdin Books, 1988)
The Cricket in Times Square, George Selden (Farrar Straus & Giroux, 1981)
Goodnight Moon, Margaret Wise Brown (Harper & Row, 1947)
Gwinna, Barbara Berger (Philomel, 1990)
James and the Giant Peach, Roald Dahl (Knopf, 1989)

The Little House on the Prairie, Laura Ingalls Wilder (HarperCollins, 1991)

Look Inside: How the Body Works, David Sachs (Aspen, 1972)

The Magic School Bus on the Ocean Floor, Joanna Cole (Scholastic, 1992)

The Missing Piece, Shel Silverstein (HarperCollins, 1995)

Mr. Popper's Penguins, Richard Atwater (Dell, 1982)

My Side of the Mountain, Jean Craighead George (Scholastic, 1969)

The Mystery on the Train, Gertrude Chandler Warner (Scholastic, 1996)

Pinocchio, Carlo Collodi (Penguin, 1996)

The Tooth Book, Theo. LeSieg (Beginner Books, 1981)

Tooth Truth: Fun Facts and Projects, Jennifer Storey Gillis (Storey Communications, 1996)

Winnie the Pooh: Two Favourite Stories, A. A. Milne (Ladybird, 1995)

The Wizard of Oz, Lyman Frank Baum (Umadevan, 1962)

Wonderful Alexander and the Catwings, Ursula K. Le Guin (Scholastic, 1996)

Eight Years Old

Anne of Green Gables, L. M. Montgomery (David Campbell, 1995)

Baby-Sitters Club: Dawn and the Impossible Three, Ann M. Martin (Scholastic, 1987)

The Calvin and Hobbes Tenth Anniversary Book, Bill Watterson (Scholastic, 1995)

Goosebumps, R. L. Stine (Hippo, 1994)

A Light in the Attic, Shel Silverstein (HarperCollins, 1981)

The Little House on the Prairie, Laura Ingalls Wilder (HarperCollins, 1991)

Lydia, Queen of Palestine, Uri Orlev (Puffin Books, 1995)

Martin Luther King, Benoit Marchon (Centurion/Astrapi, 1995)

Matilda, Roald Dahl (Alfaguara, 1992)

My Father's Dragon, Ruth Stiles Gannett (Trumpet Club, 1988)

The Mystery on the Train, Gertrude Chandler Warner (Scholastic, 1996)

Stuart Little, E. B. White (HarperCollins, 1990)

World's Most Baffling Puzzle Book, Charles Townsend (Sterling, 1991)

Nine Years Old

Blubber, Judy Blume (Simon & Schuster, 1974)

Bus Station Mystery, Gertrude Chandler Warner (A. Whitman, 1974)

Brighty of the Grand Canyon, Marguerite Henry (McNally, 1970)

Charlotte's Web, E. B. White (HarperCollins, 1980)

The Clue of the Leaning Chimney, Carolyn Keene (Armada, 1995)

Ella of All of a Kind Family, Sydney Taylor (Dell, 1978)

From Sea to Shining Sea, Dennis B. Fradin (Children's Press, 1993)

The Indian in the Cupboard, Lynne Reid Banks (Avon Books, 1995)

The Lion, the Witch and the Wardrobe, C. S. Lewis (Macmillan, 1986)

The Little House on the Prairie, Laura Ingalls Wilder (HarperCollins, 1991)

Number the Stars, Lois Lowry (Houghton Mifflin, 1996)

The Phantom Tollbooth, Norton Juster (Random House, 1989)

The Scarlet Slipper Mystery, Carolyn Keene (Armada, 1995)

What Manner of Man: A Biography of Martin Luther King, Jr., Lerone Bennett (Johnson, 1989)

The Witches, Roald Dahl (Weekly Reader Books, 1983)

The Yearling, Marjorie Kinnan Rawlings (Aladdin Paperbacks, 1986)

Ten Years Old

Anne of Green Gables, Lucy Maud Montgomery (David Campbell, 1995)

Are You There God? It's Me, Margaret, Judy Blume (Macmillan Books for Young Readers, 1990)

Cherry Tree, Philippe Jaccottet (Delos, 1991)

The Chronicles of Narnia, C. S. Lewis (Harper Trophy, 1994)

The Dark Is Rising, Susan Cooper (Aladdin, 1973)

Fear Street: The Sleepwalker, R. L. Stine (Pocket Books, 1990)

Goosebumps, R. L. Stine (Hippo, 1994)

I Am Regina, Sally M. Keehn (Dell, 1993)

The Indian in the Cupboard, Lynne Reid Banks (Avon Books, 1995)

Journey to Topaz, A Story of the Japanese-American Evacuation, Yoshiko Uchida (Scott Foresman, 1994)

The Little House on the Prairie, Laura Ingalls Wilder (HarperCollins, 1991)

Many Waters, Madeleine L'Engle (Dell, 1987)

Eleven Years Old

Dorothy Returns to Oz, Thomas L. Tedrow (Family Vision Press, 1993)
The Giver, Kathleen Fischer (Learning Links, 1995)
Goosebumps, R. L. Stine (Hippo, 1994)
The Indian in the Cupboard, Lynne Reid Banks (Doubleday, 1980)
The Little House on the Prairie, Laura Ingalls Wilder (HarperCollins, 1991)
Little Women, Louisa May Alcott (Smithmark, 1995)
Macbeth, William Shakespeare (Oxford University Press, 1995)
Meet Addy, an American Girl, Connie Rose Porter (Pleasant, 1993)
The Once and Future King, Terence Hanbury White (Dell, 1960)

Twelve Years Old

The Giver, Lois Lowry (Learning Links, 1995)
The Joy Luck Club, Amy Tan (Minerva, 1990)
Lost Moon: The Perilous Voyage of Apollo 13, Jim Lovell (Houghton Mifflin, 1994)
Pride and Prejudice, Jane Austen (Sceptre, 1995)
Watership Down, Richard Adams (Penguin, 1974)
A Wrinkle in Time, Madeleine L'Engle (Puffin, 1995)

BOOKS (Boys)

Six Years Old

The Alaskan Adventure, Franklin W. Dixon (Pocket Books, 1996)
Amazing Birds of Prey, Jemima Parry-Jones (Dorling Kindersley, 1993)
Bible Stories, J. McKissack (Simon & Schuster Children's Books, 1998)
The Calvin and Hobbes Tenth Anniversary Book, Bill Watterson (Scholastic, 1995)
Dinosaur 2: A Simulation Using Time-telling Skills to Unravel the Mysteries of Prehistoric Life, Myron Flindt (Interact, 1995)
Dinosaurs: Living Monsters of the Past, Michael Benton (Smithmark, 1995)
Goosebumps, R. L. Stine (Hippo, 1994)
Great Whales: The Gentle Giants, Patricia Lauber (H. Holt, 1993)
He-Man and the Memory Stone, Jason Kingsley (Ladybird, 1985)

Hide and Seek with Anthony Ant, Lorna Philpot (Random House, 1995)

I Spy Managing Information: Information Is All Around Us (Scholastic, 1996)

I Wonder How Parrots Can Talk: And Other Neat Facts About Birds, Mary Packard (Western, 1992)

Laura Ingalls Wilder's Little House Books, Laura Ingalls Wilder (Harper Trophy, 1994)

The Legend of King Arthur: A Young Reader's Edition of the Classic Story by Howard Pyle, David Borgenicht (Courage Books, 1996)

Mystery Ranch, Gertrude Chandler Warner (A. Whitman, 1986)

Why Did the Chicken Cross the Road? And Other Riddles, Old and New, Joanna Cole (Scholastic, 1995)

Yukon Ho!: A Calvin and Hobbes Collection, Bill Watterson (Scholastic, 1991)

Seven Years Old

The Adventures of Huckleberry Finn, Mark Twain (Globe Books, 1993)

The Bears' Christmas, Stan Berenstain and Janice Berenstain (Beginner Books, 1970)

Bus Station Mystery, Gertrude Chandler Warner (A. Whitman, 1974)

The Cat in the Hat, Dr. Seuss (Random House, 1985)

Charlie and the Chocolate Factory, Roald Dahl (Knopf, 1964)

Charlotte's Web, E. B. White (HarperCollins, 1980)

A Christmas Carol, Charles Dickens (Bloomsbury, 1995)

Dinotopia: The World Beneath, James Gurney (Scholastic, 1995)

Do You Know Me?, Nancy Farmer (Orion Children's Books, 1995)

Dragons, Gods and Spirits from Chinese Mythology, Tao Tao Liu Sanders (P. Bedrick Books, 1995)

Family Math, Jean Kerr Stenmark (Lawrence Hall of Science, 1986)

Fat Men from Space, Daniel Manus Pinkwater (Dell, 1980)

Gone-away Lake, Elizabeth Enright (Scholastic, 1957)

Goosebumps, R. L. Stine (Hippo, 1994)

The Hobbit: Or, There and Back Again, J. R. R. Tolkien (Galahad Books, 1993)

My Father's Dragon, Ruth Stiles Gannett (Random House, 1948)

Nate the Great and the Halloween Hunt, Marjorie Weinman Sharmat (Coward-McCann, 1989)

Owen, Kevin Henkes (Troll Associates, 1993)

The Puppy Who Wanted a Boy, Jane Thayer (Hippo, 1991)

Puzzle Train, Susannah Leigh (EDC, 1995)

Rin Tin Tin's Rinty, Julie Campbell (Whitman, 1954)

Search Out Science, Mary Horn (BBC, 1990)

Sheila Rae, the Brave, Kevin Henkes (Puffin Books, 1988)

Stuart Little, E. B. White (Dell, 1972)

The Adventures of Tom Sawyer, Mark Twain (Steck-Vaughn, 1991)

The Way Things Work, David Macaulay (Houghton Mifflin, 1988)

What Your First Grader Needs to Know: Fundamentals of a Good First Grade Education, E. D. Hirsch, Jr. (Doubleday, 1991)

Eight Years Old

The Alaskan Adventure, Franklin W. Dixon (Pocket Books, 1996)

All for the Boss, Ruchoma Shain (Feldheim, 1984)

The BFG, Roald Dahl (Puffin Books, 1984)

Bus Station Mystery, Gertrude Chandler Warner (A. Whitman, 1974)

Charlie and the Chocolate Factory, Roald Dahl (Knopf, 1964)

Dinotopia: The World Beneath, James Gurney (Scholastic, 1995)

Dragon's Gate, Laurence Yep (HarperCollins, 1993)

Dunc and Amos Hit the Big Top, Gary Paulsen (Dell, 1993)

Fantastic Mr. Fox, Roald Dahl (Puffin Books, 1988)

Goosebumps, R. L. Stine (Hippo, 1994)

I Left My Sneakers in Dimension X, Bruce Coville (Hodder Children's, 1995)

Johnny Tremain, Esther Forbes (Sundance, 1992)

Keys for Kids: A Learning Packet for Self-Care, Latch Key Children and Their Parents, (Ohio Cooperative Extension Service, 1985)

The Little Grey Mouse, George Sutton (Storytime Publications, 1989)

The Magic School Bus at the Waterworks, Karen M. Gabler (Sundance, 1990)

Mariel of Redwall, Brian Jacques (Putnam, 1992)

Math Curse, Jon Scieszka (Viking, 1995)

Moby Dick, Herman Melville (Landoll, 1995)

The Monopoly Companion, Philip Orbanes (Adams, 1988)

Sing Down the Moon, Scott O'Dell (Dell, 1976)

The Adventures of Tom Sawyer, Mark Twain (Steck-Vaughn, 1991)

The Way Things Work, David Macaulay (Houghton Mifflin, 1988)

Windchaser, Scott Ciencin (Red Fox, 1995)

The Wedding of Mistress Fox, Philip H. Bailey (North-South Books, 1994)

The World Beneath Us, Anita McConnell (Orbis, 1985)

Nine Years Old

The Adventures of Tom Sawyer, Mark Twain (Smithmark, 1995)

Bus Station Mystery, Gertrude Chandler Warner (A. Whitman, 1974)

Dinotopia: The World Beneath, James Gurney (Scholastic, 1995)

Family Math, Jean Kerr Stenmark (Lawrence Hall of Science, 1986)

Farmer Boy, Laura Ingalls Wilder (HarperCollins, 1989)

Goosebumps, R. L. Stine (Hippo, 1994)

Heaven Cent, Piers Anthony (Avon Books, 1988)

James and the Giant Peach, Roald Dahl (Knopf, 1989)

The King's Fifth, Scott O'Dell (Houghton Mifflin, 1994)

Knight's Castle, Edward Eager (Harcourt Brace Jovanovich, 1984)

The Lion, the Witch and the Wardrobe, C. S. Lewis (Macmillan, 1986)

The Magic School Bus Inside the Earth, Joanna Cole (Scholastic, 1993)

The Magic School Bus on the Ocean Floor, Johanna Cole (Sundance, 1995)

Mariel of Redwall, Brian Jacques (Putnam, 1992)

Mossflower, Brian Jacques (Philomel Books, 1988)

Mrs. Frisby and the Rats of NIMH, Robert C. O'Brien (Atheneum, 1972)

My Side of the Mountain, Jean Craighead George (Scholastic, 1969)

My Teacher Fried My Brains, Bruce Coville (Minstrel Books, 1988)

The New View Almanac: The First All-Visual Resource of Vital Facts and Statistics! Bruce Glassman, ed. (Blackbirch Press, 1996)

Puzzle Island, Paul Adshead (Child's Play, 1990)

Ribsy, Beverly Cleary (Houghton Mifflin, 1993)

Salamandastron, Brian Jacques (Hutchinson, 1992)

Sideways Stories from Wayside School, Louis Sachar (Avon Books, 1985)

The Sign of the Beaver, Elizabeth George Speare (Houghton Mifflin, 1983)

Stuart Little, E. B. White (Seedlings, 1991)

Wildlife Fact File Yearbook (International Masters, 1990)

Ten Years Old

Bagthorpes Liberated, Helen Cresswell (Puffin, 1990)

The Book of Atrus, Rand Miller (Hyperion, 1995)

Boy: Tales of Childhood, Roald Dahl (Penguin, 1992)

The Bugman Lives!, R. L. Stine (Pocket Books, 1996)

Bus Station Mystery, Gertrude Chandler Warner (A. Whitman, 1974)

Creepy Castle, Wes. Magee (Heinemann Educational, 1996)

Eastern Sun, Winter Moon: An Autobiographical Odyssey, Gary Paulsen (Gollancz, 1996)

First Light: The Search for the Edge of the Universe, Richard Preston (Random House, 1996)

Goosebumps, R. L. Stine (Hippo, 1994)

Insomnia, Stephen King (Grijalbo, 1995)

Grimm's Fairy Tales, Jacob Grimm (Penguin, 1995)

Jurassic Park, Michael Crichton (Knopf, 1995)

Making a Go-Cart, John D. Fitzgerald (Wright, 1993)

Mariel of Redwall, Brian Jacques (Putnam, 1992)

More Sideways Arithmetic from Wayside School, Louis Sachar (Scholastic, 1994)

Myst: The Pearls of Lutra, Brian Jacques (Philomel Books, 1997)

The Redwall, Brian Jacques (Avon Books, 1990)

The Secret of the Tunnel, Franklin W. Dixon (Macdonald & Co., 1969)

Stephen Biesty's Incredible Cross Sections, Stephen Biesty (Knopf, 1992)

Tales of the Greek Heroes, Roger Lancelyn Green (Puffin Books, 1989)

Technological Change from Inside: A Review of Breakthroughs! Ashoka Mody (Industry and Energy Dept, World Bank, 1989)

The Witches of Worm, Zilpha Keatley Snyder (Atheneum, 1983)

Eleven Years Old

The Calvin and Hobbes Tenth Anniversary Book, Bill Watterson (Scholastic, 1995)

Fahrenheit 451, Ray Bradbury (Buccaneer Books, 1990)

Grant Hill: On the Court, Matt Christopher (Little Brown, 1996)

The Great Automatic Grammatizator and Other Stories, Roald Dahl (Viking, 1996)

The Hobbit, J. R. R. Tolkien (Houghton Mifflin, 1989)

The Indian in the Cupboard, Lynne Reid Banks (Avon Books, 1995)

Lad, a Dog: The Best Dog in the World, Margo Lundell (Scholastic, 1997)

Mariel of Redwall, Brian Jacques (Putnam, 1992)

Math Curse, Jon Scieszka (Viking, 1995)

Old Yeller, Fred Gipson (Harper Trophy, 1990)

Twelve Years Old

The Alaskan Adventure, Franklin W. Dixon (Pocket Books, 1996)

Dinotopia: The World Beneath, James Gurney (Turner, 1995)

The Education of Little Tree, Forrest Carter (University of New Mexico Press, 1986)

The Hobbit, J. R. R. Tolkien (Houghton Mifflin, 1989)

Jurassic Park, Michael Crichton (Knopf, 1995)

Kids Travel: A Backseat Survival Guide (Klutz Press, 1994)

The Lord of the Rings Trilogy, J. R. R. Tolkien (Ballantine Books, 1970)

The Lost World, Michael Crichton (Century, 1995)

Mariel of Redwall, Brian Jacques (Putnam, 1992)

1984, George Orwell (Harcourt Brace Jovanovich, 1984)

The Phantom Tollbooth, Norton Juster (Bullseye Books, 1988)

Tortilla Flat, John Steinbeck (Penguin, 1965)

The Way Things Work, David Macaulay (Houghton Mifflin, 1988)

When the Tripods Came, John Christopher (Trumpet Club, 1991)

A Wrinkle in Time, Madeleine L'Engle (Puffin, 1995)

GAMES AND TOYS (Girls)

Six Years Old

crazy eights
character figures
dolls
dress-up clothes
go fish
horse figurines
jump rope
play kitchen
solitaire
stuffed animals
tire swing
21 card game
American Girls dolls (Pleasant
    Company)
Barbie dolls (Mattel)
Candyland (Milton Bradley)
Carmen Sandiego Junior
    Edition (University Games)
Clue (Parker Brothers)
Clue Junior (Parker Brothers)
Connect Four (Milton
    Bradley)
Geosafari (Educational
    Insights)
Grocery Store (Little Tikes)
Guess Who? (Milton Bradley)
Hi-Ho Cherry-O (Parker
    Brothers)
Legos (Lego)
Littlest Pet Shop (Kenner)
Mancala (Great American
    Trading Corp.)
Memory (Milton Bradley)
Monopoly (Parker Brothers)
Monopoly Junior (Parker
    Brothers)

Pocahontas (Disney)
Ravensburger games
    (Ravensburger)
Rollerblades (Rollerblades)
Safely Home (Quin Crafts)
Scrabble Junior (Milton
    Bradley)
Snow White and the Seven
    Dwarfs (Disney)
Uno (Mattel)

Seven Years Old

bead kits
board games
children's theater
dollhouse and accessories
dolls
fuzzy rabbit
globe
horse figurines
microscope
sewing supplies
shells
solitaire
stones
teddy bear
toy microphone
American Girls dolls (Pleasant
    Company)
Barbie dolls (Mattel)
Barbie Mini Van (Mattel)
Brain Bash (Tiger Electronics
    Toy)
Brain Quest (Workman)
Candyland (Milton Bradley)
Chess (Pavilion)
Chinese Checkers (Pavilion)

Chutes and Ladders (Milton
   Bradley)
Clue (Parker Brothers)
Guesstures (Milton Bradley)
Guess Who? (Milton Bradley)
Herd Your Horses (Aristoplay)
Littlest Pet Shop (Kenner)
Mancala (Great American
   Trading Corp.)
Memory (Milton Bradley)
Monopoly (Parker Brothers)
Monopoly Junior (Parker
   Brothers)
Mouse Trap (Milton Bradley)
Muffy Bears (North American
   Bear Co.)
Nintendo Entertainment
   System (Nintendo)
Polly Pocket Doll (Mattel)
Scrabble (Milton Bradley)
Talking Alphabet Soup (Play-
   school)
Uno (Mattel)

Eight Years Old

animal figures
antique baby doll
cards
dollhouse
dolls
porcelain doll
puppets
stuffed animals
war
Amazing Laybrinth
   (Ravensburger)
American Girls dolls (Pleasant
   Company)

Bibbity Bop (8)
Chess (Pavilion)
Clue (Parker Brothers)
Dungeons and Dragons (TSR,
   Inc.)
Four Square (Sport Fun)
Gameboard (Carrom)
Geosafari (Educational
   Insights)
Curious George the Monkey
   (Gund)
Husker Du (Parker Brothers)
Jenga (Milton Bradley)
K'Nex (K'Nex)
Labyrinth (Pavilion)
Legos (Lego)
Mancala (Great American
   Trading Comp.)
Monopoly Junior (Parker
   Brothers)
Rollerblades (Rollerblades)
San Franciscopoly (Global
   Games)
Scattergories (Milton Bradley)
Scrabble (Milton Bradley)
Stratego (Milton Bradley)

Nine Years Old

bat (rubber)
lanyards
remote control car
snake (rubber)
stuffed animals
Amazing Labyrinth
   (Ravensburger)
American Girls dolls (Pleasant
   Company)

Author Cards (Woodkrafter kits)
Barbie dolls (Mattel)
Capsela (Play Tech)
Clue (Parker Brothers)
Clue: The Great Museum Caper (Parker Brothers)
Dapples horse (Breyer)
Dominoes (Pressman)
Herd Your Horses (Aristoplay)
K'Nex (K'Nex)
Madame Alexander dolls (Alexander Doll Co.)
Mastermind (Pressman)
Monopoly (Parker Brothers)
My Little Pony figures (Hasbro)
Scattergories Junior (Milton Bradley)
Scrabble (Milton Bradley)
Talk Boy Fx Plus (Tiger)
Toy Story (Sega)
Uno (Mattel)
Where in the World Is Carmen Sandiego Junior (University Games)
Yahtzee (Milton Bradley)

Addy and Felicity American Girls dolls (Pleasant Company)
Barbie dolls (Mattel)
Brain Quest (Workman)
Chess (Pavilion)
Chinese Checkers (Pavilion)
Clue (Parker Brothers)
Elmo stuffed animal (Tyco)
Guess Who? (Milton Bradley)
Legos (Lego)
Master Labyrinth (Ravensburger)
Mastermind (Pressman)
Mille Bornes (Parker Brothers)
Monopoly (Parker Brothers)
Mouse Trap (Milton Bradley)
Nerf Bow and Arrow (Kenner)
101 Dalmations stuffed animal (Disney)
Playmobil Indians (Playmobil)
Playmobil Medical Set (Playmobil)
Scrabble (Milton Bradley)
Stratego (Milton Bradley)
Taboo (Milton Bradley)
Tri Bond (Big Fun A Go Go)

Ten Years Old

animal figures
bunny
cardboard
diary
dollhouse
eyeball ball
horse figurines
stuffed animals
yo-yo

Eleven Years Old

card games
clay
dollhouse
soccer
word games
American Girls dolls (Pleasant Company)
Hackey Sack (Mattel)
Labyrinth (Pavilion)

Legos (Lego)
Magic 8-ball (Tyco)
Mancala (Great American
    Trading Corp.)
Mastermind (Pressman)
Monopoly (Parker Brothers)
Poker (Pavilion)
Scattergories (Milton Bradley)
Scrabble (Milton Bradley)
Set (Set Enterprises)
Tripole (Cadaco)
Trouble (Milton Bradley)
Up Words (Milton Bradley)

Twelve Years Old

computer
dice
dolls
playing cards
playing pretend
stuffed animals
Amazing Labyrinth
    (Ravensburger)
Erector set (Meccano)
Life (Milton Bradley)
Rook (Parker Brothers)
Uno (Mattel)
Where in the World Is Carmen
    Sandiego (University
    Games)

GAMES AND TOYS (Boys)

Six Years Old

blocks
cards
cat's cradle string
go fish

hide-and-seek
jet plane
jigsaw puzzles
loom
no peeking
pogs
rubber ball
stuffed animals
stuffed kangaroo puppet
tag
Air Hockey (Carrom)
Allowance Kit (World of
    Money)
Amazing Labyrinth
    (Ravensburger)
Author Cards (Woodkrafter
    Kits)
Brick by Brick (Binary Arts)
Candyland (Milton Bradley)
Capsela (Play Tech)
Checkers (Pavilion)
Chess (Pavilion)
Chinese Checkers (Pavilion)
Circuit Board (Radio Shack)
Concentration (Hasbro)
Erector set (Meccano)
G.I. Joe action figures
    (Kenner)
Game Boy video games (Sega)
Geosafari (Educational
    Insights)
K'Nex (K'Nex)
Knights and Castles Lego set
    (Lego)
Lego Castle (Lego)
Legos (Lego)
Mancala (Great American
    Trading Corp.)

Marble Works (Discovery Toys)
Matchbox cars (Tyco)
Mega Man (Nintendo)
Memory (Milton Bradley)
Micromachines (Galoob)
Monopoly (Parker Brothers)
Monopoly Junior (Parker Brothers)
Othello (Pressman)
Playmobil toys (Playmobil)
River Roads and Rails (Ravensburger Games)
Rollerblade Hockey (Rollerblade)
Scrabble (Milton Bradley)
Smath (Pressman Toys)
Spiderman figures (Toy Biz)
Stratego (Milton Bradley)
Super Nintendo (Nintendo)
Tinker toys (Playskool)
Uncle Wiggley (Milton Bradley)
Uno (Mattel)
X-Men figures (Toy Biz)
Yahtzee (Milton Bradley)
Zolo Creative Building Sets (E Market)

Seven Years Old

gin rummy
hearts
stuffed animals
tepee
trampoline
word searches
Aggravation (Milton Bradley)

Amazing Labyrinth (Ravensburger)
Batman figures (Kenner)
Battleship (Milton Bradley)
Brain Quest (Workman)
Brio Train set (Brio)
Capsela (Play Tech)
Checkers (Pavilion)
Chess (Pavilion)
Cribbage (Pavilion)
Dinorama (American Museum of World History)
Donkey Kong (Nintendo)
Enforcer remote control car (Nikko)
Erector set (Meccano)
Flexibears (Flexitoys)
Gameboy (Nintendo)
Gear's Fun (Fun-N-Learn)
Guess Who? (Milton Bradley)
Hangman (Milton Bradley)
K'Nex (K'Nex)
Legos (Lego)
Matchbox cars (Tyco)
Memory (Milton Bradley)
Micromachines (Galoob)
Monopoly (Parker Brothers)
Monopoly Junior (Parker Brothers)
Playmobil Zoo (Playmobil)
Poker (Pavilion)
Power Rangers (Ban Dai)
Robotix 2000 (Learning Curve)
Sand Surprises (Kenner)
Scrabble (Milton Bradley)
Scrabble Junior (Milton Bradley)
Splat (Milton Bradley)

Toobers and Zots (Kenner)
Where in the World Is Carmen
  Sandiego? (University
  Games)
Yahtzee (Milton Bradley)

Eight Years Old

action figures
anagrams
blocks
electric train
geology
paper airplanes
plastic reptiles
remote control cars
stuffed animals
tic-tac-toe
toy soldiers
Chess (Pavilion)
Chutes and Ladders (Milton
  Bradley)
Clue (Parker Brothers)
Connect Four (Milton
  Bradley)
Cribbage (Pavilion)
Donkey Kong (Nintendo)
Erector set (Meccano)
15 Classic Board Games (Klutz
  Press)
Geosafari (Educational
  Insights)
Jumanji (Milton Bradley)
K'Nex (K'Nex)
Koosh Basketball (Oddz On
  Products)
Labyrinth (Pavilion)
Legos (Lego)
Lego Aquazone (Lego)

Lego Knights Horses and
  Castles (Lego)
Life (Milton Bradley)
Magic Works (Milton Bradley)
Master Labyrinth
  (Ravensburger)
Micromachines (Galoob)
Monopoly (Parker Brothers)
Monopoly Junior (Parker
  Brothers)
Mortal Kombat 3 (Nintendo)
Ninja Zord (Ban Dai)
Parcheesi (Milton Bradley)
Pente (Decipher)
Playmobil toys (Playmobil)
Rollerblade Hockey
  (Rollerblade)
Sega video games (Sega)
Set (Set Enterprises)
Sorry (Parker Brothers)
Super Nintendo (Nintendo)
Taboo (Milton Bradley)
Take Off! (Take Off Inc.)
Yahtzee (Milton Bradley)

Nine Years Old

baseball cards
bicycle
handball
hearts
pinochle
race car track
soccer
By Jove (Aristoplay)
Chess (Pavilion)
Clue (Parker Brothers)
Command and Conquer
  (Westwood)

Erector sets (Meccano)
Godzilla action figure
   (Trendmasters)
K'Nex (K'Nex)
Koosh (Oddz On Products)
Legos (Lego)
Life (Milton Bradley)
Magic Cards: The Gathering
   (Wizards of the Coast Inc.)
Mancala (Great American
   Trading Corp.)
Medical Monopoly (Parker
   Brothers)
Micromachines: Millenium
   Falcon (Galoob)
Mission: Survival (Atari)
Monopoly (Parker Brothers)
Nerf toys (Kenner)
Othello (Pressman)
Payday (Parker Brothers)
Risk (Parker Brothers)
Skip-Bo (Mattel)
Space Shooters (D. Jackal)
Star Wars figures (Galoob)
Stratego (Milton Bradley)

Ten Years Old

action figures
bicycle
gin rummy
go
imaginary play
remote control car
stuffed animals
touch football
toy soldiers
Battleship (Milton Bradley)
Brain Quest (Workman)

Brick by Brick (Binary Arts)
By Jove (Aristoplay)
Capsela (Play Tech)
Chess (Pavilion)
Dungeons and Dragons (TSR,
   Inc.)
Erector set (Meccano)
G.I. Joe action figures
   (Kenner)
K'Nex (K'Nex)
Legos (Lego)
Life (Milton Bradley)
Magic Cards: The Gathering
   (Wizards of the Coast Inc.)
Mancala (Great American
   Trading Corp.)
Master Labyrinth
   (Ravensburger)
Micromachines Military
   (Galoob)
Micromachines Space
   (Galoob)
Monopoly (Parker Brothers)
Nick the Greek Casino (Athol
   Research Group)
Parcheesi (Milton Bradley)
Playmobil Civil War series
   (Playmobil)
Poker (Pavilion)
Risk (Parker Brothers)
Scrabble (Milton Bradley)
Star Trek Video Interactive
   games
Star Wars figures (Galoob)
Stratego (Milton Bradley)
Super Nintendo (Nintendo)
Super Soaker (Larami)
Uno (Mattel)
Woody doll (Disney)

Yahtzee (Milton Bradley)
Zolo (E Market)

Eleven Years Old

action figures
bean bags for juggling
computer
Chess (Pavilion)
Erector set (Meccano)
Legos (Lego)
Magic: The Gathering
   (Wizards of the Coast Inc.)
Mastermind (Pressman)
Monopoly (Parker Brothers)
Poker (Pavilion)
Risk (Parker Brothers)
Rollerblades (Rollerblades)
Solar Quest (Universal Games)
Sorry (Parker Brothers)
Super Nintendo (Nintendo)
Take Off! (Take Off Inc.)

Twelve Years Old

microscope
remote control car
telescope
Battledome (Parker Brothers)
Battleship (Milton Bradley)
Capsela (Play Tech)
Chess (Pavilion)
Clue: Museum Madness
   (Parker Brothers)
Crack the Case (Milton
   Bradley)
Domino Rally (Pressman)
Garfield (Dakin)
Hail to the Chief (Aristoplay)
Lego Aquazone (Lego)

Lego Century Skyway (Lego)
Lego Technic (Lego)
Legos (Lego)
Magic Cards: The Gathering
   (Wizards of the Coast Inc.)
Micromachines: Star Wars
   (Galoob)
Monopoly (Parker Brothers)
Scrabble (Milton Bradley)
Solar Quest (Universal Games)
Super Nintendo (Nintendo)

MODELS AND PUZZLES (Girls)

Six Years Old

animal puzzles
floor puzzles
dollhouse
horse puzzle
Moses puzzle
sea otter puzzle
USA puzzle
Disney puzzles (Disney)
Legos (Lego)
Playmobil Indian Village
   (Playmobil)
Playskool wooden puzzle
   (Playskool)
Pocahontas 3-D puzzle
   (Disney)
Ravensburger puzzles
   (Ravensburger)

Seven Years Old

cats puzzle
clock puzzle
doggies in a basket puzzle

jigsaw puzzle
sea life puzzle
styrofoam bird model
Lego Building Sets (Lego)
Legos (Lego)
Little Tike Doll House (Little Tike)
Minnie Mouse puzzle (Disney)
Pattern Blocks (Cuisinnaire)
Ravensburger puzzles (Ravensburger)
Triazzle (Da Mert Co.)

Eight Years Old

airplane model
dinosaur skeletons
dollhouse furniture
human body model
math puzzles
mazes
1000-piece puzzle
planets
reef puzzle
spaceship model
Styrofoam bird
Tyrannasaurus Rex
USA puzzle
Disney puzzle (Disney)
Labyrinth (Pavilion)
Lego Robot (Lego)
Pocahontas puzzle (Disney)
Jungle puzzle (Ravensburger)
Ravensburger puzzles (Ravensburger)

Nine Years Old

airplane model
1500-piece puzzle horse

insect puzzle with magnifying glass
interlocking metal puzzle
skeleton model
3-D puzzles
USA puzzle with capitals
Jungle Scene puzzle (Lauri)
Lion King jigsaw puzzle (Disney)
Micromachines Star Wars (Galoob)

Ten Years Old

animal puzzle
car model
dollhouse
fighter plane
mazes
papier-mâché
relief maps
robot model
rocket model
model of Spanish mission
six-sided cube
string games
3-D puzzle of Victorian house
USA puzzle
world puzzle
Egyptian Adventure (Running Press)
Geo Logs (Binary Arts)
Indian Village (Playmobil)
Mind Trap (Pressman)
Owl and the Pussycat puzzle
Ravensburger puzzle

Eleven Years Old

crossword puzzle
dollhouse
find-a-word puzzle
1000-piece jigsaw puzzle
papier-mâché model of the
    (local) San Francisco Bay
    Area
poster puzzle
3-D puzzles of capitol building
wooden model of human body
The Night Sky (David
    Chandler)
Rubik's Cube (Oddz On)
Triazzle (Da Mert Co.)

Twelve Years Old

dollhouse
Indian Village
Parthenon (self-designed)
stage sets
3-D puzzles
USA puzzle
Ravensburger Sailboat puzzle
    (Ravensburger)

MODELS AND PUZZLES (Boys)

Six Years Old

Apache helicopters
flying bird
car models
dinosaur puzzle
eagle model (wood)
floor puzzles
foam puzzles

helicopter model (solar-
    powered)
homemade puzzle
human body model
magic trick puzzles
mazes
100-piece jigsaw puzzles
paper sawmill
shark puzzle
USA puzzle
wooden puzzles
Erector set Junior (Meccano)
Highlights Puzzlemania
    magazine (Highlights)
K'Nex (K'Nex)
Legos (Lego)
Lego Race Car (Lego)
Lego Royal Drawbridge (Lego)
Ravensburger Knight's Castle
    puzzle (Ravensburger)
Ravensburger puzzles
    (Ravensburger)
Tangrams (Creative Toys Ltd.)

Seven Years Old

brain teaser puzzle
car model
dinosaur puzzle
dinosaur models
500-piece jigsaw puzzle
mazes
Noah's Ark puzzle
space shuttle puzzle
Statue of Liberty puzzle
swan jigsaw puzzle
3-D nine-square slide puzzle
USA puzzle
Wooly Mammoth (wood)

word searches
Capsela (Play Tech)
Donald Duck puzzle (Disney)
Frantic Ants (Parker Brothers)
K'Nex (K'Nex)
Legos (Lego)
Lego Space Shuttle (Lego)
Power Rangers jigsaw puzzle
    (Ban Dai)
Ravensburger Dinosaur puzzle
    (Ravensburger)
Starship Enterprise
    (Playmates)
Steel Tech moving models
    (Remco)
Triazzle puzzle (Da Mert)
Whitewings (AG Industries)

Eight Years Old

airplane models
cars
dinosaur model
dinosaur (wood kit)
generator
jigsaw puzzle
motor
Native American puzzle
origami safari
pinewood derby car
police car model
rain forest
skeleton model
3-D puzzles
trains
USA puzzle
word searches
Brain Ticklers (Wild Goose)
Capsela (Play Tech)

Fisher Price Technics (Fisher
    Price)
K'Nex (K'Nex)
K'Nex Windmill (K'Nex)
Legos (Lego)
Legos Space series (Lego)
Pattern Blocks (Cuisinnaire)
Penny Press puzzles (Penny
    Press)
Ravensburger puzzles
    (Ravensburger)
Tetris (Nintendo)
Triazzle (Da Mert Co.)

Nine Years Old

aircraft models
airplane (Monogram kit)
B-52 bomber
battleship model
Civil War soldiers
dinosaur puzzle
Eiffel Tower 3-D puzzle
Glow-in-the-Dark Night Sky
helicopter
home model train set
human body model
jigsaw puzzle
matching puzzle
model cars
nature jigsaw puzzle
pinewood derby car
robot
rockets
San Francisco puzzle
spaceships
3-D puzzles
300-piece jigsaw puzzle
train model (electric)

truck model
USA puzzle
word searches
Ducktales puzzle (Disney)
Erector sets (Meccano)
Legos (Lego)
Lego Roboguardian (Lego)
Millenium Falcon (Galoob)
New Pyramid Cubed 3-D
   puzzle (InterActive Arts,
   Inc.)
Rubik's Cube (Oddz On)
Tangoes puzzle (Rex Games)
Triazzle (Da Mert Co.)
Whitewings (AG Industries)

Ten Years Old

airplane
car models
carpentry projects
Challenger rocket model
Dream Team puzzle
electric motor kit
hidden picture jigsaw puzzle
highway patrol car model
physics problems
rocket model
submarine model
truck model
windmill
IQ Collection Soma Cube
   (Family Games)
K'Nex (K'Nex)
Legos (Lego)
Legos Space Satellite (Lego)
Mystery jigsaw puzzle (Buffalo
   Games Inc.)

Ravensburger puzzles
   (Ravensburger)
Rubik's Cube (Oddz On)
Science Wizardry for kids
   (Barron's)
Tangoes (Rex Games)
Tangrams (Creative Toys Ltd.)
Triazzle (Da Mert Co.)
Visible Man model (Skilcraft)

Eleven Years Old

airplane
American Presidents puzzle
beach puzzle
dinosaur model
manipulative puzzles
mazes
rain forest puzzle
rocket model
sea life jigsaw puzzle
train model
Legos (Lego)
Legos Model Team (Lego)
Move Its: Piper Mouse
   Robotics (Elekit)
Snafooz foam squares (Idea
   Group Inc.)
Triazzle (Da Mert Co.)

Twelve Years Old

African rain forest jigsaw
   puzzle
airplane
alpine castle 3-D puzzle
coral reef paper model
dig puzzle
mansion 3D puzzle
Medal Tavern puzzle

metal car model
mule team model
1000-piece puzzles
rocket models
3-D jigsaw puzzles
tramboard
White House 3D puzzle
Erector sets (Meccano)
How Amazing (Snape and
    Scott)
Legos (Lego)
Lego Technic Super Car
    (Lego)
Star Wars (Galoob)
Star Wars: Battle of Hoth
    Scene (Galoob)
Tangrams (Creative Toys Ltd.)
Whitewings (AG Industries)

MUSICAL INSTRUMENTS (Girls)

Six Years Old

guitar
harp
keyboard
piano
recorder
violin
voice
whistle

Seven Years Old

Balinese percussion
    instruments
drums
harmonica
horn

keyboard
lap harp
percussion instruments
piano
recorder
song flute
taiko (Japanese drums)
violin
voice

Eight Years Old

guitar
keyboard
piano
recorder
violin
voice

Nine Years Old

cello
clarinet
flute
lap harp
piano
ukulele
violin
voice

Ten Years Old

clarinet
flute
oboe
piano
recorder
trumpet
violin

Eleven Years Old

flute
piano
recorder
violin
voice

Twelve Years Old

flute
piano
violin

MUSICAL INSTRUMENTS (Boys)

Six Years Old

drums
electric guitar
guitar
keyboard
mandolin
organ
piano
recorder
ukulele
violin
voice
wood blocks

Seven Years Old

drums
drumsticks
flute
guitar
harmonica
keyboard
pencil on containers and jars
piano

recorder
saxophone
violin
voice

Eight Years Old

baritone horn
cello
clavinova
drums
electric guitar
guitar
keyboard
marimba
piano
recorder
trumpet
xylophone

Nine Years Old

bass
cello
clarinet
drums
flute
guitar
keyboard
piano
recorder
saxophone
trumpet
violin
voice

Ten Years Old

cello
clarinet
drums

piano
recorder
saxophone
trumpet
violin

Eleven Years Old

drums
piano
saxophone
trombone
violin

Twelve Years Old

cello
clarinet
drums
flute
piano
recorder
saxophone
trumpet

ART MATERIALS (Girls)

Six Years Old

art kits
cardboard
Chinese water paints
clay
collage materials
coloring books
crayons
decoupage
glitter
knitting needles and yarn
markers
origami

paints
paper
sand art
Mr. Sketch scented markers

Seven Years Old

bead loom
cardboard
clay
collage materials
color pencils
color pens
crayons
drawing supplies
fabric
glitter crayons and paints
glue
India ink
markers
oil paints
paints
paper
pastels
pencils
pens
rubber stamps
rulers
sidewalk chalk
sketch book
watercolor crayons
watercolors

Eight Years Old

clay
color pencils
colored construction paper
drawing tools and supplies
glitter

glitter crayons
markers
mosaic tiles
origami paper and patterns
paints
paper
pencils
pens
scented markers
watercolor paint

Nine Years Old

clay
colored pencils
crayons
diorama supplies
markers
paints
papier mâché materials
pencils
rubber stamps
sand painting supplies
watercolor paints
Fimo clay (Eberhardt Faber)
thin point markers (Pentel)

Ten Years Old

art book
calligraphy set
clay
clay book
collage paper
colored pencils
crayons
markers
oil paints
paint
paper

paper flowers
pastels
pencils
scissors
sewing materials
sketch book
stencils
watercolors
Fimo clay (Eberhardt Faber)

Eleven Years Old

colored pencils
drawing pencils
drawing supplies
marker
origami paper
papermaking kit
stitchery
watercolors
weaving
Fimo clay (Eberhardt Faber)

Twelve Years Old

beading materials
clay
pastels
pencils of varying thicknesses
pens

ART MATERIALS (Boys)

Six Years Old

art kits
clay
claymation clay
colored pencils
construction paper
crayons

fine-tip markers
glitter
glue
markers
oil pastels
paints
paper
pencils
recycled paper
scissors
tape
unfinished cubes
watercolors
weaving and knitting supplies

Seven Years Old

acrylic paints
canvas
cardboard
clay
colored pencils
crayons
drawing materials
drawing pad
glitter
glue
India ink
markers
origami paper
paintbrushes
paints
paper
pencils
pens
scented markers
soapstone and carving tools
stickers
watercolors

Eight Years Old

charcoal
clay
colored pencils
coloring books
crayons
drawing supplies
glue
glitter
markers
overwriter markers
paints
paper
pastels
pencils
rock sculpting
scissors
woodworking supplies
Berol Watercolor Felt Pens
Fimo clay (Eberhardt Faber)
Kidpix (Broderbund)
Play-Doh (Playskool)
Play-Doh molds and presses
    (Playskool)
Sculpey clay (Polyform
    Products)

Nine Years Old

canvas
chalk
changeable markers
clay
colored pencils
dough
glitter crayons
hammer
markers
nails

origami supplies
paints
paper
pastels
pencils
plaster casting supplies
plastic beads
tracing paper
wood
Fimo clay (Eberhardt Faber)
Lego blocks (Lego)
Play-Doh (Playskool)
Sculpey clay (Polyform
   Products)

Ten Years Old

acrylics
aluminum foil
canvas
clay
colored pencils
crayons
erasable white board
erasers
drawing kit
markers
mechanical pencils
oil paints
paintbrush
paper
pencils
wood
Fimo clay (Eberhardt Faber)

Eleven Years Old

calligraphy
clay
colored pencils

drawing supplies
paints
paper
pencils
pens

Twelve Years Old

acrylic paints
art set
calligraphy pens
chalk
colored pencils
fine-tip colored pens
ink
oil paints
origami paper
paper
pastels
pencils
pens
sand art
scratch board
watercolor paints
Fimo clay (Eberhardt Faber)
Sculpey clay (Polyform Products)

LESSONS AND CLASSES (Girls)

Six Years Old

animals class
art
ballet
clay/ceramics
computers
dinosaurs
flower making
hip-hop dance

gymnastics
Irish dancing
Mandarin
math
piano
pond ecology
quantum science
science
sewing
Spanish
swimming
whales
zoo camp

Seven Years Old

animals class
art
ballet
chemistry
chess
cooking
creative dance
drama
Ecole Bilingual
folkdance
gymnastics
ice-skating
Kids and Clay
Kumon math tutoring
Kwanzaa celebration
making a terrarium
making glow-in-the-dark goop
math
piano
Polynesian dance
reader's workshop
recorder
religious school

science
soccer
soccer camp for girls
swimming
how to take care of pets
tap dancing
winter solstice
Kindershul

Eight Years Old

acting
advanced math
anatomy
art
bubbleology
chess
computer
crime camp
drama
emergency procedures
family history
gymnastics
insects and ancestors
karate
Mandarin
math
multiplication tables
physical education
piano
religion
soccer
song and dance
Sunday school
swimming

Nine Years Old

acrobatics
art

ballet
ceramics
choir
cooking
computer
dance
drawing
electricity assembly
endangered species
horse camp
horse riding
ice-skating
jazz dance
karate
math
music
pandas
physical education
piano
reading
science
Scottish country dancing
sculpture
sewing
sports
swimming

Ten Years Old

acting
art
ballet
ceramics
crime camp
flute
gymnastics
history
karate
knitting

math
music
oceanography
piano
poetry
pottery
science
soccer
Spanish
sports
swimming lesson
violin
writing

Eleven Years Old

algebra
Ancient Egypt
art camp
ballet
colonial America
chemistry
dance
gymnastics
math
mythology (Indian, Norse)
physical education
quilting
rocketry
science for girls
Shakespeare in the schools
social studies
swimming
violin

Twelve Years Old

geography
gymnastics
horseback riding

Kumon math
Latin
manipulatives
math
microbiology
science
social studies
taekwondo
world history

LESSONS AND CLASSES (Boys)

Six Years Old

arithmetic
art
church choir
clay
computer
developmental kindergarten
    class
drama
French
growing plants
karate
marine biology
math
mazes
music
physical education
physical science for
    preschoolers
piano
music
reading
sculpture
sharks
skiing
swimming

tennis
zoo camp

7 Years Old

art
ballet for boys
beginning mechanics
biology
boomerang
carpentry
chemistry
chess
circus skills
computer
cooking
gardening
gymnastics
history
journal writing
judo
karate
library and reading
mask making
math
math tile games
music
nature
origami
painting
physical education
poetry
reptiles
roller hockey
science
sound magic (special music
    class)
swimming
violin

volts and jolts (science center class)

Eight Years Old

after-school algebra
animals
art
birds
Brazilian dance
chess
computers
geography (maps and map reading)
Hebrew school
insect terrariums
karate
math
natural science
papier-mâché animals
physical education
piano
quantum science
reading
science
sculpting
swimming
taekwondo
tennis
volcanoes
writing

Nine Years Old

aikido
algebra
art
boat camp
Brazilian dance
carpentry

city building
clarinet
computer keyboarding
drawing
electricity
fun science
Greek mythology
gymnastics
history
horseback riding
karate
Lego building (science center)
math
math games (science center)
migrations of Polynesians
music
physical education
piano
racquetball
reading
rock climbing
roller hockey
science
science camp
Spanish
speech therapy
spelling
swimming
tap dancing
watercolor
woodworking
writer's workshop
zoo camp

Ten Years Old

algebra
animal dissection
art

basketball
chemistry
choir
clarinet
computers
drums
English
experiments
history
karate
Latin
math
painting
physical education
piano
politics
reading
science
solar system
spelling
taekwondo
starlab classes
survival class
swimming
table tennis
violin
writing

Eleven Years Old

algebra
art
clay
designing a tree house
drawing
drums
Dungeons and Dragons
journal writing
kayaking

Latin
light wizardry
marine biology (science
    center)
math
magic squares
music
painting
physical education
robotic arm class (science
    center)
science
skiing
swimming
tennis

Twelve Years Old

advanced math problems
art
building a speaker
circulatory system
diving
flute
gizmos and gadgets (science
    center)
golf
instrumental music
lacrosse
Lego Buggy Robotics
math
oceanography club
    (aquarium)
physical education
piano
rain forest
rockets
role-play
sailing

science
sculpting
Spanish
speed-reading
star camp (science center)
swimming
youth group at church

OUTINGS AND TRIPS (Girls)

Six Years Old

bat exhibit (science center)
beach
camping
fairs
hiking
ice-skating
lake
movies
national parks
nature study area
park
playground
sleepover at a friend's
vacation
Bishop Museum (Hawaii)
California Academy of
    Sciences
Discovery Museum
Disneyland
Exploratorium
Lawrence Hall of Science
    (U.C. Berkeley)
Marine World

Seven Years Old

abandoned mine
art center

backpacking
backstage tour of the
    Nutcracker
baseball games
beach
bike riding
camping
Girl Scout field trips
hiking
ice skating
Magic Flute
mammal center
A Midsummer Night's Dream
movie
museum
national parks
Phantom of the Opera
river rafting
skiing
tide pooling
zoo
Discovery Museum
Disneyland
Lawrence Hall of Science
Marine World (via ferry)
Monterey Bay Aquarium
Sea World
University Art Museum (U.C.
    Berkeley)

Eight Years Old

abandoned mine
aquarium
ballet
bats exhibit (science center)
beach
bike riding
cabin

camping (with Brownie group)
cruise (Caribbean)
day camp
field trips
fishing
geology
history museums
national park
Native American history
overseas
parades
rafting
sailing
science center
science museums
shopping
symphony
theater
zoo
Discovery Museum
Disneyland
Exploratorium
Monterey Bay Aquarium

Nine Years Old

antique schooner ship
around the world
bat exhibit
beach
bike riding
camping
caverns
fossil hunting
Girl Scout campout
gold panning
horseback riding
mountains
outdoor storytelling

picnic lunches
skiing
Disneyland
Discovery Museum
Exploratorium
Lawrence Hall of Science

Ten Years Old

beach
blackberry picking
Campfire Girls ski trip
camping
farm
gold panning
high tea
hiking
ice rink
mountains
museums
planetarium
tidepooling
redwood groves
seashore
Tommy Tune musical
waterslides
Disney World
Exploratorium
Indian Camp (California
    Academy of Sciences)
Lawrence Hall of Science
Marine World
Museum of Modern Art
    (Houston)

Eleven Years Old

across America
backpacking
biking

camping
canoeing (in wildlife
    sanctuary)
car show
Chinese immigration museum
geysers
gold panning
hiking
ocean cruise
overnight field trip (on a boat)
seashore
skiing
whale watching
Disneyland
Exploratorium

Twelve Years Old

beach
skiing
sushi bars
whale watching
Chicago Institute of Art
Monterey Bay Aquarium
Museum of Modern Art (San
    Francisco)

OUTINGS AND TRIPS (Boys)

Six Years Old

bats exhibit (science center)
beach
biking
camping
canoeing
crabbing
ferry on San Francisco Bay
fishing
hiking

mountains
nature trails
Nutcracker
parks
Picasso exhibit
pinball places
restored Indian village
rock climbing
seashore
skiing
wildlife museum
California Academy of
    Sciences
Discovery Museum
Discovery Zone
Disneyland
Exploratorium
Hands-On Museum
Lawrence Hall of Science

Seven Years Old

aircraft carrier show
beach
bike riding
camping
dude ranch (Montana)
fishing
hiking
ice-skating
lighthouse
movies
national parks
parks
planetarium
ranch
sailing
serpentarium
submarine tour

teddy bear factory
waterslides
woods
zoo
Discovery Zone
Disneyland
Exploratorium
Lawrence Hall of Science
Marine World
Monterey Bay Aquarium
Sacramento Train Museum
Universal Studios

Eight Years Old

beach
bike riding
birdwatching
camping
cotton farm
Cub Scout overnighter
dude ranch (Montana)
grandparents' house
hidden villa
hiking
horseback riding
ice-skating
lakes laser show
mountain lake (fishing, camp-
    ing, sailing)
movies
museums
national parks
old-fashioned general store
planetarium
railroad museum
redwood groves
sailboat cruise
skiing

sledding
stargazing
train trip cross-country
Disneyland
Disney World
Exploratorium
Lawrence Hall of Science
Monterey Bay Aquarium

Nine Years Old

antique schooner ship
beach
baseball game
biking
camping
dude ranch (Wyoming)
hiking
hockey camp
skating rink
kayaking
lakes
marine reserve
mountains
movies
museums
ocean cruise
parks
plane trips
planetarium
rafting
seashore
science museums
skiing
tidepools
grandparents house
whale watching
Bishop Museum (Hawaii)

California Academy of
  Sciences
Discovery Museum
Disneyland
Lawrence Hall of Science
Marine World
Monterey Bay
Aquarium
Sacramento Train Museum
Wild Animal Park (San Diego)

Ten Years Old

bike riding
camping
campover on island
crabbing
cruise ship
Cub Scout overnighter
fishing
football game
grandmother's house
historical places
hiking
hydroelectric dams
ice-skating
lakes
lava beds
Les Miserables
missions of California
Nutcracker
overnight field trip
Phantom of the Opera
skiing
tidepools
Disneyland
Epcot Center (Orlando,
  Florida)

Exploratorium
Great America
Lawrence Hall of Science
Universal Studios

Eleven Years Old

aquarium
backpacking
bike riding
camping
kayaking
lakes
ranch
restaurants
seashore
summer camp
Exploratorium
Lawrence Hall of Science

Twelve Years Old

aquarium
backpacking with Boy Scouts
botanical gardens
Boy Scout camping
cattle ranch
ice-skating
inland sea marine lab
jet skiing
Latin convention
lava beds
national parks
seashore
skiing
snow camping
wetlands
whale watching
Discovery Museum

Disneyland
Exploratorium
Kennedy Space Center
Lawrence Hall of Science
San Francisco Museum of
    Modern Art
Tech Museum

SPORTS EQUIPMENT (Girls)

Six Years Old

balls
baseball bat
bicycle
bouncing ball (large)
ice skates
in-line skates
jump rope
monkey bars
roller skates
skis
soccer ball
swing set
tennis equipment

Seven Years Old

bicycle
climbing structure
downhill skis
fishing pole
ice skates
in-line skates
jump rope
roller skates
soccer ball
swim goggles
tennis racquet

Eight Years Old

ball
baseball and bat
bicycle
chinning bar
ice skates
in-line skates
jump rope
old rowboat
roller skates
snow tube
soccer ball
vault

Nine Years Old

balls
basketball
bicycle
boots
canoe
gymnastics equipment
in-line skates
riding helmet
skis
soccer ball
swimming pool (YMCA)
tennis racquet
tetherball

Ten Years Old

baseball
basketball
bicycle
catcher's mitt
chin-up bar
gymnastics equipment
in-line skates
rock climbing equipment

ski equipment
skis
soccer ball
softball
tennis racquet
volleyball

Eleven Years Old

basketball
bicycle
bowling ball
in-line skates
skis
soccer ball
swimming pool
trampoline

Twelve Years Old

basketball
golf club
gymnastics mat and bar
ice skates
sailboat
soccer ball
volleyball

SPORTS EQUIPMENT (Boys)

Six Years Old

ball
baseball
basketball
bicycle
bicycle-built-for-two
football
in-line skates
kickballs
rock climbing rope

skis
soccer ball
swimming pool
swing set
tennis racquet
tricycle
Nerf football (Kenner)
Whoosh (OddzOn Products)

Seven Years Old

badminton set
ball
baseball
baseball bat and glove
basketball
bicycle
bicycle helmet
bow and arrow
bowling ball
football
in-line skates
karate
rollerskates
soccer ball
T-ball
tennis racquet
Nerf football (Kenner)

Eight Years Old

balls
baseball
baseball bat and glove
bicycle
bicycle helmet
football
hockey stick
in-line skates
karate

lacrosse stick
roller hockey
rollerskates
sailboat
snorkel
soccer ball
soccer equipment
swim goggles
tennis racquet

Nine Years Old

balls
baseball glove and bat
basketball
basketball hoop
bicycle
football
fox tails
hockey equipment
in-line skates
homemade miniature sailboat
lacrosse stick
martial arts equipment
skateboard
sled
soccer ball
softball

Ten Years Old

balls
baseball
baseball glove and bat
basketball
basketball hoop
bicycle
bow and arrow
football
ice hockey skates and stick

in-line skates
lacrosse stick
rock climbing harness
sled
skis
soccer ball
T-ball
tennis racquet
trampoline
wetsuit
Vortex football (OddzOn)

Eleven Years Old

balls
baseball
basketball
bicycle
cross-country skis
in-line skates
skateboard
soccer ball
swimming pool
tennis racquet

Twelve Years Old

basketball
bicycle
in-line skates
mountain bike
protective pads
rope climbing equipment
skateboard
soccer ball
street hockey equipment
swimming pool
tennis racquet
Hackey Sack (Mattel)
Vortex football (Oddzon)

CDs/TAPES/RECORDS (Girls)

Six Years Old

children's music
Christmas tapes
sing-along tapes
Al the Alligator
Disney stories
Gary Lapow
Gray Goose
Lullaby: A Collection
Pocahontas sound track
Schoolhouse Rock series
Seventh Day, The Sound of Music
Wee Sing Dinosaur tape
Why Hippo Is Hairy

Seven Years Old

classical music
Polynesian music
reggae
soft rock
Ace of Base
BBC Lady Bird Classics Christmas Carols
Beethoven Lives Upstairs
Dinosaurs
Green Day
Jim Wise's Tales on Tape
Joel Ben Izzy Stories
The Lion King sound track
The Little Thinker
Nutcracker Suite
The Phantom of the Opera
Pocahontas sound track
Sing-Along Lion King
Trout Fishing in America
Yanni

Eight Years Old

Broadway show tunes
classical
Jewish music and stories
tape of own drama production
    in the park
Beethoven Lives Upstairs
Boys II Men
Classical for Kids series
Design of a Decade
El Primero
Gray Goose
Janet Jackson
Joel Ben Izzy tapes
Let's Sing Yiddish Songs
The Lion King sound track
The Lion, the Witch and the Wardrobe
Michael Jackson
Pachelbel Canon in D Major
Smiling Island of Songs
Stokowsky (ballet music)
Tchaikovsky Discovers America
Waterfalls

Nine Years Old

classical music
fairy tale tapes from around
    the world
Aerosmith
Fantasia
The Lion King sound track
Live at the BBC
Lord of the Rings
Phantom of the Opera
Sleeping Beauty
Waiting to Exhale sound track
Wee Sing Around the World

Wee Sing Dinosaur
Young Country

Learnables
Weird Al Yankovich

Ten Years Old

classical music
Greek myths
nature tapes
weird music
Beach Boys
Boys II Men
Forrest Gump sound track
Hard Day's Night
Jimmy Buffett
Les Miserables
Learnables
Music Man sound track
Pecos Bill
Sing We Xmas
Waterfalls
The Wizard of Oz sound track

Eleven Years Old

folk songs
musical sound tracks
Beethoven Lives Upstairs
Brandy
Clueless sound track
Coolio
Daydream
Disney movie sound tracks
Little Richard

Twelve Years Old

Apollo 13 sound track
Call of the Wild sound track
Cranberries
Green Day

CDs/TAPES/RECORDS (Boys)

Six Years Old

Books on tape
classical music
dinosaur songs
rock and roll
singing with guitar
tape of mom's stories
Ants
Beach Boys
Beatles
Call of the Dolphin
Chuck Berry's Greatest Hits
Classical Kid's series
Gary Lapow
Jumanji sound track
Kris Kross
Let's Pretend Fairy Tales
The Lion King sound track
Little Proto
Mickey Mouse Club Sing Along
Nightmare Before Christmas
   sound track
Peter and the Wolf
Peter Paul and Mary
Rabbit Ears Radio storytapes
Scorpions
Tim Cain
Who's Next

Seven Years Old

classical music
folk songs
oldies

rock and roll
A Walk in the Forest (sounds of
    nature)
Acropolis Live
Beethoven Lives Upstairs
Black Beauty sound track
Bonnie Raitt
Boomerang sound track
Boys II Men
Disney Classics (volume 2)
Getting Along
Green Day
Harry Connick
Junior Christmas Album
Lead Belly
The Lion King sound track
Mendelsohn's Italian Symphony
Ring of Mystery
Robin Williams
*They Came Singing: Songs from
    California's History*
Travelling Tunes
Waterfalls
Wee Sing series
Witches
Yellow Submarine

Eight Years Old

Abriendo Puertas
Animals
Batman sound track
Beach Boys
Big Bands of the 40's
Chikvng Meditations
Chuck Berry
Country for Kids
Crazysexycool
Faletha MacKenzie

For the Children
Green Day
The Lion King sound track
MC Hammer
Peter Pan Broadway sound track
Soulful Christmas
Super Mario Brothers sound
    track
Wee Sing series

Nine Years Old

cello solo
rock and roll
story tapes
1812 Overture
Ace of Base
Adventures in Odyssey series
Banana Slug String Band
Beach Boys
Beatles
Beethoven Lives Upstairs
Bible story tapes
Blues Traveler
Boys II Men
Christmas Revels
Eyewitness series
Fantastic Voyage
Frank Zappa
Greek myths
Green Day
Hank the Cowdog
John Williams
Ken Burns' Baseball
Nutcracker
REM
Rock and Learn Multiplication
They Might Be Giants

Ten Years Old

Books on tape
movie sound tracks
Aesop's Fables
Alapalooza
Andy Belling
Beatles
Call of the Dolphin
Dinotopia
Disney Christmas Songs
Green Day
Hamlet
Lord of the Rings
Machines That Work
Mr. Bach Comes to Call
Nirvana
16 Stone
Regulate
Rolling Stones
TLC
Top Gun sound track
Weird Al Yankovich
White Fang sound track

Eleven Years Old

Folk songs
Beatles
Boys II Men
Buddy Holly
Chuck Berry
Dangerous Minds sound track
Gilbert and Sullivan musicals
Going Going Gone (baseball
    music)
Hank the Cowdog
Joe Scruggs
Mozart's sonatas
Smashing Pumpkins

Snowman
Weird Al Yankovich

Twelve Years Old

Adventures in Odyssey series
Boys II Men
Cool Runnings sound track
Dangerous Minds sound track
Frank Zappa
Green Day
Nirvana
North Sound (nature tape)
Offspring
The Phantom of the Opera sound
    track
Pink Floyd
Pulse of the Planet
Roberta Flack
Time Warp
Waterfalls

VIDEOS (Girls)

Six Years Old

Professional ice-skating
Aladdin
Cooking for Kids
Dinosaurs
Fantasia
Firefighter
GEO Kids
Little Mermaid
PBS
Princess Bride
Return of Jafar
School House Rock series
The Secret Garden
The Sound of Music

Star Wars
Totoro

Seven Years Old

Polynesian dance show videos
Barney Live
Congo
Ghostwriter
Gift of the Whales
Land Before Time
Lantern Hill
The Lion King
The Little Princess
Little Women
National Geographic Kids
    (Tropical Rain Forest, Really
    Wild Animals)
Our Gang
The Secret Garden
The Swan Princess

Eight Years Old

Big Green
BBC French language course
Beethoven Lives Upstairs
Carmen Sandiego
Dinosaurs
Escape to Witch Mountain
Fantasia
The Little Princess
Little Women
The Magic School Bus
Mary Kate and Ashley
National Geographic: In the
    Shadow of Mount Vesuvius
Oliver
The Sound of Music

Stars to the Rescue (drug
    prevention video)
The Sword in the Stone

Nine Years Old

videos on manners
videos on values
Apollo 13
Carousel
Jumanji
Jurassic Park
K9 Cop
The Lion King
Little Women (1949 and 1994
    versions)
Mask
Mrs. Doubtfire
Santa Clause
Star Wars

Ten Years Old

sports videos
Allas Guta
Apollo 13
Batman Forever
Benji
Big
Fiddler on the Roof
Finite Oceans
Forrest Gump
The Indian in the Cupboard
Ishi (history tape)
Jumanji
Little Women
Malcolm X
Pollyanna
Rubberstamping (how to)

The Secret Garden
The Secret of Roan Inish

Eleven Years Old

musicals
Clueless
Dumbo
A League of Their Own
The Little Princess
Little Women
Much Ado About Nothing
Sleeping Beauty
Speed
Winnie the Pooh

Twelve Years Old

Allas Guta
Apollo 13
Disney Classics
Forrest Gump
Jurassic Park
Tin-Tin
To Live (Chinese video)

VIDEOS (Boys)

Six Years Old

Nature shows
Cool Runnings
Daniel Boone
Eyewitness: Bird
Free Willy
Johnny Appleseed
Jurassic Park
The Lion King
Little Rascals
Lost Trousers
Lost World Wonders

Magic School Bus series
Mighty Morphin Power Rangers
*National Geographic Really Wild
Animals*
The Nightmare Before Christmas
Peter and the Wolf
Santa Clause
Seventh Voyage of Sinbad
Shelly Duval Bedtime Stories
The Sound of Music
Star Wars Trilogy
The Tempest
There Goes a Monster Truck
Thomas the Tank Engine

Seven Years Old

Aladdin
Angels in the Outfield
Apollo 13
Breaking Away
Castle
Christopher Churchmouse series
Donkey Kong
Forrest Gump
Fox and the Hound
Home Alone
Homeward Bound
Incredible Suckers
Indiana Jones
Kilauea Volcano
The Lion King
Magic School Bus series
Marx brothers' movies
Mathematic Land
Miracle on 34th Street
My First Science Projects
National Geographic Kid's videos

National Geographic Season of the Sea
National Geographic Swinging Safari
Pele Soccer Games
Santa Clause
Star Wars Trilogy
Thomas the Tank Engine
Three Stooges
Tornadoes

Eight Years Old

Adventures of Yellow Dog
Bambi
Charlotte's Web
Eat Drink Man Woman
Free Willy 2
Honey I Shrunk the Kids
Jane Fonda's Workout
The Lion King
Little Shop of Horrors
Mask
Mortal Kombat
National Geographic Reptiles
Night at the Opera
PBS
Power Rangers
Seal Morning
Star Wars Trilogy
Three Musketeers
Winnie the Pooh

Nine Years Old

Batman Forever
Beatles movies
Bill Nye: The Human Body
Cool Runnings

Crimson Tide
D2
Eye Witness series
Grammar Rock
Jurassic Park
The Lion King
Mortal Kombat
The Nightmare Before Christmas
Pulp Fiction
Star Wars Trilogy
Tom and Jerry the Movie

Ten Years Old

Ace Ventura
Aladdin
Apollo 13
Batman Forever
Castle and Cathedral
Forrest Gump
Free Willy
Gettysburg
International Tournament of Animation I and II
Judge Bao (Chinese)
Jumanji
The Little Princess
Lord of the Rings
Magic School Bus series
Mask of Phantasm
Miracle on 34th Street
Mortal Kombat
National Geographic
The Nightmare Before Christmas
Predator
Rocketeer
Sea Life: Submarines
Secrets of the Deep: Shark Attack
Sports Bloopers

Star Trek
Star Wars Trilogy

Eleven Years Old

Apollo 13
Clueless
Dumb and Dumber
Forrest Gump
Jurassic Park
Mask
Mrs. Doubtfire
Sesame Street
Snowman

Twelve Years Old

Apollo 13
Dumb and Dumber
Forrest Gump
Jurassic Park
Mask
Men in Tights
Mrs. Doubtfire
Pink Panther
Roswell
Star Wars Trilogy
Toy Story

SOFTWARE (Girls)

Six years old

Around the World in 80 Days
    (Electronic Arts)
Kid Pix (Broderbund)
Kid's Math
Lion King (Disney)
Math Blaster (Davidson)
Millie's Math House (Edmark)
Reader Rabbit (Learning Co.)

Scooter's Magic Castle
    (Electronic Arts)
The Playroom (Broderbund)
Thinkin' Things (Edmark)
Thinkin' Things II (Edmark)
Where in the World Is Carmen
    Sandiego? (Broderbund)

Seven years old

A.D.A.M. (Mindscape)
Arthur's Teacher Trouble (Living
    Books)
Kid Pix (Broderbund)
Magic School Bus series
    (Microsoft)
Math Blaster (Davidson)
Math Workshop (Broderbund)
Oregon Trail (MECC)
Ozzie's World (Digital Impact)
Putt Putt's Fun Pack
    (Humongous)
Reader Rabbit (Learning Co.)
Storybook Weaver (MECC)
Thinkin' Things (Edmark)
Treasure Math Storm (Learning
    Co.)

Eight years old

Aladdin Activity Pack (Disney)
Amazon Trail (MECC)
Explorapedia: The World of
    Nature (Microsoft)
Fine Artist (Microsoft)
Gizmos and Gadgets (Learning
    Co.)
Kid Pix (Broderbund)
Mario Teaches Typing (Interplay
    Productions)

Math Blaster (Davidson)
Mavis Beacon Teaches Typing (Mindscape)
Oregon Trail (MECC)
Print Shop (Broderbund)
Sim Farm (Maxis)
Sim Town (Maxis)
Treasure Math Storm (Learning Co.)
Where in the World Is Carmen Sandiego? (Broderbund)

Nine years old

Creative Writer (Microsoft)
Fine Artist (Microsoft)
Kid Pix (Broderbund)
Mario Teaches Typing (Interplay)
Maya Quest (MECC)
Oregon Trail (MECC)
Reader Rabbit (Learning Co.)
Recess in Greece (Morgan Interactive)
Sim City (Maxis)
Thinkin' Things (Edmark)
Treasure Mountain (Learning Co.)

Ten years old

Encarta (Microsoft)
Fine Artist (Microsoft)
Kid Pix (Broderbund)
Magic School Bus series (Microsoft)
Math Blaster (Davidson)
Math Blaster II (Davidson)
Number Munchers (MECC)
Oregon Trail (MECC)

Sim City (Maxis)
Thinkin' Things (Edmark)
Treasure Math Storm (Learning Co.)
Where in the World is Carmen Sandiego? (Broderbund)

Eleven years old

Creative Writer (Microsoft)
Lost Mind of Dr. Brain (Sierra)
Mac Write (Macintosh)
Magic School Bus series (Microsoft)
Mario Teaches Typing (Interplay)
Oregon Trail (MECC)
Oregon Trail II (MECC)
Print Shop Deluxe (Broderbund)
Sim City (Maxis)
Sim City 2000 (Maxis)
Sim Tower (Maxis)
Tetris Gold (Philips Interactive)
Where in the World Is Carmen Sandiego? (Broderbund)

Twelve years old

Kid Pix 2 (Broderbund)
Lost Mind of Dr. Brain (Sierra)
Myst (Broderbund)
Sim City 2000 (Maxis)
Where in the World Is Carmen Sandiego? (Broderbund)

Software (Boys)

Six years old

Arthur's Teacher Trouble (Living Books)

Crayola Paintbox (Micrografix)
Flying Colors (Davidson)
Gizmos and Gadgets (Learning Co.)
Kid CAD (Davidson)
Kid Desk (Edmark)
Kid Pix (Broderbund)
Math Blaster (Davidson)
Number Munchers (MECC)
Paintbrush (Microsoft)
Playroom (Broderbund)
Reader Rabbit (Learning Co.)
Sim Town (Maxis)
Treasure Math Storm (Learning Co.)
Treasure Mountain (Learning Co.)
Where's Waldo (Warner Active)

Seven years old

Brain Quest (Workman)
Encarta (Microsoft)
Gizmos and Gadgets (Learning Co.)
Kid Pix (Broderbund)
Mac Draw (Macintosh)
Magic School Bus series (Microsoft)
Math Blaster (Davidson)
Math Workshop (Broderbund)
Myst (Broderbund)
Oregon Trail (MECC)
Paintbrush (Microsoft)
Putt Putt (Humongous)
Reader Rabbit (Learning Co.)
Recess in Greece (Morgan Interactive)
Ruff's Bone (Living Books)

Sim City (Maxis)
Sticky Bear Reading (Philips Media)
Super Solvers Spellbound (Learning Co.)
Storybook Weaver (MECC)
Super Munchers (MECC)
Thinkin' Things (Edmark)
Thinkin' Things II (Edmark)
Treasure Cove (Learning Co.)
Treasure Math Storm (Learning Co.)
Tree House (Broderbund)
Wiggleworks (Apple)

Eight years old

Amazon Trail (MECC)
Arthur's Birthday Party (Learning Co.)
Dr. Brain (Sierra)
Gizmos and Gadgets (Learning Co.)
Kid Pix (Broderbund)
Kid Pix Studio (Broderbund)
Lost Mind of Dr. Brain (Sierra)
Math Blaster (Davidson)
Myst (Broderbund)
NFL Math (Sanctuary Woods)
Oregon Trail (MECC)
Sim City (Maxis)
Sim City 2000 (Maxis)
Super Solvers (Learning Co.)
The Treehouse (Broderbund)
Thinkin' Things II (Edmark)
Treasure Mountain (Learning Co.)
What's the Secret (3M Software)

*Where in the USA Is Carmen
    Sandiego?* (Broderbund)

Nine years old

Arthur's Teacher Trouble (Living
    Books)
Encarta (Microsoft)
Flying Colors (Davidson)
Gizmos and Gadgets (Learning
    Co.)
Kid Pix Studio (Broderbund)
Magic School Bus series (Micro-
    soft)
Mario Teaches Typing
    (Interplay)
Math Blaster II (Davidson)
Myst (Broderbund)
NFL Math (Sanctuary Woods)
Odell Down Under (MECC)
Oregon Trail (MECC)
Oregon Trail II (MECC)
Ozzie's World (Digital Impact)
Sim City (Maxis)
Sim City 2000 (Maxis)
Sim Earth (Maxis)
Sim Life (Maxis)
Treasure Math Storm (Learning
    Co.)
*Where in the World Is Carmen
    Sandiego?* (Broderbund)

Ten years old

Alien Tales (Broderbund)
Gizmos and Gadgets (Learning
    Co.)
Kid Pix 2 (Broderbund)
Lost Mind of Dr. Brain (Sierra)
Myst (Broderbund)
Oregon Trail (MECC)
Oregon Trail II (MECC)
Sim Ant (Maxis)
Sim City (Maxis)
Sim City 2000 (Maxis)
Storybook Weaver (MECC)
*Where in the World Is Carmen
    Sandiego?* (Broderbund)

Eleven years old

Myst (Broderbund)
Oregon Trail (MECC)
Sim Ant (Maxis)
Sim City (Maxis)
Sim City 2000 (Maxis)
*Where in the World Is Carmen
    Sandiego?* (Broderbund)

Twelve years old

Eagle Eye Mysteries (Creative
    Wonders)
Myst (Broderbund)
Sim Earth (Maxis)
*Where in the World Is Carmen
    Sandiego?* (Broderbund)

SELECTIONS FOR ADOLESCENTS

BOOKS (Girls)

Thirteen Years Old

Are You There God? It's Me, Margaret, Judy Blume (Bradbury Press, 1974)
The Clan of the Cave Bear, Jean M. Auel (Bantam, 1980)
The Giver, Kathleen Fischer (Learning Links, 1995)
Homecoming, Cynthia Voigt (Atheneum, 1981)
Liftoff! Mike R. Mullane (Silver Burdett Press, 1995)
Shabanu: Daughter of the Wind, Suzanne Fisher Staples (Random House, 1991)
Tiger Eyes, Robyn Donald (Harlequin Books, 1995)

Fourteen Years Old

An Anthology of Poetry by Women: Tracing the Tradition (Cassell, 1994)
Jane Eyre, Charlotte Bronte (Folio Society, 1991)

Fifteen Years Old

The Chalice and the Blade, Riane Eisler (Harper San Francisco, 1994)

BOOKS (Boys)

Thirteen Years Old

The Chronicles of Narnia, C. S. Lewis (Harper Trophy, 1994)
Foundation's Friends: Stories in Honor of Isaac Asimov (Grafton, 1991)
Great Works of Sir Arthur Conan Doyle, Arthur Conan Doyle (Chatham River Press, 1987)
Hatchet, Gary Paulsen (Houghton Mifflin, 1996)
Star Wars: Children of the Jedi, Barbara Hambly (Bantam, 1996)

Fourteen Years Old

Dungeons and Dragons Sea People (TSR Inc., 1990)

El Mundo Perdido, Arthur Conan Doyle (Anaya, 1994)
Ghost Movies II, Dean R. Koontz (Severn House, 1996)
The Great Columbia River, William Dietrich (University of Washington Press, 1996)
Northwest Passage: The Clan of the Cave Bear, Jean M. Auel (Bantam, 1991)
The Ray Bradbury Chronicles, Ray Bradbury (Nantier Beall Minoustchine, 1994)
Three Complete Novels by Peter Benchley, Peter Benchley (Wings Books, 1994)

Fifteen Years Old

Atlas Shrugged, Ayn Rand (Penguin, 1992)
Mariel of Redwall, Brian Jacques (Putnam, 1992)
Much Ado About Nothing, William Shakespeare (Wordsworth, 1995)
Robotech, Jack McKinney (Ballantine Books, 1994)
20,000 Leagues Under the Sea, Jules Verne (Landoll, 1993)

GAMES AND TOYS (Girls)

Thirteen Years Old

boombox
CD player
3-D puzzles
American Girls dolls (Pleasant Company)
Breyer horses (Breyer)
Checkers (Pavilion)
Chess (Pavilion)
Football (Sega Game)
Mille Bornes (Parker Brothers)
Nintendo Entertainment System (Nintendo)
Parcheesi (Milton Bradley)
Set (Set Enterprises)
Take Off! (Take Off Inc.)
Uno (Mattel)

Fourteen Years Old

tetherball
Mind Trap (Pressman)
Monopoly (Parker Brothers)
Silly Putty (Binney and Smith)

Sixteen Years Old

charades
wooden pattern blocks

GAMES AND TOYS (Boys)

Thirteen Years Old

computer
electronic kit
Chess (Pavilion)
Clue (Parker Brothers)
Legos (Lego)

Risk (Parker Brothers)
Rollerblades (Rollerblades)
Scattergories (Milton Bradley)
Sequence (Jax Unlimited)
Supremacy (Supremacy
  Games, Inc.)
Tri Bond (Big Fun A Go Go)

Fourteen Years Old

remote control car
Brick By Brick (Binary Arts)
Chess (Pavilion)
Dungeons and Dragons (TSR,
  Inc.)
Legos (Lego)
Magic Cards: The Gathering
  (Wizards of the Coast Inc.)
Micromachines (Galoob)
Monopoly (Parker Brothers)
Nintendo (Nintendo)
Risk (Parker Brothers)
Sega (Sega)
Uno (Mattel)

Fifteen Years Old

dirt bike
lacrosse
Chess (Pavilion)
Legos (Lego)
Magic Cards: The Gathering
  (Wizards of the Coast Inc.)
Tangle (Mattel)

MODELS AND PUZZLES
(Girls)

Thirteen Years Old

Corvette (1990)
horse figurines

Hubble space telescope model
jigsaw puzzles
mind puzzles
rocket model
3-D puzzles
Crazy Cats (Price, Stern, &
  Sloan)

Fourteen Years Old

Jenga (Milton Bradley)

MODELS AND PUZZLES
(Boys)

Thirteen Years Old

a-wing
airplanes
bird of prey puzzle
car models
1000-piece puzzle
rocket models
ship models
3-D puzzles
2000-piece puzzle
Book of Games (Games
  Magazine)
Triazzle (Da mert Co.)

Fourteen Years Old

airplane model
Corvette model
engine model
fish tank
1000-piece jigsaw puzzle
Pianer
P-51D Mustang
USA flags puzzle
world map puzzle

Star Trek: Deep Space Nine
  (Playmates)
Triazzle (Da Mert Co.)

Fifteen Years Old

mind puzzles
plastic apple 3-D puzzle
3-D puzzles
WW II planes
Legos (Lego)
Rubik's Cube (Oddz On)

MUSICAL INSTRUMENTS (Girls)

Thirteen Years Old

clarinet
flute
keyboard
piano
recorder

Fourteen Years Old

flute
guitar
violin

Sixteen Years Old

piano
voice

MUSICAL INSTRUMENTS (Boys)

Thirteen Years Old

electric guitar
guitar

piano
saxophone
trumpet

Fourteen Years Old

clarinet
drums
piano
saxophone
voice

Fifteen Years Old

cello
drums
keyboard
oboe
piano
saxophone
trombone

ART MATERIALS (Girls)

Thirteen Years Old

calligraphy pens
candle making materials
charcoal
colored pencils
felt pens
paper
pastels
pencil
watercolors
wood
Fimo clay (Eberhardt Faber)

Fourteen Years Old

clay
colored pencils

felt pens
paint

Sixteen Years Old

charcoal
sketch pad

ART MATERIALS (Boys)

Thirteen Years Old

craft supplies
glue gun
oil paints
origami paper
paint
pencil
Fimo clay (Eberhardt Faber)

Fourteen Years Old

drawing pencils
modeling clay
oil paints
sewing costumes
wood projects

Fifteen Years Old

clay
origami paper
pencil
sketch pad
woodworking materials

LESSONS AND CLASSES (Girls)

Thirteen Years Old

ballet
animal care

drama
English
family chores
history
horseback riding
language
ice-skating
math
poetry
quilting
sculpture
woodshop

Fourteen Years Old

geometry
music
swimming
tennis

Sixteen Years Old

ballet
jazz
writing workshop (creative
    writing)

LESSONS AND CLASSES (Boys)

Thirteen Years Old

art school (summer program)
Bar Mitzvah training
electronics (science center)
geometry
guitar
math
orchestra
photography
physics

rocketry
saxophone
science
shop
social studies
woodworking

Fourteen Years Old

atmospheric science
biology
Brazilian dance
encyclopedia
English
geometry
karate
music
science
sports
wood shop
young actor's workshop
youth group at church

Fifteen Years Old

cognitive science seminar
karate
math applications in science
science
soccer
Spanish
wood shop

OUTINGS AND TRIPS (Girls)

Thirteen Years Old

backpacking
beach
camping
gold panning field trip

hiking
kayaking
mountains
movies
river rafting
Space Academy (Level 1)

Fourteen Years Old

mall

Sixteen Years Old

whale watching

OUTINGS AND TRIPS (Boys)

Thirteen Years Old

camping
field trips
fishing
football games
kayaking
overnight camp
professional ice hockey game
sex education overnight (local
    Middle School)
skiing
snorkeling
summer backpacking camp
Exploratorium
Lawrence Hall of Science
Space Camp (Alabama)

Fourteen Years Old

beach
laser show
movies
professional ice hockey game

river rafting
skiing
summer science camp
Texas
Lawrence Hall of Science

Fifteen Years Old

bike trip
downhill skiing
hiking
houseboat for water skiing
jet skiing
train trip across country
Space Camp
Virtual World

SPORTS EQUIPMENT (Girls)

Thirteen Years Old

badminton equipment
balls
baseball mitt
basketball
gymnastics equipment
karate gear
mountain bike
soccer ball

Fourteen Years Old

skiis
swimming suit
volleyball

Sixteen Years Old

ice-skates

SPORTS EQUIPMENT (Boys)

Thirteen Years Old

basketball
bicycle
hockey equipment
in-line skates
martial arts equipment
skateboard
skis
soccer ball

Fourteen Years Old

football
in-line skates
skateboard

Fifteen Years Old

bicycle
cross-country running shoes
in-line skates
rowing machine
skis
soccer ball
swimming pool
weights and heavy bag
Nerf football (Kenner)

CDs/TAPES/RECORDS (Girls)

Thirteen Years Old

classical flute
foreign language tapes
Beatles' music
Boys II Men
Daydream
El Primero
Jack London stories on tape

Phantom of the Opera
Waiting to Exhale sound track

Fourteen Years Old

Aerosmith
Daydream
Madonna

Sixteen Years Old

A Circle Is Cast

CDs/TAPES/RECORDS (Boys)

Thirteen Years Old

rock music
Jagged Little Pill
President of the United States
Prince
Rage Against the Machine
Weird Al Yankovich

Fourteen Years Old

rock and Roll
Ray Bradbury stories on tape
They Might Be Giants

Fifteen Years Old

comedians on tape
Alanis Morissette
Heavy Like Lead
Jefferson Airplane
The Well Tempered Clavier

VIDEOS (Girls)

Thirteen Years Old

Apollo 13
City Slickers II
Father of the Bride
Henry VIII and His Wives
Little Women
Maverick
A River Runs Through It
The Secret Garden

Fourteen Years Old

Forrest Gump
The Nutcracker

VIDEOS (Boys)

Thirteen Years Old

Ace Ventura
Blown Away
Goldfish
Goonies
Man with One Red Shoe
Mask
Monty Python: Life of Brian
Outbreak
Star Trek Generations

Fourteen Years Old

Ace Ventura
Interview with a Vampire
Mortal Kombat
Star Trek Generations
Young Frankenstein

Fifteen Years Old

Braveheart
Free Jack
Jurassic Park
Star Trek series

SOFTWARE (Girls)

Thirteen Years Old

African Trail (MECC)
Creative Writer (Microsoft)
Myst (Broderbund)
Oregon Trail (MECC)
*Where in the World Is Carmen
    Sandiego?* (Broderbund)

Fourteen Years Old

Myst (Broderbund)

SOFTWARE (Boys)

Thirteen Years Old

Sim City (Maxis)
Sim City 2000 (Maxis)

Fourteen Years Old

Sim City 2000 (Maxis)
Sim Tower (Maxis)

Fifteen Years Old

Myst (Broderbund)
Sim City 2000 (Maxis)

Notes

Chapter One: Trees That Grow So Fair

p. 15. **This seemed to coincide:** H. Brody, "Organization of the Cerebral Cortex III: A Study of Aging in the Human Cerebral Cortex," *Journal of Comparative Neurology,* 102 (1955): 511–556.

p. 16. **Finally, a third neurologist:** G. Leboucq, "Le Rapport entre Lepoids et la Surface de L'hemisphere Cerebral chez L'homme et les Singes," *Mem. Acad. R. Med. Belg.* 10 (1929): 55. Also, B. D. Burns, *The Mammalian Cerebral Cortex* (London: Arnold, 1958).

p. 23. **In their 1964 article:** M.C. Diamond, D. Krech, and M. R. Rosenzweig, "The Effects of an Enriched Environment on the Histology of the Rat Cerebral Cortex," *Journal of Comparative Neurology,* 123 (1964): 111–120.

Later that same year: R. L. Holloway, "Dendritic Branching: Some Preliminary Results of Training and Complexity in Rat Visual Cortex," *Brain Research,* 2 (1966): 393–396.

p. 24. **He found more higher-order branches:** W.T. Greenough, F. Volkman, and J. M. Juraska, "Effects of Rearing Complexity on Dendritic Branching in Frontolateral and Temporal Cortex of the Rat, *Experimental Neurology,* 41 (1973): 371–378.

p. 27. **Connor saw that the spines resembled:** James R. Connor, and Marian C. Diamond, "A Comparison of Dendritic Spine Number and Type on Pyramidal Neurons of the Visual Cortex of Old Adult Rats from Social or Isolated Environments, *The Journal of Comparative Neurology,* 210 (1982): 99–106.

A researcher at the University of California at Davis: Richard G. Coss, John G. Brandon, and Albert Globus, "Changes in Morphology of Dendritic Spines on Honeybee Calycal Interneurons Associated with Cumulative Nursing and Foraging Experiences," *Brain Research,* 192 (1980): 49–59.

p. 28. **Richard Coss found similar changes:** Richard G. Coss, Albert Globus, "Spine Stems on Tectal Interneurons in Jewel Fish Are Shortened by Social Stimulation," *Science,* 200 (1978): 787–789. Also, J. W. Burgess and R. G. Coss, "Crowded Jewel Fish Show Changes in Dendritic Spine Density and Spine Morphology, *Neuroscience Letters* 17: (1980) 277–281.

a change from lollipop to umbrella-like spines: G. Rausch, and H. Scheich, "Dendritic Spine Loss and Enlargement During Maturation of the Speech Control System in the Mynah Bird," *Neuroscience Letters,* 29 (1982): 129–133.

A third group found that: J. J. Pysh, and G. M. Weiss, "Exercise During Development Induces an Increase in Purkinje Cell Dendritic Tree Size," *Science,* 206 (1979): 230–232.

Finally, several researchers have studied: Dominick P. Purpura, "Dendritic Spine 'Dysgenesis' and Mental Retardation," *Science,* 186 (1974): 1126–1128. Also, Brian S. Scott, L. E. Becker, and T. L. Petit, "Neurobiology of Down's Syndrome," *Progress in Neurobiology,* 21 (1983): 199–237.

The nubbin spines may represent: Telephone conversation with Richard Coss. Also, R. G. Coss, and Donald H. Perkel, "The Function of Dendritic Spines: A Review of Theoretical Issues." *Behavioral and Neural Biology,* 44 (1985): 151–185.

p. 33. **in the part of the cortex concerned with . . . speech:** Roderick J. Simonds, and Arnold B. Scheibel, "The Postnatal Development of the Motor Speech Area: A Preliminary Study," *Brain and Language,* 37 (1989): 42–58.

p. 34. **Second, a graduate student in Scheibel's lab:** Bob Jacobs, Matthew Schall, and Arnold B. Scheibel, "A Quantitative Dendritic Analysis of Wernicke's Area in Humans. II. Gender, Hemispheric, and Environmental Factor," *The Journal of Comparative Neurology,* 327 (1993): 97–111.

They also explored a third brain region: Arnold Scheibel, Tracy Conrad, Sondra Perdue, Uwami Tomiyasu, and Adam Wechsler,

"A Quantitative Study of Dendrite Complexity in Selected Areas of the Human Cerebral Cortex," *Brain and Cognition*, 12 (1990): 85–101.

Chapter Two: An Enchanted Thing

p. 39. **By Thursday, the embryo would consist of thirty cells:** William J. Larsen, *Human Embryology* (New York: Churchill Livingstone 1993), Ch. 13.

p. 41. **Our neocortex is divided into five lobes:** Kathleen R. Gibson and Anne C. Peterson, eds., *Brain Maturation and Cognitive Development: Comparative and Cross-Cultural Perspectives* (New York: Aldine de Gruyter, 1991), Chapters 1 and 2. Also, Larsen (1993).

p. 42. **The other two-thirds have become tucked inside:** Mark F. Bear, Barry W. Connors, and Michael A. Paradiso, *Neuroscience: Exploring the Brain* (Baltimore: Williams and Wilkins, 1996), Ch. 18.

p. 46. **The struggle is so reminiscent:** G. M. Edelman, *Neural Darwinism: The Theory of Neuronal Group Selection* (Basic Books, New York, 1987).

An initial hooking-up takes place: Carla Shatz, "The Developing Brain," *Scientific American*, September 1992; 61–67.

p. 47. **By the best estimates:** Peter R. Huttenlocher, "Morphometric Study of Human Cerebral Cortex Development," in *Brain Development and Cognition: A Reader*, Mark H. Johnson, ed. (Cambridge, MA: Blackwell, 1993).

It weighs 370 grams at birth: Harry T. Chugani, "Development of Regional Brain Glucose Metabolism in Relation to Behavior and Plasticity," in *Human Behavior and the Developing Brain*, Geraldine Dawson and Kurt W. Fischer, eds. (New York: The Guilford Press, 1994).

p. 51. **Next he saw a startling tenfold explosion:** P. R. Huttenlocher and Ch. de Couten, "The Development of Synapses in Striate Cortex of Man," *Human Neurobiology*, 6 (1987): 1–9.

When Huttenlocher looked: Peter R. Huttenlocher, "Synaptic Density in Human Frontal Cortex: Developmental Changes and Effects of Aging," *Brain Research*, 163 (1979): 195–205.

During Phase Two: Peter R. Huttenlocher, "Synaptogenesis in Human Cerebral Cortex," in Dawson and Fischer (1994).

p. 53. **He found that in newborn babies:** Harry T. Chugani, Michael E. Phelps, and John C. Mazziotta, "Positron Emission Tomagraphy Study of Human Brain Functional Development," *Annals of Neurology,* 22 (1987): 487–497.

p. 55. **the dismantling of unused circuits:** Chugani, in Dawson and Fischer (1994). Also, Chugani in Developmental Neuroimaging, Robert Thatcher, et al. (Eds.) New York: Academic Press, Inc. (1997).

The pruning of neural connections in adolescence: Mark R. Rosenzweig, Arnold L. Leiman, and S. Marc Breedlove, *Biological Psychology* (Sunderland, MA: Sinauer Associates, Inc., 1996), p. 707. Also, Joel L. Swerdlow, "Quiet Miracles of the Brain," *National Geographic,* June 1995; 27–30.

p. 58. **Or by simultaneous impulses from both eyes.** Norman K. Wessells and Janet L. Hopson, *Biology* (New York: Random House, 1988), p. 997–1000.

However, if it was closed from day thirty: D. H. Hubel and T. N. Wiesel. "The Period of Susceptibility to the Physiological Effects of Unilateral Eye Closure in Kittens," *Journal of Physiology* (London), 206 (1970): 419–436.

p. 59. **Ophthalmologists usually recommend:** Nigel W. Dau, *Visual Development* (New York: Plenum, 1995).

p. 61. **Some are tuned to brief sounds, some to sustained:** Larsen (1993).

Neville's research group sought out families: Helen J. Neville, "Developmental Specificity in Neurocognitive Development in Humans," in *The Cognitive Neurosciences,* Michael S. Gazzaniga, ed., (Cambridge, MA: MIT Press, 1995).

p. 62. **One group . . . produced laboratory hamsters:** Douglas O. Frost, "Sensory Processing by Novel, Experimentally Induced Cross-Modal Circuits," in *The Development and Neural Bases of Higher Cognitive Function,* A. Diamond, ed., (New York: New York Academy of Sciences Press, 1991) p. 92–112.

And another research group found that in monkeys: James Shreeve, "Touching the Phantom," *Discover* (June 1993): 38.

Chapter Three: Feed My Brain

p. 67. **One recent study of American children:** Ron Kotulak, "Epidemic of Violence and Stress Devastating Children's Brains," *Chicago Tribune,* (Special Reprint, 1993); 5.

a mother who gives birth to her first child: Kotulak (1993). Also, Kristin A. Moore, "Facts at a Glance," January 1996, Child Trends, Inc., Washington, DC.

p. 68. **The women who most need preconception services:** Brian W. Jack, and Larry Culpepper, "Preconception Care: Risk Reduction and Health Promotion in Preparation for Pregnancy," *Journal of the American Medical Association,* 264 (1990): 1147–1149.

p. 69. **The U.S. Public Health Service estimates:** "Make Folacin a Household Word," *University of California at Berkeley Wellness Letter,* 12, No. 8 (1996): 1–2.

Of the nearly 200,000 babies born: Mike Samuels and Nancy Samuels, *The Well Pregnancy Book* (New York: Summit Books, 1986), Ch. 7.

p. 70. **Researchers spent more than two years tracing:** Larsen, (1993).

Despite the strident warnings: Janet L. Hopson, and Norman K. Wessells, *Essentials of Biology,* (New York: McGraw-Hill, 1990), Ch. 17.

p. 71. **surveys conducted in the mid to late 1980s:** Matthew J. Ellenhorn, and Donald G. Barceloux, *Medical Toxicology,* (New York: Elsevier, 1988), Ch. 8.

A separate study: Ellenhorn (1988).

p. 72. **Antidepressants taken late in pregnancy:** Ellenhorn, (1988).

p. 74. **In addition to the baby's physical paralysis:** John H. Postlethwait, and Janet L. Hopson, *The Nature of Life,* 2nd Ed. (New York: McGraw-Hill 1992), Ch. 27. Also, Janice Hutchinson, "What Crack Does to Babies," *American Educator,* (Spring 1991); 31–32. And "The Compound Cost of Prenatal Cocaine," *Brainwork: The Neuroscience Newsletter,* Charles A. Dana Foundation (July–August 1996); 7.

p. 75. **Joan's recklessness:** Diana Korte, *Every Woman's Body: Everything You Need to Know to Make Informed Choices About Your Health* (New York: Fawcett Columbine, 1994); p. 453.

With 10 million Americans dabbling: Lucile F. Newman, and Stephen L. Buka, "Clipped Wings," *American Educator,* (Spring 1991); 27–33, 42, In *Human Development* (Guilford, CT 95/96, Karen L. Freiberg, ed.: Dushkin Publishing Group, 1995).

p. 76. **After weighing the evidence on all sides:** Brenda Eskenazi, *Journal of the American Medical Association,* 270, No. 24 (1993): 2973–2974.

few . . . have studied how a father's drug use: Anne Merewood, "Sperm Under Siege," *Health* (April 1991); 76–77.

p. 77. **the phenomenon cuts across:** Elisabeth Rosenthal, "When a Pregnant Woman Drinks," *New York Times Magazine* (February 4, 1990); 30, 49, 61, in Freiberg, (1995).

Some physicians fear: Rosenthal (1990), cited above. Also, Stephen Braun, "New Experiments Underscore Warnings on Maternal Drinking," *Science,* 273 (1996): 738–739.

Alcohol . . . is considered a major cause: Rosenthal (1990).

p. 78. **Tobacco researchers estimate:** Newman and Buka, (1991).

these can cut the amount of oxygen: K. A. Fackelmann, "Mother's Smoking Linked to Child's IQ Drop," *Science News* (February 12, 1994); 101.

p. 79. **And in some parts of the country:** Samuels and Samuels (1986), cited above. Also, Janet Raloff, "Banned Pollutant's Legacy: Lower IQ," *Science News* (September 14, 1996); 165.

p. 81. **Stress also makes preexisting brain diseases:** Robert Sapolsky lecture (see list, page 449). Also, see bibliography. And Robert M. Sapolsky, "Why Stress Is Bad for Your Brain." *Science,* 273 (1996): 749–750.

Ironically, many couples who defer pregnancy: Korte (1994), cited above, p. 89.

The ancient Japanese Taikyo tradition: Marian C. Diamond, Enriching Heredity (New York: Free Press, 1988), Ch. 5.

p. 82. **The malnutrition . . . in industrialized countries:** Calvin J. Hobel, "Factors During Pregnancy that Influence Brain Development," in John M. Freeman, ed., *Prenatal and Perinatal Factors Associated with Brain Disorders,* National Institutes of Health Publication No. 85–1149 (April 1985).

Teenagers . . . prone to poor prenatal nutrition: Hobel (1985).

Deprivation in the third trimester: Brian Morgan and Kathleen Gibson, "Nutritional and Environmental Interactions in Brain Development," in *Brain Maturation and Cognitive Development: Comparative and Cross-Cultural Perspectives*, (New York: Aldine de Gruyter, 1991), Ch. 5.

p. 83. **Hospital records confirm:** Jared Diamond, "War Babies," *Discover* (December 1990): 70–75.

The answer is yes: Morgan (1991), cited above.

p. 84. **It is this lack of environmental stimulation:** J. Larry Brown and Ernesto Pollitt, "Malnutrition, Poverty and Intellectual Development," *Scientific American* (February 1996); 38–43.

p. 87. **Anthony DeCasper:** Interview with Anthony DeCasper (see list, page 448). Also, Anthony J. DeCasper and Melanie J. Spence, "Prenatal Maternal Speech Influences Newborn's Perception of Speech Sounds," *Infant Behavior and Development*, 9 (1986): 133–150.

p. 91. **In the early 1980s, Van de Carr described:** Rene Van de Carr and Marc Lehrer, "Enhancing Early Speech, Parental Bonding and Infant Physical Development Using Prenatal Intervention in Standard Obstetric Practice," *Pre- and Peri-Natal Psychology*, 1, No. 1 (1986): 20–30.

p. 92. **At twenty-one months of age, one prenatally stimulated little girl:** Donald Shetler, "The Inquiry into Prenatal Music Experience: A Report of the Eastman Project, 1980–1987," in Frank R. Wilson and Franz L. Roehmann, eds., *Music and Child Development*, Proceedings of the 1987 Denver Conference.

p. 94. **Researchers in Virginia:** Merry J. Sleigh and Robert Lickliter. "Augmented Prenatal Visual Stimulation Alters Postnatal Auditory and Visual Responsiveness in Bobwhite Quail Chicks," *Developmental Psychobiology*, 28, No. 7 (1995): 353–366.

This, writes Als in a recent article: Heidelise Als, "The Preterm Infant: A Model for the Study of Fetal Brain Expectation," in Jean-Pierre Lecanuet, William Fifer, Norman Krasnegor, and William Smotherman, eds. *Fetal Development: A Psychobiological Perspective* (Hillsdale, NJ: Lawrence Erlbaum 1995), Ch. 24.

p. 95. **French researcher Jean-Pierre Lecanuet:** Jean-Pierre Lecanuet, Carolyn Granier-Deferre, and Marie-Claire Busnel,

"Human Fetal Auditory Perception," in Lecanuet, Fifer, Krasnegor, and Smotherman (1995), p. 239.

Chapter Four: Dreaming Eyes of Wonder

p. 104. **Today, more than half of all women:** Susan Chira, "Baby-
Mom Bonding—Day Care No Risk," *San Francisco Examiner*
(May 12, 1996), p. 1, from *New York Times* wire service.

For 48 percent, it is a relative: Associated Press, "Working Moms
Relying More on Day Care, Census Says," In *San Francisco Chronicle* (April 24, 1996), Section A: 5.

They obtained brain specimens: Roderick J. Simonds and Arnold
Scheibel, "The Postnatal Development of the Motor Speech
Area: A Preliminary Study," *Brain and Language*, 37 (1989): 42–58.

p. 105. **It is therefore a classic case of dendritic growth:** Arnold
Scheibel, "Some Structural and Development Correlates of Human Speech," Gibson and Peterson (1991), Ch. 13, pp. 345–353.

p. 110. **And according to a panel of pediatricians:** American
Academy of Pediatrics, *Caring for Your Baby and Young Child,*
Steven P. Shelov, ed. (New York: Bantam Books, 1994), p. 179.

p. 113. **A few insightful scientists:** Sidney J. Segalowitz, "Developmental Psychology and Brain Development, A Historical Perspective," in Dawson and Fischer (1994), Ch. 2.

Piaget is equally well known for basing: Herbert P. Ginsburg and
Sylvia Opper, *Piaget's Theory of Intellectual Development,* 3rd Ed.
(Englewood Cliffs, NJ: Prentice-Hall, 1988).

p. 114. **These skills, in turn, feed back as experience.** Kurt Fischer
and Samuel Rose, "Dynamic Development of Coordination of
Components in Brain and Behavior," in Dawson and Fischer
(1994), Ch. 1.

p. 116. **Nonmobile babies, on the other hand:** Roseann Kermoian and
Joseph J. Campos, "Locomotor Experiences: A Facilitator of Spatial
Cognitive Development," *Child Development,* 59 (1988): 908–17.

Joseph Campos, in an earlier study: Bennet I. Bertenthal and
Joseph J. Campos, "New Directions in the Study of Early Experience," *Child Development,* 58 (1987): 560–567.

p. 117. **In a second test, called "Object Retrieval":** Adele Diamond, Development time course in human infants and infant monkeys, and the neural bases, of inhibitory control in reaching. *Annals of the New York Academy of Sciences, 608,* (1990) 637–676.

By eleven to twelve months: Adele Diamond, "Frontal Lobe Involvement in Cognitive Changes During the First Year of Life," in Gibson and Peterson (1991), Ch. 7. Also, Adele Diamond, "Neuropsychological insights into the meaning of object concept development." In S. Carey & R. Gelman (Eds.), *The epigenesis of mind: Essays on biology and knowledge* (1991): 67–110. Hillsdale, NJ: Lawrence Erlbaum Associates. Reprinted in Mark H. Johnson (Ed.) (1993), *Brain Development and Cognition: A Reader.* Cambridge, MA: Basil Blackwell.

This fact allowed Yale researcher: Patricia Goldman-Rakic, "Working Memory and the Mind," *Scientific American* (September, 1992): 111–117.

p. 118. **In their tests, this area "lights up":** Martha Ann Bell and Nathan A. Fox, "Brain Development Over the First Year of Life," in Dawson Fischer (1994), Ch. 10.

p. 119. **Another five-year-cycle sweeps:** Robert W. Thatcher, "Cyclic Cortical Reorganization: Origins of Human Cognitive Development," in Dawson and Fischer (1994), Ch. 8.

Then, she theorizes, the profiles switch: Harriet W. Hanlon, "Topographically Different Regional Networks Impose Structural Limitations on Both Sexes in Karl Pribram, ed. Early Postnatal Development," in Learning as Self-organization, (Hillsdale, NJ: L. Erlbaum Publishers, 1996).

p. 121. **Much to some people's surprise:** Elizabeth Spelke, "Initial Knowledge: Six Suggestions," *Cognition,* 50 (1994): 431–445.

Now, when . . . the baby sees two Mickeys: Karen Wynn, "Origins of Numerical Knowledge," *Mathematical Cognition,* 1 (1995): 54–63.

p. 124. **Again, EEGs of the children showed:** Richard J. Davidson, "Temperament, Affective Style, and Frontal Lobe Asymmetry," in Dawson and Fischer (1994), Ch. 16.

Her baby is much more likely to have right frontal activity: Geraldine Dawson, "Development of Emotional Expression and Emotion Regulation in Infancy," in Dawson Fischer (1994), Ch. 11.

p. 125. **Physicians Susan Farrell of the University of North Carolina:** Susan E. Farrell and Ada I. Pimentel, "Interdisciplinary Team Process in Developmental Disabilities," in Arnold J. Capute and Pasquale Accardo, eds. *Developmental Disabilities in Infancy and Childhood*, 2nd ed., Vol. 1, (Baltimore: Paul H. Brookes, 1996).

Students of the brain know a great deal about the roles: Geraldine Dawson, in Dawson and Fischer (1994), Ch. 11.

p. 126. **Writes Aimée Liu:** American Academy of Pediatrics (1994), p. 133.

Many experts on child development are convinced: Richard Davidson, "Asymmetric Brain Function, Affective Style, and Psychopathology: The Role of Early Experience and Plasticity," *Development and Psychopathology*, 6 (1994): 741–758.

p. 129. **Significantly, infant rhesus monkeys:** Sandra Blaskeslee, "In Brain's Early Growth, Timetable May Be Crucial," *New York Times* (August 29, 1995), Section C; 1. Also, Lee J. Martin, et al., "Social Deprivation of Infant Rhesus Monkeys Alters the Chemoarchitecture of the Brain: Subcortical Regions," *Journal of Neuroscience*, 11 (1991): 3347–3358.

p. 130. **"I really haven't cared about people my whole life":** Steven A. Chin, "Oregon's Killing Suspect: Murder's Interesting," *San Francisco Examiner* (December 17, 1995), Section A; 1.

p. 131. **Bruce Perry estimates that more than 3 million American children:** Bruce Perry, "Psychophysiological 'Archaeology' and the Impact of Abuse and Neglect on the Developing Brain," in M. Murburg, ed., *Catecholamines in PTSD*. (Washington, DC: APA Press, 1994), p. 253–276.

Psychologist Raymond Starr, Jr., of the University of Maryland: Raymond H. Starr, Jr., "The Lasting Effect of Child Maltreatment," in Freiberg (1995), Article 31.

p. 133. **"Language learning is not really something that the child does":** N. Chomsky, *Language and Problems of Knowledge* (Cambridge, MA: MIT Press, 1988).

French linguist Jacques Mehler and others: Jacques Mehler and Anne Christophe, "Maturation and Learning of Language in the First Year of Life," in Gazzaniga (1995), Article 61, p. 943–958.

p. 134. **At the tender age of two months:** Bruce Bower, "Tots Take Rhythmic Stock Before Talk," *Science News*, 146 (1994): 196.

Another study shows that this is already beginning: Patricia Kuhl, et al., "Linguistic Experience Alters Phonetic Perception in Infants by Six Months of Age," *Science*, 255 (1992): 606–608.

p. 135. **Psychologists recently reported significantly higher scores:** Chris Ravashiere Medvescek, "Toddler Talk," *Parents* (December 1992); 73–77, in Freiberg (1995), Article 17. Also, Bruce Bower, "Talkative Parents Make Kids Smarter," *Science News* (August 17, 1996); 100.

p. 136. **But, says Jim Trelease, author of *The Read-Aloud Handbook:*** David M. Schwartz, "Ready, Set, Read—20 Minutes Each Day Is All You'll Need," *Smithsonian Magazine* (October 1995): 82–92.

Educator and writer Colin Greer: Colin Greer, "Read to Your Children—It's a Family Value," *Parade Magazine* (December 17, 1995); 17.

p. 137. **By age ten, most children spend less than 1 percent:** Schwartz (1995).

p. 140. **"They want to *tell* someone about them":** Linda Acredolo and Susan Goodwyn, *Baby Signs: How to Talk with Your Baby Before Your Baby Can Talk*. Lincolnwood, Illinois: NTC/Contemporary Publishers, 1996.

p. 144. **In a recent sociological study:** K. Alison Clarke-Stewart, "A Home is Not a School: The Effects of Environment on Development," in Michael Lewis and Saul Feinman, eds., Social Influences and Socialization in Infancy, (New York: Plenum Press, 1991), Ch. 3.

Chapter Five: These Become Part of the Child

p. 152. **The "terrible twos" still apply at this point:** Theresa Caplan and Frank Caplan, *The Early Childhood Years: The 2- to 6-Year-Old*, (New York: Bantam Books, 1984), p. 187–188.

This is an age of little fibs, tall tales: American Academy of Pediatrics, (1994).

p. 153. **A four- to five-year-old child can also get bossy:** Caplan (1984), Ch. 6 and 7.

p. 154. **The young child's explosion of synapses or contact points:** Peter Huttenlocher, "Morphometric Study of Human Cerebral Cortex Development," in Johnson (1993).

The running, playing, chattering preschooler: Harry T. Chugani, "Development of Regional Brain Glucose Metabolism in Relation to Behavior and Plasticity," Dawson and Fischer (1994).

Brain-wave measurements by EEG: Kurt Fischer and Samuel Rose, "Dynamic Development of Coordination of Components in Brain and Behavior," in Dawson and Fischer (1994), Ch. 1.

p. 155. **Robert Thatcher of the University of South Florida:** Robert W. Thatcher, "Cyclic Cortical Reorganization: Origins of Human Cognitive Development," in Dawson and Fischer (1994), Ch. 8.

p. 156. **In fact, the group discovered using their own sociological analyses:** Pamela Burdman, "UC Scholars Turn 'Bell Curve' Upside Down," *San Francisco Chronicle* (August 12, 1996): A.2.

Once again, though, follow-up studies years later showed: Anne C. Lewis, "The Payoff from a Quality Preschool," *Phi Delta Kappan* (June 1993); 746–749.

Social worker Joanne Nurss: Joanne Nurss, "More Than Baby-Sitting: A Homeless Children's Day Shelter Program," *Children Today,* 22: 2 (1993): 7–9. Also, personal communication from Joanne Nurss (February 1, 1995).

p. 158. **The caregivers at the Frank Graham Porter Center:** Joseph Sparling and Isabelle Lewis, *Learningames for the First 3 Years: A Guide to Parent-Child Play.* (New York: Walker, 1979).

The reading and math scores of the fifteen-year-old Abecedarians: Frances A. Campbell and Craig T. Ramey, "Cognition and School Outcomes for High-Risk African American Students at Middle Adolescence: Positive Effects of Early Intervention," *American Educational Research Journal,* 32: 4 (1995): 743–772.

p. 160. **Adults must encourage children to explore:** Sharon Landesman Ramey and Craig T. Ramey, "Early Educational Intervention with Disadvantaged Children: To What Effect?" *Applied and Preventive Psychology,* 1 (1992): 131–140.

p. 161. **Five-year-old Skye is also what many child development professionals call:** I. E. Sigel, "Does Hothousing Rob children of Their Childhood?" *Early Childhood Research Quarterly*, 2: 211–225 (1987).

p. 162. **Leslie Rescorla of Bryn Mawr College:** *Academic Instruction in Early Childhood: Challenge or Pressure?* Eds. Leslie Rescorla, Marion C. Hyson, and Kathy Hirsh-Pasek. New Directions for Child Development, Number 53 (San Francisco: Jossey-Bass, Fall 1991).

p. 165. **Marion Hyson of the University of Delaware:** "Building the Hothouse: How Mothers Construct Academic Environments," by Marion Hyson. In *Academic Instruction in Early Childhood.*

p. 167. **Educational researcher Kathy Hirsh-Pasek at Temple University:** "Pressure or Challenge in Preschool: How Academic Environments Affect Children," by Kathy Hirsh-Pasek, in *Academic Instruction in Early Childhood.*

p. 168. **Depressingly, they replied that** *one out of three:* Ernest L. Boyer, *Ready to Learn: A Mandate for the Nation,* Carnegie Foundation for the Advancement of Teaching (Princeton, NJ 08540, 1991).

p. 171. **Even more surprisingly, the children she studied:** Karin Stromswold, "The Cognitive and Neural Bases of Language Acquisition," in Gazzaniga (1995), Article 55, pp. 855–867.

She continues to use her vocabulary in sentences like: Steven Pinker, *The Language Instinct: How the Mind Creates Language* (New York: HarperPerennial, 1994), p. 293.

Nevertheless, as Pinker explains: Pinker (1994), p. 53.

p. 172. **He can, however, hear and understand thousands of words:** Stromswold in Gazzaniga (1995), p. 861.

To add to this argument, psychologist Elissa Newport: Elissa Newport, "Maturational Constraints on Language Learning," *Cognitive Science*, 14 (1990): 11–28.

p. 173. **If they arrived between ages eleven and fifteen:** Jacqueline Johnson and Elissa L. Newport, "Critical Period Effects in Second Language Learning: The Influence of Maturational State on the Acquisition of English as a Second Language," *Cognitive Psychology*, 21 (1989): 60–99.

Out of nine well-documented histories of "feral" children: Stromswold in Gazzaniga (1995).

Feral children and deaf children deprived of language: Helen Neville, "Developmental Specificity in Neurocognitive Development in Humans," in Gazzaniga (1995), Article 13, pp. 219–231.

p. 175. **Several years ago, Shaw heard a lecture:** Krishna V. Shenoy, Jeffrey Kaufman, John V. McGrann, and Gordon L. Shaw, "Learning by Selection in the Trion Model of Cortical Organization," *Cerebral Cortex,* 3 (1993): 239–248.

p. 176. **The results earned headlines all over the world:** Frances H. Rauscher, Gordon L. Shaw, and Katherine N. Ky, "Listening to Mozart Enhances Spatial-Temporal Reasoning: Towards a Neurophysiological Basis," *Neuroscience Letters,* 185 (1995): 44–47.

p. 177. **They tested the same children . . . after the program had ended:** Frances H. Rauscher, Gordon L. Shaw, Linda J. Levine, and Katherine N. Ky, "Music and Spatial Task Performance: A Causal Relationship," presented at American Psychological Association, Los Angeles, 1994. Also, Frances H. Rauscher, Gordon L. Shaw, Linda J. Levine, Eric L. Wright, Wendy R. Dennis, and Robert L. Newcomb, "Music Training Causes Long-Term Enhancement of Preschool Children's Spatial-Temporal Reasoning," *Neurological Research,* 19: 2–8 (1997).

p. 178. **But, Case explains, if you don't show any beans:** Robbie Case lecture (see list, page 448).

p. 179. **Case and Griffin created a series of games:** Sharon Griffin, Robbie Case, and Robert Siegler, "Rightstart: Providing the Central Conceptual Prerequisites for First Formal Learning of Arithmetic to Students at Risk For School Failure," in Kate McGilly, ed. *Classroom Lessons: Integrating Cognitive Theory and Classroom Practice* (Cambridge MA: M.I.T. Press, 1994), Ch. 2.

p. 182. **Yale University child psychologist Jerome Singer:** Jon Spayde, "Make-Believe Buddies," *Parents:* (March 1996); 116–118.

Psychologists estimate that one fifth to three fifths of all the remarks children make: Laura E. Berk, "Why Children Talk to Themselves," *Scientific American* (November 1994); 78–83.

p. 183. **Honoring the child's imaginative efforts:** Thomas Armstrong, "Sparking Creativity in Your Child," *Ladies Home Journal* (October 1993): 122–124.

p. 184. **New research employing PET scans:** Marcia Barinaga, "Brain Researchers Speak a Common Language," *Science,* 270 (1995): 1437.

Chapter Six: Letting the Future In

p. 193. **Boys, on the other hand, reach only 80 percent of adult height:** Elizabeth Fenwick and Tony Smith, *Adolescence: The Survival Guide for Parents and Teenagers* (New York; DK Publishing, 1996).

p. 194. **In the visual region of the cerebral cortex:** Peter Huttenlocher, "Morphonmetric Study of Human Cerebral Cortex Development," in Johnson (1993).

This is reflected in its slowly fading ability: Harry T. Chugani, "Development of Regional Brain Glucose Metabolism in Relation to Behavior and Plasticity," in Dawson and Fischer (1994).

p. 195. **The child, in other words, is relating several ideas to each other:** Kurt Fischer and Samuel Rose, "Dynamic Development of Coordination of Components in Brain and Behavior," in Dawson and Fischer (1994), Ch. 1.

Thatcher sees the brain as fairly quiescent and balanced: Robert W. Thatcher, "Cyclic Cortical Reorganization: Origins of Human Cognitive Development," in Dawson and Fischer (1994), Ch. 8.

p. 196. **The Dutch team found that the older a child:** Maurits W. Van der Molen and Peter C. M. Molenaar, "Cognitive Psychophysiology: A Window to Cognitive Development and Brain Maturation," in Dawson and Fischer (1994), Ch. 14.

p. 198. **Jacqueline Johnson of the University of Virginia:** Jacqueline S. Johnson and Elissa L. Newport, "Critical Period Effects on Universal Properties of Language: The Status of Subjacency in the Acquisition of a Second Language," *Cognition,* 39 (1991): 215–258.

p. 200. **Tallal, in fact, thinks the 15 percent or nearly 20 million American children:** John Travis, "Let the Games Begin," *Science News* (February 17, 1996): 104–105.

Over time, the "ear glasses" challenge and gradually train the brain: Michael M. Merzenich, William M. Jenkins, Paul Johnson, Christopher Schreiner, S. L. Miller, and Paula Tallal, "Temporal

Processing Deficits of Language-Learning-Impaired Children Ameliorated by Training," *Science*, 271 (1996); 77–80. Also, Paula Tallal, et al., *Science* 271 (1996): 81–84, and Madeleine J. Nash, "Zooming in on Dyslexia," *Time* (January 27, 1996); 62.

p. 201. **Logic continues to develop throughout childhood:** Jonas Langer, "Logic," *Encyclopedia of Human Behavior*, Vol. 3, (New York: Academic Press 1994).

p. 202. **Observers of science education describe:** Joe Alper, "The Pipeline Is Leaking Women All Along the Way," *Science* 260 (1993): 409–411.

For example, nearly 40 percent of women chemists: Marguerite Holloway, "A Lab of Her Own," *Scientific American* (November 1993); 94–103.

She drew confidence from her parents' strong support: "The Making of a Female Scientist," *Science*, 262 (1993): 1815.

p. 203. **One researcher in this field, for instance:** Lynn A. Cooper and Roger N. Shepard, "Turning Something Over in the Mind," in *The Workings of the Brain: Development, Memory, and Perception*, (New York; Freeman 1990).

p. 205. **Perfect pitch may be centered there:** Rachel Nowak, "Brain Center Linked to Perfect Pitch," *Science*, 267 (1995): 616.

According to this study, it seems that early music training: Gottfried Schlaug, et al., "In Vivo Evidence of Structural Brain Asymmetry in Musicians," *Science*, 267 (1995): 699–701.

p. 206. **After that age there was almost no difference:** Thomas Elbert, et al., "Increased Cortical Representation of the Fingers of the Left Hand in String Players," *Science*, 270 (1995): 307–305.

Concludes an editorial in *Director*: "Neuroscience: Start Early on Instruments," *Director*, 15 (1996): 15.

p. 207. **"Fat camps" are growing in popularity:** Sally Squires, "Too Many Youngsters Too Fat," *San Francisco Chronicle* (Oct. 2, 1995): A3, reprinted from *Washington Post*. Also, Kate Zernick, "Fat Camp Is No Big Deal," *Boston Globe* (September 16, 1996), reprinted in *San Francisco Chronicle*: A2. September 17, 1996.

p. 208. **Pressure to excel and win:** Susan Gilbert, "Sports Your Child Shouldn't Play," *Redbook* (April 1996); 154–157.

In terms of developing skills: Chuck Hogan, "The Intelligence of Play," *Touch the Future* (Spring, 1996).

p. 209. **The healthiest children, psychologists tend to agree:** Wray Herbert, "The Moral Child," *U.S. News and World Report* (June 3, 1996); 52–59.

Children can also be directly encouraged: Joan Leonard, "Raising Responsible Kids," *Parents* (March 1996); 79–82. Also, Rick Epstein, "Whose Chore Is It, Anyway?" *Parents* (March 1996); 85–86. And Jenny Friedman, "What Helping Out Teaches Your Children About Others and Themselves," *Parents* (March, 1996); 89–93.

p. 211. **Sociological studies show that for children under age nine:** Susan Goff Timmer, Jacquelynne Eccles, and Keith O'Brien, "How Children Use Time," in F. Thomas Juster and Frank P. Stafford, eds., *Time, Goods, and Well Being* (Ann Arbor, University of Michigan Survey Research Center, Institute for Social Responsibility, 1985).

p. 212. **A group at the University of Illinois and Loyola University:** Reed Larson and Maryse Richards, "Daily Companionship and Early Adolescence: Changing Developmental Contexts, *Child Development,* 62 (1991): 284–300.

Boys spend most of the balance alone: Larson and Richards (1991).

According to a study commissioned by the Carnegie Council: Elliott Medrich and Carolyn Marzke, "Young Adolescents and Discretionary Time Use: The Nature of Life Outside School," Carnegie Council on Adolescent Development (Washington, D.C., 1991).

p. 217. **By age eighteen, writes Patricia Greenfield:** Patricia Greenfield, Dorathea Farrar, and Jessica Beagles-Roos, "Is the Medium the Message? An Experimental Comparison of the Effects of Radio and Television on Imagination," *Journal of Applied Developmental Psychology* 7 (1986): 201–218.

Based on her study of 349 children: Betsy J. Blosser, "Ethnic Differences in Children's Media Use," *Journal of Broadcasting and Electronic Media,* 32 (1988): 453–470.

The children in these homes, he adds, can usually watch as much TV: Elliott Medrich, "Constant Television: A Background to Daily Life," *Journal of Communication* (Summer 1979); 171–176.

They concluded that children who watch shows like *Sesame Street:* John C. Wright and Aletha C. Huston, "Effects of Educational TV Viewing of Lower Income Preschoolers on Academic Skills, School Readiness, and School Adjustment One to Three Years Later," Report to Children's Television Workshop (May, 1995).

p. 218. **Among parents of all socioeconomic levels:** Richard Zoglin, "Chips Ahoy," *Time* (February 19, 1996); 58–61.

Experts debate the negative consequences of watching violence: "Television Violence and Kids: A Public Health Problem?" *ISR Newsletter* (February 1994); 5–7, in Freiberg (1995), pp. 176–178.

They recorded violence on 57 percent of all broadcast programs: Zoglin (1996).

These statistics helped push the Federal Communications Commission: Paul Farhi, "Study Finds Violence All Over TV," *Washington Post,* reprinted in *San Francisco Chronicle,* (February 13, 1996); A6. Also, "Parents Find Violent TV a Turnoff," *San Francisco Chronicle,* (September 10 1996); C7. Also, Jane Hall, "FCC Finally Adopts Guidelines for Kids," *Los Angeles Times,* reprinted in *San Francisco Chronicle* (August 9, 1996): A3.

Putnam recently told a *People* magazine reporter: "Our Separate Ways," *People* (September 25, 1995): 125–128.

p. 219. **Too much food linked with too little exercise:** Carl Suplee, "Despite Diet Craze, U.S. Getting Fatter," *Washington Post,* reprinted in *San Francisco Chronicle* (March 7, 1997): A1.

Those who watched an average of one hour per day: Robert K. and Leslie L. Cooper, *Low Fat Living,* (Emmaus, PA; Rodale Press, 1996), pp. 24, 61, 62.

These educational shows promoted a mild degree of creative play: Greenfield (1986), p.295.

p. 220. **When it comes to kids and imagination:** Greenfield (1986).

"Like most things," the mother wrote: Deborah Diamond, "Life Without TV," *Parents* (January 1996); 87–88.

p. 221. **In 1991, 34 percent of all American homes:** Patricia Greenfield, "Video Games as Cultural Artifacts," *Journal of Applied Developmental Psychology,* 15 (1994): 3–12.

The games act as "cognitive socialization": Kaveri Subrahmanyam and Patricia M. Greenfield, "Effect of Video Game Practice on Spatial Skills in Girls and Boys," *Journal of Applied Developmental Psychology*, 15 (1994): 13–32. Also, Journal of Communication, #2, 38: 71–92 (1988).

Greenfield's team found that video games don't train children: Patricia Greenfield, et al., "Cognitive Socialization by Computer Games in Two Cultures: Inductive Discovery or Mastery of an Iconic Code?" *Journal of Applied Developmental Psychology*, 15 (1994): 59–86.

Brain researchers have found that action video games: Greenfield (1994): 3–12.

And teenagers who play violent video games: Sandra L. Calvert and Siu-Lan Tan, "Impact of Virtual Reality on Young Adults' Physiological Arousal and Aggressive Thoughts: Interaction Versus Observation," *Journal of Applied Developmental Psychology*, 15 (1994): 125–139.

p. 222. And many parents worry about inappropriate free advertising: "Young Internet Users Lured by Ads, Group Says," Reuters News Service, *San Francisco Chronicle* (March 7, 1997); A3. Also, Carin Rubenstein, "Internet Dangers," *Parents*, (March 1996); 145–148.

p. 224. With Reid at the controls, the Cessna went down: Jonathan Alter, "Jessica's Final Flight," *Newsweek* (April 22, 1996): 24–27. Also, Richard Stengel, "Fly Till I Die," *Time* (April 22, 1996): 34–39.

The National Transportation Safety Board: Michael McGabe, "Flight Instructor Blamed for Child Pilot's Crash," *San Francisco Chronicle* (March 5, 1997); A1.

"Now, I feel my job is to help them learn": Stengel (1996), p. 35.

p. 225. "You'd almost have to kill that child": Elizabeth Gleick, "Every Kid a Star," *Time* (April 22, 1996); 39–41.

p. 226. Inherent in this transition, writes Larson: Reed Larson, Mark Ham, and Marcela Raffaelli, "The Nurturance of Motivated Attention in the Daily Experience of Children and Adolescents," In *Advances in Motivation and Achievement: Motivation Enhancing Environments*, 6 (1989): 45–80.

But, Larson believes that over time both external rewards and punishments: Larson (1989): 49.

p. 227. **While "wrapped up" in a favorite pastime:** Reed Larson and Douglas A. Kleiber, "Structured Leisure as a Context for the Development of Attention During Adolescence," *Society and Leisure,* 16 (1993): 77–98.

Chapter Seven: Plant Another Tree

p. 235. **More than one-third of seventeen-year-olds smoke cigarettes:** "Teens Increase Use of Drugs, Cigarettes," *San Francisco Chronicle* (December 16, 1995); C16.

As a group, 3.1 million adolescents smoke 1 billion packs: "Teens Sensitivity to Tobacco Ads Emphasized in Study," *San Francisco Chronicle* (April 4, 1996): A2.

And tobacco firms, these critics continue: Sheryl Stolberg, "Clinton Puts New Limits on Tobacco," *Los Angeles Times,* reprinted in *San Francisco Chronicle* (August 21, 1996): A1. Also, "Sorry Pardner," by J. H. Smolowe, *Time,* June 30, 1997, p. 24–29.

At least two million teens have serious drinking problems: David Elkind, "Waah! Kids Have a Lot to Cry About," *Psychology Today* (May/June, 1992): 38–41, in Freiberg (1995).

p. 236. **Illicit drug use by teenagers has risen by nearly 80 percent:** Karen Schoemer, "Rockers, Models, and the New Allure of Heroin," *Newsweek* (August 26, 1996); 52.

Eighteen percent of teens say they now use illegal drugs: Associated Press, "Teenage Drug Use Highest Ever Study Found," *San Francisco Chronicle* (September 26, 1996); A4. Also, Lorri Montgomery, "Drug Czar Quits as Use Grows," *Desert Times* (May 23, 1996); A1.

The United States has the highest rate of teen births: Bulletin issued by Child Trends, Inc. (Washington, D.C. 20008, July, 1996).

While overall crime rates in the United States have dropped: Fox Butterfield, "FBI Reports Lower Crime Rate But Warns of New Surge," *New York Times,* reprinted in *San Francisco Examiner* (November 23, 1995): A1.

p. 237. **Divorce claims about half of all American marriages:** David Gelman, "A Much Riskier Passage," *Newsweek* (Special Edition, Summer/Fall, 1990): 10–16, in Freiberg (1995), pp. 190–193.

In fact, a Northwestern University professor who studied: Gelman (1990), p. 191.

Nevertheless, even today's untroubled teens: Laura Shapiro, "Parents Take Heart," *Newsweek* (April 8, 1996), p. 56–57.

While these behaviors are a necessary part of growing up: Fenwick and Smith, (1996).

Partly because their sex hormones are surging: Reed Larson and Douglas Kleiber, "Daily Experience of Adolescents," in eds., Patrick Tolan and Bertram Cohler eds., Handbook of Clinical Research and Practice with Adolescents (New York; Wiley, 1993, Ch. 6, pp. 125–145.

p. 240. The peaks are accompanied, as well, by a maturing of moral judgment: William Hudspeth, and Karl Pribram, "Psychophysiological Indices of Cerebral Maturation," *International Journal of Psychophysiology* 12 (1992): 19–29.

The brain's frontal lobes are increasingly active during adolescence: Kurt Fischer and Samuel Rose, "Dynamic Development of Coordination of Components in Brain and Behavior, in Dawson and Fischer (1994), Ch. 1.

p. 241. The U.S. Department of Health and Human Services estimates: Michele Ingrassia "Waiting to Exhale," *Newsweek* (May 1, 1995); 76.

This onslaught reduces the oxygen-carrying capacity of the blood: Lowell Ponte, "How Cigarettes Cloud Your Brain," *Reader's Digest* (March 1995): 128–130.

p. 242. By affecting the prefrontal and temporal lobes of the brain: J. B. Peterson, J. Roth Fleisch, and R. O. Pihl, "Acute Alcohol Intoxication and Cognitive Functioning," *Journal of Studies on Alcohol* 51 (1990): 114–22.

Heavy drinking also carries a less obvious risk: M. Hillbom, et al., "Recent Alcohol Consumption, Cigarette Smoking, and Cerebral Infarction in Young Adults," *Stroke* 26 (1995): 40–45.

This, again, suggests an impact on the brain's frontal lobes: M. E. Bates and J. I. Tracy, "Cognitive Functioning in Young Social Drinkers: Is There Impairment to Detect?" *Journal of Abnormal Psychology* 99 (1990): 242–249. Also, D. L. Pogge, J. Stokes, and P. D. Harvey, "Psychometric Versus Attentional Correlates of Early Onset Alcohol and Substance Abuse," *Journal of Abnormal Child Psychology* 20 (1992): 151–162.

p. 243. **The team members speculate that cannabinoids:** N. Solowij, P. T. Michie, and A. M. Fox, "Differential Impairments of Selective Attention Due to Frequency and Duration of Cannabis Use," *Biological Psychiatry* 37 (1995): 731–739.

The team found that people who smoke marijuana daily: R. I. Block and M M Ghoneim, "Effects of Chronic Marijuana Use on Human Cognition," *Psychopharmacology* 110 (1993): 219–228.

In a recent study of MDMA: "Rave Drug Could Damage Brain," *San Francisco Chronicle* (Aug. 11, 1995): A7, reprinted from *New York Times*.

Fully half the people between ages twenty-five and thirty: Eugene Brown, Jordan Prager, Hsin-Yi Lee, and Ruth Ramsey, "CNS Complications of Cocaine Abuse: Prevalence, Pathophysiology, and Neuroradiology," *American Journal of Roentgenology* 159 (1992): 137–147.

p. 244. **A terrifying 80 percent of the time:** Brown, Prager, Lee, and Ramsey (1992): 137.

But the most frightening aspect of cocaine use: Brown, Prager, Lee, and Ramsey (1992): 137. Also, John Leo, "How Cocaine Killed Leonard Bias," *Time* (July 7, 1986): 52.

One research group found that teenage girls who used drugs: R. E. Tarter, A. C. Mezzrich, Y. S. Hsieh, and S. M. Parker, "Cognitive Capacity in Female Adolescent Subculture Abusers," *Drug and Alcohol Dependence* 39 (1995): 15–21.

The researchers were surprised that the effects were mild: B. Bernal, A. Ardila, and J. R. Bateman, "Cognitive Impairments in Adolescent Drug Users," *International Journal of Neuroscience* 75 (1994): 203–212.

p. 246. **Researchers at the University of Arizona found that 90 percent:** Michele Ingrassia, "The Body of the Beholder," *Newsweek* (April 24, 1995): 66–67.

By some estimates, one in four teens: Elkind (1995): 171.

Clothes, grooming, and attitude: Ingrassia (1995): 67.

p. 247. **There appear to be at least four gender-based differences:** Sharon Begley, "Gray Matters," *Newsweek* (March 27, 1995): 48–53.

Various structures in the male's limbic system: Begley (1995): 49–50.

p. 248. **Females, on the other hand, were equally good:** Begley (1995): 54. Also, Bennet Shaywitz, et al., "Sex Differences in the Functional Organization of the Brain for Language," *Nature* 373 (1995): 607–609.

Girls and women are better at recalling landmarks: Doreen Kimura, "Sex Differences in the Brain," *Scientific American* (September, 1992): 119–124.

p. 249. **Teenage girls were slightly stronger in reading comprehension:** Larry Hedges and Amy Nowell, "Sex Differences in Mental Test Scores: Variability and Numbers of High Scoring Individuals," *Science* 269 (1995): 41–45.

p. 250. **But this crashed to 29 percent by age fifteen to sixteen:** Bruce Bower, "Teenage Turning Point," *Science News* (March 23, 1991): 184–186, in Freiberg (1995), pp. 194–196.

These feelings may clash with the competitiveness: Bower (1991): 195.

This sudden awareness may undermine: Reed Larson and Maryse Richards, *Divergent Realities: The Emotional Lives of Mothers, Fathers and Adolescents* (New York; Basic Books, 1994), Ch. 4, pp. 79–104.

Both boys and girls reported feeling "very happy": Larson and Richards (1994), p. 82.

p. 251. **By fifteen, say Larson and Richards:** Larson and Richards (1994), p. 85.

p. 252. **In Russia and Japan, behavior researchers report:** Carla M. Leone and Maryse H. Richards, "Classwork and Homework in Early Adolescence: The Ecology of Achievement," *Journal of Youth and Adolescence* 18 (1989): 531–548.

In a country like Taiwan, 27 percent of eleventh graders: Andrew Fuligni and Harold W. Stevenson, "Time Use and Mathematics Achievement Among American, Chinese, and Japanese High School Students," *Child Development* 66 (1995): 830–842.

Several hundred American teens in one survey: Larson and Richards (1984), pp. 89, 98.

p. 253. **Even this modest investment in physical activity:** Carol E. Kirshnit, Mark Ham, and Maryse Richards, "The Sporting Life: Athletic Activities During Early Adolescence," *Journal of Youth and Adolescence* 18 (1989): 601–615.

Ironically, teenagers frequently report that sports: Larson and Kleiber in Tolan and Cohler (1993), p. 129.

Those who stay with organized sports throughout high school: Larson and Kleiber in Tolan and Cohler (1993), p. 131.

So are sitting on the bench: Kirshnit (1989): 602.

This is less clear, but sports may be a victim: Lawrence Chalip, et al., "Variations of Experience in Formal and Informal Sport," *Research Quarterly for Exercise and Sport* 55 (1984): 109–116.

p. 254. **These can be relaxing and help a teenager:** Larson and Richards (1994), p. 104.

p. 255. **Underused synapses will go on disappearing:** Kolb, Bryan, *Brain Plasticity and Behavior*, (NJ; Lawrence Erlbaum, 1995), pp. 25–32. Also, Marian Diamond, *Enriching Heredity* (New York; Free Press, 1988). And Peter Huttenlocher, "Morphometric Study of Human Cerebral Development," in *Neuropsychologia*, (Elmsford, NY: Pergammon Press, 1990), pp. 517–527.

Chapter Eight: Learning Not by Chance

p. 266. **And three-quarters of recent recruits to the Armed Services:** Milton Goldberg and James Harvey, "A Nation at Risk: The Report of the National Commission on Excellence in Education." *Phi Delta Kappa* (September 1983): 14–19.

p. 267. **History scores have continued to fall:** Lynell Hancock and Pat Wingert, "A Mixed Report Card," *Newsweek* (January 13, 1995): 69.

Schools do, however, seem to be a bit safer: Rene Sanchez, "Schools Falling Short of Ambitious Goals," *Washington Post*, reprinted in *San Francisco Chronicle* (November 10, 1995): A2.

Large corporations can train graduates in specific vocational skills: Paul Gray, "Debating Standards," *Time* (April 8, 1996): 40.

p. 268. **This tied with Louisiana for the worst grade school reading scores:** Louis Freedburg, "U.S. Schools Bracing for Huge Influx," *San Francisco Chronicle* (August 22, 1996): A1. Also, Nanette Asimov, "Alarming Statewide Test Results," *San Francisco Chronicle* (April 5, 1995): A1. And, Robert B. Gunnison and Greg Lucas, "Plan to Boost Reading Scores," *San Francisco Chronicle* (July 28, 1996): A1.

The college school year has also shrunk by 20 percent: Debra J. Saunders, "Dumbing Down America from the Top," *San Francisco Chronicle* (March 13, 1996): A16.

Fully half of those polled no longer trust the public schools: Tamara Henry, "Public Attitudes Seem to Favor Private Schools," *USA Today* (October 11, 1995): 4A.

Typical fifth graders in Taipei: Jonathan Marshall, "How Homework Really Pays Off," *San Francisco Chronicle* (May 20, 1996): C2.

p. 269. **A researcher from the University of California at San Diego:** Marshall (1996).

p. 270. **Despite our democratic ethos, a child's home life is strongly correlated:** David W. Grissner, et al., "Student Achievement and the Changing American Family" (Rand/MR-488-LE. Santa Monica, CA, 1994), pp. 105–106. Also, Bruce Bower, "Talkative Parents Make Kids Smarter," *Science News* (August 17, 1996): 100. And Leah Garchik, "Family's Effect on Scholarship," *San Francisco Chronicle* (August 27, 1996), reporting a study on divorce and academic achievement by Jennifer Gerner and Dean Lillard of Cornell University.

p. 272. **A 1996 report in *Science* magazine states that:** Hiroo Imura, "Science Education in Japan," *Science* 274 (1996): 15.

p. 274. **Along with the nineteenth-century push toward democracy:** "History of Education," *Encyclopedia Britannica,* Macropedia, Vol. 18 (1992).

p. 278. **Pogreba credits some of the changeover to a paid consultant:** Patricia Wolfe and Marny Sorgen, "Mind, Memory, and Learning: Implications for the Classroom" (80 Crest Road, Fairfax, CA 94930) (1990).

p. 281. **John Bruer also cites a seventh-grade boy named Charles:** John T. Bruer, "The Mind's Journey from Novice to Expert," *American Educator* (Summer 1993): 6–15, 38–46.

p. 283. **It, in turn, drew ideas from Peninsula School in Menlo Park:** Mary Anne Raywid, "Why Do These Kids Love School?" *Phi Delta Kappan* (April 1992): 631–633.

Students need "interaction with ideas and the environment": John Abbott, "Children Need Communities, Communities Need Children," *American Journal of Educational Leadership* (May 1995).

Chapter Nine: As Morning Shows the Day

p. 286. **Using a wrinkled, hairless lab animal called the nude mouse:** Gary O. Gaufo and Marian C. Diamond, "Prolactin Increases CD4/CD8 Cell Ratio in Thymus-Grafted Congenitally Athymic Nude Mice," *Proceedings of the National Academy of Sciences,* USA 93 (1996): 4165–4169. Also, Gary O. Gaufo and Marian C. Diamond, "Thymic Graft Reverses Morphological Deficits in Dorsolateral Frontal Cortex of Congenitally Athymic Nude Mice," *Brain Research* 756 (1997): 191–199.

p. 287. **Well, working in collaboration with Joe's team in Texas:** William Brooks, J. Meilandt, Mark R. Rosenzweig, Marian Diamond, and Joe L. Martinez, Jr., "Subtraction Cloning of a Learning-related cDNA Encoding a Highly Conserved Site-Specific Recombinase," *Science* (submitted).

p. 298. **By the year 2010, they predict this will increase to a 60 percent majority:** Ramon G. McLeod, "U.S. Growth Rate of New Households at 14-Year Low," *San Francisco Chronicle* (May 3, 1996): A2.

Only 39 percent of parents with dependent children at home voted: Elizabeth Gleick, "The Children's Crusade," *Time* (June 3, 1996): 31–35.

p. 299. **In California, 47 percent of those living below the poverty level:** Teresa Moore, "Alarming Outlook for Children," *San Francisco Chronicle* (May 3, 1996): A2.

In 1995, that level was officially defined: Ramon McLeod, "Poverty Fell, Income Rose in U.S. in 1995," *San Francisco Chronicle* (September 27, 1996): A1.

Nationally, more than one of every four: Ruth Sidel, *Keeping Women and Children Last* (New York; Penguin Books, 1996), p. xiv.

Among children under age three: James Collin, "The Day Care Dilemma," *Time* (February 3, 1997): 58.

By 1993, half of all household income: Sidel (1996). 14. The richest 5 percent of Americans: Stephanie Coontz, *The Way We Never Were* (New York; Basic Books, 1992).

Head Start is the largest and best known: Hillary Clinton, *It Takes a Village and Other Lessons Children Teach Us* (New York; Simon &

Schuster, 1996), p. 78. Also, David A. Hamburg, *Today's Children* (New York; Times Books, 1992), p. 67.

p. 300. **These all-day schools attempt to provide:** Margot Hornblower, "It Takes a School," *Time* (June 3, 1996): 36–38.

Although Lisbeth Schorr has concluded that Americans: Gleick (1996): 35.

Two months later, President Clinton: George J. Church, "Ripping Up Welfare," *Time* (August 12, 1996): 18–22.

If what *Time* magazine writer George Church calls: Church (1996): 18.

p. 301. **Children's Defense Fund president:** Church (1996): 20.

Every year, over 700,000 teenagers drop out of school: Hamburg (1992), p. 198. Also, Hillary Clinton (1996), p. 265.

Premature babies born to young mothers: Coontz (1992), p. 287.

In 1992, then-presidential candidate Bill Clinton: Bill Clinton and Al Gore, *Putting People First: How We Can All Change America* (New York; Times Books, 1992).

In October 1996, President Clinton also proposed: "Clinton Reveals Plan for Children to Have Work-Study Tutors," *San Francisco Chronicle* (October 26, 1996): A3.

Interviews and Lectures

Extensive quotations from the following individuals throughout the text, when not otherwise cited, are taken from unpublished interviews conducted by the authors and from lectures given by these experts:

Linda Acredolo and Susan Goodwyn. Transcript of interview conducted November 7, 1995, Davis, California.

Bruce Alexander. Transcript of telephone interview conducted July 3, 1996.

Jane Holmes Bernstein. Transcript of interview conducted October 24, 1995, Cambridge, MA.

Roger Brindle. Transcript of telephone interview conducted August 28, 1996.

John Bruer. Transcript of telephone interview conducted February 15, 1996.

Frances Campbell. Transcript of interview conducted October 3, 1995, Chapel Hill, NC.

Robbie Case. Lecture in series "Brain Mechanisms Underlying School Subjects," June 1995, Eugene, OR, sponsored by the James S. McDonnell Foundation, St. Louis, MO, and the Institute of Cognitive and Decision Sciences, University of Oregon, Eugene, OR.

Harry Chugani. Transcript of interview conducted October 30, 1995, Detroit, MI.

Philip Cogen. Transcript of telephone interview conducted April 24, 1996.

Richard Coss. Transcript of telephone interview conducted March 21, 1996.

Anthony DeCasper. Transcript of telephone interview conducted April 24, 1996.

Adele Diamond. Transcript of interview conducted October 20, 1995, Cambridge, MA.

Glenn Doman and Janet Doman. Transcript of interviews conducted October 8, 1995, Berkeley CA, and October 17, 1995, Philadelphia, PA.

Glenn Doman. Lecture given at Second Annual Symposium on the Human Brain, sponsored by the Education Department of the University of California Extension, October 7–8, 1995.

Kurt Fischer. Transcript of interview conducted October 24, 1996, Cambridge, MA.

Rochel Gelman. Transcript of interview conducted October 2, 1995, Los Angeles, CA.

Kathleen Gibson. Transcript of interview conducted October 11, 1995, Houston, TX.

Norman Krasnegor. Transcript of telephone interview conducted April 23, 1996.

Helen Neville. Transcript of interview conducted November 16, 1995, Eugene, OR.

Bruce Perry. Transcript of interview conducted October 12, 1995, Houston, TX.

Martha Pierson. Transcript of interview conducted October 11, 1995, Houston, TX.

Claudia Pogreba and Harriet Green. Transcript of interview conducted January 30, 1996, Seattle, WA.

Ernie Prindel. Transcript of telephone interview conducted September 17, 1996.

Mary Rothbart. Transcript of interview conducted November 15, 1995, Eugene, OR.

Robert Sapolsky. Lecture given at Cognitive Neuroscience Society meeting, April 1, 1996, San Francisco, CA.

Arnold Scheibel. Transcript of interview conducted September 23, 1995, Berkeley, CA.

Gordon Shaw. Transcripts of interviews conducted August 2, 1996, by telephone, and September 26, 1995, Irvine, CA.

Donald Shetler. Transcript of telephone interview conducted March 13, 1996.

Elizabeth Spelke. Transcript of interview conducted October 9, 1995, Ithaca, NY.

James Stigler. Lecture at University of California Department of Psychology, October 12, 1995.

F. Rene Van de Carr. Transcript of interview conducted February 16, 1996, Hayward, CA.

Norman K. Wessells. Transcript of telephone interview conducted April 24, 1996.

Karen Wynn. Transcript of interview conducted August 26, 1995, Tucson, AZ.

Index

Page numbers in **boldface** refer to
   illustrations

Abbott, John, 283
Abecedarian Project, 157–59,
   299–300
Abstract thought, 126, 154, 195, 240
Abuse and neglect, 127–33, 299
Academic Instruction in Early Childhood
   (Rescorla, Hyson, and Hirsh-
   Pasek), 162
Academics
   and American students, 253–54,
      266–68, 270
   and males vs. females, 249
   and middle years, 192
   and preschoolers, 162–70, 296
Acetaminophen, 72
Acne medication (Accutane), 70–71
Acredolo, Linda, 137–40, 145
Acremant, Robert, 130
Adams, Abigail, 264, 283
Adolescents or teens (age 13–19),
   31, 233–63
   activities, 296
   and brain, 7–8, 50, 238–41
   and social problems, 235–38
   drugs and brain of, 241–46
   enrichment and, 7–8, 254–59

enrichment recommended for,
   259–63, 411–19
and music vs. TV, 212–13
and sex differences, 246–51
synaptic pruning in, 55–56
time use by, 252–54
violence, 218, 221
Adrenaline (epinephrine), 80
Affective retardation, 130
African-Americans, 207, 217, 241,
   246, 250
After-school activities, 211, 214–16,
   252, 297–98
Aggression, 79, 126, 218, 221
AIDS, 68, 81, 236
Alcohol, 5
   and fetus, 88
   and pregnancy, 66, 67, 69, 70,
      76–78, 98, 99
   and teens, 235–36, 241, 242, 260
   and violence, 130
Alertness, 126
Alexander, Bruce, 206–7
Alexander, Robert, 233, 234, 256–57,
   258, 261
Als, Heidelise, 94–95
Alzheimer's disease, 81
American children
   and abuse and neglect, 131–32

American children (*cont.*)
  academic scores of teens, 251
  and education, 266–73
  and nutrition, 82
  and obesity, 207
  and reading skills, 137
  and societal problems, 8, 291–94,
    297–300
  and teen births, 236
  and television, 216–17
  and time use of teens, 252–53
American Medical Association, 76,
  218
American Sign Language, 172, 174
American Youth Soccer
  Organization, 207
Amphetamines, 75
Amygdala, 41, **41**, 125–27, 129
Anencephaly, 68
Anesthetics, 79
Anorexia, 246
"A not B" test, 116–17, 118
Antacids, 71
Anterior commissure, 247
Antiasthma drugs, 71
Antibiotics, 71, 72, 73
Anticoagulants, 71
Antidepressants, 71, 72
Antinausea medicine, 71
Antiseizure medicines, 71
Anxiety, 131
Apprenticeships, 283
"Approach" emotions, 124
Arsenic, 79
Art
  and babies and toddlers, 147
  and middle years, 231
  and preschoolers, 169, 187
  and teens, 260, 262, 263
Aspirin, 72–74
"At-risk" children, 149, 155–61,
  299–300
Attachment, 131
Attention, 79, 94, 136, 141, 196,
  226–27
Attention span, 152
Auditory cortex, 60–61, 62
"Authoritarian control," 159–60
Autoimmune diseases, 286
Avance, 300

Axon, 21–22, 25–26, **26**, 39
  in fetus, 43–45
  and myelin, 48, 49, 153

Babbling, 134
Babies and toddlers (birth to age 2),
  101–47
  and abuse and neglect, 127–33
  brain maturation of, 46–48, 53
  brain development and growth
    spurts in, 112–19
  dendritic branching, 104–5, **106**
  and developmental milestones,
    109–12
  early environment, 103–4
  emotions, and brain structure,
    122–27, 132–33
  enriching environment, 106–9
  enrichment recommended for,
    140–47, 332–38
  innate knowledge of, 120–22
  and language, 133–40
  and touch, 129
Baby Signs, 137–40, 141
Baby Signs (Acredolo and Goodwyn),
  139, 145
Bach, J. S., 100
Bacteria, 79
Barceloux, Donald, 71
Beethoven, 100, 188
Behavioral problems, 77, 127
Bell, Martha Ann, 118
Bell Curve, The (Herrnstein and
  Murray), 156
Bell's palsy, 78
Bennett, Edward, 12, 14, 19z
Bernstein, Jane Holmes, 166
Bertenthal, Bennett, 116
Best of the Best for Children (American
  Library Association), 222
"Better Baby" movement, 161–65,
  166, 167
Betts, Julian, 269
Bias, Len, 244
Birth control pills, 71
Birth defects, 69, 70–72
Blosser, Betsy, 217
Board games, 180, 185, 187, 230
Books
  for babies and toddlers, 147,
    332–333

on child rearing, 141, 144, 181,
   310–16
for middle years, 200, 229–30,
   360–68
for preschoolers, 186, 338–42
for teens, 262, 411–12
Bootstrapping, 115–16, 194
Boredom, 150–51, 241
Bouton, 25, **26**
Brain, 10–35
   and adolescence, 238–51, 255–56
   anatomy of, 16–20, 39–42, **40**, **41**
   of babies and toddlers, 47, 51,
      112–19
   cells, death in embryo, 46–47
   changeability of, 288–89
   in childhood, 113–19
   circuits developed, 55
   close-up view of, 37–42
   critical periods in, 56–64
   and drinking and drugs, 242–46
   and embryo and fetus, 38–47, **43**,
      45
   and emotional abuse, 128–29
   and enrichment research, 2,
      12–14, 26–27, 30–35, 63
   growth, 6–8, 15–16
   growth spurts, 113–118, 194–95,
      240
   human vs. rat, **18**
   and language, 133–40
   and malnutrition, 83–84
   and maturation, 48–50, 52–53, 240
   metabolism, 52–56, 59, 154
   and middle years, 191, 194–96
   modularity of, 63
   and music, 175–77
   and nurturing, 129
   and nutrition, 85
   plasticity of, 56–64, 194, 255–56
   pleasure center, 74–75
   and poverty, 299–300
   prenatal development of, 66–70
   and preschoolers, 150–55
   research, and education, 265–66,
      274–75
   shaped by experience and
      stimulation, 2–3 and *passim*
   shrinkage with age, 15–16
   substitute circuits in, 56
   of talented humans, 32–33

   thin "bark" layer of, 17–19
   and video games, 221
   weight and size, 47–49, 52
"Brain-based education," 266, 273,
   275–80, 283, 304
Brain stem, **10**, 17, **18**, **40**, 49, 53, 77,
   125, 131
Branching. *See* Dendritic branching
Breaking the Silence (Hartley), 127
Breast-feeding, 79, 85
Brindle, Roger, 269
Broca's area, 33, 154
Brooks, Seth, 286–87
Bruer, John, 272–73, 280–82
Buka, Stephen, 75, 77
Bulimia, 246
Bush, George, 267

Caffeine, 66, 76, 98
Caine, Geoffrey, 275
Caine, Renate Nummela, 275
California Proposition 13, 297
California schools, 267–68
Call to Character, A (Greer), 136–37
Campbell, Frances, 157, 159
Campos, Joseph, 116
Caplan, Frank, 109, 146
Caplan, Theresa, 109, 146
Caring for Your Baby and Young Child,
   110
Carnegie Council on Adolescent
   Development, 212–13
Carnegie Foundation for the
   Advancement of Teaching, 168
Carughi, Arianna, 83–84
Case, Robbie, 177–80, 281
Cataracts, 59
Cat in the Hat, The (Dr. Seuss), 88
Cats, 17, 58–60
Caucasians (whites), 217, 241, 250
Centers for Disease Control, 219
Cerebellar cortex, and pons, 42
Cerebellum, 17, **18**, **40**, 42
   lack of, 37, 56
   metabolism, 53
   myelin buildup in, 49
Cerebral aqueduct, **40**, 41
Cerebral cortex
   and boys vs. girls, 247
   branches and synapses, 23–25,
      51–52

Cerebral cortex *(cont.)*
    defined, 17–19
    effect of experience on, 33–35 and
        passim
    and emotion, 126
    in embryo and fetus, 42–45, **45**,
        66, 77
    and middle years, 191, 198
    and immune system, 286
    and language, 198
    loss of, 56
    metabolism in children, 53
    and music, 175–77, 205–6
    myelination of, 153
    and pons, 42
    and preschool years, 105, **106**,
        150–51
    of rats, 13–15, **18**, 19–20, 31, 84
    shrinkage, 15–16, 31
    and spines, 28–29
    and teen years, 239
    thickness of, 19, 23, 31, 150–51
Cerebral hemispheres, 17, **18**, 42–43,
    43
Chemical exposure, 79
Chesterton, G. K., 65
Child. *See* Adolescents and teens;
    Babies and toddlers; Fetus and
    embryo, Grade school children;
    Prenatal care; Preschoolers
Child care, 104, 144
Children's Defense Fund, 300, 301
Children Today (magazine), 156
Child Trends, Inc., 67
Choice, 108
Chomsky, Noam, 133, 135
Chugani, Harry, 52–56, 154, 194,
    206, 225, 239, 294–95
Church, George, 300–301
Cingulate gyrus, 248
Cleft palate, 76
Clinton, Bill, 235, 300, 301
Clinton, Hillary, 236, 291
Cocaine, 236, 243–45, **245**
    and pregnancy, 66, 74–75, 76, 98
Cochlea, 61
Codeine, 71
Cogen, Philip, 97
Cognitive bootstrapping, 115–16
Cognitive development
    and drugs in pregnancy, 72, 77

and middle years, 192
and prenatal stimulation, 92
and teen years, 239
See also Development
Cognitive neuroscience, 113, 117
Cognitive science, and educational
    research, 281–83
Colleges and universities, 268
Computer
    and middle years, 221–23
    and teens, 260, 262
    time spent at, 186, 215, 219, 228
*Computer Museum Guide to the Best
    Software for Kids,* 222
Computer software
    for babies and toddlers, 147
    for middle years, 222–23, 232
    for preschoolers, 184, 185, 188
    for teens, 263
Concentration difficulties, 77, 78
Concrete Operational period, 113
Conel, Jesse, 48–49
Connor, James, 27
Conscience, 192
"Constant television households,"
    217
Constituency for Enrichment, 301–2
Coordination, 151–52
Corpus callosum, 39, **40**, 247
Corpus striatum, 39
Cortisol, 80, 81
Coss, Richard, 27–28, 29
Cough and cold medicines, 71
Crack, 75
Crawling, 110, 111, 115–16, 141, 143
Creativity
    and pregnancy, 81
    and preschooler, 182–84
    and talking to baby, 135
    and TV, 219, 220
Crib, 141
Critical periods
    for color, 63
    defined, 57
    for hearing, 60–63
    for motion, 63
    for music, 206–207
    for vision, 58–60, 63
Cystic fibrosis, 68, 69
Cytomegalovirus, 73

Darwin, Charles, 46
Davidson, Richard, 123–24
Daw, Nigel, 63
Dawson, Geraldine, 124
Deafness
    and language, 172–74, 198–99
    prenatal causes of, 73–74
DeCasper, Anthony, 87–88, 95,
    164–65
Decision making, 119, 126, 135
Dendritic branching, 20–25
    in babies and toddlers, 105, **106**,
        107
    and child development theory, 114
    defined, 23
    dwindling of, 29
    and experience, 28
    higher-order, in preschoolers,
        150–51
    and language, 33–34
    and learning, 31
    lower-order, vs. higher-order,
        24–25
    in middle years, **193**, 194–95
    in Phase One and Two, 52
    and prenatal nutrition, 83
    and stress, 80, 81
    in teens, 239–41, 246, 255–56
    and visual cortex, 51
Dendrites, **21**
    and child development, 56
    continued growth of, 51, 56
    defined, 21
    in fetus, 43, 44, 45
    and maturation of brain, 50
    and neuron communication,
        25–26, **26**
Development, 180
    and babies and toddlers, 109–112
    books on, 141
    and preschoolers, 151–53
    and middle years, 6–12, 191–96
    Piaget's stages, 113
    and TV viewing, 216–20
*Developmentally Appropriate Practice in
    Early Childhood Programs*
    (NAEYC), 168–70
Dewey, John, 274, 283
Diabetes, 68, 69, 76
Diamond, Adele, 116–18, 132
Diamond, Dick, 11, 12

Diamond lab, 14–15, 19, 23, 27,
    30–31, 49, 93, 104, 150, 240–41,
    265, 275
Dickens, Charles, 2–3
Dickenson, Emily, 37–38
Diet, 8, 15
    and brain growth, 113–14
    and enriched vs. impoverished
        environment, 107–8
    in pregnancy, 66, 67, 69, 296
    and TV, 219
Diet pills, 71
Dilulio, John, Jr., 237
Dioxin, 79
Director (magazine), 206
Dissociation, 131
Distractibility, 55
Diversity, 269–70
Divorced parents, 237, 270
Doman, Glenn, 166, 167
Dorsal lateral prefrontal cortex, 286
Down's syndrome, 28, 69
Drugs, medicinal, and pregnancy,
    69–74, 79, 98, 99
Drugs, recreational, 290, 296
    and brain, 241–46
    and pregnancy, 5, 67, 69, 70,
        74–76, 98, 99, 295
    and schools, 267
    and teenagers, 236, 260
Dubroff, Jessica, 223–24
Dubroff, Lloyd, 223–24
Dyslexia, 44, 200

"Each One Teach One" program,
    213–14, 293
Eastin, Delain, 268
Eastman School of Music Talent
    Education Program, 91–92
Eating disorders, 246–47
Ecstasy (drug), 236, 243, 245
Ectoderm, 39
Edelman, Gerald, 46
Edelman, Marian Wright, 301
Education 2000 Trust, 283
Education, 264–84, 291
    and at-risk preschoolers, 155–61
    brain-based, 273–80
    and brain research, 8, 265–66
    and dendritic branching, 34, 35

Education *(cont.)*
  problems of American, 266–73
  reforms, 273–84
Educational television, 217
"Effects of Enriched Environments
    on the Histology of the
    Cerebral Cortex" (Diamond,
    Krech, and Rosenzweig), 14, 16
Eidetic imagery, 33
Electrical-chemical signals, **26**
Elkind, David, 167, 242
Ellenhorn, Matthew, 71
Ellis, Albert, 127
Emotional Intelligence (Goleman), 126
Emotions
  and abuse and neglect, 127–33
  and babies and toddlers, 103,
    124–28
  and brain regions, 125, 127–30
  and brain structure, 67
  and critical periods, 63
  and impoverishment, 108
  needs of children, 107, 290–91,
    296
  needs of perschoolers, 181–82
  and prenatal environment, 70,
    74–77
  and reading, 136
  and teen years, 237, 250–51
  and temperament, 123
Empathy, 182
English-as-second-language, 198
Enrichment
  and American child, 5
  and at-risk preschoolers, 155–61
  and babies and toddlers, 106–9,
    132–33, 135–40, 140–41
  building constituency for, 301–5
  controversy over preschool,
    150–51
  defined, 106–8
  and genes, 287–88
  and higher-order vs. lower-order
    branches, 24–25
  history and potential of, 5–6
  and human brain, 32–35
  impact of, on brain, 31
  and middle years, 7, 211–13
  and nutrition, 84–85
  and preschoolers, 149–50, 181

  and rats' brains, 13–15, 16, 19,
    30–32, 56, 84
  and society, 290–302
  and teens, 240–41, 254–61
Enrichment recommendations
  for babies and toddlers, 140–47,
    332–38
  for fetus, 97–100
  for language, 135
  for middle years, 228–32, 360–410
  for preschoolers, 180–88, 338–59
  for teens, 259–63, 411–19
Environmental toxins, 79
Epilepsy, 44, 52, 69, 81
  and aspirin, 73–74
"Essential daily ingredients," 160
"Essentialism," 274
Estrogen, 246
Event-related potentials (ERPs), 173
Experience, and brain, 3, 27–29, 33,
    62–63, 83–84
Exploration, 108, 141, 160, 166,
    168–69, 182, 296
Extroversion, 123
Eye contact, 129

Facial paralysis, 78
"Fade-out," 156
Families
  decrease in, 298
  discussions, 209
  and school performance, 270
Family planning, 68
Family time, 211
Family traditions, 296
Farrell, Susan, 125
Father, 76–88
Federal Communications
    Commission, 218
Federal Drug Administration, 235
Feldman, David, 225
"Feral" children, 173
Fetal alcohol syndrome, 70, 77–78
Fetus and embryo
  and alcohol, 70, 76–78
  brain development in, 38–47
  and environmental toxins, 79
  and hearing, 60
  and learning, 87–89, 96
  and medicinal drugs, 70–74
  and mother's health, 68–70

and music, 91–93
and nutrition, 82–85
and overstimulation, 94–97
and preconception education,
    67–68
and recreational drugs, 74–77
and smoking, 78–79
and stress, 80–82
Fifer, William, 87
First trimester, 71–74, 77, 82, 83, 87
First Twelve Months of Life, The
    (Caplan and Caplan), 109, 146
Fischer, Kurt, 113–14, 119, 132–33,
    154, 167, 194–95, 240
Fischer, Seth, 113–14
"Flow," 227, 228
Folic acid (folacin), 68–69, 85
Forebrain region, 39, 42–44
Foreign languages, 134–35, 172–73,
    184, 198
Formal Operational period, 113, 240
"Fossilized history" of dendritic
    growth, 105
Fox, Nathan, 118
Fractions, 201–2
Frames of Mind (Gardner), 197, 228,
    275
Frank, Anne, 259
Frank Graham Porter Child
    Development Center, 157–60
Freedman, Dorothy, 185
Free time, 291
    and middle years, 211–16, 228
    and teen years, 252–54
Frontal cortex, **107**, 125, 194,
    195–96, 243
Frontal lobe, **40**, 50
    and abuse and neglect, 129, 130
    and drinking, 242
    growth of synapses in, 51
    metabolism of, 53
    and teen years, 240
    and temperament, 123–24, 125

Gallagher, James, 157
Games
    and babies and toddlers, 147
    and middle years, 230
    and preschoolers, 160
    and teens, 262

Gardner, Howard, 197, 207, 208,
    210, 228, 275, 283
Gaufo, Gary, 285–86
Gelman, Rochel, 201–2
Gender differences
    and abuse, 131
    and brain and behavior, 247–50
    and crosstalk, 155
    and maturation, 192–94
    and self-esteem of girls, 250–51
    and spatial reasoning skills, 119
    and "traveling waves" theory, 119,
        195
    and video games, 221
Genes
    and behavior, 249–50
    and enrichment, 287–88
    and grammar, 172
    and IQ, 3, 155, 156
    and language, 133, 134
    and synapses in children, 54
    and temperament, 123
Genetic disorders, 68, 69
German measles, 68, 73
Gestural language, 102, 145. See also
    Baby Signs
Gibson, Kathleen, 49, 50
Girls
    and computer or video games, 221
    and math and science, 190, 202
    and puberty, 246–47
    See also Gender differences
Glia, 37, 43, 44, **45**, 48
Goldman-Rakic, Patricia, 117, 153
Goleman, Daniel, 126
Golgi stain, 22
Goodwyn, Susan, 137, 138–40, 145
Grade school children (age 6–12,
    middle years), 189–232
    developmental and brain changes,
        191–96
    enrichment recommended for,
        228–32, 360–410
    growing intelligence of, 196–210
    and interpersonal and
        intrapersonal skills, 208–10
    and knowledge of nature, 210
    and language, 197–200
    and math, 201–3
    and music, 204–7
    and physical skills, 207–8

Grade school children *(cont.)*
  and pressure and motivation,
    223–27
  and spatial intelligence, 203–4
  and time use, 211–16
  time use survey, 213–16
  and TV and computer games,
    216–23
Grammar, 170–74
Gray matter, **18**, 19
Green, Harriet, 277, 278–80, 294
Greene, Graham, 189
Greenfield, Patricia, 217, 219–21
Greenough, William, 24
Greer, Colin, 136–37
Griffin, Sharon, 179, 281
"Growers," 114
Growth spurts, 114–15
  and "traveling wave" theory,
    118–19
Guatemalan stimulation study, 84–85
Gymnastics, 146, 147, 189, 225

Hamburg, David, 301
Hand coordination, 152
Handel, 100
Hand-eye coordination, 83, 118
Hand/finger cortex region, 34
"Hanging out," 213, 241, 253, 268
Hanlon, Harriet, 119, 195
"Hardwiring," 55, 57, 59, 72–74
Hartley, Mariette, 127
Hathaway, Lisa, 223, 224
Head growth, 113, 114, 154
Head Start, 155–56, 299, 301
Hearing, 41
  and cerebral cortex, 19, 33
  critical periods for, 57, 60–63
  in fetus, 87–88
  and language, 198–200
  and medicinal drugs, 72–74
  and prenatal nutrition, 83
  and visual system, 62
Hebb, Donald, 12–13
Hepatitis, 68
Heroin, 75, 98, 236
Herrnstein, Richard, 156
Hidden toys skill, 111, 116–17, 118
Higher-order branches, 24–25, 105
High/Scope Educational Research
    Foundation, 156

Hindbrain, 41–42
Hippocampus, 41, **41**, 50
Hirsh-Pasek, Kathy, 162, 167–68
Hispanic children, 217, 241, 250
History education, 267
Hobbies and interests, 296
  and middle years, 192, 225–27
  and preschoolers, 187
  and teens, 254
Hogan, Chuck, 208
Holloway, Ralph, 23
Home resource specialists, 158,
    159–60
Homework, 215, 228, 251, 260,
    268–69, 296
Honeybee studies, 27, 29
Hormones, 238
Hothousing, 161–68
Hubel, David, 57, 58, 59
Hudspeth, William, 239–40
Hurried Child, The (Elkind), 167
Huston, Aletha, 217
Hutchin, Robert, 274
Hutchinson, Dr. Jamie, 74
Huttenlocher, Peter, 51–52, 54, 194
Hydrocephalus, 36, 78
Hyperactivity, 55, 72, 77
Hyperlexia, 171
Hypothalamus, 11, 39, **40**, 125
Hyson, Marion, 162, 165

Imaginary friends, 182
Imagination, 136
  how to encourage, 182–84
  and preschoolers, 152, 153, 154
  and teens, 261
  and TV, 219–20
"Immersion" workshops, 277
Immune system, 80, 286, 288
Impoverished condition, 30, 108–9
  consequences of, 290–91
  and teen years, 241
Impulsiveness, 77, 126, 131
Independence, 112, 128–29
"Inductive discovery," 221, 222
Infant Mind, The (Restak), 43
Inferior colliculus, **40**, 41
Inhibitory ability, 118, 130, 196
Innate knowledge, 120–22
Intelligence
  and at-risk preschoolers, 155–61

and cerebral cortex, 17–19, 29, 31
and frontal lobes 196
and middle years, 196–210
and pruning in prefrontal cortex,
    154
See also IQ; Multiple intelligences
    theory
Interest centers, 158
Internet, 222
Interpersonal skills, 208–10
Intracranial "crosstalk," 155
Intrapersonal skills, 209–10
Introverts, 123
IQ scores
    and absence of nurturing, 129
    and drugs in pregnancy, 72
    and lack of stimulation, 84
    and music for preschoolers,
        175–77
    as poor measure of talent, 197
    and premature birth, 94, 95
    and prenatal nutrition, 83, 84
    and preschool for at-risk children,
        149, 155–61
    and smoking, in pregnancy, 78
    and talking to baby, 135
Irritable babies, 72, 75, 76, 81
It Takes a Village (Clinton), 236

Jacobs, Bob, 34
James, William, 115
Japan, 134, 252–53, 267, 269,
    270–72, 282
Japanese Taikyo tradition, 81
Jefferson, Thomas, 274
Jobs, of teens, 252–53, 268
Johnson, Jacqueline, 172, 198
Johnson, Lyndon, 155
*Journal of the American Medical
    Association,* 68

Kagan, Jerome, 123
Kanamycin, 73
Keeping Women and Children Last
    (Sidel), 301
Kelly, Marguerite, 192, 195, 208–9
Kermoian, Roseanne, 116
"Kick Game," 86, 90, 93
Kidsgardening (Raftery and Raftery),
    210
Kimura, Doreen, 248

Kinesthetic skills, 207, 208, 219. *See
    also* Physical skills
Kipling, Rudyard, 10
Kohl, Herbert, 136
Koresh, David, 128–29
Krasnegor, Norman, 96
Krech, David, 12, 13, 14, 19

Lag gene, 287–88
Langer, Jonas, 201
Language
    and babies and toddlers, 105, 111,
        112, 115, 119, 133–40, 145
    and brain regions, 126
    and cerebral cortex, 33–34
    and critical periods, 57, 63
    delayed, 140
    and dendritic branching, 105
    and fetal alcohol, 77
    and girls, 119, 249
    and middle years, 197–200
    and prefrontal cortex pruning, 154
    and preschoolers, 151–53, 160,
        169–74, 184
    and teens, 261
Language and Problems of Knowledge
    (Chomsky), 133
Language Instinct, The (Pinker), 133,
    170, 171
Language-learning impairment
    (LLI), 199–200
Larson, Reed, 226, 227, 250–51
Lawrence Hall of Science, 146, 203,
    285–86
Laxatives, 71
Learning
    areas of, 42
    capacity of brain, 29
    and genes, 287
    need for science of, 280–81
    and prenatal nutrition, 83, 84
"Learningames," 158, 160
Learning and behavioral problems,
    67, 70, 77–79, 84, 94
Learning centers, 169
Learning styles, 279
Lecanuet, Jean-Pierre, 95
Left and right hemispheres
    and girls vs. boys, 248
    and sweeping model, 118–19,
        195–96

Left frontal lobe, 124
Left hemisphere
  and dendritic branching, 105
  and language, 133–34, 173
  loss of, 4
  and music, 205
  and preschoolers, 151
  and speech, 34
  and stimulation, 119
Lehrer, Marc, 86
Lesher, Susan, 185
Lewis, Isabelle, 157, 158
Limbic system, 41, **41**, 77, 125, 126, 131, 248
Linne, Carl von, 233, 255, 259
Liu, Amee, 126
Living Stage Theatre Company, 233–34, 256–59
Logic, 34, 201, 240
"Long-term potentiation" protein, 287
Love, 131–33, 141, 144–45, 181–82, 229
Low birth weight, 76, 77, 78, 79
Lower-order branches, 24, 105
Lupus erythematosus, 286

McDonnell Foundation, 282–83
McLuhan, Marshall, 220
Magnetic resonance imaging (MRI), 247–48
Making Connections (Caine and Caine), 275–76
Malnutrition, 83–84, 299
Marijuana, 75, 76, 98, 236, 243
Martinez, Joe, 287
Math
  babies and reasoning, 121–22
  and board games, 180
  and girls, 190, 202–3, 248–50
  and homework, 269
  and journaling, 278
  and marijuana, 243
  materials recommended for, 185
  and middle years, 197, 201–3
  and preschoolers, 158, 163, 166, 177–80, 181
  scores, 252, 266–68
  teaching methods, 270–72, 282
  and teens, 248–50, 252, 261

Math for the Very Young (Polonsky, Freedman, Lesher, and Monison), 185
MDMA (Ecstasy), 243
Media, 237, 254
Medical Toxicology (Ellenhorn and Barceloux), 71
Medrich, Elliott, 217
Medulla oblongata, 17, **40**, 42, **43**
Mehler, Jacques, 133, 134, 135
Memory, 50, 79, 81, 119, 125, 243
Mental passivity, 219
Mental retardation, 70–71, 77, 157–58, 159, 160
Merzenich, Michael, 200
Metabolism of brain
  Chugani's study of, 53–55, 154
  and middle years, 194
  and preschoolers, 154
  and teen years, 239
  and vision, 58–59
Microcommunities, 277–78, 283
Midbrain, 41, 49
"Migration" of neurons, 44, **45**
Mill, John Stuart, 167
Millie's Math House (CD-ROM), 185
Milton, John, 285, 290
Minority students, 190
Minstrell, Jim, 281–82
Miseducation: Preschoolers at Risk (Elkind), 167
Modularity of brain, 63
Monison, Kate, 185
Montessori, Maria, 274
Mood, 131
Moore, Marianne, 5, 36
Morality, 209
Mother, 67, 87, 114, 137, 299
  and babies' temperament, 123–25
Mother's Almanac II (Kelly), 192
Motivation
  and attention state, 226–27
  and education, 270, 283, 284
  and teen years, 251
Motor cortex, 118
Motor skills, 49, 72, 118, 152
Mozart, 100, 175–77, 204
Multiple intelligences theory, 197–213, 228, 275, 283
Murray, Charles, 156

Music
and babies and toddlers, 134, 142, 147
and middle years, 197, 204–7
and fetus, 91–93, 96, 99–100
and free time, 212–13
and preschoolers, 148–49, 169
and teens, 260, 261–62
Musical instrument
as boost to IQ, 174–77
critical period for, 63
and middle years, 204–7, 230–31
and practicing, 225–26
and teens, 263
and preschoolers, 181, 185, 187
Music recordings
and middle years, 232
and teen years, 254, 263
and preschoolers, 188
Myelin
accumulation (myelination), 48–50, 52, 56, 82–83, 114, 115, 153
defined, 19, 48

Nader, Ralph, 301
Narcotic pain relievers, 71
National Academy of Sciences, 82
National Assessment of Educational Progress, 267
National Association for the Education of Young Children (NAEYC), 168, 181
National Association of Scholars (NAS), 268
National Cancer Institute, 241
National Coalition for Music Education, 204–5, 206
National Commission on Excellence in Education, 266
National Institute of Child Health and Human Development, 96
Nation at Risk, A (NCEE report), 266
Natural cell death, 46–47
Nature appreciation, 197, 210
Nelson, Jennifer, 233
Neocortex, 20, 41, 50
Neo-Piagetians, 113
Nerve growth factor, 45
Netherlands, 83
Neural Darwinism, 46

Neural defects, and toxins, 79
Neural language, and music, 175–76
Neural migration, 44
Neural sculpting, 57
Neural surface area, 22–23
Neural tube defects, 68, 69, 71, 82, 83, 85
Neurologists, 15–16
Neurons (nerve cells)
anatomy of, in brain, 6–7
in auditory cortex, 61
branching, 20–25, **21**, 51, **106**
communication as specialty of, 25–27, **26**
in fetus, 43, 82
measuring, in cerebral cortex, 20
migration of, in fetus, 44–45
number of, in brain, 37
and stress, 80–81
viewing through microscope, 22
in visual cortex, 57–58
See also Dendrite branching; Dendrites
Neville, Helen, 59–63, 134, 173, 174, 199
Newborn
brain, 46, 47–50, 125–26
and communication, 133–34
milestones of development, 109–10
sound preferences, 87–88
Newman, Lucile, 75, 77
Newport, Elissa, 172, 198
Newsweek, 236, 237
Nicotine, 79, 242
Noradrenaline (norepinephrine), 80
Nucleus accumbens, 74
Number games, 185, 202, 281
Nurss, Joanne, 156–57
Nutrition, and fetus, 67, 82–85, 99

Obesity, 207, 219
"Object continuity" test, 120–21
"Object Retrieval" test, 117
Occipital lobe, **40**, 50, 53
Olds, David, 78
Olfactory bulbs, 17, 24, 39, **41**
Open-ended play, 184
"Open participation plan," 283
Open-plasticity notion, 59–60
Optic nerves, 39, 57

Outgoing nature, 141
Outings
    and babies and toddlers, 147
    and middle years, 231
    and preschoolers, 169, 185–88
    and teens, 263
Ovaries, 246
Overconnectedness, 54–55
Over-scheduled child, 228–29
Over-the-counter drugs, 71, 98

Pain relievers, 71
Painting, 79
Parents
    and adjustment to learning, 165
    and brain development, 127
    and emotion, 124–28
    importance of loving, 126–28,
        132–33
    and language skills, 136–38
    and morality, 209–10
    and preschool enrichment, 159–60
    role of society vs., 294–95
    and teen enrichment, 260
    and TV viewing, 216
    and voting, 298
Parents as Teachers program, 300
Parents magazine, 220
Parent support group, 141
Parietal lobe, **40**, 50
Passive vs. active involvement, 108
Pattern recognition, 110, 142
    and math-smart kids, 201–2
Paxton, Tom, 100
PCBs, 79
Peer group, 260
Peninsula School (California), 283
People, 218
Pepto Bismol, 74
Perfect pitch, 205
Performance anxiety, 168
Peripheral vision, 62
Perry, Bruce, 127–32, 292–94
Perry Preschool, 156
Personality, 103
Pesticides, 79
PET scanner, 52–53, 55–56
Photography, 79
Physical change
    and adolescence, 246-47
    and middle years, 192

Physical skills
    and baby and toddler, 145–46
    and middle years, 197, 207–8
    and preschoolers, 152
    and teen years, 253–54, 260, 262
    and TV, 219
Physics teaching, 281–82
Piaget, Jean, 113, 114, 120
Pierson, Martha, 72–74, 209–10
Pimentel, Ada, 125
Pinker, Steven, 133, 135, 137, 170,
        171, 172
Pipher, Mary, 237
Pituitary gland, 246
Planning, 19, 34
Planum Temporale, 205
Play, 168, 169, 182, 184, 215
    effect of TV on, 212–13, 219
Playpen, 141
Pogreba, Claudia, 264, 276–78, 283
Pollit, Ernesto, 84–85
Polonsky, Lydia, 185
Pons, **40**, 42
Poverty, 67, 291–94
    enrichment for children in,
        155–61, 299–302
    and public recreation, 298–99
    See also Socioeconomic factors
Praise, 160, 181
Preckwinkle, Sue, 265, 281, 283
"Preconception care," 67–68, 78, 97
Prefrontal cortex, 117–18, 123, 126,
        153, 154, 221
Pregnancy (prenatal environment),
        7, 65–100
    and alcohol, 76–78
    and caffeine, 76
    and environmental exposure, 79
    and medicinal drugs, 70–74
    and music, 91–93
    and nutrition, 82–85
    and preconception care, 67–68
    and prenatal enrichment, 65–66,
        86–97, 99–100, 292, 296
    and recreational drugs, 74–76
    and smoking, 78–79
    and stress, 80–82
    and temperament, 292–93
Premature infants, 94, 95
Prenatal care, poor, 299, 301
Prenatal Classroom (Van de Carr), 86

Pre-Operational period (age two to seven), 113
Preschool enrichment controversy, 150–51, 161–70, 173
  and poor, 155–61
Preschoolers (age 2 to 5), 148–88
  and abuse, 131
  academic schooling for, 161–70
  at-risk, enrichment for, 155–61
  brain structure of, 7, 153–55
  developmentally appropriate activities for, 168–70, 180
  developmental milestones, 151–53
  enrichment recommended for, 180–88, 338–59
  and language, 170–74
  and math gap, 177–80
  and music, 174–77
  and preschool, enrichment, 150–51
Preschools, 181, 296, 300
Prescription drugs, 70–71, 98
Pressure, 208, 223–27
Pribram, Karl, 127, 239–40
"Private speech," 182–83
Problem-solving, 55, 117, 135, 152, 154, 166, 169
Protein, 84–85, 99
Pruning, 48, 52–56, 63
  and Fischer model, 114
  in middle years, 194
  in newborn, 47
  in prefrontal cortex, 154
  in teens, 239, 255
  in visual cortex, 51, 154
Psychological counseling, 132
Psychology Today, 242
Puberty
  age for girls, 192–93
  and identity, 246–47
  and neural pruning, 55–56
Public education, 274, 297
Punishment, 141, 144–45, 181–82, 226–27
Putnam, Robert, 218
Puzzles, 187, 230, 262

Radiation exposure, 79
Radio, 220
Raftery, Kevin and Kim, 210
Rakic, Pasko, 44

Ramey, Craig, 157–58, 160
Rat studies, 6, 12–20, 30–32, 72–74, 84
Rauscher, Frances, 175–77, 204
Read-Aloud Handbook (Trelease), 136
Reading, 8, 135–38
  and at-risk preschoolers, 158, 163–64
  and babies and toddlers, 136
  early, 149, 162–63
  and middle years, 200, 215–16, 229–30
  and preschoolers, 181, 184
  scores, 268
  and TV, 217
Reading to child
  and baby, 136–37, 141, 145
  and middle years, 200, 229–30
  and preschoolers, 181, 184
Reasoning, 53, 126, 192
Reciprocal teaching, 265, 281
Recreational programs, cutbacks, 297–98
Red nucleus, 41
Reid, Joe, 223, 224
Relearning, 288
"Representational mapping," 154–55
Rescorla, Leslie, 162
Resource Mothers of South Carolina, 300
Responsibility, 209
Restak, Richard, 43, 47
Reticular formation, 125–26
Retina, 39, 46, 57
Rewards, 226–27
Rhesus monkey studies, 49–50, 129
Richards, Maryse, 250–51
Richardson, David, 126–27
Right brain, 105, 119
Right-brain, left-brain studies, 17, 275
Right frontal lobe, 124
Right hemisphere removal, 36–37, 56
"Rightstart Program," 179–80
Rose, Samuel, 113
Rosenzweig, Mark, 12, 13, 14, 19
Rothbart, Mary, 122–23
Rozman, Deborah, 127
Rumanian orphanages, 129–30
Russia, 252

Sacks, Oliver, 198–99
Sandel, Oran, 257–59
Sapolsky, Robert, 80–81
Schaefer, Earl, 157
Schall, Matthew, 34
Scheibel, Arnold, 22, 24, 32–35, 37,
    44, 104–5, 134, 150, 165–66
Scheibel, Madge, 32
Schizophrenia, 44, 55
School
    academic preschool and, 168
    failure, 299, 301
    funding, 273
    hours in, 252, 268
    and middle years, 216, 228
    and music education, 206–7
    public vs. private, 268
    and teens, 251–53, 260
    toddlers, 150
    See also Education
Schools for Thought (Bruer), 281
Schorr, Lisbeth, 299, 300, 301
Science, 12, 272
Science education, 266, 268, 274,
    282, 304
    and girls, 190–91, 202
Scientific American, 248
Second trimester, 69, 72–74, 82
Secret Garden (video), 232
Seeing Voices (Sacks), 198
Selective attention, 243
Self-awareness, 111, 112, 192, 209,
    250
Self-consciousness, 238, 254
Self-control, 126
Self-defense reflexes, 109
Self-esteem, 127, 132
    and girls, 250–51, 254, 258
Self-image, 237, 238
Self-reliance, 238
Sense, 94, 108, 142
Sensorimotor period, 113
Sensorimotor responses, 114–15
Sensory defects, 72
Sensory deprivation, 108
Serotonin, 243
Sesame Street (TV show), 217, 219
Sex, and teen brain, 246–51
Sex hormones, 247, 249
Sexual behavior, 126
Sexual curiosity, 192

Sexual maturation, 237, 251
Shakespeare, 16, 81
Shatz, Carla, 46
Shaw, Gordon, 174–77, 177, 204
Shetler, Donald, 91–93, 100
Shyness, 101, 122–25, 141
Sickle-cell anemia, 68
Sidel, Ruth, 301
Sigel, Irving, 161
Signs or word labels, 136–38, 145
Simonds, Roderick, 104–5
Singer, Bobbie, 213
Singer, D. G., 219
Singer, J. L., 219
Singer, Jerome, 182
Singer, Marcus, 11–12
Singing to child, 137, 184
Single parents, 80, 149, 237
Skinner, B. F., 127
Sleep, 126, 131
Smoking
    and pregnancy, 66, 67, 69, 78–79,
        98, 99
    and teenagers, 235, 241–42, 260
Smotherman, William, 88
Social interaction, 108, 153
Social isolation, 27, 108
Socialization, and teenagers, 237, 252
Social policies, 156, 297–98
Social skills
    and middle years, 192, 197
    and preschoolers, 182
Society, and enrichment, 291–302
Socioeconomic factors
    and alcohol, 77
    and developmental problems, 67
    and enrichment, 291–93
    and IQ, 156
    and math gap, 179–80
    and preschoolers, 155–61
    and reading for pleasure, 215–16
    and TV viewing, 215, 217–18
    See also Poor and poverty
Sound, and fetus, 96, 97
Sound-induced seizures, 72, 73
Sparling, Joe, 157, 158
Spatial intelligence, 197, 203–4, 221,
    248–49
    in babies, 116–17
    and gender, 119
    and Mozart, 175–77, 185

Speech, 19, 83, 92, 94, 95, 138, 154
Speech centers, 74–75
Spelke, Elizabeth, 120–21, 122, 166, 225–26
Spilich, George, 241–42
Spina bifida, 68, 82
Spinal cord, 17, **40**
Spines, **21**, **26**, 27–29, 31, 32, 51, 56
    and stress, 80, 81
    and teens, 239, 246
"Spoiling" baby, 144
Sports. *See also* Physical skills
Sports, 296
    and babies and toddlers, 147
    and middles years, 231–32
    and preschoolers, 188
    and teens, 253–54, 260, 263
Starr, Raymond, Jr., 131
Startle reflex, 109
Stigler, James, 267, 270–73
Stranger anxiety, 53
Stress, 108, 182, 286–87
    prenatal, 67, 69, 80–82, 98
Stromswold, Karin, 171, 172
Structured activities, 215, 225–29, 231, 254, 263
Superior collicullus, **40**, 41, 117–18
Support groups, 82
Suzuki, Shinichi, 92, 205
Synapses, 56
    and brain growth, 114–15
    defined, 25
    and fetus, 44–45, 46, 83
    and first year, 126–27
    growth of, in childhood, 51–52, 54, 63
    and metabolism of brain, 54
    and middle years, 194
    and neural communication, 25–26
    number of, 37
    overconnectedness of, 46–48, 54–55, 73
    and preschoolers, 154
    and spines, 27
    and teens, 55–56, 59, 238–39, 255–56

Tacitus, 3
Taiwan, 252–53
Talking to child, 135–41, 145, 184. *See also* Language; Speech

Tallal, Paula, 199, 200
Taub, Edward, 205–6
Tay-Sachs disease, 68
T-cells, 286
Teachers, 271–75
Tectum, 41
Teen pregnancy, 82, 233–34, 236, 254–58, 296, 299, 300
Teeth, 93
Tegmentum, **40**, 41
Television, 8, 29, 109, 268
    how much to allow, 220, 227, 228
    and language, 137
    and middle years, 192, 212–13, 215, 216–20
    and physical skills, 207
    and preschoolers, 186
    and socialization, 237
    and teens, 254, 260, 262
    unplugging, 227, 296
Temperament, 103, 112, 122–33, 292–93
Temporal lobe, **40**, 50, 247
Teratogen, 70
"Terrible twos," 52, 54–55, 112, 152
Testes, 246
Testosterone, 246
Thalamus, 39, **40**, 42, 53, 125
Thalidomide, 69
Thatcher, Robert, 118–19, 155, 195
Theme learning, 169
"Theory of mind" skills, 154–55
Thinking, 34, 50, 81, 131
Third trimester, 69, 72–74, 77, 82–83
Time, 300
Times of London, 224
Today's Children (Hamburg), 301
Touch, 19, 129
Toxic agents, 69, 70, 78, 79, 98, 99
Toxoplasmosis, 68, 73
Toys
    for babies, 110, 111, 147, 333–34
    for middle years, 230, 369–76
    for preschoolers, 183–84, 187, 342–45
    for teens, 262, 412–13
Tranquilizers, 71
"Traveling wave" theory, 46, 118–19, 195–96
Trelease, Jim, 136, 137
Tremors in fetus, 72

Trion model, 175–77
"Triune brain" theory, 275
Tutoring programs, 301
Tylenol, 72

U.S. Congress, 300
U.S. Department of Health and
    Human Services, 235, 241
U.S. Food and Drug Administration,
    71, 76
U.S. Public Health Service, 69, 76–77
University of North Carolina, Chapel
    Hill, early infancy enrichment
    program, 157–58
Unschooled Mind, The (Gardner), 275

Van de Carr, F. Rene, 86, 88–91, 93,
    95, 96, 100, 291–92
"V chip," 218
Ventricles of brain, 41
Verbal ability, 243, 249–50
Video games, 227
Videos
    for babies and toddlers, 147, 338
    for middle years, 232, 403–407
    for preschoolers, 188, 356–58
    for teens, 254, 263, 418–19
Violence, 67, 130–31, 218, 221, 299
Viruses, 79
Vision, 41, 53
    of babies, 110, 118, 142
    and cerebral cortex, 19
    critical periods for, 57–63
    and gender, 119

Visual cortex, 33, 51, 57–60, 62, 63,
    118, 154, 194
Vitamins, 68, 85, 99
Vocabulary
    of babies and toddlers, 135, 136
    of preschoolers, 151, 152, 154, 170
Vocalizing, 110–11
Vogt, Oscar and Cecille, 32–33
"Voluntary attention," 226
Volunteer work, 260, 262

Walking, 111, 153
War on Poverty, 155
Watson, John B. family, 127–28
Welfare, end of, 300–301
Wernicke's area, 34, 154
Wessells, Norman, 93–94
White matter, 18, 19, 39
Whitman, Walt, 148, 151
Wiesel, Torsten, 57, 58, 59
Williams syndrome, 171
Winn, Marie, 227
Within Our Reach (Schorr), 299
Wooodway Elementary Micro-
    Community, 277–78
Working mothers, 104
Wright, John, 217
Writing skills, 135, 138, 258, 268
Wynn, Karen, 121–22, 201

YMCA, 146

Zigler, Edward, 300
Zill, Nicholas, 67